CONTENTS

How to use this book

KU-316-691

HOW TO USE THIS BOOK

The material is organised into main **subject areas**. Each has its own colour key which is shown on the contents list on page 3 and on the contents lists appearing at the beginning of each subject area.

Core text is material suitable for students of a wide ability range. However, not all of the core text will be suitable for all syllabuses and teachers should be aware of this.

Investigations which the authors have found to be particularly useful or enjoyable have been chosen. The instructions are detailed enough to be followed by most students without further help. However, instructions for drawing up results tables and graphs have been deliberately omitted in several cases, so that the student's ability to do this can be assessed.
In some places measurements are shown as fractions rather than decimals. This has been done deliberately to make it easier for students to understand.

20 RESPIRATION

Respiration is a process which occurs in all living cells. Respiration releases energy from food.

Every living cell respires

Each living cell in every living organism needs energy. Energy is needed to drive chemical reactions in the cell. It is needed for movement. It is needed for building up large molecules from small ones. If a cell cannot get enough energy it dies. Cells get their energy from organic molecules such as glucose. The chemical process by which energy is released from glucose and other organic molecules is called **respiration**. Every cell needs energy. Each cell must release its own energy from glucose. So each cell must respire. Every cell in your body respires. Every living cell in the world respires.

Fig. 20.1 Florence Griffith-Joyner ('Flo-Jo') winning the 100 m at the Seoul Olympics. The energy which she is using comes from respiration in her muscle cells.

INVESTIGATION 20.1

Getting energy out of a peanut

1 Spear a peanut on the end of a mounted needle. Be careful – it is easy to break the peanut.
2 Put some cold water into a boiling tube. Support the boiling tube in a clamp on a retort stand, with the base of the tube about 30 cm above the bench top. Take the temperature of the water and record it.
3 Set light to the peanut by holding it in a Bunsen burner flame. (Keep the Bunsen burner well away from the boiling tube.) When the peanut is burning hold it under the boiling tube. Keep it there until it stops burning.
4 Immediately take the temperature of the water and record it.

Fig. 20.2 Burning a peanut

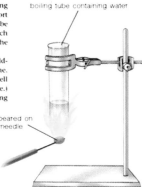

boiling tube containing water

peanut speared on mounted needle

Questions

1 Why should you keep the Bunsen burner away from the tube of water?
2 By how much did the temperature of the water rise?
3 What type of chemical reaction was occurring as the peanut burnt?
4 Put these words in the right order, and join them with arrows, to show where the heat energy in the water came from:

energy in peanut molecules

energy in glucose in peanut leaf

sunlight energy

heat energy in water

5 Put the following words over two of the arrows in your answer to question 4:

photosynthesis   oxidation
6 Do you think all the energy from your peanut went into the water? If not, explain what else might have happened to it.
7 How could you improve the design of this experiment to make sure that more of the peanut energy went into the water?

┌─ EXTENSION ┐
8 People often want to know exactly how much energy there is in a particular kind of food. The amount of energy is measured in kilojoules.
4.18 J of energy will raise the temperature of 1 g of water by 1 °C.
Design a method for finding out the amount of energy per gram in a particular type of food.

Apparatus Lists for the investigations will be found on pages 200–202. These lists also include other notes for teachers, such as particular safety points or ways in which the investigation might be slightly altered or extended. These notes should be read before attempting any experiments.

COORDINATED SCIENCE

SECOND EDITION

Biology

Mary Jones & Geoff Jones

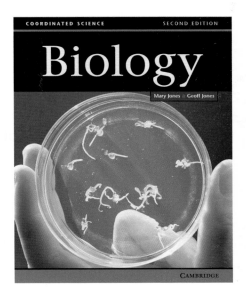

CAMBRIDGE
UNIVERSITY PRESS

PUBLISHED BY THE PRESS SYNDICATE OF THE UNIVERSITY OF CAMBRIDGE
The Pitt Building, Trumpington Street, Cambridge CB2 1RP, United Kingdom

CAMBRIDGE UNIVERSITY PRESS
The Edinburgh Building, Cambridge CB2 2RU, United Kingdom
40 West 20th Street, New York, NY 10011-4211, USA
10 Stamford Road, Oakleigh, Melbourne 3166, Australia

First published 1993
Second edition 1997

Printed in the United Kingdom at the University Press, Cambridge

A catalogue record for this book is available from the British Library

ISBN 0 521 59981 4

Prepared for the publishers by Stenton Associates

Cover photograph: Genetically engineered seedlings,
Weiss/Jerrican/Science Photo Library

Notice to teachers
It is illegal to reproduce any part of this work in material form
(including photocopying and electronic storage) except under the
following circumstances:
(i) where you are abiding by a licence granted to your school or
institution by the copyright Licensing Agency;
(ii) where no such licence exists, or where you wish to exceed the
terms of a licence, and you have gained the written permission of
Cambridge University Press;
(iii) where you are allowed to reproduce without permission
under the provisions of Chapter 3 of the Copyright, Designs and
Patents Act 1988.

Respiration is an oxidation reaction

You can do an experiment to release energy from food if you do Investigation 20.1. When a peanut burns, the energy in the peanut is released as heat energy. But how do your cells release energy from food such as peanuts?

Obviously, you do not burn peanuts inside your cells! But you do something very similar. The chemical reactions of burning and respiration are very like each other.

First, think about what happens when you burn the peanut. The peanut contains organic molecules, such as fats and sugars, which contain energy. When you set light to the peanut you start off a chemical reaction between these molecules and oxygen in the air. The peanut molecules undergo an **oxidation** reaction. They combine with oxygen. As they do so, the energy in them is released as **heat energy**.

When you eat peanuts, your digestive system breaks the peanut into its individual molecules. Your blood system then takes these molecules to your cells. Inside your cells the molecules combine with oxygen. They undergo an oxidation reaction. This is respiration. The energy in the molecules is released. But, unlike the burning peanut, much of the energy is *not* released as heat energy. It is released much more gently and gradually, and stored in the cell.

So, the burning of a peanut, and the respiration of 'peanut molecules' in your cells are both oxidation reactions. In both of them the peanut molecules combine with oxygen. In both of them the energy in the peanut molecules is released. But in your cells the reaction is much more gentle and controlled.

ATP is the energy currency in cells

Respiration releases energy from food. Each cell must do this for itself. Every living cell respires to release the energy it needs. The energy released in respiration is not used directly for movement or any of the other activities of the cell. It is used to make a chemical called **ATP**. ATP is short for adenosine triphosphate. ATP, like glucose, contains chemical energy.

chemical energy in glucose → chemical energy in ATP

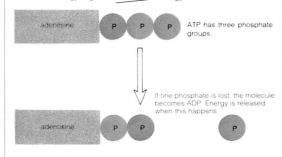

ATP has three phosphate groups.

If one phosphate is lost, the molecule becomes ADP. Energy is released when this happens.

Fig. 20.3 ATP and ADP

ATP is the ideal energy currency in a cell. The energy in an ATP molecule can be released from it very quickly – much more quickly than from a glucose molecule. The energy is released by breaking ATP down to **ADP**. ADP is short for adenosine diphosphate. Another good reason for using ATP as an energy supply is that one ATP molecule contains a much smaller amount of energy than one glucose molecule. If a cell needs just a small amount of energy, then it can break down just the right number of ATP molecules. The amount in a glucose molecule might be too much, and energy would be wasted. Each cell produces its own ATP by the process of respiration. ATP is not transported from cell to cell.

The respiration equation

Respiration is a chemical reaction. The word equation for the reaction with glucose is:

$$glucose + oxygen \longrightarrow carbon\ dioxide + water + energy$$

The balanced molecular equation for the reaction is:

$$C_6H_{12}O_6 + 6O_2 \longrightarrow 6CO_2 + 6H_2O + energy$$

Questions

1 Respiration is a chemical reaction.
 a Where does it take place?
 b What type of chemical reaction is it?
 c Why is it so important to living cells?

2 List two similarities, and one difference, between the burning of a peanut and the respiration of 'peanut molecules' in your cells.

3 a Write down the word equation for respiration.
 b Write down the balanced molecular equation for respiration.

4 Respiration releases energy from food. Explain how the energy came to be in the food.

5 a What is ATP?
 b Why do cells use ATP as an energy store?
 c A muscle cell uses glucose to provide energy for movement.
  i List all the energy changes involved in this process, beginning with energy in sunlight.
  ii Energy is 'lost' at each transfer. What do you think happens to this 'lost' energy at each stage?

Extension text is material which only more able students need to consider. It includes such things as rearranging formulae, performing calculations, or understanding more difficult concepts. However, there is no sharp dividing line between core and extension material and individual teachers may well disagree with us in particular instances. Weaker students may be able to cope with some of the extension material if sufficiently motivated.

Questions are included in most topics. They range widely, from relatively simple structured questions, through comprehensions, to open-ended questions requiring considerable planning, and perhaps further research by the student.

In addition, each subject area ends with a range of structured questions relating to all the topics within it. Teachers should be able to find questions to suit students of a wide ability range.
Answers to numerical questions will be found on page 202.

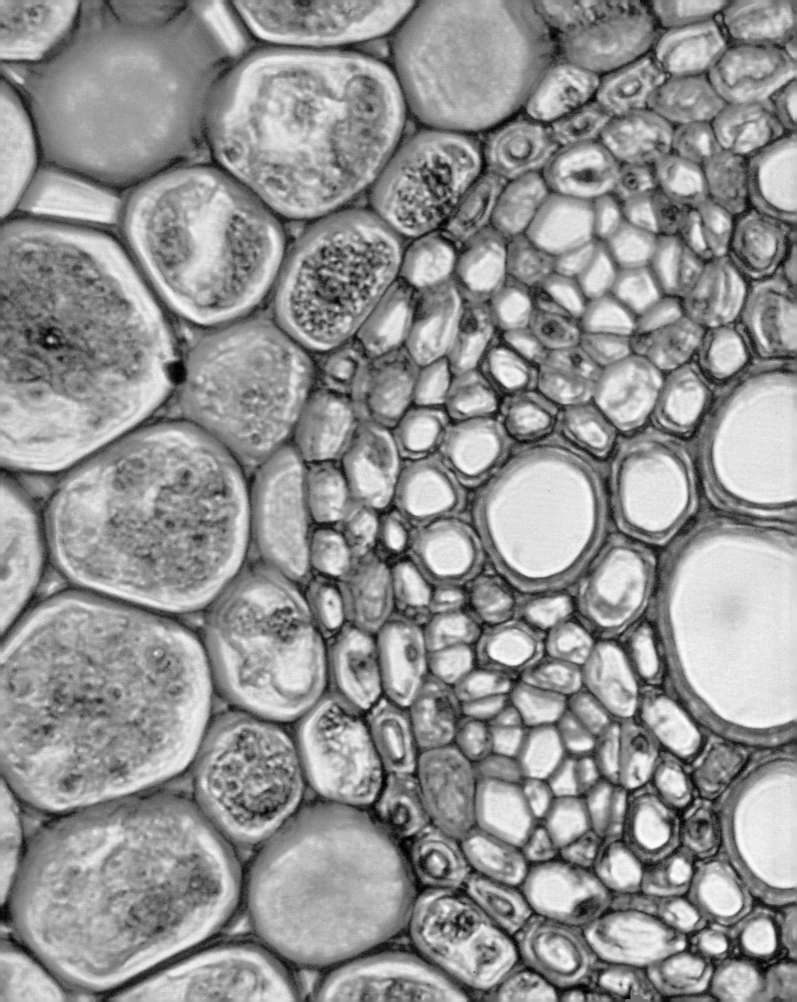

CELLS AND TRANSPORT

1 LIFE PROCESSES

All living things carry out seven processes. Non-living things do not carry out all of these processes. Living things are also known as organisms.

Fig. 1.1 What can you see here that is alive? What is not alive? Do any of the non-living things share some of the 'life processes' of the living organisms?

Living things include plants and animals

If you look around you, you will see many things which are alive and many which are not alive. Living things are often known as **organisms**. The living things you can see might include people and other **animals**, and also **plants**. There may also be other, smaller living things around you. For example, there are **bacteria** almost everywhere. And there are probably some **fungi** (such as toadstools) not too far away.

All of these living things carry out seven vital processes. These processes are special to living things – they are not all carried out by non-living things. They are called **life processes**. The seven life processes are **nutrition**, **respiration**, **excretion**, **sensitivity**, **movement**, **reproduction** and **growth**.

Nutrition includes feeding and photosynthesis

All living things need to take in substances from around them. They use the atoms in these substances to build the molecules which make up their bodies. Taking in substances for this purpose is called **nutrition**.

For animals (including humans), nutrition involves **feeding**. We eat substances which we call 'food'. Food is material containing substances such as proteins, fats and carbohydrates. These substances have been made by plants. You can read more about feeding in humans in Topics 26 to 29.

For plants, nutrition involves **photosynthesis**. Plants do not need to eat food – they make what they need from carbon dioxide and water, plus some minerals. They use energy from sunlight to help them to convert these substances into the molecules they need. You can read more about photosynthesis in Topic 16.

Respiration releases energy from food

Living things do not only need atoms to build up their bodies. They also need **energy**. All living organisms get the energy they need by breaking down certain molecules, such as glucose molecules. The glucose molecules contain energy, and when they are broken down, in a series of chemical reactions, the energy is released. This process is called **respiration**. It takes place in every cell in every living organism. You can read more about respiration in Topic 20.

Movement may involve all or part of the body

Living things can **move**. You can see this most clearly in animals, most of which can move around from place to place. Plants do not move their whole bodies around like this, but parts of their bodies can move. For example, the petals of many flowers close up at night. You can read more about movement in Topic 82.

Excretion removes waste products of metabolism from the body

Respiration is one example of a series of chemical reactions that takes place inside living cells. The chemical reactions which happen in living organisms are called **metabolic reactions**. Some metabolic reactions produce harmful substances, which the living organism does not want and must get rid of. For example, respiration produces carbon dioxide. The removal of waste products of metabolism, such as carbon dioxide, from the body, is called **excretion**. You can read more about excretion in animals in Topic 85.

Reproduction is the formation of new organisms

Living organisms are able to produce new organisms from themselves. This is called **reproduction**. Sometimes, a single organism just grows a new organism from its body. This is called **asexual reproduction**. For example, a spider plant grows new spider plants. Sometimes, the organisms produce sex cells called **gametes**, which fuse together in a process called **fertilisation**. This produces a new cell, which then divides to form a new organism. This is called **sexual reproduction**. You can read more about reproduction in Topics 35 to 44.

Sensitivity involves responding to stimuli

Living things are able to detect changes in their environment. This is called **sensitivity**. For example, plants and animals are sensitive to light. The light is a **stimulus**, which may cause the plant or animal to **respond** to it in some way. In an animal, the response might be a movement. In a plant, the response might be by growing in a particular way. You can read more about sensitivity and responses in Topics 75 to 78.

Growth is a permanent increase in size

When a new organism is first formed, it is usually small. As it gets older, it gets bigger. This is called **growth**. Growth happens as the individual cells in an organism get bigger, and also as these cells divide to produce more cells. You can read more about growth in Topic 40.

Questions

1 Match each term with its description.
    terms:
    nutrition, growth, sensitivity, reproduction, excretion, movement, respiration.
    definitions:
    • a permanent increase in size, brought about by an increase in the size of individual cells, and also an increase in the number of cells.
    • the production of new individuals from one or more parents; it may be asexual or sexual.
    • the release of energy from food, which takes place in every living cell.
    • the removal of waste products of metabolism from the body; some of these products would be toxic (poisonous) if allowed to accumulate inside the body.
    • the ability to detect changes in the environment, called stimuli, and to respond to them.
    • changing the positions of parts of the body, or of the whole body.
    • taking in substances containing atoms and molecules which can be used to build new molecules that make up the structure of the body; and which can also be used to provide energy.

2 Which characteristics of living things does a computer have? Why isn't a computer a living thing?

All cells are made of cytoplasm surrounded by a cell surface membrane. Most have a nucleus. Plant cells also have a cell wall around them.

Cells are the building blocks for living things

All living things are made up of cells. A cell is a very small piece of transparent jelly-like substance, surrounded by a thin covering. The jelly is called **cytoplasm**. The covering is called a **membrane**. Most cells also have a dark area inside the cytoplasm, called a **nucleus**.

An average size for a cell is about $\frac{1}{100}$ mm across. Some cells, for example bacterial cells, are a lot smaller than this. Some may be much larger. Some of the largest cells of all are egg cells. As cells are so small, it takes many of them to make up a large organism such as yourself. Your body contains several million cells. Other organisms are so small that their whole body is made of just one cell.

Plant cells always have cell walls

The cells in every kind of living organism are very similar. But plant and animal cells do have some important differences between them. One of these differences is that all plant cells have a **cell wall** outside their cell surface membrane. The cell wall is made of fibres which criss-cross over one another. This makes a strong, protective covering around the plant cell. The fibres are made of a carbohydrate called **cellulose.**

Fig. 2.1   An animal cell as seen through a light microscope.

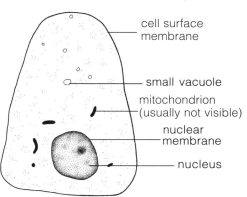

- cell surface membrane
- small vacuole
- mitochondrion (usually not visible)
- nuclear membrane
- nucleus

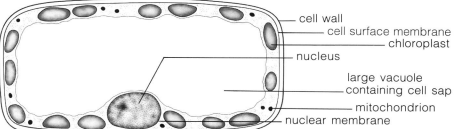

- cell wall
- cell surface membrane
- chloroplast
- nucleus
- large vacuole containing cell sap
- mitochondrion
- nuclear membrane

Fig. 2.2   A plant cell as seen through a light microscope.

Fig. 2.3   A 3-D view of a plant cell.

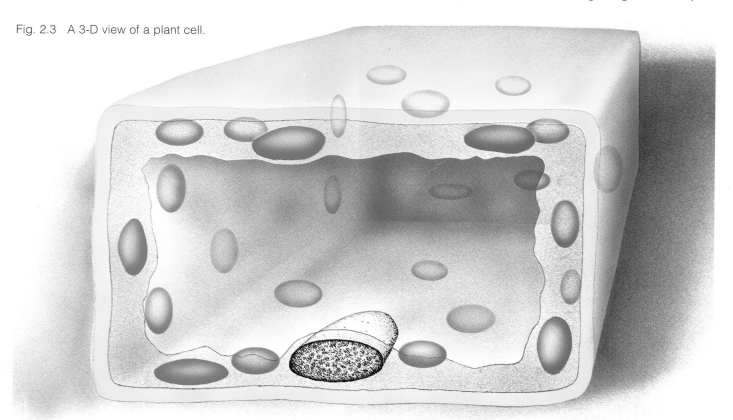

Plant cells may have chloroplasts and large vacuoles

Many plant cells contain small, green objects inside their cytoplasm. These are **chloroplasts**. They are green because they contain a green colour or pigment called **chlorophyll**. It is chlorophyll which makes plants look green. Only the parts of the plants which are above ground contain chlorophyll. Chlorophyll absorbs light energy, which is used in photosynthesis.

Most plant cells also contain a large fluid-filled area called a **vacuole**. The vacuole contains a sugary liquid called **cell sap**.

Animal cells never have cell walls, never have chloroplasts and never have vacuoles as large as those in plant cells.

Question

Copy and complete this table.

Structures contained in		
all cells	all plant cells but not animal cells	some plant cells but not animal cells

Question

Which of these groups of cells are animal cells, and which are plant cells? Give a reason for each of your answers.

Fig. 2.4   Cells from plants and animals.

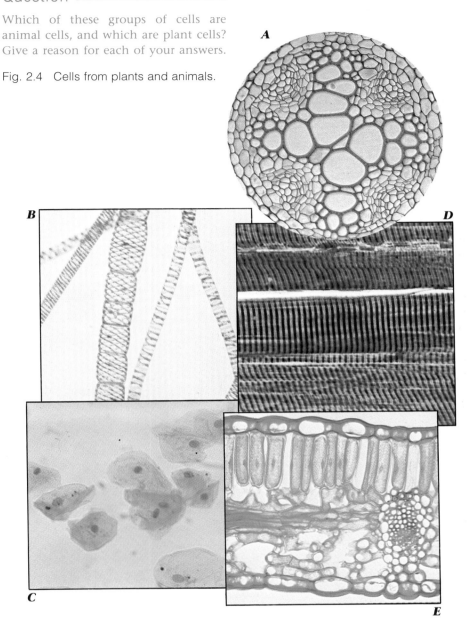

Sizes of cells

As cells are so small, they are usually measured in micrometres. A micrometre is one thousandth of a millimetre. The shorthand way of writing 'micrometre' is µm.

Questions

1   Which is the smallest of the cells shown?
2   How many times larger is the cheek cell than the bacillus?
3   How many micrometres are there in 1 cm?
4   How many micrometres are there in 1 m?

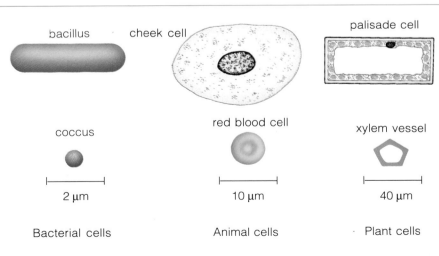

3 USING A MICROSCOPE

As cells are very small, a microscope is needed to see them clearly. Using a microscope is an important skill which all scientists should have.

INVESTIGATION 3.1

Using a microscope

These instructions may look long and complicated, but you **must** follow them every time you use a microscope if you want to be sure of seeing things quickly and clearly. As you work through them, use the labels on the large diagram to find the different parts of the microscope.

1 Place the microscope so that it is facing towards a source of light. This could be a window, or a lamp.

2 Swivel the objectives until the smallest one (the lowest power) is over the centre of the stage.

Fig. 3.1 How to use a microscope

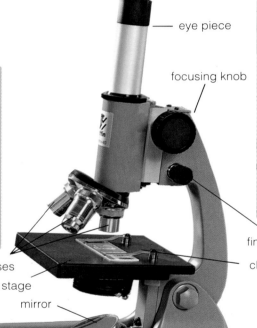

— eye piece

— focusing knob

fine focusing knob

objective lenses

stage

mirror

clips to hold slide in position

4 Put your slide on the stage. Put the part you want to look at in the middle of the stage.

5 Looking from the *side* of the microscope, *not* down the eyepiece, turn the focusing knob to bring the stage close to the objective lens.

3 Look down through the eyepiece, and move the mirror until everything looks bright.

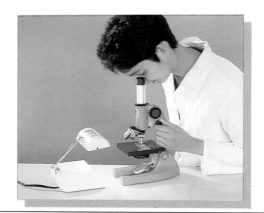

6 Now look down the eyepiece, and gradually move the stage *away* from the objective until the slide is in focus.

7 If you want to use a higher magnification, make sure that the piece of the object you want to look at is right in the middle of your field of view. Then swing a higher powered objective lens into place over the stage. Focus as before. You will need to bring the objective lens so close to the slide that it almost touches it.

Making a microscope slide

1. Make sure that the microscope slide you are going to use is clean.
2. Put the object you are going to look at in the centre of your slide. The object must be so thin that light can pass right through it. Thick objects cannot be seen clearly through an ordinary microscope.
3. If the object is not already liquid, it must have liquid added to it. This could be water or it could be a stain. Add the liquid carefully, using a pipette. Add just enough to cover the object.
4. Now, gently, lower a cover slip over the liquid on the slide. The diagram shows how to do this without trapping air bubbles.
   The cover slip is important for several reasons. It holds the object flat, making it easier to focus on it. It stops the liquid evaporating from the slide. It also stops the liquid getting on to the lenses of the microscope. *Always* use a cover slip when you make a slide.

5. Finally, use filter paper to mop up any excess liquid on the slide, or on top of the cover slip. This is important, because if liquid gets on to the objective lenses on your microscope, you will not be able to see through them properly.

Fig. 3.2   Lowering a coverslip

Fig. 3.3   A microscopist using a scanning electron microscope. Electron microscopes work in a similar way to light microscopes, but use electron beams instead of light beams. The beams are focused with electromagnets instead of glass lenses. The image on these screens shows a grid of known size, used to calibrate the microscope.

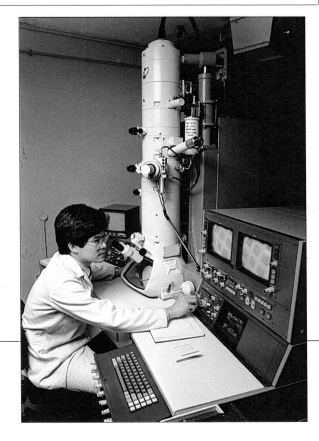

Looking at plant cells

1. Take a clean microscope slide, and put a drop of water into the centre of it.
2. Cut a piece about 1 cm² from a section of onion bulb. Using fine forceps, carefully pull away the very thin inner lining, or **epidermis**, from your piece of bulb. Working quickly, put the piece of epidermis into the drop of water on the slide, trying not to let it curl up.
3. Take a cover slip, and gradually lower it over the epidermis, as shown in the diagram. Doing it this way allows any air bubbles to escape.

4. Use filter paper to soak up any water which has seeped out from under the cover slip.
5. Set up a microscope and look at your slide on low power.
6. Make a labelled drawing of what you can see.
7. Now take a piece of pond weed, and put this on to a slide in the same way as you did for the onion cells. Again, cover with a cover slip, and look at it under the microscope. Draw and label what you can see.

Questions

1. Which were the larger – onion epidermis cells or pond weed cells?
2. What colour were
   a the onion cells
   b the pond weed cells?
3. What is the reason for this difference in colour?

4 THE PARTS OF CELLS

Every part of a cell has its own part to play in the smooth running of the cell's activities.

The cell surface membrane controls what enters and leaves the cell

The cell surface membrane is one of the most important parts of a cell. It makes sure that the contents of the cell stay inside. It also stops unwanted substances outside the cell from entering. But it must allow some substances into the cell. These substances include water, oxygen and food materials. It must also allow waste substances, such as carbon dioxide, to get out. So the membrane lets some substances through, but not others. It is called a **partially permeable** membrane.

Chemical reactions take place in the cytoplasm

The cytoplasm is a jelly made of proteins dissolved in water. Many chemical reactions go on in the cytoplasm. These reactions are called **metabolic reactions**.

The nucleus contains inherited information

Most cells also have a nucleus. The nucleus contains thin threads called **chromosomes**. Chromosomes contain information, inherited from the parent cell or cells, which give information to the cell about what it does. Usually, the chromosomes in the nucleus are so long and thin that they cannot be seen

Mitochondria release energy from food

The cytoplasm contains small objects called **mitochondria**. Inside mitochondria, sugar and oxygen react together to release energy. The number of mitochondria in a cell can often give you a clue about what that particular cell does. Muscle cells, for instance, contain huge numbers of mitochondria, because they need so much energy.

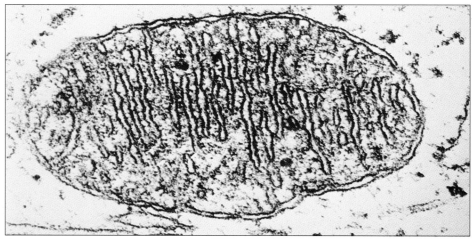

Fig. 4.1 A photograph of a mitochondrion, taken with an electron microscope. The reactions of aerobic respiration take place in the space inside it, and on the folded membranes. The actual size of a mitochondrion can be about 2 micrometres long. By how much has this one been magnified?

except with an electron microscope. But when the cell divides, they thicken. You can then see them with a light microscope.

Chloroplasts make food by photosynthesis

All the structures described so far are found in every cell. But some plant cells also contain very important structures called **chloroplasts**. Chloroplasts are quite large – often as big as the nucleus. They are always green because they contain the green pigment **chlorophyll**. Their function is to make sugar and other types of food, using energy from sunlight, water and carbon dioxide. Chlorophyll is essential for this, because it traps energy from sunlight. The process is called **photosynthesis.**

Many plant cells contain starch grains

Plant cells which live underground have no use for chloroplasts, as there is no sunlight for them to absorb. These cells may have other structures, similar to chloroplasts, but with no chlorophyll in them. These structures contain food stores. Potato cells, for example, contain many **starch grains**. The cells in the potato plant's leaves, which do contain chloroplasts, make sugar by photosynthesis. Some of this sugar is carried down to the potato underground. It is then converted to starch and stored there to be used later on. Chloroplasts can also store starch grains.

Specialised cells

Many cells have their own special jobs to do. Their sizes, shapes and contents are often different from other cells, to enable them to do their job really efficiently.

Palisade cells from a leaf are rectangular in shape. They contain large numbers of chloroplasts, often arranged around the edge of the cell where they can get the most sunlight for photosynthesis.

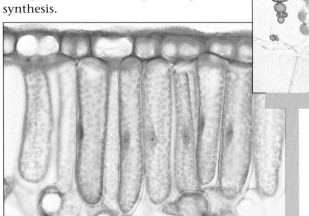

Potato cells store starch. The starch grains fill most of the cell. The starch may be used to provide energy for the potato to begin to grow new shoots next year.

Muscle cells are usually long and thin. They contain enormous numbers of mitochondria, to provide the energy they need for movement.

INVESTIGATION 4.1

The effect of heat on plant cell membranes

Beetroot cells contain a red pigment (colour). The cell surface membrane keeps this pigment inside the cell. High temperatures damage the cell surface membrane, allowing the pigment to leak out.

1 Take a raw beetroot, and cut a cylinder out of it using a cork borer. Wash the cylinder very thoroughly, until no more red colour comes out of it.

2 Set up a Bunsen burner, tripod and gauze. Put some sand into a sand tray, and put this on the gauze. Half fill a beaker with water, and stand this in the sand in the sand tray.

3 Put the piece of washed beetroot into the beaker of water. Light the Bunsen burner. Hold a thermometer in the water, and watch the beetroot carefully as the temperature rises. As soon as any red colour begins to come out of the piece of beetroot, stop heating, and note the temperature of the water.

Questions

1 Why must the piece of beetroot be washed thoroughly?
2 Why does some red colour come out of the piece of beetroot *before* it is heated?
3 Why is the beaker of water heated in sand?
4 At what temperature did red colour begin to leak from the beetroot?
5 What was happening to the beetroot cells at this temperature?
6 Vegetables which have been boiled for a long time contain fewer nutrients than raw or lightly cooked vegetables. Can you explain why?

Questions

1 Which part of a cell performs each of the following functions:
   a releases energy from sugar and oxygen?
   b controls what enters and leaves the cell?
   c makes food by photosynthesis?
   d contains information inherited from the cell or cells that produced it?

2 Below is a list of cells.

A cheek cell   B leaf cell
C muscle cell   D onion epidermis cell
E carrot root cell   F human liver cell

Which of the cells from this list would you expect to contain each of the structures below? Give a reason for each of your answers.
   a cell membrane
   b chloroplasts
   c mitochondria
   d nucleus
   e cell wall

5 GROUPS OF CELLS

Large organisms are made of many different kinds of cells, each specialising in a different job. Cells doing the same job are often grouped together into a tissue.

A group of similar cells is called a tissue

In a single-celled organism, like *Amoeba*, the one cell has to carry out all the jobs which need doing. But in a large organism, such as yourself, there are millions of cells. Most of these cells are specialised to carry out just a few functions really efficiently. Muscle cells, for example, are specialised to produce movement. Nerve cells carry messages.

The cells lining your digestive system digest food.

Cells which specialise in the same function are usually grouped together. A group of similar cells is called a **tissue**. The onion epidermis which you looked at in Investigation 3.3 is an example of a tissue. The cells lining your stomach are another example.

A group of tissues can form an organ

Tissues themselves are often grouped together to form even larger structures. A group of tissues working together to carry out a particular function is called an **organ**. An eye is an example of an organ. If you look at Figure 77.2, you can see some of the tissues that it contains. The sclera, the choroid, the conjunctiva and most of the other structures labelled on the diagram are all tissues.

Plants have organs too. A leaf is an organ. The different tissues – for example, the epidermis and palisade layer – are labelled in the diagram on page 45.

A group of organs which all work together to perform a particular function is called an **organ system**, or just a system. For example, you have a digestive system, containing organs that are shown on page 74. Other systems in the human body include the nervous system, excretory system, circulatory (blood) system and breathing system.

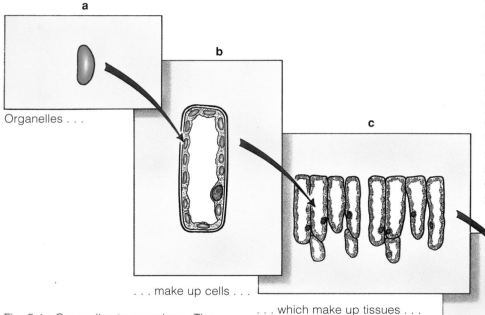

Organelles . . .

. . . make up cells . . .

. . . which make up tissues . . .

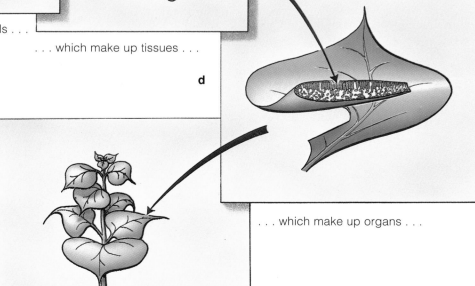

. . . which make up organs . . .

. . . which make up organisms.

Fig. 5.1 Organelles to organisms. The small structures found inside cells are called organelles.

Can you name:
a the organelle shown in diagram a?
b the cell shown in diagram b?
c the tissue shown in diagram c?
d the organ shown in diagram d?

Questions

1 Copy and complete this paragraph.

All cells contain a jelly-like substance called .... which is surrounded by a ....Within the cell are smaller structures called organelles. The largest organelle is usually the ..... This contains ....., which hold inherited information about what the cell should do.

In addition, plant cells contain green organelles called ..... These contain a green pigment called ..... which traps energy from ..... This energy is used to make food, in the process known as .....

Unlike animal cells, plant cells always have a .... outside their cell surface membrane. This is made of ....

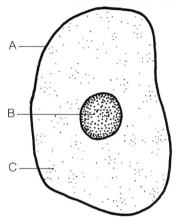

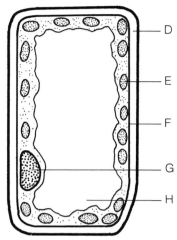

2 Name the structures labelled on the diagrams above.

3 The following instructions for looking at a slide under a microscope on high power, are in the wrong order. Write down the letters in the correct sequence. One of them needs to be used twice.

a Put the slide on to the stage.

b Turn to the highest power objective lens.

c Focus the microscope.

d Position the microscope facing a light source.

e Look from the side, and bring the stage and the objective lens close together.

f Adjust the mirror to fill the field of view with light.

g Turn to the lowest power objective lens.

4 Below is a photograph of some human cheek cells taken through a light microscope.

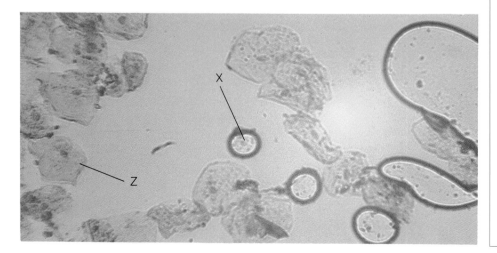

4 a Give two reasons why you could tell that these were animal and not plant cells.

b What are the structures labelled X?

c Describe how the slide should be made to make sure that there are not too many of these structures.

d Make a drawing of Cell Z, and label its nucleus, cytoplasm and cell surface membrane.

e A human cheek cell is about 10 μm or 0.01 mm across. By how much has Cell Z been magnified in this photograph?

5 The following list contains two organelles, two cells, two tissues, two organs and two organisms. Which is which?

onion epidermis	oak tree
heart	chloroplast
mitochondrion	cheek cell
pig	conjunctiva
leaf	red blood cell

EXTENSION

6 Identify the structures labelled A to E on this electron micrograph of a plant cell. (An electron micrograph is a photograph taken using an electron microscope. Electron microscopes use beams of electrons instead of beams of light, and can show clearly much smaller objects than light microscopes.)

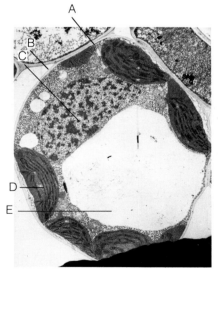

17

Moving particles spread around

A smell will slowly spread across a room. We can explain this by imagining that the smell is made of moving particles of a smelly substance. The molecules move around, filling the room. This movement is called **diffusion**. Diffusion can be defined as *the movement of particles from a place where there is a high concentration of them, to a place where there is a lower concentration of them.* Diffusion tends to spread the particles out evenly.

You can watch diffusion happening if you use a substance, such as potassium permanganate, which has coloured particles. If a crystal of potassium permanganate is carefully dropped into a beaker of water, it dissolves. The particles in the crystal separate from each other and slowly move through the water. The colour only spreads slowly. The particles keep bumping into the water molecules. They do not travel in straight lines. Eventually the colour fills the whole beaker, but this takes a very long time.

Diffusion happens faster in gases than in liquids

In a gas the molecules are not so close together as in a liquid. If a coloured gas is mixed with a clear one, the colour spreads. This happens faster than in a liquid, because fewer particles get in the way. You can watch this happening with bromine, as it diffuses through air. Bromine is a brown gas. It covers about 2 cm in 100 s. If it diffuses into a vacuum, it goes even faster, because there are no particles to get in the way. It then travels 20 km in 100 s!

Fig. 6.1 Potassium permanganate diffusing in water. A crystal has just been dropped into the gas jar on the left. The potassium permanganate has been diffusing for about 30 minutes in the centre jar, and for 24 hours in the jar on the right.

Fig. 6.2 An experiment showing the diffusion of bromine gas. On the left, the two gas jars are separated by a glass lid. The lower one contains bromine, and the upper one contains air. On the right, the lid has been removed. The bromine and air diffuse into one another.

Questions

1 a Which part of a plant cell requires oxygen for respiration?

b If the oxygen concentration outside a cell is higher than the oxygen concentration inside the cell, then oxygen will diffuse into it. List, in order, the parts of a plant cell through which oxygen will diffuse, until it reaches the part you have named in a.

c Which gas will diffuse *out* of a respiring cell?

INVESTIGATION 6.1

How quickly do scent particles move?

If a bottle of perfume is opened, the smell spreads across a room. Design an experiment to find out how quickly the smell spreads from a particular type of perfume.

You will need to consider how you will decide when the scent has reached a particular part of the room. Would the same group of experimenters always get the same results? Would you get the same results in a different room? Or in the same room on a different day? Try to take these problems into account when you design your experiment.

Get your experiment checked, and then carry it out. Record your results in the way you think best. Discuss what your results suggest to you about the speed at which scent particles (molecules) move.

Diffusion of two gases

This experiment will be demonstrated for you, as the liquids used should not be touched.

A piece of cotton wool is soaked in hydrochloric acid. A second piece of cotton wool is soaked in ammonia solution. The two pieces of cotton wool are pushed into the ends of a long glass tube. Rubber bungs are then pushed in, to seal the ends of the tube.

The hydrochloric acid gives off hydrogen chloride gas. The ammonia solution gives off ammonia gas. (Both of these gases smell very unpleasant, and should not be breathed in in large quantities.)

Fig. 6.3 Diffusion of two gases

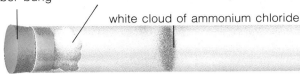 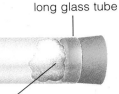

rubber bung — cotton wool soaked in hydrochloric acid — long glass tube

white cloud of ammonium chloride

cotton wool soaked in ammonia solution

Questions

1 Hydrogen chloride and ammonia react together to form a white substance called ammonium chloride. Nearest which end of the tube does the ammonium chloride form?

2 How had the two gases travelled along the tube?

3 Which gas travelled faster?

4 The molecules of ammonia are smaller and lighter than the molecules of hydrogen chloride. What does this experiment suggest about how the size and mass of its molecules might affect the speed of diffusion of a gas?

5 If this experiment could be repeated at a higher temperature, would you expect it to take a longer or shorter time for the ammonium chloride to form? Explain your answer.

EXTENSION

Cells can use energy to move substances by active transport

Cells may need to take in substances that are present in a low concentration. For example, a plant requires nitrate ions. Plant roots have fine, single-celled **root hairs**, which absorb water and minerals such as nitrate ions from the soil. The concentration of nitrate ions is often much lower in the soil than inside the root hair. So you would expect the nitrate ions to diffuse out of the root hair into the soil, down their concentration gradient.

But, despite this, the root hairs are still able to take in nitrate ions. They have special protein molecules, called **transporter proteins**, in their cell surface membranes, into

which nitrate ions fit perfectly. When a nitrate ion bumps into a transporter protein on the outer surface of the cell surface membrane, the cell uses energy to change the shape of the transporter and so push the nitrate ion into the cell (Figure 6.4). The energy comes from a molecule called **ATP**, which the cell makes by respiration (see Topic 20.).

All living cells use active transport to move ions and other substances into or out of the cell, against their concentration gradient. They have many different transporter proteins in the cell surface membranes, each one shaped so that a particular ion or molecule fits perfectly.

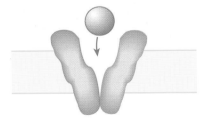

1. The nitrate ion enters the transporter protein.

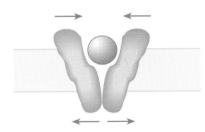

2. The transporter protein changes shape. The energy needed for this comes from ATP, produced in respiration in the cell.

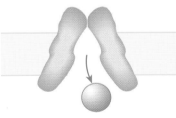

3. The change of shape of the transporter protein pushes the nitrate ion into the cell.

Fig. 6.4 Active transport

7 OSMOSIS

Water molecules are small. The molecules and ions of solutes are often much larger. This means that water molecules can get through holes through which solute molecules are too large to pass.

Water molecules are smaller than most solute molecules

A water molecule is made up of two hydrogen atoms and one oxygen atom. Hydrogen atoms are the smallest atoms which exist. Oxygen atoms are not particularly large, either. So water molecules are quite small as molecules go.

All sorts of substances can dissolve in water. Many of these substances have quite large molecules. Sugar is one example. A molecule of cane sugar (the sort you put in tea or coffee) has 12 carbon atoms, 22 hydrogen atoms and 11 oxygen atoms. So you can see that a sugar molecule is quite enormous compared with a water molecule.

Water molecules can diffuse through very small holes

Figure 7.1 shows a sugar solution. The sugar molecules are spread amongst the water molecules. The sugar solution is separated from some pure water by a thin piece of material called a **membrane**. This particular membrane is a piece of **visking tubing**. Visking tubing has extremely small holes in it. The holes are big enough to let water molecules through. But sugar molecules are much too big to pass through the holes. A membrane like this, which will let some molecules through but not others, is called a **partially permeable membrane**.

What will each kind of molecule do? The sugar molecules cannot do very much at all. They move around on their side of the membrane, bumping into each other, into water molecules, and into the membrane. But they cannot cross on to the other side of the membrane. The water molecules also move around, bumping into other molecules and the membrane. Some of them will 'bump into' a hole in the membrane, and go through to the other side. Water molecules from both sides of the membrane will cross on to the other side. There is a two-way traffic of water molecules from one side of the membrane to the other.

But there are far more water molecules on side A than on side B. On average, more water molecules on this side will bump into holes in the membrane, because there are more of them. So more water molecules will go from side A to side B than will go the other way. The water molecules **diffuse** from the pure water into the sugar solution.

This is the same process as a gas diffusing across a room. The water molecules diffuse from where there are a lot of them to where there are not so many. The sugar molecules would do the same if they could. But they cannot.

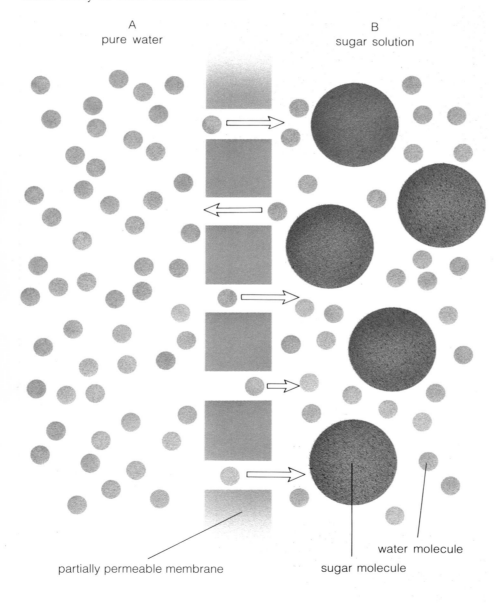

A
pure water

B
sugar solution

partially permeable membrane

sugar molecule

water molecule

Fig. 7.1 Osmosis

The net movement of water molecules into the sugar solution is called osmosis

The overall result of all this bumping around of molecules is that water molecules move from the pure water into the sugar solution. This process is called **osmosis**.

Osmosis can be defined as *the net movement of water molecules, through a partially permeable membrane, from a place where there is a high concentration of water molecules to a place where there is a lower concentration of water molecules.*

Osmosis is really just a special sort of diffusion, where only water molecules can diffuse through a membrane.

INVESTIGATION 7.1

Osmosis and visking tubing

Fig. 7.2

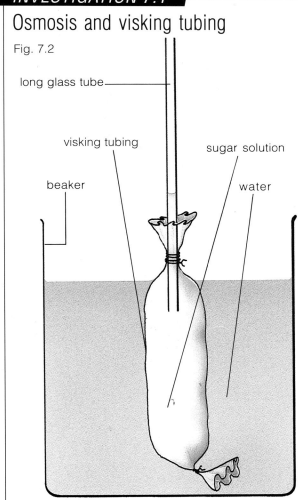

long glass tube

visking tubing

sugar solution

beaker

water

1   Set up the apparatus as in Figure 7.2. You must take great care to tie your knots very tightly, so that there is no chance that any liquid can leak out. You must also wash the outside of the visking tube after filling it and before putting it into the beaker, in case any sugar solution has got on to the outside of it.
2   Mark the level of the liquid in the tube. At 2 min intervals, measure any increase in height above this initial height. Record your results in a chart.
3   When you have about 15 readings, or when the liquid has stopped rising, stop collecting results. Draw a line graph of your results.

Questions

1   Explain, as fully as you can, why the liquid rises up the glass tube.
2   Did the liquid rise at a steady rate? If not, suggest some reasons for any variations.
3   What would you expect to happen, and why, if you set up this experiment:
   a with pure water in the tubing, and a concentrated sugar solution in the beaker?
   b with equal concentrations of sugar solution in the tubing and the beaker?
   c with a concentrated sugar solution in the tubing and a dilute sugar solution in the beaker?

Questions

1 Write down definitions of:
   a diffusion   **b** osmosis

---EXTENSION---

2   A piece of visking tubing is filled with starch solution. The tubing is tied tightly at both ends, and then put into a beaker. The beaker is filled with iodine solution. The concentration of water molecules in the two solutions is the same.
   a Draw a labelled diagram of what the apparatus would look like at this stage.
   Starch molecules are too big to get through visking tubing. Iodine molecules can get through.

   b Explain what you think will happen to:
      i the water molecules
      ii the starch molecules
      iii the iodine molecules
   When starch and iodine are mixed together, a blue-black colour is produced. Iodine solution is brown.
   c Draw and colour the apparatus as it would look at the end of the experiment.

8 OSMOSIS AND LIVING CELLS

All living cells are surrounded by a partially permeable membrane. Osmosis can occur through this membrane.

Living cells are surrounded by a partially permeable membrane

All living cells are surrounded by a **cell surface membrane**. This membrane is partially permeable. It will let water molecules through, but many other molecules are not allowed to pass through freely. The contents of a living cell are a fairly concentrated solution of proteins, sugars and other substances in water. These solute molecules are not allowed out of the cell. They cannot get through the cell surface membrane.

Fig. 8.2 A plant cell in pure water. The cell swells and becomes turgid. The strong cell wall stops it from bursting.

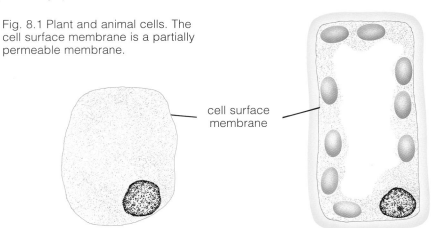

Fig. 8.1 Plant and animal cells. The cell surface membrane is a partially permeable membrane.

cell surface membrane

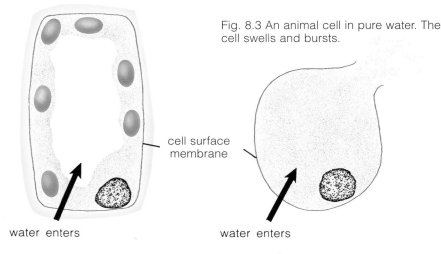

cell surface membrane

water enters

Fig. 8.3 An animal cell in pure water. The cell swells and bursts.

cell surface membrane

water enters

Cells take up water if put into pure water

What might happen if you put a cell into pure water? The situation is like that in Figure 7.1. Water molecules will tend to move from where they are in high concentration – outside the cell – to where they are in a lower concentration – inside the cell. Water moves by osmosis into the cell. As the cell surface membrane will not let other molecules out, the cell gets fuller and fuller. If this goes on for long, it may even burst. This does actually happen if you put red blood cells in pure water. Water goes into them by osmosis and they burst.

A red blood cell is an animal cell. Plant cells also have partially permeable membranes. So plant cells also take up water by osmosis if you put them into pure water. But they do not burst. This is because every plant cell has a tough, outer covering called a **cell wall**. The cell wall is strong enough to stop the cell bursting, even if it takes up a lot of extra water. Plant cells in pure water simply get very full. The extra water which goes into them makes the contents of the cell push out against the cell wall. The cell becomes firm and rigid. It is said to be **turgid**.

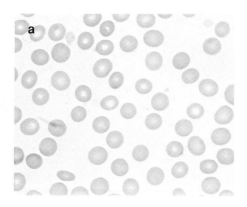

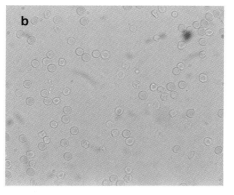

Fig. 8.4 Red blood cells in (a) a solution of the same concentration as their cytoplasm, and (b) in pure water. The cells in (a) look normal. Because the solutions on either side of their cell surface membranes are of equal concentration, they neither gain nor lose water. The cells in (b) are bursting. Water is entering them by osmosis, making them swell and break their membranes.

Cells in a concentrated solution tend to lose water

Imagine a cell in a solution which is more concentrated than itself. Now the higher concentration of water molecules is *inside* the cell. So water molecules tend to diffuse out of the cell. Remember, many molecules dissolved in water, either inside the cell or outside, cannot get through the cell surface membrane. Only the water molecules are allowed through. As water leaves the cell, the cell starts to shrink. A red blood cell in a concentrated sugar solution looks very shrivelled. Other animal cells behave in the same way.

But, once again, the cell wall of a plant cell makes it behave rather differently. Just as in an animal cell, water leaves the plant through its partially permeable membrane. The contents of the cell shrink. But the cell wall stays quite firm. It collapses inwards a bit, but not much. As the cell loses water, it becomes less rigid. It gets floppy, or **flaccid**. If the plant cell loses a lot of water, its contents may shrink so much that the inside parts pull away from the cell wall. This is called **plasmolysis**.

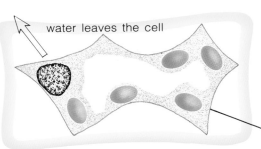

Fig. 8.6 A plant cell in a concentrated solution. The cell contents (but not the cell wall) shrink. The cell becomes flaccid. If the contents shrink so much that the cell surface membrane is pulled away from the cell wall, the cell is said to be plasmolysed.

Fig. 8.7 Red blood cells in a concentrated solution. Water has moved out of their cytoplasm, by osmosis, through their cell surface membranes into the solution surrounding them. The cells have become shrunken.

Fig. 8.5 An animal cell in a concentrated solution. The cell shrinks.

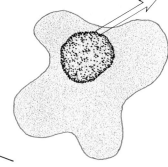

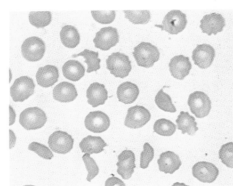

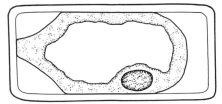

INVESTIGATION 8.1

Osmosis and raisins

Raisins are dried grapes. They are made up of plant cells. The grapes are left in the sun to dry. A lot of the water inside their cells evaporates, leaving each cell full of a very concentrated sugar solution.

1 Draw a raisin.
2 Put some raisins into a petri dish and cover them with water. Leave them until your next lesson.
3 Draw a raisin after soaking it in water.

Questions

1 Where were the following when you put the raisins into water:
   a a concentrated solution
   b an extremely dilute solution
   c partially permeable membranes?
2 Explain, as fully as you can, why the raisins became swollen after soaking in water.

Questions

1 The diagram below shows a plant cell which has just been put into a concentrated sugar solution.

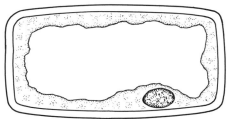

a Copy the diagram and label: concentrated sugar solution; cell wall; cell surface membrane; fairly concentrated solution.
b The diagram below shows the same cell after being in the solution for 30 minutes. Copy the diagram and label: concentrated sugar solution (in two places); cell wall; cell surface membrane.

c Which part is the partially permeable membrane?
d Which cell is the flaccid cell?
e How could you make the flaccid cell turgid?

2 *Amoeba* is a single-celled organism made up of a cell about 0.1 mm across. It lives in fresh-water ponds. Like all cells, it is surrounded by a partially permeable cell surface membrane, surrounding a fairly concentrated solution of proteins and other substances in water. *Amoeba* has a small, water-filled space inside it called a contractile vacuole. The contractile vacuole keeps filling up with water, and then emptying this water outside the cell. It does this non-stop, at frequent intervals.

a Explain why you think that *Amoeba* needs a contractile vacuole, and what might happen to it if it did not have one.
b A different kind of *Amoeba* lives in the sea. It does not have a contractile vacuole. Why do you think this is?

23

9 SUPPLYING CELLS

Cells need water, food and oxygen. In small organisms cells can get these things by diffusion. In large organisms a transport system is needed.

Cells need a supply of water, food and oxygen

All cells need water and food. Most cells need oxygen. These substances get into the cell through its cell surface membrane. A cell on its own, such as *Amoeba*, gets its food, water and oxygen from the water in which it lives. The molecules go into the cell by **diffusion**. Because cells are very small it takes hardly any time at all for the molecules to diffuse right into the middle of the cell.

Large organisms need transport systems

In a large organism, such as fish, the cells in the middle of its body are a long way from the water around it. It would take far too long for oxygen to diffuse into them from the water. So large animals and plants need a **transport system**. The transport system carries substances around their bodies and supplies every cell with whatever it needs. In many animals, including humans, this transport system is the **blood system** or **circulatory system**.

The human blood system is made up of the heart and blood vessels

The blood system is made up of thousands of tubes which carry blood to every cell in the body. These tubes are called **blood vessels**. There are several different sorts of blood vessels. There is a pump (the heart) which keeps the blood moving swiftly through these vessels. It works continuously throughout life.

Humans have a double circulatory system

The heart is really two pumps side by side. One side pumps blood to the head and body. The other side pumps blood to the lungs.

The two pumps are closely joined together, and pump with exactly the same rhythm. But blood cannot get directly from one side to the other.

To understand how the system works, look at Figure 9.1. Begin in the right-hand side of the heart (the left-hand side of the diagram). The heart pumps blood out of its right-hand side, along a vessel to the lungs.

In the lungs, the blood collects oxygen from the air you breathe in. The blood goes back along another vessel to the heart. This time it goes into the left-hand side of the heart.

This side pumps the blood out along another vessel, this time to the head or some other part of the body. Here, cells will take oxygen from the blood. The blood which has had some oxygen removed flows along yet another vessel which carries it back to the right-hand side of the heart. The whole journey now begins again.

So, on one complete journey round the body, the blood goes through the heart twice – first one side and then the other. This arrangement is called a **double circulatory system**. All mammals have a blood system like this.

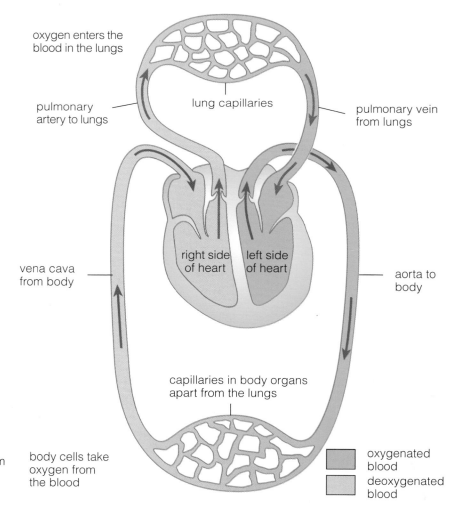

oxygen enters the blood in the lungs

pulmonary artery to lungs

lung capillaries

pulmonary vein from lungs

vena cava from body

right side of heart

left side of heart

aorta to body

capillaries in body organs apart from the lungs

body cells take oxygen from the blood

oxygenated blood

deoxygenated blood

Fig. 9.1 The double circulatory system of a mammal.

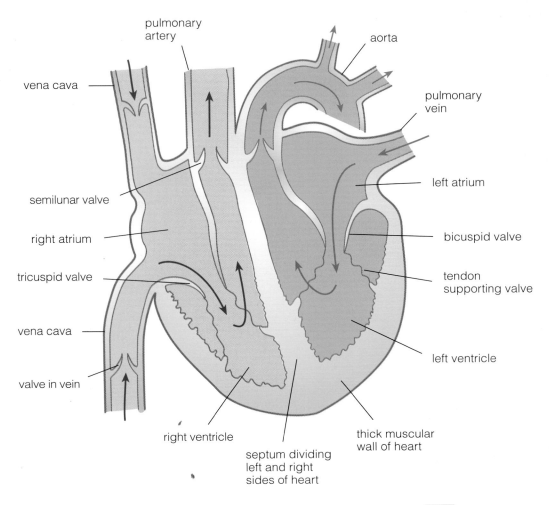

pulmonary artery

aorta

vena cava

pulmonary vein

semilunar valve

left atrium

right atrium

bicuspid valve

tricuspid valve

tendon supporting valve

vena cava

left ventricle

valve in vein

right ventricle

thick muscular wall of heart

septum dividing left and right sides of heart

Fig. 9.2 A vertical section through a mammal's heart.

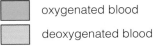

oxygenated blood

deoxygenated blood

─ EXTENSION ─

Double circulatory systems keep blood moving fast

Fish do not have a double circulatory system. Their blood goes only once through the heart on one complete journey round the body. The heart pumps the blood to the gills. It picks up oxygen from the gills. From the gills, the blood continues around the body, without going back to the heart first.

A double circulatory system is a really good arrangement for keeping blood moving at a good pace around the body. Blood has to go to the lungs to collect oxygen before it goes to the other cells in the body, or it would not have any oxygen to give them. But if it went straight to these cells from the lungs, it would lose a lot of the speed

and pressure which the heart had given it. By going back to the heart again after going to the lungs, the blood is given another boost to push it round the body quickly. This enables the blood to carry its oxygen swiftly to all the cells which need it. It is no coincidence that it is the most active, fast-moving animals such as birds and mammals, which have double circulatory systems. The quick, efficient supply of oxygen to all their cells means that these cells can respire rapidly, producing energy for movement and keeping warm.

Questions

1 Besides speed, what other advantage does a double circulatory system have over the type found in fish?

2 Suggest how the structure of a fish's heart might differ from the structure of a mammal's heart. Find out if you are right.

Your heart beats all your life, pumping up to 25 litres of blood every minute. Like all pumps, it has a power source – the heart muscle – and valves to ensure flow in one direction.

The most reliable pump ever!

Mass:
  between 250 g and 400 g
Flow rate:
  up to 25 dm³/min
Pressure developed:
  right side up to 5 kPa
  left side up to 26 kPa
Rate of beating:
  65 beats per minute on average
Total number of beats in a 70 year lifetime:
  2 391 480 000
Fuel:
  glucose and oxygen
Fuel consumption:
  26 cm³ oxygen per minute at cruising speed
  150 cm³ oxygen per minute at high speed
Servicing intervals:
  with care, should last a lifetime
Maintenance instructions:
  use regularly at higher beat rates; keep supply vessels clear by avoiding saturated fats in diet; do not smoke; keep body weight at reasonable level.

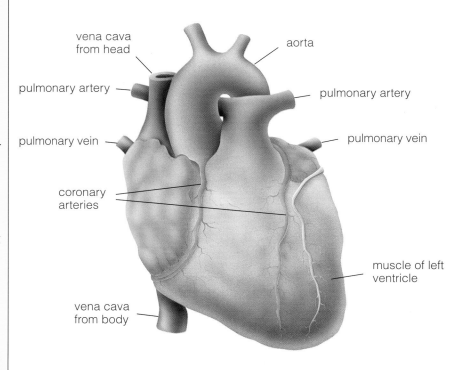

vena cava from head

aorta

pulmonary artery

pulmonary artery

pulmonary vein

pulmonary vein

coronary arteries

muscle of left ventricle

vena cava from body

Fig. 10.1   External view of the human heart

The heart has four chambers

The heart contains four spaces called chambers. The two upper ones are small, with thin walls. These are the right and left **atria**. These are the parts of the heart into which blood flows first.

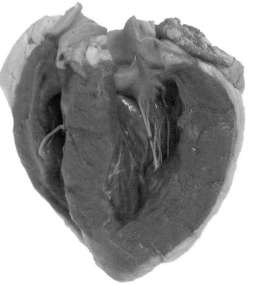

Fig. 10.2   A sheep's heart, cut open to show the chambers and valves. Try to identify: left and right ventricles; left atrium (this is very small, and has not been cut open); openings to the aorta and the pulmonary artery; semi-lunar valve in the aorta; bicuspid or mitral valve at the top of the left ventricle; tendons supporting this valve. Notice how thick the wall of the left ventricle is, and the septum which separates the two sides of the heart.

Beneath the atria are the two **ventricles**. These are the real powerhouses of the heart. Their thick walls are made of cardiac muscle. When this muscle shortens or contracts, it squeezes inwards on the blood inside the ventricles. This pushes the blood out of the heart. The left ventricle is quite a bit larger than the right ventricle. The main reason for this is that the left ventricle has to be able to produce a much bigger force, as it has to push blood all around the body. The right ventricle has to push blood only to the lungs, which are very close to the heart. To produce a big force, a lot of muscle is needed, so the left ventricle has extra thick walls.

The atria need only thin walls, as they have to produce only enough force to push blood into the ventricles below them.

Valves keep blood moving in the right direction

All pumps need valves, to keep the fluid they pump moving in one direction. The heart has four sets of valves.

Two of these sets are between the atria and the ventricles. On the left side is the **mitral** or **biscuspid** valve. The one on the right is the **tricuspid** valve. These valves make sure that blood can flow easily from the atria into the ventricles, but not in the opposite direction. Figure 10.3 shows how they work.

The other two sets of valves are in the entrances to the two large arteries through which the blood leaves the heart. They are called **semi-lunar** (half-moon) valves because of their shape. They allow blood to flow out of the ventricles into the arteries, but not back the other way.

Fig. 10.3 How the bicuspid valve works. Only the left-hand side of the heart is shown.

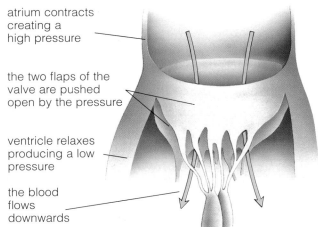

atrium contracts creating a high pressure

the two flaps of the valve are pushed open by the pressure

ventricle relaxes producing a low pressure

the blood flows downwards

atrium relaxes

blood is forced up against the valve flaps pushing them together

ventricle contracts producing a high pressure

the tendons attached to the valves will hold them, so that they cannot swing too far upwards

a When the ventricle relaxes and the atrium contracts, blood is squeezed against the flaps of the valve. This pushes the flaps downwards, and the blood flows through from the atrium to the ventricle.

b When the ventricle contracts, it pushes the blood up against the valves. They will be pushed upwards. The two flaps will be pushed tightly together, so no blood will be able to flow upwards.

Tendons hold valves in position

The valves between the atria and the ventricles have strong cords attaching them to the wall of the ventricle. These cords are called **tendons**. The tendons stop the valves from swinging too far up into the atria. When the ventricles contract, blood is squeezed up against the valves. The valves are pushed upwards. They swing up until the tendons are pulled taut. The tendons hold them in just the right position to make a barrier so that blood cannot get through.

INVESTIGATION 10.1

Looking at a mammal's heart

Sheep and pig hearts are sold in super-markets and butcher's shops.

1 Describe the shape and size of the heart.

2 The heart is made almost entirely of dark red muscle. What is the name of this kind of muscle?

3 Running over the surface of the heart are branching blood vessels. What are these called?

4 If the heart has not been too badly damaged, you will be able to find the two atria at the top of it. How thick are their walls compared with the thickness of the ventricle walls? Why is there a difference between them?

5 Look at the large tubes coming out of the top of the heart. These are the **aorta** and the **pulmonary artery**. Push a pencil – or better still, a finger – down through these tubes to find out which part of the heart they are coming from. Which part is it? Where would each of these arteries take blood to in the living animal?

6 Using scissors, cut through the walls of the aorta, continuing the cut to cut right through the wall of the left ventricle. Look for the thin, floppy **semi-lunar valves** in the wall of the aorta. What is their function?

7 The inside of the ventricle has little bumps on it. Attached to these are white cords, called **tendons**. What is their function? Attached to the top of the tendons, at the top of the ventricle, are more valves. What is the function of these valves?

8 Cut into the right ventricle. Is it bigger or smaller than the left ventricle? Why?

9 Notice the thick wall of muscle which separates the right and left ventricles. What is this dividing wall called? There is no way for blood to get through it. So how does blood get from one side of the heart to the other?

11 HEART-BEAT

Your heart beats at around 65 times a minute. It speeds up or slows down according to how much work you are doing. A blockage in the vessels supplying the heart muscle with oxygen can cause a heart attack.

Heart rate is controlled by a pacemaker

The rate at which your heart beats is controlled by a patch of muscle in the right atrium, called the **pacemaker**. When you are resting, the pacemaker beats at a speed of about 65 beats per minute (yours might be slower or faster than this). When you exercise, the brain sends messages along nerves to the pacemaker to make it beat faster.

Sometimes, the heart's pacemaker does not work properly, perhaps because it has become diseased. A person with this problem can be fitted with an artificial pacemaker. This is a small, battery-powered device which gives out electrical signals at regular intervals. The heart muscle responds to the signals by contracting at the same rate.

Electrocardiograms

Electrocardiograms, or ECGs, give information about the way the heart is beating. Electrodes attached to the skin of the chest, near the heart, pick up electrical signals from it as messages travel from the pacemaker to the rest of the muscles. ECG A is a normal one, showing a normal steady heartbeat. ECG B shows a heart which is contracting in an un-coordinated, haphazard way. This is called **fibrillation**, and is fatal if not treated immediately.

Fig. 11.1 Electrocardiograms

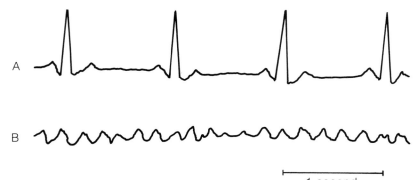

A

B

|— 1 second —|

EXTENSION

INVESTIGATION 11.1

How does exercise affect the rate at which your heart beats?

The more exercise you do, the more oxygen your muscles need. To supply them with this extra oxygen, your heart beats faster than usual. This pushes blood quickly to the lungs to collect oxygen, and then to the muscle cells to deliver it.

Fig. 11.2 Finding your pulse. Let your left wrist flop downwards. Using two or three fingers of your right hand – not your thumb – find the tendon near the outside of your wrist. Feel down in the hollow beside it.

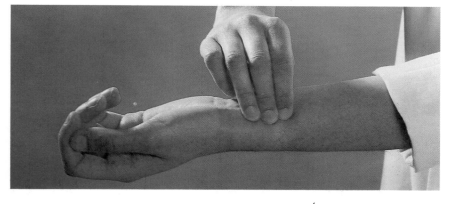

1 Rest quietly, until you are really relaxed. Find your pulse and count how many times your heart beats in 1 min. Record this in a results chart.
2 Still resting, record your pulse rate again, and fill it in on your chart.
3 Carry out some exercise until you feel slightly out of breath.

You could do some press-ups, or step up and down on to a chair.
4 As soon as you finish exercising, take your pulse rate again. Keep taking it every minute, filling in each result on your chart. Keep taking the rate until you have two readings which are nearly the same as the ones you began with.

Questions

1 Draw a line graph to show your results.
2 What is your normal pulse rate at rest?
3 What was your maximum pulse rate during this investigation?
4 After you stopped exercising, how long did it take your pulse rate to return to normal?
5 Explain why your heart beats faster then normal when you exercise.

Heart sounds give information about how the valves are working

When a person has a medical checkup, the doctor will usually listen to their heartbeat. A normal heartbeat has two sounds when heard through a stethoscope. The first is made by the valves between the atria and ventricles as they snap shut. The second is a similar, but slightly quieter, sound made by the closure of the valves in the aorta and pulmonary artery.

Sometimes, an extra sound can be heard. This is called a **heart murmur**. Many people who have heart murmurs are perfectly healthy. But sometimes a murmur may be caused by turbulence as blood flows past a faulty valve. If the problem is very bad, then artificial heart valves can be put into the heart to replace the faulty ones.

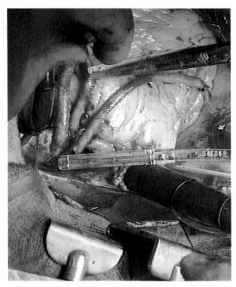

Fig. 11.3 Heart surgery being carried out.

Heart attacks are caused by damaged coronary arteries

The muscle in the heart needs a continuous supply of oxygen. If it does not get it, it may stop beating, or begin to beat very irregularly. This is a **heart attack**, or **cardiac arrest**.

Oxygen is supplied to the heart muscle by the coronary arteries (see Figure 10.1). If these are blocked, then the amount of blood flowing through them is reduced, and the heart muscle runs out of oxygen. The most usual cause of a blockage in a coronary artery is the build-up of a fatty substance called **cholesterol**, which narrows the artery and stiffens its wall. This is most likely to happen in people who smoke, or eat a lot of animal fat (such as butter), and who do little exercise. If the problem is realised in time, a badly damaged coronary artery can be by-passed. A healthy piece of blood vessel is taken from another part of the patient's body. This is often a leg. It is then attached to the heart in such a way that it carries blood past the damaged artery to the heart muscle which needs it. Coronary by-pass operations have saved many lives.

Heart attacks are still one of the major causes of death in Britain. You can cut down your chances of having a heart attack when you are older by the way you live now. Do not smoke; do not eat too much animal fat; and do some regular exercise.

Questions

Read the following passage. Use the information in the passage, and your own knowledge, to answer the questions.

The benefits of by-pass surgery

The coronary artery supplies the muscles of the heart with oxygenated blood. Several smaller coronary vessels branch off from the coronary artery. These vessels sometimes become partially blocked. The narrowing of the coronary vessels reduces blood flow to the heart muscles. One symptom of coronary artery problems is pain in the region of the heart and left arm. This pain is called angina. Patients with poor coronary circulation are unable to perform vigorous exercise, because the supply of oxygen to the heart muscle is inadequate. They run a high risk of a heart attack, which could be fatal.

It has been accepted for some time that coronary by-pass surgery can relieve the pain of angina and improve the quality of life of sufferers from coronary artery problems. Comparative studies have been carried out to see what happened to patients who had this surgery, or were just treated with drugs. The studies found that, five years after treatment, 92% of patients who had had coronary by-pass surgery were still alive. Only 83% of those treated with drugs were still alive. Twelve years after treatment, 71% of surgery patients and 67% of those treated with drugs were still alive.

This suggests that coronary by-pass surgery is a better treatment for sufferers from coronary problems than the use of drugs alone. However, twelve years after treatment the difference between the two groups is not very great. This is partly because the by-pass grafts tend to deteriorate with time. This may mean that a second by-pass operation is needed, which is much riskier than the first. The implication of these studies is that mild coronary problems are probably better treated at first with drugs rather than surgery. This means that if a by-pass operation does turn out to be needed later, there is less likelihood that a second, risky, one will have to be used. But severe coronary artery disease should be treated immediately with by-pass surgery.

1 a Why does coronary artery disease limit a person's ability to perform vigorous exercise?
  b Give one symptom of coronary artery disease.
  c Give two factors which may increase a person's risk of suffering from coronary artery problems.
  d What is 'coronary by-pass surgery'?
  e What evidence is there from this study that coronary by-pass surgery is more successful than the use of drugs in treating coronary artery disease?
  f Explain why it is recommended that mild coronary artery disease should initially be treated with drugs rather than surgery.

12 BLOOD VESSELS

Blood is carried around the body in tubes called blood vessels. Arteries take blood away from the heart. Veins return blood to the heart. Capillaries, which link arteries and veins, deliver blood to the body tissues.

Blood vessels take blood all over the body

In humans, the blood is contained in tubes called **blood vessels**. There are three types – arteries, veins and capillaries.

Blood leaves the heart by one of two large **arteries**. These are the **pulmonary artery**, which goes to the lungs, and the **aorta**, which goes to the rest of the body. The pulmonary artery divides into two, one branch going to each lung. But the aorta splits into many smaller arteries, each delivering blood to one of the many body organs. Figure 12.7 shows just some of these many branches.

On reaching its destination, each artery divides into many tiny vessels called **capillaries**. These penetrate right inside every tissue, forming a network which takes blood close to every individual cell. A network of capillaries is sometimes called a **capillary bed**.

The capillaries then gradually join up with each other to form larger vessels called **veins**. Veins carry blood back to the heart. The veins from the body empty into one of the two large veins called **venae cavae**, which empty into the right hand side of the heart. The veins from the lungs are called **pulmonary veins**, and these empty into the left-hand side of the heart.

Arteries have muscular walls

Arteries carry blood away from the heart. This blood is at high pressure, travelling fast, so the walls of arteries must be strong. Artery walls are also elastic, as this allows them to give a little as the blood surges through. You can feel this happening when you feel your pulse. Each surge of blood from the heart pushes outwards on the artery wall, and in between surges the wall recoils inwards again. This helps to keep the blood flowing smoothly, as the elastic recoil of the wall gives the blood an extra 'push' in between the pushes from the heart.

Capillaries have very thin walls

The job of capillaries is to deliver oxygen, food and other substances to body tissues, and to collect waste materials from them. So their walls must be really thin, to let these substances move into and out of them. Often, these walls are only one cell thick. They have small gaps in them, too, to make it even easier for substances to pass through. Capillaries are very tiny, in many cases only 7 µm (0.007 mm) in diameter.

Fig. 12.1 An artery

thick outer wall

thick layer of muscles and elastic fibres

small lumen

smooth lining

Fig. 12.2 A capillary

very small lumen

wall made of a single layer of cells

Fig. 12.3 A vein

fairly thin outer wall

thin layer of muscles and elastic fibres

large lumen

smooth lining

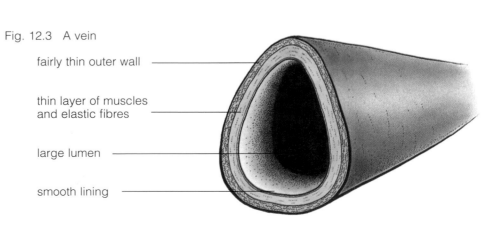

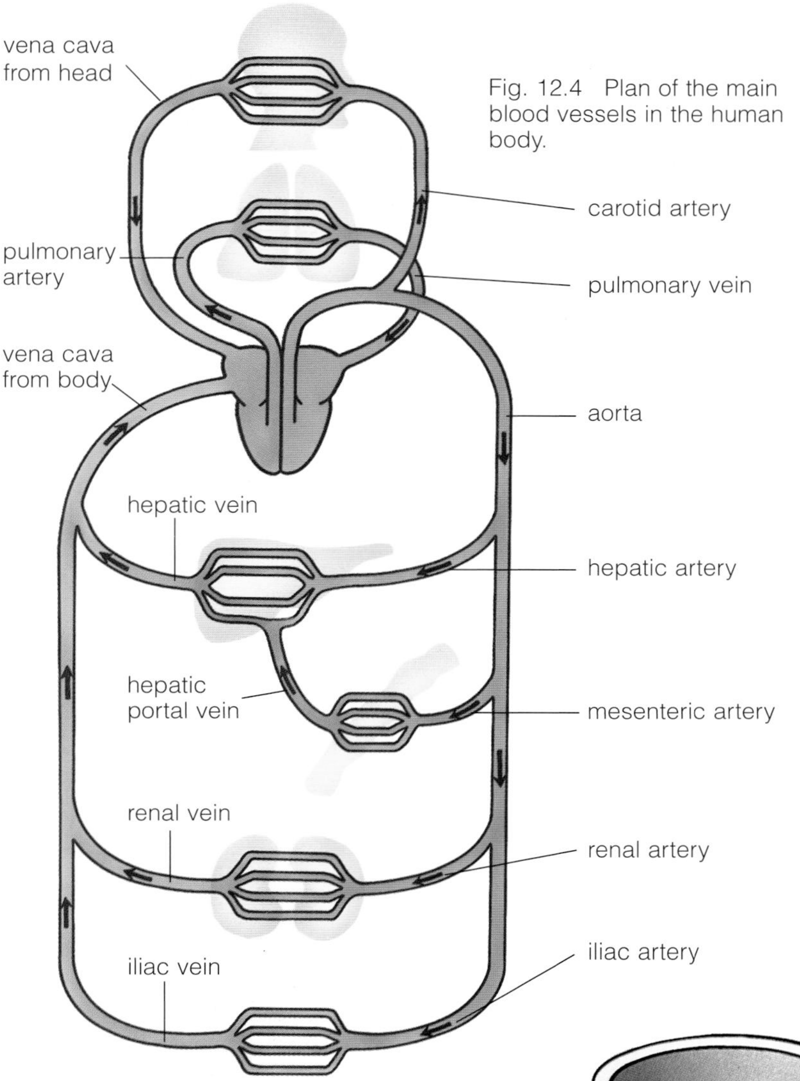

vena cava from head

pulmonary artery

vena cava from body

hepatic vein

hepatic portal vein

renal vein

iliac vein

Fig. 12.4 Plan of the main blood vessels in the human body.

carotid artery

pulmonary vein

aorta

hepatic artery

mesenteric artery

renal artery

iliac artery

Veins have thin walls, and valves

Veins carry blood back to the heart from the tissues. By the time it enters the veins, the blood has lost most of its impetus, and is travelling quite slowly at low pressure. So veins do not need to have strong, elastic walls like arteries. Instead, they are wide and have valves to help the blood to flow through them easily. The valves stop blood going backwards, and make sure that blood flow is always towards the heart. Many veins lie between muscles and this also helps to keep the blood flowing in them. The big veins in your legs lie between the leg muscles. When you walk, the movements of these muscles squeeze in on the veins, pushing the blood along inside them.

Fig. 12.5 Valves in a vein

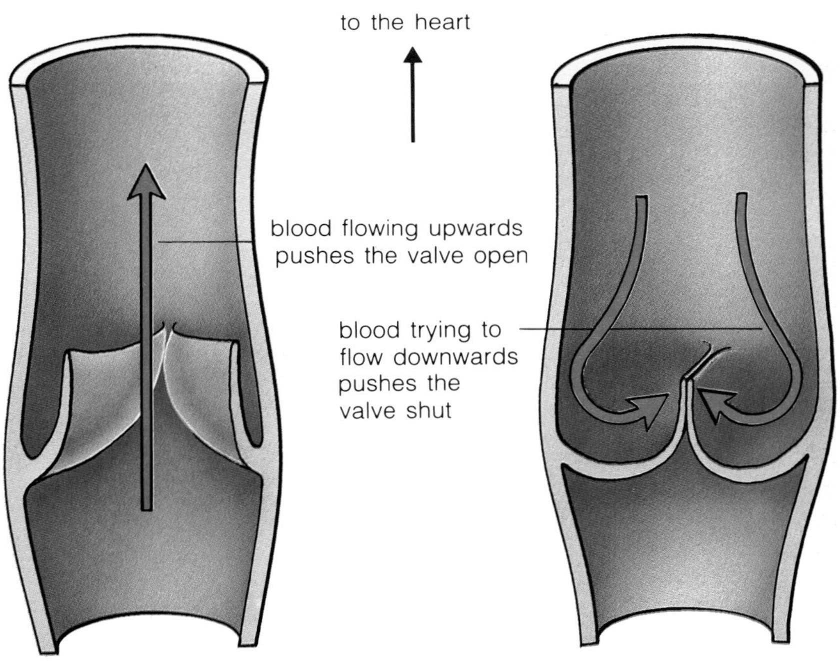

to the heart

blood flowing upwards pushes the valve open

blood trying to flow downwards pushes the valve shut

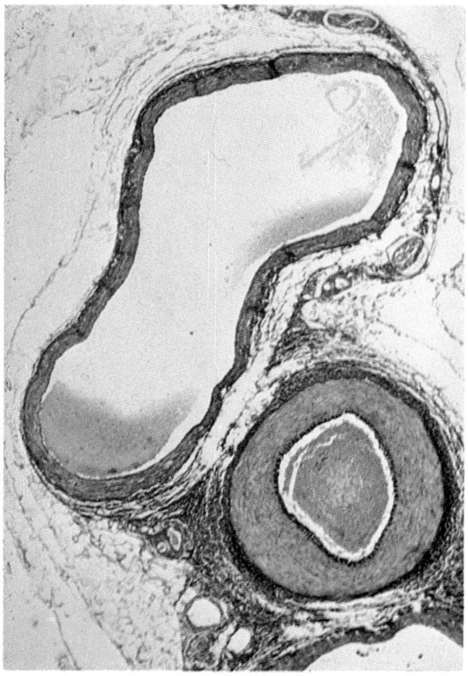

Fig. 12.6

Question

1 The photograph in Figure 12.6 shows a section through two blood vessels. One is an artery and one a vein. Which is which? Give as many reasons as you can for your choice.

Problems with blood vessels

Problems with blood vessels are one of the commonest medical complaints, especially in people who are overweight and unfit. However, you do not need to be overweight or unfit to suffer from a **bruise**. A bruise is caused when blood capillaries in or just under the skin are broken, and blood leaks from them. The dark colour is the blood seen through the skin. As the blood is gradually broken down the bruise changes colour.

Varicose veins are raised veins near the surface of the skin, usually on the legs. They are caused when the valves in the leg veins stop working properly, allowing blood to flow the wrong way. The blood collects in these veins instead of flowing back to the heart, and stretches their walls.

Hardening of the arteries is medically known as **atherosclerosis**. It is a stiffening of the artery walls so that they cannot stretch and recoil as the blood pulses through. It can be caused by a build-up of cholesterol. If this happens in the coronary arteries a heart attack may result. The artery walls become weaker, and are more likely to burst if the blood inside them is at high pressure. If this happens in the brain, blood spills out and damages brain cells. This is called a **stroke**.

A **thrombosis** is a blood clot. Blood clots inside blood vessels can be dangerous, because they may block important vessels such as the coronary arteries, causing a heart attack.

Questions

1 For each of the following, state whether they are associated with arteries, veins or capillaries:

a valves
b pulsating, muscular walls
c blood taken away from the heart
d walls made of a single cell

e blood taken towards the heart
f blood taken very close to every cell
g leaky walls

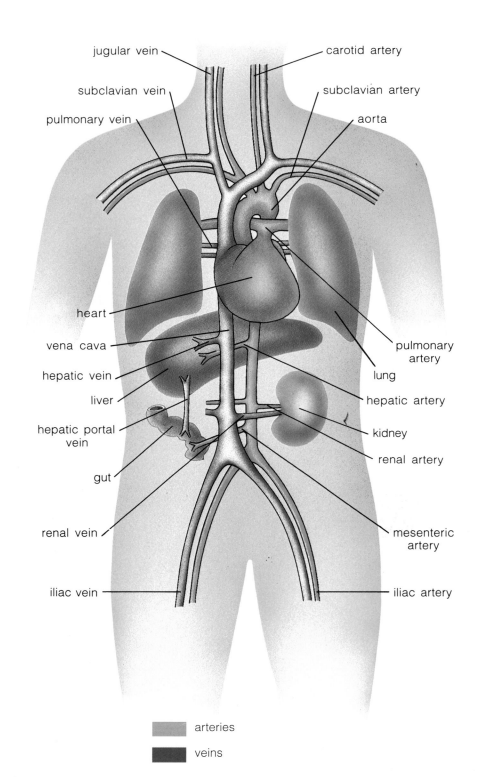

Fig. 12.7 The positions of some of the main vessels in the human body

arteries

veins

13 BLOOD

Blood is made of a liquid in which float several kinds of cells. It transports all sorts of substances around the body, and defends you against diseases.

The liquid part of blood is called plasma

You might be forgiven for thinking that blood is a red liquid. But, in fact, if you see blood under a microscope you realise this is not quite true. The red part of blood is not actually liquid at all. Blood looks red because it contains red cells, which float in a pale yellowish liquid. The liquid part of the blood is called **plasma**. Plasma is mostly water. Many different substances are dissolved in the water. They include glucose, amino acids, vitamins, ions such as sodium and chloride, and blood proteins. These blood proteins have some important roles to play in helping the blood to clot, and in fighting disease.

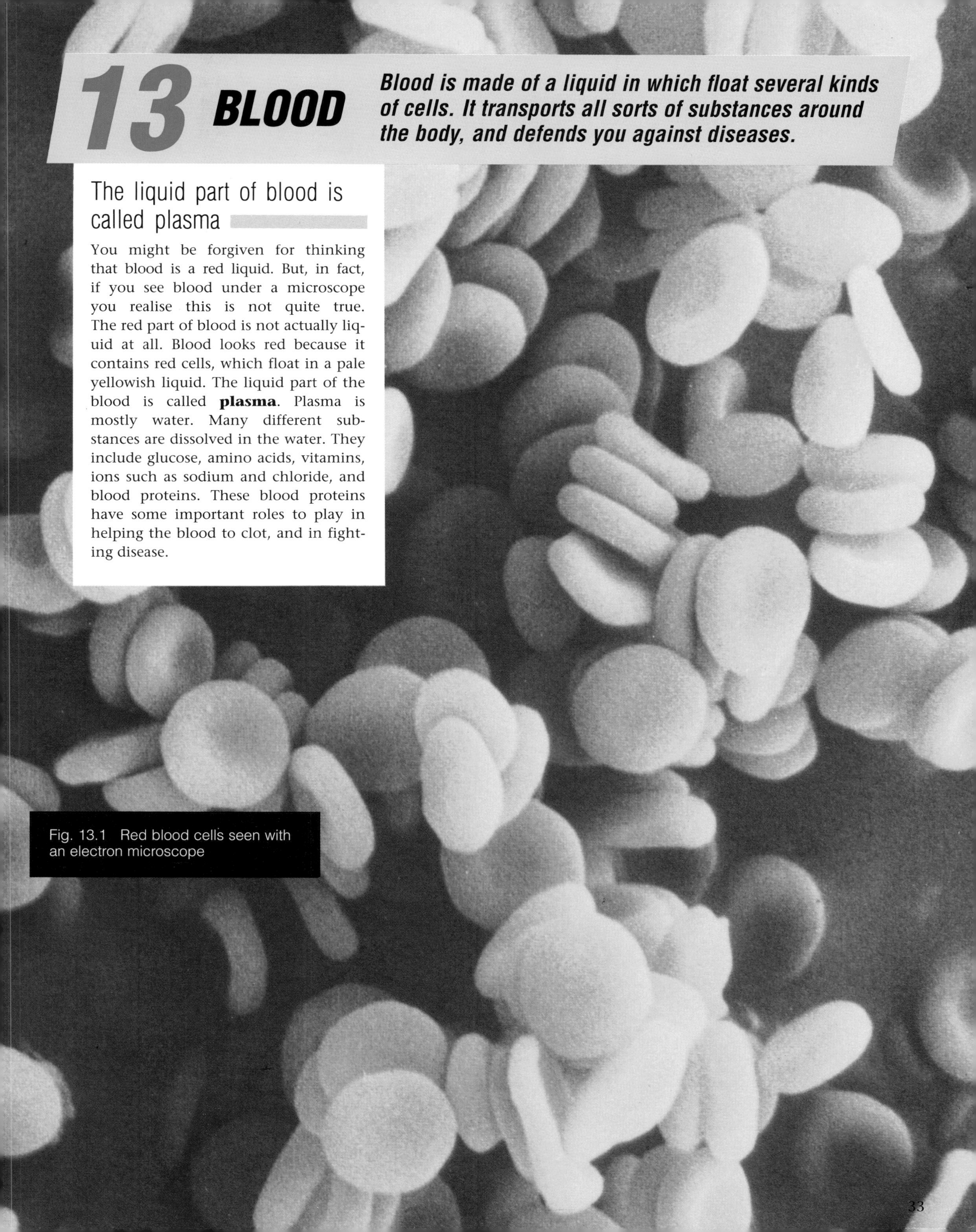

Fig. 13.1　Red blood cells seen with an electron microscope

Red blood cells transport oxygen

Red blood cells are much the most common cells in your blood. They are very small cells. You have about 5 million of them in 1 ml of blood!

Red cells are red because they are full of a protein called **haemoglobin**. Haemoglobin is sometimes called **Hb** for short. Hb combines with oxygen as the blood flows through the lungs, becoming **oxyhaemoglobin** or **oxyHb**. The blood flows out of the lungs, back to the heart, and then round the body. As it passes through the capillaries, the oxyHb gives up its oxygen to the body cells, becoming Hb again. OxyHb is bright red, and Hb is purplish red, so your blood actually changes colour as it goes round and round the body.

Red cells are very unusual because they have no nucleus. This is thought to be so that there is more room to pack in as much Hb as possible. Their shape gives them a large surface area, so that a lot of oxygen can get in or out of them very quickly. Their small size, and the fact that they are quite flexible, makes it possible for them to squeeze along even the smallest capillaries. They may have to go in single file if the capillaries are very tiny, but this is useful because it means that every red cell gets very close to the cells to which it is delivering oxygen.

Blood transports carbon dioxide

The blood also transports carbon dioxide. Body cells produce carbon dioxide when they respire. The carbon dioxide diffuses into the blood. Most of the carbon dioxide is transported in solution in the blood plasma. Some of this is in the form of carbon dioxide molecules, but most of it is as hydrogencarbonate ions. A small amount of the carbon dioxide combines with the haemoglobin inside the red blood cells. So red cells are not the main way of transporting carbon dioxide, but they do help. When the blood reaches the lungs, the carbon dioxide leaves the blood and diffuses into the air spaces in the lungs, before being breathed out.

Fig. 13.2   Red blood cells

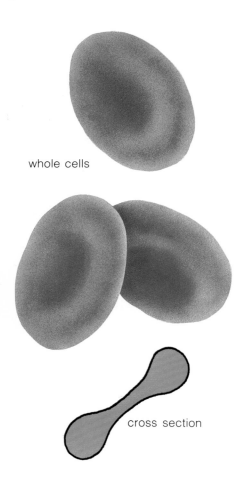

whole cells

cross section

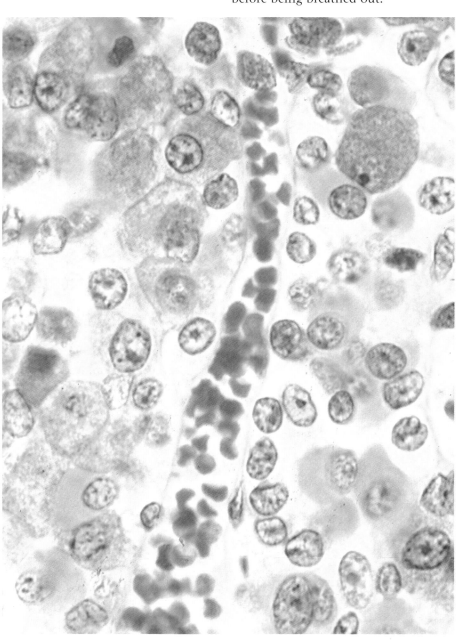

Fig. 13.3   Red blood cells in a capillary. The capillary runs from top to bottom through the centre. On either side are cells making up the tissue through which the capillary runs. Notice how small the red blood cells are, in comparison with the tissue cells.

White cells fight disease

There are far fewer white cells than red cells in your blood. White cells are slightly larger than red cells and they always have a nucleus. There are several different sorts, which can be divided into two main groups.

Phagocytes are irregularly shaped white cells, often with a lobed nucleus. They crawl actively around the body, squeezing in and out of capillary walls, and finding their way into every bit of you. Their job is to find and 'eat' any invading bacteria, or any of your own cells which have become damaged or worn-out. They do this by flowing around the bacterium, enclosing it in a vacuole, and then secreting enzymes on to it to digest it.

Platelets help in blood clotting

As well as red and white cells, the blood contains little cell fragments called **platelets**. These are smaller than red or white cells, and they do not have a nucleus – just cytoplasm surrounded by a cell surface membrane. Platelets come into action when a blood vessel is damaged, for example if you cut your skin. They react by secreting chemicals which stimulate the formation of a blood clot, and which encourage white cells to attack any bacteria that might invade through the broken skin. The platelets also help to block the wound by sticking to each other, to other blood cells, and to the walls of the damaged blood vessel.

Blood diseases

Some people don't have enough red cells in their blood. This makes them look pale, and they feel tired because not enough oxygen is being carried around their body. The disease is called **anaemia**. One very common cause of anaemia is not having enough iron in the diet. Iron is needed to make haemoglobin, the major component of red blood cells.

Leukaemia is a type of cancer which affects the white cells. So many white cells are made that there is not enough room in the blood for red cells. Leukaemia can be fatal, but is often treated successfully.

Lymphocytes also attack bacteria, but in a different way. They make proteins called **antibodies**. These are carried around the body in the blood and destroy foreign invading cells.

You can read more about how white cells help you to fight disease in Topic 62.

Fig. 13.4   White blood cells

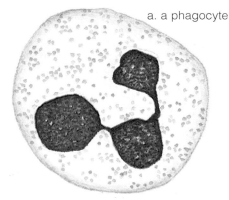
a. a phagocyte

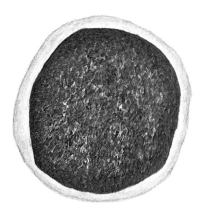
b. a lymphocyte

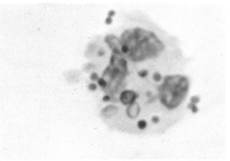

Fig. 13.5   A phagocytic white blood cell. The purple areas are the lobed nucleus. The smaller, redder objects are organisms which have been engulfed by the cell.

AIDS is another disease which affects the white cells. The AIDS virus reproduces inside lymphocytes and destroys them. This means that the body has lost its defence system, and is open to attack from any germs which come along. A person with AIDS eventually dies from one of these infections. You can find more about AIDS on pages 153–154.

Haemophilia is an inherited disease in which the blood does not clot properly. It can cause all sorts of problems. One of the most painful problems is caused by bleeding into the joints. Haemophilia is a sex-linked disease – only men suffer from it. It can be kept under control by giving regular doses of a substance called Factor 8, which is obtained from the blood of unaffected people. Haemophilia cannot be cured.

Fig. 13.6   Blood collected from donors is carefully labelled before storage. What information do you think needs to go on the label?

Questions

1   Briefly list the function of:
   a blood plasma
   b red blood cells
   c white blood cells
2   Explain why:
   a blood is red
   b blood in arteries is bright red, whereas blood in veins is purplish red
   c people feel tired if they do not have enough iron in their diet
   d someone with AIDS is likely to suffer from many different infections.

14 TISSUE FLUID AND LYMPH

Blood plasma leaks out of capillaries and forms tissue fluid. This is collected in lymphatic capillaries and returned to the blood.

Spaces between your cells are filled with tissue fluid

Capillaries leak. Tiny gaps in their walls allow blood plasma to leak out as the blood flows through them. The leaked blood plasma fills all the spaces between your cells. It is called **tissue fluid**.

Tissue fluid helps to carry substances between the blood and the body cells. Oxygen and glucose, needed by the cells for respiration, move from the blood to the cells. Carbon dioxide and other waste substances move from the cells to the blood.

The concentration of substances like glucose and water in the blood plasma is kept just right, in the processes known as **homeostasis**. As tissue fluid is made from blood plasma, it too has the correct concentrations of these important substances. So the cells are bathed in a fluid containing the correct concentrations of the substances that they need, allowing them to work really efficiently.

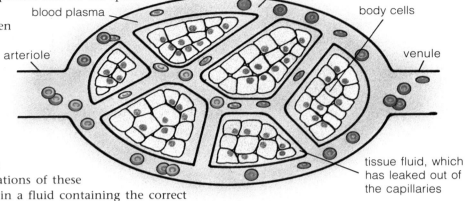

Fig. 14.1 A capillary bed

Fig. 14.2 Gas exchange through tissue fluid

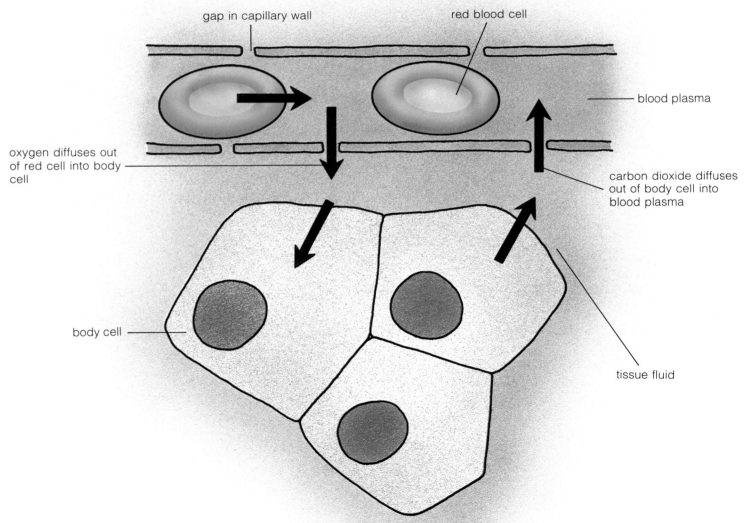

36

Tissue fluid is returned to the blood in lymph vessels

Blood capillaries are not the only tiny vessels running in amongst the body cells. There are also **lymphatic capillaries**. These collect up the tissue fluid from between the cells and drain into the lymphatic capillaries. These carry it to the neck. Here, they empty the fluid back into the blood. Lymphatic vessels have no pump to keep the fluid moving in them. They use the same method as veins. They lie between muscles, so that when the body moves, the muscles squeeze in on them. Valves in the lymphatic vessels make sure that the fluid only goes in one direction.

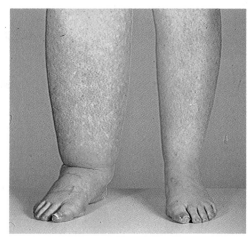

Fig. 14.3 This person has oedema. The tissue fluid between the cells in their right leg is not being carried away in the lymphatic vessels. The fluid builds up, making the leg swollen and puffy.

EXTENSION

Questions

The chart shows the changes in pressure inside the left atrium and left ventricle of a human heart during one heart beat.

a How long does one heart beat last?

b How many beats will there be in 1 min?

c For what proportion of one heart beat is the ventricle contracting?

d What is the maximum pressure reached in the ventricle in this heart beat?

e What is the maximum pressure reached in the atrium in this heart beat?

f Make a simple copy of this graph. On it, show the time in which you think the atrium is contracting. Show it in the same way as the ventricular contraction has been shown.

g Draw a vertical line on the graph to mark the time at which you think the valve between the atrium and ventricle will close.

h Draw another vertical line on the graph to mark the time at which you think this valve will open.

i Explain why you have drawn the two vertical lines in these positions.

j This graph shows what is happening in the left-hand side of the heart. Will the events in the right-hand side of the heart show a similar pattern at the same time?

k Will the pressures in the right-hand side of the heart be the same, higher or lower than shown on this graph? Explain your answer.

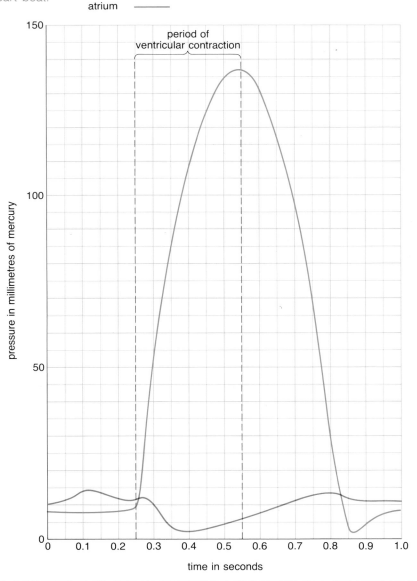

ventricle ———
atrium ———

period of ventricular contraction

pressure in millimetres of mercury

time in seconds

15 TRANSPORT IN PLANTS

Plants have two transport systems. Xylem transports water and minerals. Phloem transports sugars and amino acids. Transpiration pulls water up through the plant.

Plants have two transport systems

Plants have two separate transport systems. A network of **xylem vessels** transports water and mineral ions from the roots to all the other parts of the plant. **Phloem tubes** transport food made in the leaves to all other parts of the plant. Neither of these systems has a pump. Plants can manage without a heart to pump substances around their bodies, because they are not so active as animals. Muscle cells in an animal need rapid supplies of food and oxygen, but plant cells do not.

Neither xylem nor phloem transports oxygen. Plants do not have a special oxygen transport system. Oxygen gets to a plant's cells by diffusion. Both stems and roots contain xylem vessels and phloem tubes. In a stem, these are grouped into **vascular bundles** arranged in a ring. In a root, they are in the centre, forming a structure called the **stele**.

The **epidermis** is a layer of protective cells on the outside of the stem and root. The cells of the **cortex** are quite large, and often store starch. **Cambium** cells can divide, so that the root or the stem can grow wider.

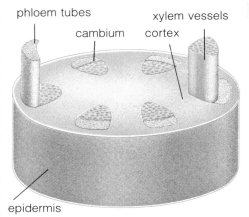

Fig. 15.1 Transverse section through a stem

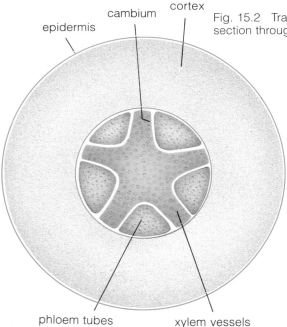

Fig. 15.2 Transverse section through a root

Xylem vessels carry water and minerals from the roots

Water gets into a plant through its roots. Near the tip of each branch of a root, there are thousands of tiny **root hairs**. Water from the soil moves into these hairs by osmosis. The small size and large number of root hairs gives them an enormous surface area. So a lot of water can get into the plant very quickly.

Mineral ions are dissolved in the water. These might include nitrate, phosphate, calcium and magnesium ions. These also enter the root hairs. They travel into the plant dissolved in water.

Once inside the plant's root, the water and ions move into the xylem vessels. The xylem vessels are like long drainpipes reaching all the way from the root to the tip of every leaf. They are made of dead cells, joined end to end.

Phloem vessels carry sugars from the leaves

The leaves of a plant make sugars by photosynthesis. These sugars are carried to other parts of the plant by the phloem vessels. Phloem vessels run from the leaves to every part of the plant. They also carry other substances made by the plant's cells, such as amino acids.

Phloem and xylem vessels often run side by side. A group of phloem and xylem vessels is called a **vascular bundle**. The veins in a leaf are vascular bundles.

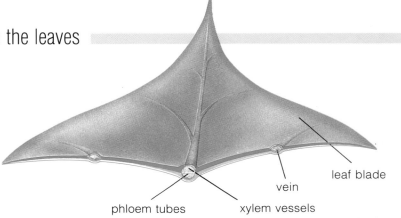

Fig. 15.3 A leaf, cut through to show the veins. The veins are vascular bundles. They branch all over the leaf, taking water and collecting food from the leaf cells. The rigid, dead xylem vessels also act as a skeleton supporting the leaf blade.

Transpiration pulls water up through xylem vessels

Plants have no heart to pump water through their xylem vessels. Yet water travels upwards very fast through them. Try standing a piece of freshly-cut leafy celery in a beaker of ink. If your celery is healthy, you can actually watch the ink moving up through the vascular bundles.

What makes water move up through xylem vessels? When the water reaches the top of the xylem vessels it goes into the leaves. Leaves contain large air

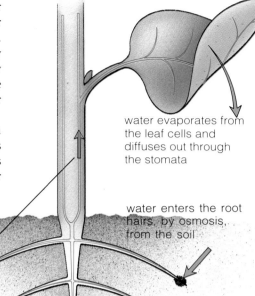

water evaporates from the leaf cells and diffuses out through the stomata

Fig. 15.4   The transpiration stream

the water travels up through the xylem vessels in the root, stem and leaf

water enters the root hairs, by osmosis, from the soil

spaces. They also have hundreds of small holes on their undersides, called **stomata**. Water from the xylem vessels evaporates when it gets to the leaves. It turns into gas. The gas diffuses out through the air spaces and stomata, into the air. This process is called **transpiration**. So water is constantly evaporating from a plant's leaves. To replace this water, more water moves out from the top of the xylem vessels. This pulls water in at the bottom of the xylem vessels. It is as though someone were 'sucking' water up the plant.

Plants may need to reduce transpiration

Transpiration is useful to a plant. It helps to draw water into the roots, and through the plant. Another useful effect of transpiration is that the evaporation of water from the leaves has a cooling effect. This may be very important to plants growing in hot conditions.

But if water is lost from a plant by transpiration faster than it can be taken up through the roots, then the plant's cells may become short of water. The cells become flaccid (Topic 8). When the cells are full of water, they are firm and rigid and help to support soft parts of the plant, such as its leaves. But when the cells are flaccid, the leaves become soft and floppy. The plant wilts. If the plant is short of water for too long, it may die.

Most plants are able to reduce the rate of transpiration if water is in short supply. They can close their stomata, so water vapour cannot escape through them from the leaves. They usually have a layer of wax on their leaves, so water vapour cannot escape through the leaf surface. Plants which live in dry places, such as deserts, may have a very thick layer of wax, and also other special features to help to cut down the loss of water from their leaves.

INVESTIGATION 15.1

Using a potometer to compare rates of water uptake

A potometer measures water uptake. There are many different types of potometer. But all of them have a tube into which a plant shoot can fit tightly. The tube is full of water. It is connected to a capillary tube. By watching how fast the water moves along the capillary tube, you can see how fast the shoot is taking up water.

1 Fill your potometer with water. There must be no air bubbles, and any joints must be completely airtight. Put Vaseline around any that you are not sure about.

2 Cut a leafy shoot from a plant. (Wash any Vaseline off your fingers first.) Try to choose a shoot of the right thickness to fit into your potometer. A slanting cut is often more successful than a straight one.

3 Push your shoot firmly into the potometer. It must make a really tight fit. If it does not fit, cut another shoot, or ask for help.

4 Leave the potometer for a few minutes to settle down. If everything is airtight, you should see the water meniscus moving along the capillary tube towards the plant. While you are waiting, draw up a results chart.

5 When the meniscus is moving smoothly, begin to record its position every minute for about 10 min. Record your results in a table and then draw a line graph of them.

6 If you have time, try changing the conditions around your shoot and collecting a new set of results. You could try the experiment in a cooler or warmer place, a lighter or darker place, blowing a fan on to it, or removing some of its leaves. Draw graphs to show any other results that you manage to obtain.

Questions

1 Draw a large, labelled diagram of the potometer which you used.

2 Why does the meniscus move towards the plant?

3 Why does the potometer not work properly if you fail to make everything airtight?

4 Even if you get everything airtight, the potometer will not work if a large air bubble gets trapped in the tube. Why?

5 If you managed to get more than one set of results, describe and explain any differences between them.

Questions

1 The photograph shows a blood smear from a healthy person. The blood has been stained and photographed through a microscope.

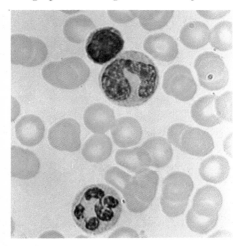

a How many white cells are visible in this photograph?

b Draw one of the white cells. Label its cell surface membrane, cytoplasm, and nucleus.

c What is the function of the type of white cell you have drawn?

d Give three ways in which the structure of red blood cells appears different from that of the white cells in this photograph.

e What is the function of red blood cells?

2 The diagram shows a vertical section through a mammalian heart.

a Copy the diagram. Add labels to each labelling line.

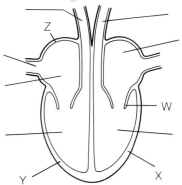

b On your diagram draw arrows to show how the blood enters, flows through, and leaves the heart. You will need to draw arrows on both sides of the heart.

c Why is the wall labelled X thicker than the wall labelled Y?

d Why is the wall labelled Z thinner than walls X and Y?

e What is the function of part W?

	Wall	Diameter	Valves	Explanation
Artery				
Vein				
Capillary				

3 Copy and complete this comparison table (above). The 'explanation' column needs plenty of space, because you may need to write quite a lot in it.

4 The graph shows how the rate of transpiration of an oak tree changed over a period of 24 hours.

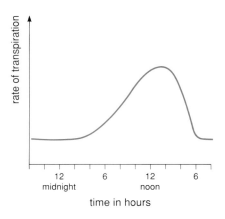

a At what time of day was the transpiration rate greatest?

b Why do you think the transpiration was highest at that time?

c The day on which these data were collected was a warm, dry day in summer. Make a copy of the graph. On your copy draw another line to show what you might expect to find on a cool, moist day in winter.

d Explain, as fully as possible, why you have chosen to draw your line in this way.

5 The photograph shows a micrograph of a transverse section through a plant stem.

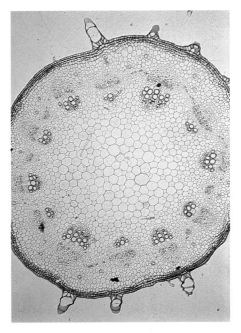

a Make a careful drawing of this photograph. You do *not* need to draw all the individual cells!

b On your diagram label the following:

epidermis   xylem
phloem   cortex

c Which of the four structures that you have labelled is made up of dead cells joined end-to-end to form long tubes?

d Which of the structures that you have labelled transports sugars from the leaves to the roots?

e Are the structures you have labelled:
A organelles
B organs
C tissues
D organisms?

PHOTOSYNTHESIS

16 PHOTOSYNTHESIS

Plant leaves are food factories. All the food in the world is made by plants and microorganisms.

All the energy of living organisms begins as light energy

All living things need energy. They need it to move, to make new cells, and to transport things around their bodies. Even plants, which do not seem to be doing very much, need energy. If you need extra energy, you eat extra food. Animals get their energy from the food they eat. Food contains energy. But where does the energy in food come from? It all begins as **sunlight**.

Plants change sunlight energy into chemical energy in food

If it were not for plants, there would be nothing at all for animals to eat. All the food in the world is made by plants. Plants use the energy in sunlight to make food. The food contains some of this energy. Animals – and plants, too – use the energy from food to stay alive. The name of the process by which plants use sunlight energy to make food is **photosynthesis**.

Fig. 16.1　Green plants harness energy from sunlight to make food. This beech wood is a giant food factory.

Fig. 16.2　A koala bear gets all its energy from that which has been trapped by eucalyptus leaves.

Plants use inorganic substances to make food

What do plants make this food from? They need two chemicals. One is **water**, which they get from the soil. The other is **carbon dioxide**, which they get from the air. They also need **sunlight energy**, which is used to make the water and carbon dioxide react together. Water and carbon dioxide are **inorganic** substances. Inorganic substances are substances which are not made by living things. They usually have small molecules.

These three things – water, carbon dioxide and sunlight – are sometimes called **raw materials**. They are the 'ingredients' from which the plant makes food.

Fig. 16.3   Some examples of inorganic substances

The inorganic raw materials are made into organic substances

The plant uses the energy in sunlight to make the water and carbon dioxide react together. This reaction produces two new substances. One is **glucose**. The other is **oxygen**.

Glucose is an **organic** substance. Organic substances have been made by living organisms. They usually have quite large molecules. They always contain carbon. The formula for one molecule of glucose is $C_6H_{12}O_6$ – so you can see that it *does* contain carbon, and it *does* have quite large molecules. The glucose contains some of the energy which started off in the sunlight. If you suck glucose sweets, you get energy from them. That energy was once sunlight energy and somewhere in the world a plant converted it into chemical energy which your body can now use. Plants are living food factories.

Fig. 16.4   Some examples of organic substances. There is also an inorganic substance here. What is it?

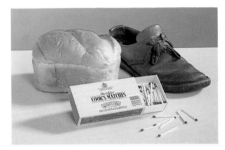

The photosynthesis equation

The raw materials for photosynthesis are water, carbon dioxide and sunlight energy. The products – the things which are made – are glucose and oxygen. This can be written as a word equation:

water + carbon dioxide $\xrightarrow{\text{sunlight energy}}$ glucose + oxygen

The balanced molecular equation for this reaction is:

$$6H_2O(l) + 6CO_2(g) \xrightarrow{\text{sunlight energy}} C_6H_{12}O_6(aq) + 6O_2(g)$$

Photosynthesis provides oxygen

Photosynthesis does not only provide all the food in the world. It also provides all the oxygen in the air.

When the Earth was first formed, the air contained gases like methane, ammonia, carbon dioxide and water vapour. There was no oxygen.

Then some tiny organisms appeared which could photosynthesise. The oxygen they made went into the atmosphere. Gradually, over millions of years, the amount of oxygen in the air built up. Now, about 20% of the air is oxygen.

We, and other animals, are completely dependent on plants. They provide us with two of the most important things we need to stay alive – food and oxygen.

Questions

1   Where does all the energy in food originate?
2 a What are the raw materials for photosynthesis?
  b What are the products of photosynthesis?
3 a Explain the differences between *organic* and *inorganic* substances.
  b Which of these substances are organic, and which are inorganic?
    wood, paper, aluminium foil, oil, a cotton shirt, a gold earring, sugar, pepper, salt, lettuce, oxygen

17 LEAVES

Photosynthesis happens in leaves. Leaves are food-making machines. They are perfectly designed to make food as efficiently as possible.

Chlorophyll absorbs sunlight

As you may have noticed, plants are green! The green colour is **chlorophyll**. All plants contain chlorophyll. Even plants like copper beech trees, which look a reddish-brown colour, have chlorophyll in their leaves.

Chlorophyll is an extremely important substance. Without it, photosynthesis could not happen. Chlorophyll absorbs energy from sunlight. Without this energy, carbon dioxide and water would not react together to make glucose. So chlorophyll is essential for photosynthesis.

Chlorophyll is kept in **chloroplasts**. Chloroplasts are organelles found in plant cells. Only cells which are above ground contain chloroplasts. Cells in roots do not contain them. There would be no point, because there is no light underground.

The cells which contain most chloroplasts are in **leaves**. Most photosynthesis happens in leaves. But other parts of plants above the ground can photosynthesise too. Stems for example may contain chloroplasts.

Fig. 17.1 The green colour of the countryside is caused by chlorophyll.

Leaves have several layers of cells

Leaves are very thin. Yet a leaf is made up of several layers of cells. Figure 17.4 shows these layers. The cells which contain chloroplasts and photosynthesise are in the middle layers. These layers are called the **mesophyll** layers. 'Mesophyll' means 'middle leaf'. There are two mesophyll layers. The one nearest the top of the leaf does most of the photosynthesis. It is called the **palisade** layer. This is where most of the chloroplasts are.

The other mesophyll layer is the **spongy** layer. These cells have big air spaces between them. They also contain chloroplasts, but not as many as the palisade layer. They too can photosynthesise.

The other two layers in the leaf are protective layers on the top and bottom. They are called the **epidermis** layers. The cells in the epidermis make a waxy substance, which spreads out over the surface of the leaf. This layer of wax is called the **cuticle**. The lower epidermis has holes in it, which open directly into the inside of the leaf. These holes are called **stomata**. They are very small, but you can see them with a microscope. Each stoma has a pair of special cells surrounding it, called **guard** cells. The guard cells can open or close the stomata.

Fig. 17.2 Leaves from a pear tree. You should be able to pick out at least five features that you can see in this picture, which help the leaves to carry out photosynthesis efficiently.

The raw materials for photosynthesis are delivered to the palisade layer

The main food-producing part of the leaf is the palisade layer. The raw materials for photosynthesis must be delivered to the cells in the palisade layer as swiftly as possible.·

Carbon dioxide gets into the leaf through the stomata. A very small part of the air – less than 0.04% – is carbon dioxide. Carbon dioxide diffuses through the open stomata into the air spaces between the cells in the spongy layer. Because the leaf is so thin, it quickly diffuses all the way to the chloroplasts in the palisade cells.

Water is brought to the leaves in tubes called **xylem vessels**. These are very long tubes, rather like drainpipes. They run all the way up from the root of the plant, through its stem, and into the leaves. The veins of a leaf contain xylem vessels. Branches of xylem vessels run close to every part of a leaf, so each palisade cell is provided with a constant supply of water. The carbon dioxide and water enter the chloroplasts in the palisade cells where chlorophyll is absorbing sunlight. The energy in the sunlight makes the carbon dioxide and water react together. Glucose and oxygen are made.

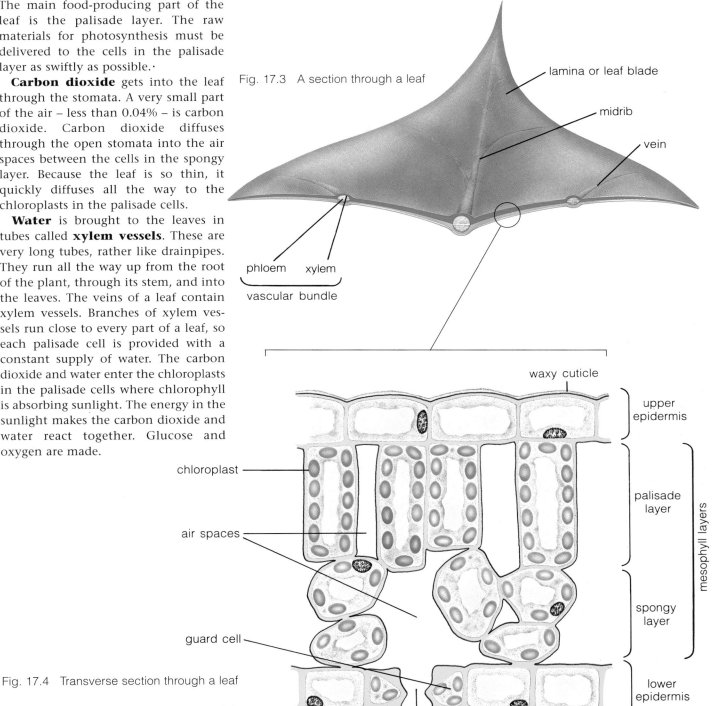

Fig. 17.3   A section through a leaf

lamina or leaf blade

midrib

vein

phloem   xylem

vascular bundle

waxy cuticle

upper epidermis

chloroplast

palisade layer

air spaces

mesophyll layers

spongy layer

guard cell

Fig. 17.4   Transverse section through a leaf

lower epidermis

waxy cuticle

stoma

Questions

1 a Precisely where is chlorophyll found?

b What does chlorophyll do?

2 Which layer(s) of a leaf:

a contain air spaces

b contain small holes called stomata

c contain most chloroplasts

d make a layer of wax

e photosynthesises

f protects the mesophyll cells?

3 Leaves are food factories. They are designed to make sure that the raw materials and energy source are supplied to the production line (the palisade layer) as swiftly as possible. Look at the photographs and diagrams of leaves on these two pages. What features of a leaf do you think:

a help to make sure that plenty of sunlight reaches the palisade layer

b help to provide plenty of carbon dioxide to the palisade layer

c help to provide plenty of water to the palisade layer

d make sure that this water does not evaporate from the leaf too quickly?

Some of the glucose made by a leaf is turned into starch and stored.

Glucose is turned into starch for storage

When plants photosynthesise they make glucose. Glucose molecules are quite small for organic molecules. They dissolve easily in water. They also react quite easily with other molecules. So they are not very good for keeping in a cell for a long time.

If a plant needs to store glucose molecules, it turns them into **starch** molecules. A starch molecule is very big. It is made of hundreds or thousands of glucose molecules linked together. Natural starch molecules do not dissolve in water. Although they are very long, they curl up tightly, so they fit into a small space. A leaf which has been photosynthesising will have a lot of starch molecules in it. The starch is in the form of **starch grains**, inside the chloroplasts in the mesophyll cells.

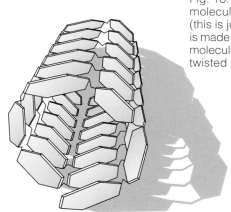

Fig. 18.1 Glucose and starch molecules. A starch molecule (this is just a small part of one) is made of hundreds of glucose molecules linked together, and twisted into a helix.

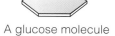

A glucose molecule

A small part of a starch molecule

Testing a leaf for starch

If you want to find out if a leaf has been photosynthesising, you can test it for starch. Starch turns blue-black when **iodine solution** is added to it. So you can add iodine solution to a leaf and see if goes blue-black. But first, you must break down the cell membranes in the leaf, so that the iodine solution can get into the chloroplasts and reach the starch. You also need to get rid of the green colour in the leaf. If you do not do this, it is very difficult to tell what colour the iodine solution turns.

Fig. 18.3 Testing a leaf for starch

Fig. 18.2 A chloroplast in a pea leaf. The dark green stripes are membranes, on which chlorophyll is spread out. The white area is a starch grain. Glucose made inside the chloroplast can be changed into starch and stored in this way.

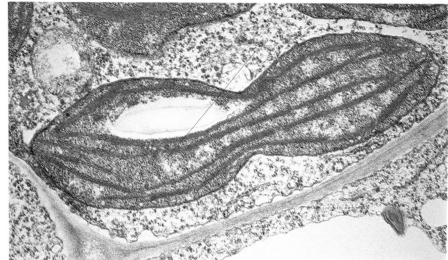

1 Heat the leaf in boiling water until it looks limp.

2 Turn out the Bunsen burner. Stand a tube of alcohol in the hot water, and put the softened leaf into the tube.

3 When the leaf has lost most of its colour, remove it gently from the alcohol. It will be very brittle, so dip it into the water to soften it.

4 Spread the leaf on to a white tile, and cover it with iodine solution. Wait a few minutes for the iodine solution to soak in. If the leaf goes black, it contains starch.

Is light needed for photosynthesis?

You are going to give part of a leaf plenty of sunlight, and keep part of it in the dark. Then you will test the leaf to see which parts of it contain starch.

1 First, remove all starch from a healthy plant. You can do this by leaving it in a dark cupboard for several days.

2 Test a leaf from your plant to check that it does not contain any starch by following these instructions.

a Boil some water in a beaker. When it is boiling, put your leaf into it. 'Cook' it for about 3-5 min. This destroys the cell membranes.

b Turn out your Bunsen burner, and put a boiling tube of ethanol into the hot water in the beaker. Ethanol has a boiling point of around 80 °C, so it will boil. Put your boiled leaf into the ethanol. The chlorophyll will dissolve in the ethanol, making it go green.

c When all the chlorophyll has come out of your leaf, take the leaf out and dip it into the water again. This is to soften it, because the ethanol makes it brittle.

d Now spread your leaf on a white tile. Cover it with iodine solution. If the leaf does not contain starch, the iodine will stay brown.

3 Now go back to your plant. Choose a healthy-looking leaf. *Leave it on the plant!* Cover part of your leaf with black paper. Cut a hole in the paper. Fasten the paper down securely, so that no light can get in round the edges.

4 Put the plant in a sunny window. Leave it for two or three days.

5 Take your leaf off the plant. Take off the black paper. Test your leaf for starch as before.

6 Make a labelled diagram of your leaf after testing it for starch.

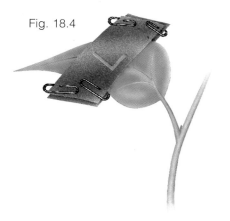
Fig. 18.4

Questions

1 Why is it important to make sure that your plant has no starch in it before you begin the experiment?

2 Why do you need to boil the leaf when testing it for starch?

3 Why do you need to put the leaf into hot ethanol?

4 Why must you not heat ethanol with a Bunsen burner?

5 Do the results of your experiment suggest that plants need light for photosynthesis?

Is carbon dioxide needed for photosynthesis?

1 Take two healthy pot plants, and destarch them by leaving them in the dark for several days. Test a leaf from each one for starch, to make sure that all the starch has gone.

2 Set up the two plants as shown in Figure 18.5. Sodium hydroxide solution will absorb all the carbon dioxide from the air. Leave the two plants in a sunny window for two or three days.

3 Test a leaf from each plant for starch.

Fig. 18.5

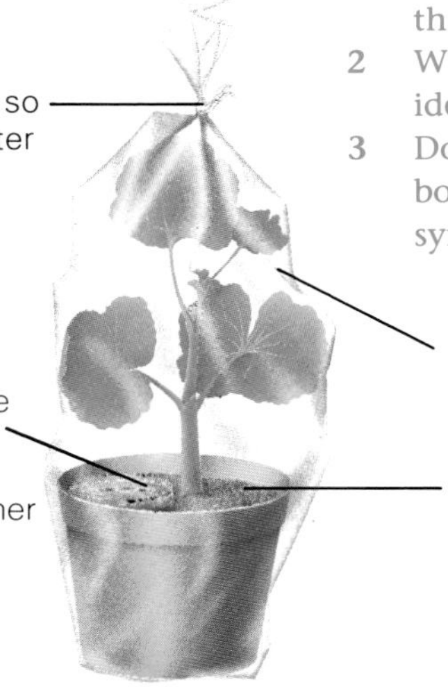

tie the bag tightly so that no air can enter or leave

Petri dish – for one plant this contains sodium hydroxide solution, for the other it contains water.

polythene bag

well-watered soil

Questions

1 Why are two plants needed in this experiment?

2 Which plant had carbon dioxide in the air surrounding it?

3 Do your results suggest that carbon dioxide is needed for photosynthesis?

Question

Some leaves have patches which do not contain chlorophyll. Such leaves are called variegated leaves. How could you use a variegated leaf to find out if chlorophyll is needed for photosynthesis? What results would you expect?

THE PRODUCTS OF PHOTOSYNTHESIS

Photosynthesis produces glucose and oxygen. The plant can then make the glucose into many other things.

INVESTIGATION 19.1

Does light intensity affect the rate of photosynthesis?

1   Set up your apparatus as shown in the diagram. Switch the lamp on.
   It is important to have a really healthy piece of pondweed. Cut its stem at an angle. If it does not produce bubbles after a couple of minutes in the tube, tell your teacher – or try another piece of pondweed!

2   When the pondweed has settled down, and is producing bubbles, start your stopclock. Count how many bubbles are produced in 2 min. Without changing anything, do the same thing twice more. Record all your readings, and work out the average number of bubbles per minute.

3   Now switch off the lamp. If the room is still bright, you can arrange some sort of shade around your apparatus. Leave the weed for at least 5 min to settle down. Then count bubbles as before. Repeat it two more times and work out the average number of bubbles per minute.

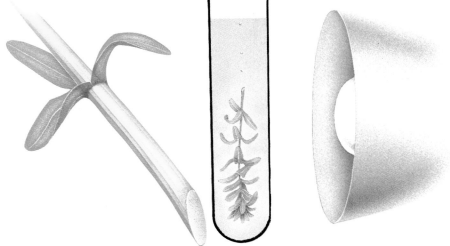

Fig. 19.1a Make a slanting cut on the stem of your piece of weed.

b Count bubbles per minute with and without the lamp.

Questions

1   Why did you take three readings each time?
2   Was there any difference in the rate of bubbling with and without the lamp?
3   Temperature can affect the rate of photosynthesis. Can you see anything wrong with this experiment? How could you solve this problem?
4   How could you collect the gas which the weed produces during this experiment? Draw a diagram to explain your ideas. How could you test it to find out what it is? What would you expect your results to be?

Limiting factors

If you try Investigation 19.1, you will probably find that the plant produces oxygen more rapidly when the light is closer to it. Plants tend to photosynthesise faster in bright light than they do in dim light. We say that light is a **limiting factor** for photosynthesis. Lack of light limits the rate at which the plant can photosynthesise.

Figure 19.2 shows this on a graph. You can see that, at very low light intensity, the plant does not photosynthesise at all. As the light intensity increases, the rate of photosynthesis increases. This is what you would expect to see if light is a limiting factor.

But, as the light intensity gets really high, the curve flattens out. The plant seems not to be able to photosynthesise any faster, no matter how much light it gets. Light is not a limiting factor any more. Something else must be stopping the plant from photosynthesising faster.

What might this be? Plants need carbon dioxide for photosynthesis, and there is only a very little carbon dioxide in the air. So, at high light intensities, it is often a shortage of carbon dioxide which limits the rate at which a plant can photosynthesise. Carbon dioxide can be a limiting factor on a bright summer day.

Temperature can also be a limiting factor. The rate of chemical reactions in a living organism slows down at low temperatures. So plants tend to photo-synthesise more slowly at low temperatures. If the temperature is raised, the rate of photosynthesis may increase. Temperature is often a limiting factor on a bright but cold day in winter.

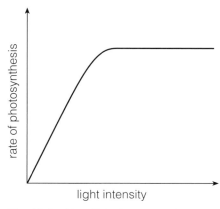

Fig. 19.2 How light intensity affects the rate of photosynthesis

Glucose is used to make other substances

When a plant photosynthesises, it makes sugars such as glucose. You have already seen that the plant changes some of the glucose to starch, which can then be stored inside the cells. But the plant makes many other substances from glucose. With the addition of a few inorganic ions (minerals) which it gets from the soil, it can make all the substances it needs.

Carbohydrates Glucose and starch are carbohydrates. Glucose can easily be changed into other carbohydrates. If the plant needs to transport carbohydrate from one part to another, the glucose or starch is changed into sucrose. Some plants use sucrose for storage, too. Carrots, sugar beet and sugar cane all do this.

Another carbohydrate is cellulose. This is the substance from which plant cell walls are made. Growing plants change a lot of the glucose they make into cellulose.

Fats and oils Glucose can be changed into fats and oils. (Oils are liquid fats.) Cell membranes contain a lot of fat, so a growing plant will need to make quite a lot of fat as it produces new cells. Fat is also used as a storage substance inside seeds. We get most of the oils we use for cooking from seeds and fruits, for example olives, sunflowers and corn.

Proteins Glucose can also be changed into amino acids, which are then used to build up proteins. To do this, the plant needs a source of nitrogen atoms, because glucose contains only carbon, hydrogen and oxygen, whereas proteins contain nitrogen as well. The plant gets its nitrogen in the form of nitrate ions from the soil. These are taken in through the root hairs. You can read about where the nitrate ions come from in Topic 57.

Other substances Glucose can be used to make many other substances, such as chlorophyll. Chlorophyll molecules contain magnesium, so plants need to take in magnesium ions from the soil. Making chlorophyll molecules also requires iron, so plants need this mineral as well. Table 19.1 lists these minerals, and also some others which plants need, in order to be able to make all the substances they need to stay healthy and grow well.

Mineral	Why it is needed	Symptoms shown by plant if mineral is deficient
nitrate	For making proteins, which are used to make cytoplasm, and as enzymes.	Stunted growth, because the plant cannot make proteins and therefore new cytoplasm. Old leaves turn yellow, as proteins are taken from them and used to supply younger leaves.
magnesium	For making chlorophyll; each chlorophyll molecule contains a magnesium atom.	Leaves turn yellow, especially older ones, because not enough chlorophyll can be made.
iron	For making chlorophyll; chlorophyll does not contain iron, but the iron is needed to help to make it.	Similar symptoms to magnesium deficiency.
phosphate	For many of the reactions of photosynthesis. Also, DNA molecules and ATP molecules contain phosphorus atoms. So do cell membranes.	Leaves become an intense green or greenish-purple. Eventually, they become mis-shaped and may develop spots of dead tissue.
potassium	To allow many enzymes to work properly, especially the ones involved in photosynthesis and respiration, making starch and making proteins.	Old leaves develop yellow spots, and then patches of dead tissue around the edges. Stems are shorter and weaker than normal.

Table 19.1 Minerals needed by plants

Questions

1 Below is a summary of some energy changes:

energy in sunlight

⤷ energy in glucose

⤷ energy in starch

⤷ energy in animal's body

⤷ movement energy

a Copy this diagram. Then write these words next to the arrows you think they fit best (you may need more than one label per arrow):
  • feeding
  • photosynthesis
  • digestion and absorption
  • respiration
b Which energy changes happen inside a plant's chloroplasts?
c Which energy changes happen inside an animal's body?

2 The diagram shows a variegated leaf, part of which has been covered with black paper. The leaf was destarched, and then left in a sunny window for four days. The leaf was then detached from the plant, and tested for starch.
Draw and label the leaf, as it would look after testing for starch.

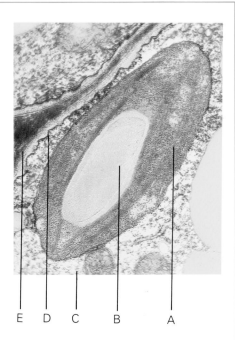

3 Explain each of the following:
a Variegated plants grow more slowly than normal ones, under the same conditions.
b Water plants in an aquarium help to oxygenate the water.
c You cannot test a leaf for starch just by adding iodine solution to it.
d Most leaves are very thin, with broad, flat surfaces.
e Plants change most of the glucose they make into starch.

5 Some tomato plants were grown in different concentrations of carbon dioxide. Their rates of photosynthesis were measured. The results are given below.

CO_2 concentration % by volume in air	Rate of photosynthesis arbitrary units
0	0
0.02	20
0.04	29
0.06	35
0.08	39
0.10	42
0.12	45
0.14	46
0.16	46
0.18	46
0.20	46

a Draw a graph showing these results.
b If the percentage of carbon dioxide in the air was 0.03 %, what is the rate of photosynthesis?
c During this experiment the light intensity was kept constant. Why was this important?
d Why does the graph level off?
e Tomato growers want their plants to photosynthesise quickly. Why?
f If tomatoes are grown in glasshouses, it is possible to increase the concentration of carbon dioxide in the air in the glasshouse. Suggest how you could do this.
g What would be the best percentage of carbon dioxide for a grower to provide in the glasshouse? Explain your answer.

6 Copy and complete these sentences. Photosynthesis is the way in which plants make ...... They use energy from ...., and some of this energy is stored in the food which they make. The plants and ..... which eat them can then use the energy from the food.
To make food, plants need carbon dioxide from the .... and water from the ...... These are ...... substances. The plants make these substances into ...... which is an .... substance. The gas .... is also made.

4 The photograph shows part of a palisade cell from a leaf. It was taken using an electron microscope. It is magnified x 2000 times. The structures labelled A are membranes inside a chloroplast. These membranes are covered with chlorophyll molecules.
a Name the structures labelled B to E.
b Is a chloroplast an organelle, a cell, or an organ?
c What is the name of the process which happens inside a chloroplast?
d What is the energy source which drives this process?
e What is the function of chlorophyll?
f Why is it useful for chlorophyll molecules to be spread out on membranes?
g Calculate the approximate width of the chloroplast.

E D C B A

RESPIRATION

20 RESPIRATION

Respiration is a process which occurs in all living cells. Respiration releases energy from food.

Every living cell respires

Each living cell in every living organism needs energy. Energy is needed to drive chemical reactions in the cell. It is needed for movement. It is needed for building up large molecules from small ones. If a cell cannot get enough energy it dies. Cells get their energy from organic molecules such as glucose. The chemical process by which energy is released from glucose and other organic molecules is called **respiration**. Every cell needs energy. Each cell must release its own energy from glucose. So each cell must respire. Every cell in your body respires. Every living cell in the world respires.

Fig. 20.1 Florence Griffith-Joyner ('Flo-Jo') winning the 100 m at the Seoul Olympics. The energy which she is using comes from respiration in her muscle cells.

INVESTIGATION 20.1

Getting energy out of a peanut

1 Spear a peanut on the end of a mounted needle. Be careful – it is easy to break the peanut.

2 Put some cold water into a boiling tube. Support the boiling tube in a clamp on a retort stand, with the base of the tube about 30 cm above the bench top. Take the temperature of the water and record it.

3 Set light to the peanut by holding it in a Bunsen burner flame. (Keep the Bunsen burner well away from the boiling tube.) When the peanut is burning hold it under the boiling tube. Keep it there until it stops burning.

4 Immediately take the temperature of the water and record it.

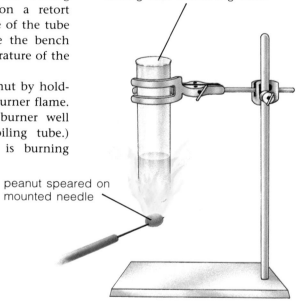

Fig. 20.2 Burning a peanut

boiling tube containing water

peanut speared on mounted needle

Questions

1 Why should you keep the Bunsen burner away from the tube of water?

2 By how much did the temperature of the water rise?

3 What type of chemical reaction was occurring as the peanut burnt?

4 Put these words in the right order, and join them with arrows, to show where the heat energy in the water came from:

energy in peanut molecules

energy in glucose in peanut leaf

sunlight energy

heat energy in water

5 Put the following words over two of the arrows in your answer to question 4:

photosynthesis   oxidation

6 Do you think all the energy from your peanut went into the water? If not, explain what else might have happened to it.

7 How could you improve the design of this experiment to make sure that more of the peanut energy went into the water?

EXTENSION

8 People often want to know exactly how much energy there is in a particular kind of food. The amount of energy is measured in kilojoules.

4.18 J of energy will raise the temperature of 1 g of water by 1 °C.

Design a method for finding out the amount of energy per gram in a particular type of food.

Respiration is an oxidation reaction

You can do an experiment to release energy from food if you do Investigation 20.1. When a peanut burns, the energy in the peanut is released as heat energy. But how do your cells release energy from food such as peanuts?

Obviously, you do not burn peanuts inside your cells! But you do something very similar. The chemical reactions of burning and respiration are very like each other.

First, think about what happens when you burn the peanut. The peanut contains organic molecules, such as fats and sugars, which contain energy. When you set light to the peanut you start off a chemical reaction between these molecules and oxygen in the air. The peanut molecules undergo an **oxidation** reaction. They combine with oxygen. As they do so, the energy in them is released as **heat energy**.

When you eat peanuts, your digestive system breaks the peanut into its individual molecules. Your blood system then takes these molecules to your cells. Inside your cells the molecules combine with oxygen. They undergo an oxidation reaction. This is respiration. The energy in the molecules is released. But, unlike the burning peanut, much of the energy is *not* released as heat energy. It is released much more gently and gradually, and stored in the cell.

So, the burning of a peanut, and the respiration of 'peanut molecules' in your cells are both oxidation reactions. In both of them the peanut molecules combine with oxygen. In both of them the energy in the peanut molecules is released. But in your cells the reaction is much more gentle and controlled.

ATP is the energy currency in cells

Respiration releases energy from food. Each cell must do this for itself. Every living cell respires to release the energy it needs. The energy released in respiration is not used directly for movement or any of the other activities of the cell. It is used to make a chemical called **ATP**. ATP is short for adenosine triphosphate. ATP, like glucose, contains chemical energy.

chemical energy in glucose → chemical energy in ATP

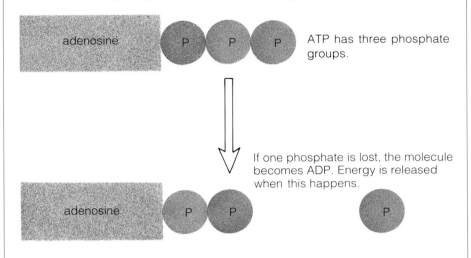

ATP has three phosphate groups.

If one phosphate is lost, the molecule becomes ADP. Energy is released when this happens.

Fig. 20.3 ATP and ADP

ATP is the ideal energy currency in a cell. The energy in an ATP molecule can be released from it very quickly – much more quickly than from a glucose molecule. The energy is released by breaking ATP down to **ADP**. ADP is short for adenosine diphosphate. Another good reason for using ATP as an energy supply is that one ATP molecule contains a much smaller amount of energy than one glucose molecule. If a cell needs just a small amount of energy, then it can break down just the right number of ATP molecules. The amount in a glucose molecule might be too much, and energy would be wasted. Each cell produces its own ATP by the process of respiration. ATP is not transported from cell to cell.

The respiration equation

Respiration is a chemical reaction. The word equation for the reaction with glucose is:

$$\text{glucose} + \text{oxygen} \longrightarrow \text{carbon dioxide} + \text{water} + \text{energy}$$

The balanced molecular equation for the reaction is:

$$C_6H_{12}O_6 + 6O_2 \longrightarrow 6CO_2 + 6H_2O + \text{energy}$$

Questions

1   Respiration is a chemical reaction.
 a Where does it take place?
 b What type of chemical reaction is it?
 c Why is it so important to living cells?

2   List two similarities, and one difference, between the burning of a peanut and the respiration of 'peanut molecules' in your cells.

3 a Write down the word equation for respiration.
 b Write down the balanced molecular equation for respiration.

4   Respiration releases energy from food. Explain how the energy came to be in the food.

5 a What is ATP?
 b Why do cells use ATP as an energy store?
 c A muscle cell uses glucose to provide energy for movement.
 i List all the energy changes involved in this process, beginning with energy in sunlight.
 ii Energy is 'lost' at each transfer. What do you think happens to this 'lost' energy at each stage?

THE HUMAN BREATHING SYSTEM

Cells need oxygen for respiration. The human breathing system gets oxygen into the blood.

Every human cell needs oxygen

Every single cell in your body needs oxygen. This is because each cell needs to release energy from glucose. It does this by combining oxygen with glucose. This is respiration.

oxygen + glucose $\longrightarrow$ carbon dioxide + water + energy

So each individual cell needs a constant supply of oxygen and glucose. These are brought to the cell in the blood system. The carbon dioxide which the cell makes is taken away in the blood.

Gas exchange occurs in the lungs

Each cell needs oxygen and produces carbon dioxide as a waste product of respiration. So your body needs to take in oxygen and get rid of carbon dioxide. The process of taking in oxygen and getting rid of carbon dioxide is called **gas exchange**. It happens in your lungs.

Lungs are made up of millions of alveoli

Lungs are like huge pink sponges. They are pink because they contain many tiny capillaries full of blood. The blood collects oxygen from the lungs and takes it to the rest of the cells in the body. The blood also brings carbon dioxide to the lungs to be removed from the body.

Lungs are like sponges because they are full of tiny air spaces. The air spaces are called **alveoli**. Air is drawn in through your nose and mouth and down your throat. It passes through a large tube called the **trachea** which divides into two smaller tubes called **bronchi**. The bronchi divide into a network of even smaller tubes called **bronchioles**. These lead into the alveoli.

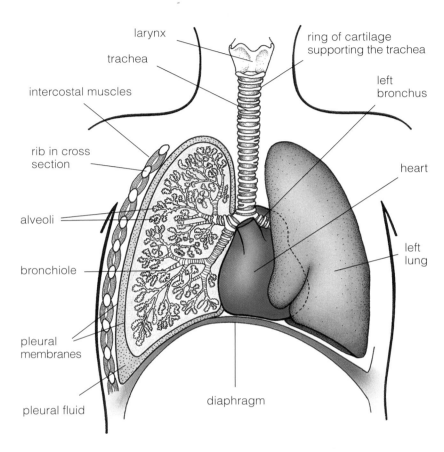

Fig. 21.1 A vertical section through the human thorax.

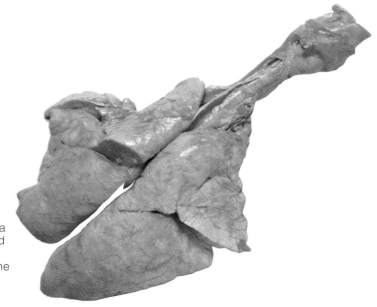

Fig. 21.2 Lungs from a pig. Try to identify: the larynx; epiglottis; trachea (cut open); rings of cartilage; left and right lungs covered with pleural membranes. You can also just see the oesophagus, running alongside the trachea.

The structure of sheep lungs

Sets of sheep lungs can be obtained from butchers. They are sometimes sold as 'lights' for dog food.

1 Describe the size, shape and colour of the lungs.

2 You will probably be able to see two tubes leading down to the lungs. One of these is the trachea, or windpipe. It has bands of gristle or **cartilage** around it to hold it open. You can feel these bands on your own trachea in your neck.

   At the top of the trachea there is a wider part. What is the name of this part? What is inside it? What does it do?

3 Covering the top of the trachea is a firm but flexible flap called the **epiglottis**. When you swallow, this flap shuts off the top of the trachea. Why is this necessary?

4 Find the other tube leading down past the lungs. What is it? Where is it leading to? How is it different from the trachea?

5 Now look at the lungs themselves. They are covered with a thin, transparent, slippery skin called the **pleural membranes**. These membranes make a fluid which allows the lungs to slide easily inside your body as they inflate and deflate. They also keep the lungs airtight.

6 Follow the trachea downwards to the lungs. Find where it divides into two tubes. What are these two tubes called? Do they have rings of cartilage, like the trachea?

7 If the lungs and trachea have not been badly cut, you can try inflating them. Put a rubber tube right down inside the trachea, and hold the top of the trachea tightly around it. Blow firmly down the tube. If the lungs do inflate, describe what they look like.

8 Cut a small piece out of one lung. Describe its appearance, weight and texture. Why does it feel like this?

Gas exchange takes place in the alveoli

The function of the lungs is to bring air as close as possible to the blood. Oxygen can then get from the air into the blood. Carbon dioxide can get from the blood into the air. This is gas exchange. Gas exchange happens in the alveoli. It is in the alveoli that the blood and air are brought really close together. The walls of the alveoli are only one cell thick. The walls of the blood capillaries are also only one cell thick. So the air and blood are separated from one another by a thickness of only two cells. The total thickness of this barrier is only about $\frac{1}{1000}$ mm.

The concentration of oxygen in the air is much greater than the concentration of oxygen in the blood in the lungs. So oxygen diffuses from the air into the blood. It diffuses into the red blood cells. Here it combines with a substance called haemoglobin to form oxyhaemoglobin. The red blood cells are swept along in the blood to every part of the body. When they arrive at a part where oxygen levels are low, the oxyhaemoglobin releases its oxygen. This is how your body cells get their supply of oxygen for respiration.

Carbon dioxide is also carried in the blood. It is brought from the body cells to the lungs. The concentration of carbon dioxide in the blood in the lungs is greater than the concentration in the air in the alveoli. So carbon dioxide diffuses into the alveoli.

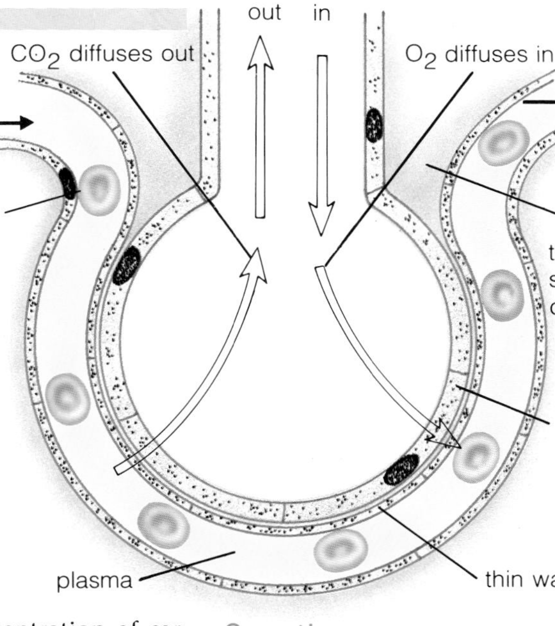

Fig. 21.3 Gas exchange in an alveolus. Notice that the walls of both the alveolus and the capillary are only one cell thick.

DID YOU KNOW?

The combined surface area of all the alveoli in both your lungs is about 70 m² (the area of a tennis court). This enormous surface area means that diffusion between the air and blood can take place very rapidly.

Questions

1 a What is gas exchange?
  b Why is gas exchange necessary?
  c Exactly where does gas exchange occur in humans?

EXTENSION

2 Discuss how the structure of the lungs, including the alveoli, is designed to make gas exchange as efficient as possible.

22 BREATHING

Breathing movements move air in and out of the lungs. This keeps the concentration of oxygen in the lungs high so that oxygen will keep diffusing into the blood.

Breathing movements supply fresh air to the alveoli

Oxygen gets into your blood by diffusion. It diffuses from the alveoli into the blood. It does this because the concentration of oxygen in the air in the alveoli is greater than the concentration of oxygen in the blood.

As the oxygen diffuses from the alveoli into the blood, the oxygen concentration in the alveoli goes down. So fresh air must be brought to the alveoli to keep the oxygen concentration high. If this did not happen, its concentration would end up the same as the concentration of oxygen in the blood. Then the oxygen would stop diffusing.

You supply fresh air to your alveoli by **breathing**. Breathing means making movements which pull and push air in and out of your lungs.

The diaphragm and intercostal muscles help in breathing

Two sets of muscles produce your breathing movements. One is the muscle in the **diaphragm**. The diaphragm is a sheet of tissue which runs across your body just below the ribs. All around the edge of it are strong muscles. When the diaphragm muscles are relaxed, the diaphragm makes a domed shape. When the diaphragm muscles contract, they pull the diaphragm flat.

The other set of muscles involved in breathing are the muscles between the ribs. They are called the **intercostal muscles**. When they are relaxed, the rib-cage slopes downwards. When the intercostal muscles contract, they pull the rib-cage upwards and outwards.

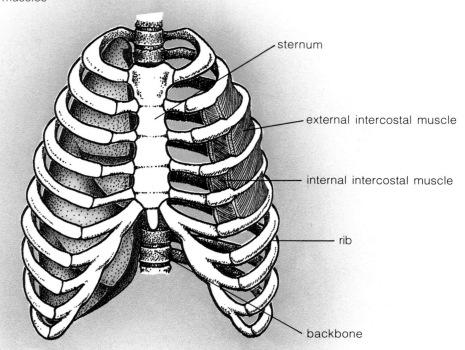

Fig. 22.1   The ribs and intercostal muscles

sternum

external intercostal muscle

internal intercostal muscle

rib

backbone

Muscles contract when you breathe in, and relax when you breathe out

How do these muscles help you to breathe? When both set of muscles are relaxed, the volume of the thorax is fairly small. But as your diaphragm and intercostal muscles contract, the shape and size of the thorax changes. The diaphragm is pulled downwards, and the ribs are pulled upwards and outwards. Both these movements increase the volume of the thorax. As the volume of the thorax *increases*, the pressure inside it *decreases*. The pressure inside the thorax becomes *lower* than the air pressure outside. So air rushes into the thorax from the atmosphere. There is only one way in. It is along the trachea and into the lungs. So air rushes into the lungs. You have breathed in.

A few seconds later, your diaphragm and intercostal muscles relax. The diaphragm springs upwards, and the rib-cage drops downwards. Both these movements decrease the volume of the thorax. The pressure inside the thorax is increased. It rises above the pressure of the air outside the body. So air inside the thorax is squeezed out. There is only one way out. Air is squeezed out of the lungs, along the bronchi and trachea, and out through your mouth or nose. You have breathed out.

DID YOU KNOW?

When you are resting breathing out requires no effort, because your lungs are elastic and spring back to squeeze air out. But if you blow a musical instrument or do strenuous exercise you need to force air out of your lungs. You can do this by using a different set of intercostal muscles, which pull the ribs downwards.

a. Expiration. Muscles relax, making the thorax volume smaller.

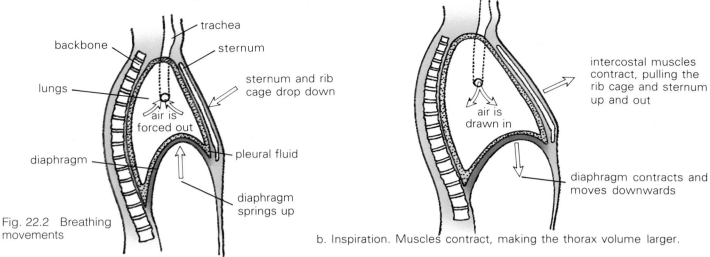

Fig. 22.2 Breathing movements

b. Inspiration. Muscles contract, making the thorax volume larger.

INVESTIGATION 22.1

Pressure and volume changes in a model thorax

1   Make a labelled diagram of the apparatus with everything relaxed. On your labels, indicate which parts you think represent the lungs, the trachea, the bronchi, the ribs and the diaphragm.
2   Pull down gently on the plastic or rubber sheet. Watch the balloons carefully. Describe what happens.

Questions

1   When you pull down on the sheet what happens to the volume and pressure inside the bell jar?
2   Use your answer to question 1 to explain why the balloons inflate when you pull down on the sheet.
3   Which important set of muscles is missing from this model of the human thorax?

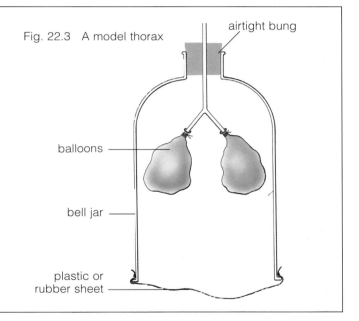

Fig. 22.3   A model thorax

INVESTIGATION 22.2

Does breathing rate increase with exercise?

You breathe to fill your alveoli with fresh air. Oxygen from this air diffuses into your blood and is carried to the body cells. The cells use this oxygen in respiration.

When cells are working hard, they need more energy. They get their energy from food, by combining it with oxygen in respiration. So cells need more oxygen when they work hard. Muscle cells work very hard when you do physical exercise.

Design and carry out an experiment to find out if your rate of breathing increases with an increasing amount of exercise. Record and explain your results as clearly as you can.

Questions

1   Explain the difference between breathing, gas exchange and respiration.
2   Copy and complete the following sentences:
When you breathe in, your .... and .... muscles .... This .... the volume and .... the pressure inside the thorax. So air rushes into the lungs.
When you breathe out, your .... and .... muscles .... This .... the volume and .... the pressure inside the thorax. So air rushes out of the lungs.

EXTENSION

3   All living things respire. Do all living things breathe? Use three or four different examples of living organisms in your answer to this question, and describe how they obtain their oxygen.

23 INSPIRED AND EXPIRED AIR

The air we breathe out contains less oxygen and more carbon dioxide than the air we breathe in. The level of nitrogen remains unchanged.

INVESTIGATION 23.1

Comparing the carbon dioxide content of inspired and expired air

Inspired air is the air you breathe in. Expired air is the air you breathe out.

You can use either lime water or hydrogencarbonate indicator solution for this experiment. Both indicate the presence of carbon dioxide. Lime water turns milky, and hydrogencarbonate indicator solution becomes yellow if carbon dioxide bubbles through it.

1   Set up the apparatus as in the diagram. The long tubes should reach right into the liquid, but the ends of the short tubes should be in the air space above.
2   Breathe in and out gently through the central tube. Watch to see which tube bubbles when you breathe in, and which bubbles when you breathe out. Make a record of which is which.
3   Keep breathing in and out until the colour of the indicator in one of the tubes changes. Record which it is.
4   Continue breathing in and out for a few more minutes. Watch the colour of the indicator in *both* tubes, and record any further changes.

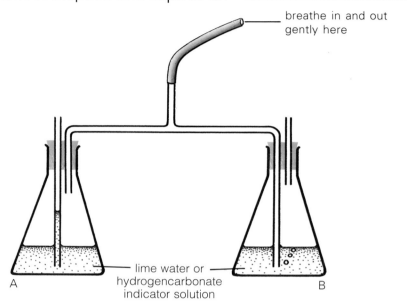

breathe in and out gently here

lime water or hydrogencarbonate indicator solution

Fig 23.1   Comparing the carbon dioxide content of inspired and expired air.

Questions

1   Try to explain why your inspired air went into one tube, and your expired air went into the other.
2   Which indicator changed first – the one with inspired air, or the one with expired air bubbling through it?
3   Which contains the most carbon dioxide – inspired air or expired air?
4   Did the indicator in both tubes eventually change colour? If so, what does this tell you?

Table 23.1   The composition of inspired and expired air

	Inspired air %	Expired air %
Nitrogen	78	78
Oxygen	21	18
Carbon dioxide	0.04	3
Noble gases	1	1

INVESTIGATION 23.2

Comparing the temperature and moisture content of inspired and expired air

1   Take the temperature of the air around you. This is inspired air.
2   Breathe out on to the bulb of a thermometer for 2 min. Do not put the thermometer in your mouth! Record the temperature of expired air.
3   Take a piece of dry cobalt chloride paper. Handle it with forceps, because any moisture on your fingers would affect the results. Wave the paper in the air around you for 2 min. Record any colour changes in the paper.
4   Take a second piece of dry cobalt chloride paper, and breathe out on to it for about 2 min. Record any colour changes in the paper.
5   Summarise your findings about the temperature and moisture content of inspired and expired air.

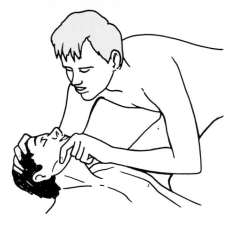

Fig. 23.2 Giving artificial respiration. Having checked that the person really is not breathing, lie them on their back. Check that the airway is not blocked, for example by loose teeth. Pull the head right back to make a clear passage from the mouth, down the trachea, to the lungs.

Either hold the nose tightly closed with one hand or cover both nose and mouth with your own mouth. Breathe firmly and steadily into the person's mouth. Do not rush your breathing – a slow and steady rate is best. Between breaths watch the person's chest to check that you are making it rise and fall. Keep going until help arrives.
If the person begins to breathe on their own, roll them onto their side into the recovery position.

Giving artificial respiration

People may stop breathing if they have an electric shock, are under water for some time or suffer some other type of accident. If this happens their body rapidly becomes short of oxygen. Brain cells are especially likely to be damaged if they get no oxygen. It is very important to help the person to begin breathing again as soon as possible.

The best way to do this is to use your own breath. You should inflate the person's lungs rhythmically. This may start their diaphragm and intercostal muscles working again. As you can see from Table 23.1, even expired air contains quite a lot of oxygen. There is plenty of oxygen in your expired air to supply an unconscious person's brain with the oxygen it needs.

Questions

1 Figure 23.3 shows some apparatus which can be used to compare the air breathed in and out by living organisms. Sodium hydroxide solution absorbs carbon dioxide. For the first experiment a mouse was put into flask C. The pump was then turned on, pulling air through the apparatus from left to right.

a What would you expect to happen to the lime water in flask B? Explain your answer.

b What would you expect to happen to the lime water in flask D? Explain your answer.

c What would happen if the tubes into flask A were put in the other way round, so that the short tube led into it and the long tube led out of it?
For the second experiment a green plant was put into flask C. The experiment was done on a sunny bench top.

d What would you now expect to happen to the lime water in flasks B and D? Explain your answer.
For the third experiment, the same green plant was left in flask C. However, the laboratory was now blacked out, and the experiment done in darkness.

e What would you now expect to happen to the lime water in flasks B and D? Explain your answer.

2 Copy and complete. There are only three different words to use, and they are all names of gases.
Expired air contains more .... and less .... than inspired air. This is because body cells use .... in the process of respiration, and produce .... as a waste product.
The percentage of .... in inspired and expired air is the same. Although body cells need this element for making proteins, they cannot use it in this form. So the .... goes into the blood, round the body, and then out again in expired air.

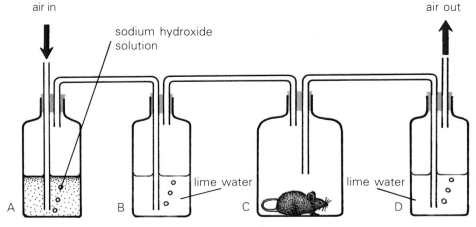

Fig. 23.3

Inspired air contains bacteria, viruses and particles of dust. The body is designed to keep harmful materials away from the lungs.

Cilia and mucus trap dust and bacteria

The air you breathe contains all sorts of things. If you live in a city, there may be carbon particles – soot – in the air. Wherever you live, there are bound to be bacteria and viruses in it.

The alveoli in your lungs are very delicate. They are easily damaged. And your lungs are a warm, moist place for bacteria to live and breed. So your breathing system is designed to protect your lungs from harmful things in the air that you breathe in. There are special cells called **goblet cells** which line the tubes leading to your lungs. They make mucus. The mucus covers the inside of your trachea. Dust and bacteria get trapped in the mucus. In between the goblet cells are other cells. These are covered with a layer of microscopic hairs. The hairs are called **cilia**. They move in a wave-like motion, sweeping the mucus upwards. The mucus, with whatever it has trapped, is swept to the back of your throat. Then you swallow it! The dirt and bacteria are destroyed in your digestive system.

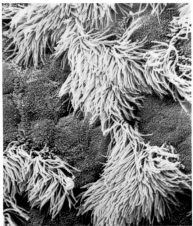

Fig. 24.2   A scanning electron micrograph of the inner surface of a human trachea. The yellow filaments are cilia. The orange parts are goblet cells, which secrete mucus. They are not really this colour!

Fig. 24.1   Cells lining the trachea

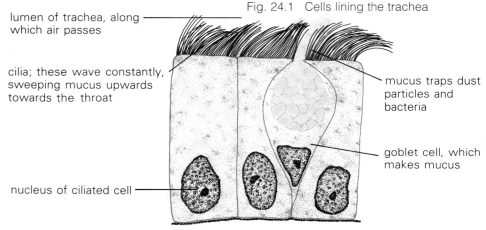

lumen of trachea, along which air passes

cilia; these wave constantly, sweeping mucus upwards towards the throat

mucus traps dust particles and bacteria

goblet cell, which makes mucus

nucleus of ciliated cell

Fig. 24.3   Two white cells patrolling the alveoli in a human lung. The spherical one is in its normal shape. Below it is an elongated white cell, about to engulf the round particle on the left.

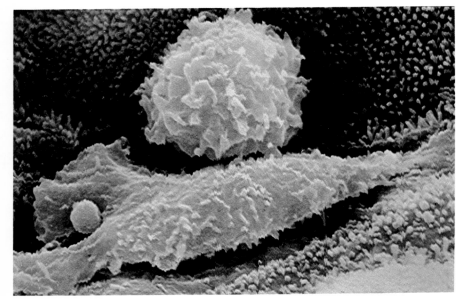

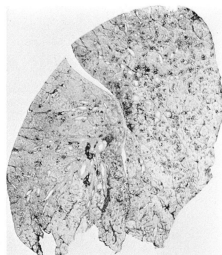

Fig. 24.4   Section through a lung of a smoker. The dark areas are deposits of tar.

White cells patrol the lungs

Despite this well-organised dust removal system, some dust and bacteria do reach the lungs. But a second line of defence now comes into operation. White blood cells constantly move around in the alveoli. They find and destroy bacteria. These white cells are called **phagocytes**.

Cigarette smoke stops cilia working

Cigarette smoke contains carbon dioxide and carbon monoxide. These substances stop the cilia from moving. If a person smokes a lot, their cilia will disappear completely. But· the goblet cells go on working. They still make mucus, and the mucus still traps dirt and bacteria. But now the mucus is not swept upwards. It trickles downwards, into the lungs. The lungs now start to fill up with mucus, bacteria and smoke particles. The person coughs to push the mucus upwards. But, very often, the organisms which cause disease stay in the lungs and the tubes leading to them. They may live and breed in the mucus. The person gets **bronchitis**.

The constant coughing of heavy smokers can also damage the delicate alveoli. Their thin walls get broken. Instead of having millions of tiny alveoli in their lungs, the smoker may end up with far fewer bigger ones. These are not very good at letting oxygen get into the blood. The person becomes short of breath. This disease is called **emphysema**.

Fig. 24.5 Emphysema can make it very difficult to get oxygen into the blood. Sufferers may need to breathe oxygen even when resting.

Fig. 24.6 Post-mortem specimens of a normal lung, and a lung destroyed by cancer. The tumour is the white part in the lower part of the lung.

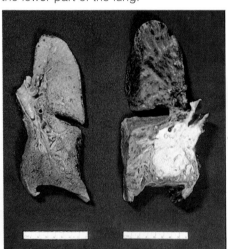

Tars in cigarette smoke may cause lung cancer

Cigarette smoke contains tars. These tars affect the cells lining the tubes leading to the lungs, and cells inside the lungs. They may make them divide more than usual. The cells go on and on dividing. They form a lump of cells called a **tumour**. Quite often, the person's white cells recognise that these dividing cells are not right. They destroy them before they cause any damage. But sometimes the tumour gets quite large. It goes on and on growing. The person now has **lung cancer**.

Many cancers can now be cured. But lung cancer is very difficult to treat. Most people who get lung cancer die from it. But most people who get lung cancer are smokers. So it is quite easy to make it almost certain that you won't get lung cancer. Don't smoke!

DID YOU KNOW?

It has been found that people who smoke are more likely to get *all* types of cancer – not just lung cancer.

Questions

1 A study was made of the incidence of upper respiratory tract infection in US Army recruits in basic training at Fort Benning, Georgia.

1230 soldiers took part in the study. The number of soldiers reporting to the troop medical clinics with upper respiratory infections were recorded over their basic training period.

Overall, it was found that soldiers who smoked were 1.46 times more likely to suffer from upper respiratory tract infection than men who did not smoke. When the smokers were subdivided into different categories, the results below were obtained:

	% of soldiers in group who reported upper respiratory infection
Group 1 - soldiers who smoked throughout basic combat training	25.3
Group 2 - soldiers who gave up smoking part way through training	36.0
Group 3 - soldiers who began smoking during training	21.4
Group 4 - soldiers who did not smoke at all	16.9

a What do you think is meant by 'upper respiratory tract infection'?

b These figures show that soldiers who smoked were more likely to suffer from upper respiratory infection than soldiers who did not smoke. Explain why you think this might be.

c The United States Army has taken a strong position against the use of tobacco by soldiers. Why do you think they have done this?

d Suggest a reason for the high figure of infection in the Group 2 soldiers.

It is possible to release energy from food without oxygen. This is called anaerobic respiration.

Energy can be released from food without using oxygen

Respiration is a chemical reaction which releases energy from food. The food is usually glucose. The reaction usually uses oxygen. The word equation for this reaction is:

glucose + oxygen → carbon dioxide + water + energy

This reaction is called **aerobic respiration**. 'Aerobic' means 'to do with air'. This reaction uses oxygen from the air.

However, it is possible to release energy from food *without* using oxygen. This method is not as good as aerobic respiration. It does not release as much energy from the food. But it is useful if oxygen is in short supply. Respiration which does not use oxygen is called **anaerobic respiration**. 'Anaerobic' means 'without air'.

Fig. 25.1 Yeast cells. This particular kind of yeast is used in bread-making. Some of the cells are producing buds, which will break off to form new cells.

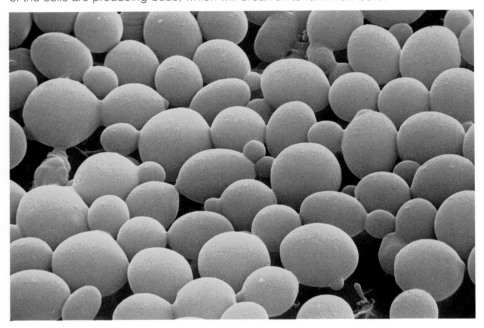

Yeast can respire anaerobically

Yeast is a single-celled fungus. Yeast lives naturally on the surface of fruit. It feeds on the sugars in the fruit. Yeast can respire anaerobically for long periods of time. It breaks down glucose, and releases energy from it, without using oxygen. The word equation for this reaction is:

glucose → carbon dioxide + ethanol + energy

You will see several differences between this reaction and the aerobic respiration reaction. Firstly, this one does not use oxygen. Secondly, this one produces ethanol. Another difference is that anaerobic respiration releases much less energy from the glucose than aerobic respiration does.

Anaerobic respiration in yeast

1 Set up the apparatus as shown in the diagram.
2 Set up an identical piece of apparatus which does not contain yeast.
3 Leave both pieces of apparatus in a warm place for at least 30 min.

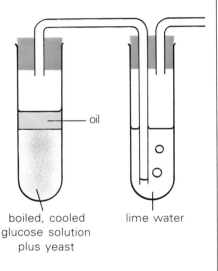

oil

boiled, cooled glucose solution plus yeast

lime water

Fig. 25.2

Questions

1 This experiment is to find out if yeast can respire anaerobically. Why was the water in the tube boiled before use?
2 Why was the boiled water cooled before the yeast was added?
3 Why is a layer of oil floated on the water?
4 Did either of the samples of limewater turn milky? What does this indicate?
5 At the end of the experiment what new substance would you expect to find in the tube containing the yeast?

Yeast is used in brewing and wine making

When yeast respires anaerobically it produces ethanol. This is used in the brewing industry to make beer. Barley grains are allowed to germinate. As they germinate they produce a sugar called maltose. The maltose is dissolved in water. Yeast is added. The yeast respires anaerobically, using the maltose. Ethanol (alcohol) is made. Hops are usually added to the liquid, to give a bitter flavour, and help to preserve it.

Yeast will also use the sugars in grapes. This is how wine is made. Both brewing and wine-making involve anaerobic respiration. Because the reaction makes alcohol, it is sometimes given another name. It is called **alcoholic fermentation**.

Fig. 25.3   In this fermentation tank, yeast is feeding on malt from barley seeds. The yeast respires anaerobically, releasing carbon dioxide and alcohol.

Yeast is used in bread-making

Yeast is also used in bread-making. This time it is the carbon dioxide which is wanted, not the ethanol. Water is added to flour to make a dough. Some of the starch in the flour breaks down to sugar. Yeast is added and respires using the sugar. It makes carbon dioxide. The carbon dioxide forms bubbles in the dough. This makes the bread rise. When the bread is baked, the yeast is killed.

Fig. 25.4   Making bread. Respiration by yeast releases carbon dioxide, which makes the dough rise.

Fig. 25.5   Athletes paying back their oxygen debt after a race.

Human muscles can respire anaerobically

Your muscle cells can respire without oxygen for a short time. They only do this when they are short of oxygen. This might happen if you run a race. Your muscles need a lot of energy, so they respire very fast. But your lungs and heart might not be able to supply enough oxygen to them. So the muscle cells have to manage without oxygen for a short while.

When muscle cells respire anaerobically, they do not make ethanol! Instead, they make **lactic acid**. The word equation for the reaction is:

glucose → lactic acid + energy

When you stop running, you will have lactic acid in your muscles and your blood. This must be broken down. Oxygen is needed to break it down. So you breathe fast to get extra oxygen into your blood to break down the lactic acid. This is why you go on breathing hard, even after you have stopped running. The extra oxygen you need to break down the lactic acid is called an **oxygen debt**.

Questions

1 **a** List three similarities between the chemical reactions of aerobic respiration and anaerobic respiration.

   b List three differences between them.

2 What is alcoholic fermentation? Give one way in which this reaction is used in industry.

3 Explain why an athlete continues to breathe faster and deeper than usual after finishing a race.

Questions

1 Copy and complete using the words listed on the right:

All the energy in living organisms begins as .... energy. This energy is trapped by the green colouring in plants, called .... The energy is used to drive the chemical reactions of .... This makes glucose and oxygen from .... and ....

The glucose contains some of the energy. The plant may change some of the glucose to .... This may be stored in the plant's seeds. An animal may eat the seeds. The animal's digestive system breaks down the starch molecules in the .... to glucose molecules. They still contain energy. The glucose molecules are taken, in the animal's .... system, to cells which need energy. Inside the cells, the glucose combines with .... This releases .... from the glucose, and produces the gas .... This reaction is called ....

Words to use:

seeds	photosynthesis
sunlight	respiration
starch	oxygen
energy	blood
water	chlorophyll
carbon dioxide (twice)	

2 The diagram shows the result of an experiment to find out how animals and plants affect the air around them.

Carbon dioxide dissolves in water to form a weak acid. Hydrogencarbonate indicator solution detects changes in acidity. It is purple with no carbon dioxide, red with a very little, and yellow with a lot of carbon dioxide present.

a In which of the tubes would you expect respiration to have been occurring?

b In which of the tubes would you expect photosynthesis to have been occurring?

c What gas is
i used
ii produced
in respiration?

d What gas is
i used
ii produced
in photosynthesis?

e In which of the tubes would you expect carbon dioxide to have been used up?

f In which tube would you expect carbon dioxide to have been made?

g Explain, as fully as you can, the reasons for the colour of the indicator in each tube.

h If a fifth tube was set up, containing both animals and plants (but covered with black paper) what results would you expect? Explain your answer.

3 a Describe how a person's lungs are kept clean.

b Explain what happens to this process if a person smokes.

c How can this damage a person's lungs?

d Briefly describe two other ways in which smoking can be harmful.

hydrogencarbonate indicator solution

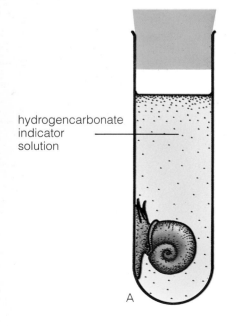

A

B

C

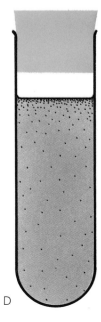

D

FOOD AND DIGESTION

26 HETEROTROPHIC NUTRITION

Animals cannot make their own food. They rely on food made by plants.

Plants use inorganic substances to make organic substances

One of the things which makes animals different from plants is the way in which they feed. Plants use **inorganic** substances. Inorganic substances are things which have not been made by living things. They often have fairly small molecules.

The inorganic substances which plants use are carbon dioxide and water. These two substances are combined to make glucose. Glucose is an **organic** substance because it contains carbon and is made by a living organism. Plants make glucose by photosynthesis.

All living things are made up of organic substances. Plants can make their own organic substances out of inorganic ones. This way of getting organic food is called **autotrophic nutrition**. 'Auto' means 'self', and 'trophic' means 'feeding'. Plants can make their own food.

Animals must eat organic food made by plants

Animals cannot make organic substances out of inorganic ones. Animals must eat organic food which plants have made. Sometimes they eat plants directly. Sometimes they eat other animals which have eaten plants. But whatever they eat, animals rely on plants to make food for them. Animals cannot make their own food. This way of feeding is called **heterotrophic nutrition**. 'Hetero' means 'other'. Animals rely on other organisms to make their organic food.

Fungi also feed heterotrophically

Fungi are another group of organisms which need organic food. Fungi cannot photosynthesise. Like animals, they rely on food that has been made by plants. Most fungi feed on organic substances that are no longer in a living organism.

The fungus which causes mildew will grow on leather boots or on paper. The leather was once an animal's skin. This animal will have eaten plants. So the organic substances in the leather were originally made by plants.

Another example of a fungus is yeast. Yeast feeds on sugars made by plants.

The mushrooms you eat are just the part of a fungus above the ground. There is a network of threads underground. These threads feed on organic substances in the soil.

Although fungi and animals both use organic food, they feed in very different ways. Fungi feed by releasing enzymes on to the food on which they grow. The enzymes help to dissolve the food. The dissolved food is absorbed into the fungus cells. This way of feeding is called **saprotrophic nutrition**. It is a special kind of heterotrophic nutrition.

Fig. 26.1   Mushrooms, like all fungi, are saprotrophs. Threads called hyphae grow underground, digesting organic substances and absorbing them.

Fig. 26.2   Mould growing on grapes. The fungus is feeding on sugar and protein from the grapes. It digests them by secreting enzymes, which will eventually reduce the fruit to a liquid.

Animals need several types of food in their diet

At first sight it may seem that the kinds of food that animals eat are very different. You, for example, would probably not be very happy with the diet that an earthworm thrives on. Earthworms eat dead leaves and soil. But there are really more similarities than differences between the diets of different animals. The kinds of food molecules which different sorts of animals need are very much the same. You and an earthworm both need the following substances in your diet:

- carbohydrates
- fats
- proteins
- vitamins
- minerals
- roughage
- water

Throughout the rest of this topic on food and digestion we will consider only humans. But do remember that all other animals use the same kinds of food, even if they eat and digest them in very different ways.

Mineral	Why you need it	Deficiency symptoms	Foods rich in it
Iron	to make haemoglobin, the red pigment in blood cells which carries oxygen	anaemia, caused by a lack of haemoglobin to carry oxygen	liver and red meat
Calcium	for bone and teeth formation	poor growth of bones and teeth	milk and other dairy products; hard water
Iodine	for making the hormone thyroxine	goitre, which is a swollen thyroid gland	sea food; table salt
Fluorine	for bone and teeth formation	more likelihood of tooth decay	milk; water in some areas; toothpaste

Table 26.1 Some minerals needed by humans

Fig. 26.3 The thyroid gland in the neck uses iodine to make the hormone thyroxine. A shortage of iodine in the diet can make the thyroid gland swell, forming a goitre.

Animals do need some inorganic substances

Two of the types of substances in the list of foods are inorganic ones. These are minerals and water.

Minerals are inorganic substances which we need in very small amounts in our diet. There is quite a large number of them. Some of them are shown in Table 26.1.

Water is needed in much larger quantities. You probably need to take in around 2–3 litres of water a day. You will not need to drink all this, because most foods contain some water. A person can live for up to 60 days without food, but will die after only a few days without any water. Water is needed for several different reasons. Firstly, the cytoplasm in your cells is a solution of proteins and other substances in water. The metabolic reactions happening in your cells will only happen in solution. So if your cells lose too much water, metabolism stops and you die.

Secondly, water is used to transport substances around your body. Blood is mostly water. If a person becomes severely dehydrated, their blood gets thicker. It travels more slowly around the body.

There are many other uses for water in the body. It is used in many different metabolic reactions. It helps in digestion. It dissolves waste products so that they can be removed in urine. It evaporates from the skin when you are hot, cooling you down.

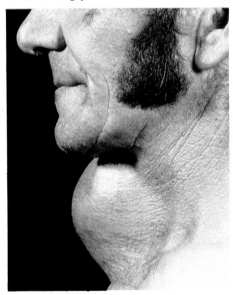

Questions

1 Explain the difference between:
   a organic and inorganic substances
   b autotrophic and heterotrophic nutrition
2 **a** List three examples of fungi.
   b On what do each of your examples feed?
   c Briefly explain how the food gets into the fungus' body.
   d What is the name for this kind of feeding?
3 **a** List the kinds of foods which animals need in their diet.
   b Which of these foods are organic?
   c Which of these foods are inorganic?
   d Give three reasons why water is needed in the diet.
   e Why does a lack of iron in the diet cause tiredness and lack of energy?

27 CARBOHYDRATES AND FATS

Carbohydrates and fats are energy foods.

Food provides energy

All the energy that you have comes from the food you eat. If you are 15 years old, you probably use up about 9500 to 12 000 kilojoules (kJ) of energy each day. A lot of this energy is used to keep you warm. The rest is used up in movement, making new cells, and other processes in your body.

Most of your energy comes from **carbohydrates** and **fats** which you eat. **Protein** provides only around 10 % of your energy. So carbohydrates and fats are sometimes called 'energy foods'.

It is important to take in the right amount of energy. If you eat food containing more energy than you need, your body stores the surplus as fat. If you do not eat enough, you lose weight and become tired and ill. Pure carbohydrate contains 17 kJ of energy in every gram. Protein also contains 17 kJ per gram. Fat, however, contains much more energy – around 39 kJ per gram. Many foods are a mixture of carbohydrates, fats, proteins and other substances. To find out how much energy they contain, they can be burnt in a calorimeter.

Fig. 27.1 Taking in more energy than you use up can lead to obesity.

Carbohydrates include sugars and starches

Sugars and starches are carbohydrates. The shape of their molecules is shown in Figure 27.2. Carbohydrates contain three kinds of atoms – carbon, hydrogen and oxygen.

The simplest kinds of carbohydrates are **sugars**. Sugars have quite small molecules. They are soluble in water and they taste sweet. Examples include glucose, sucrose – cane sugar, which you use in tea or coffee – and maltose.

Starches have much bigger molecules. They are made of thousands of glucose molecules linked in a long chain. Because the molecules are so big, they will not dissolve in water. Starch does not taste sweet.

Fig. 27.2 Carbohydrate molecules

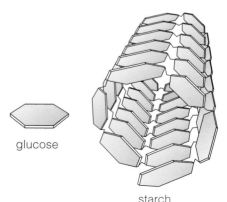

glucose

starch

INVESTIGATION 27.1

Testing foods for carbohydrates

A *Testing for starch*
1. Draw up a results chart. It should have spaces for the name of the food being tested, the colour it goes, and what you can conclude from this.
2. Collect small samples of the foods you are going to test. Take great care not to let any of the foods get mixed up.
3. Put each food in turn on to a white tile. Cover it with iodine solution. This solution is brown. If there is starch in the food, it will turn very dark blue – almost black. Record each result as you go along.

B *Testing for sugars*
1. Draw up another results chart.
2. Collect samples of food as before. This time, each food must be chopped finely, or crushed in a pestle and mortar.
3. Put a sample of the first food you are going to test into a boiling tube. Add Benedict's solution. Shake the tube to mix the food thoroughly with the Benedict's solution. This is so that any sugar molecules in the food will be able to react with the Benedict's solution easily.
4. WEAR SAFETY GLASSES. Holding your tube at an angle, heat it gently over a blue Bunsen burner flame. Shake it gently as you heat it so that each part heats evenly. If it seems to be heating too quickly take it out of the flame for a moment.

If the food contains sugar, a reddish-brown precipitate will form when the Benedict's solution boils. If there is only a little sugar, it may go green or yellowish, but not quite turn red.

Do *not* continue to boil the liquid after it has changed colour.

Questions
1. Make a list of foods which contain starch.
2. Make a list of foods which contain sugar.
3. Why do you need to chop or crush the food for the sugar test?
4. Give two reasons for shaking the solution when doing the sugar test.

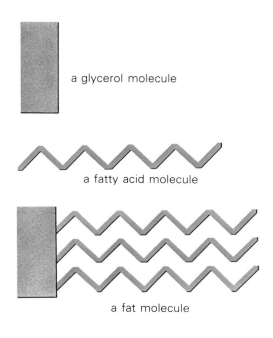

a glycerol molecule

a fatty acid molecule

a fat molecule

Fig. 27.3 Fat molecules

The wrong sort of fats can cause heart disease

Fats, like carbohydrates, contain three sorts of atoms – carbon, hydrogen and oxygen. But the way in which these atoms combine in fats is very different compared with carbohydrates. Figure 27.3 shows the structure of a typical fat molecule. Fats are not soluble in water.

Fats are sometimes called **lipids**.

Fats and oils – oils are liquid fats – should not form too large a part of a diet. Like carbohydrates they are energy foods. Too many make you fat. But you do need to eat *some* fat. Some vitamins are found only in fatty foods. Your body does need fats for making cell membranes, nerve cells and other substances.

Fats are often described as being **saturated** or **unsaturated**. Saturated fats tend to come from animals. Dairy products and meat contain a lot of saturated fat. These foods also contain a fat-like substance called **cholesterol**. People who eat a lot of saturated fats and cholesterol run a higher risk of circulatory problems (blocked blood vessels) and heart disease.

Unsaturated fats tend to come from plants. Sunflower oil, olive oil and many margarines contain unsaturated fats. These fats do not cause heart disease. In fact, there is some evidence that some of them can actually help to *stop* you getting heart disease! Olive oil, especially, is thought to help in this way. Fats from oily fish such as mackerel are also good for you.

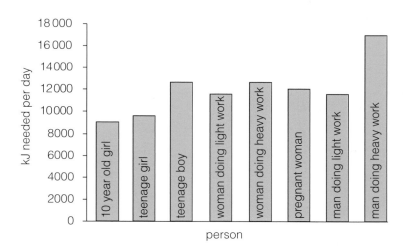

Fig. 27.4 Energy requirements. These figures are only approximate, as the amount of energy you need depends on many things, including your age, sex, weight and how much work you do. It also depends on temperature, as in a cold environment you use a lot of energy to keep warm.

Questions

1 a List four foods which are rich in carbohydrate.
b List three foods which contain almost no carbohydrate at all.
c Why do you need carbohydrate in your diet?
d Describe two properties which distinguish sugars from starches.
2 a List four foods which are rich in fat.
b List three foods which contain almost no fat at all.

c Why should you avoid too much saturated fat in your diet?
d List two foods which contain a lot of saturated fat.
e List two foods which contain unsaturated fat.
f Give two reasons why everyone should have some fat in their diet.
3 a About how much energy is needed each day by:
　i a 10-year-old girl
　ii a 15-year-old boy

　iii a pregnant woman
　iv a 40-year-old man doing a desk job
　v a 40-year-old man doing heavy work?
b Which types of food provide most of a person's energy?
c What happens if the amount of energy taken into a person's body is more than the amount of energy they use up?

28 PROTEINS AND VITAMINS

Proteins are needed for making many substances in your body. Vitamins are essential for helping metabolic reactions to take place efficiently.

Proteins are made up of amino acids

Proteins, like fats and carbohydrates, are organic substances. Like fats and carbohydrates, they are made up of carbon, hydrogen and oxygen atoms. But proteins also contain two other types of atoms. These are nitrogen and sulphur. These five types of atoms are bonded together to form **amino acid** molecules. There are about 20 different sorts of amino acids. Amino acids can join together to form chains. A short chain is called a **polypeptide**. A long chain of amino acids is called a **protein**.

There are thousands of different proteins. They are different because of the different order of the amino acids in their chains. As there are about 20 different amino acids, in a chain of 200 there are millions of possible orders in which they could be arranged. Even one amino acid difference in the chain would make a different protein! So there is almost no limit to the number of different proteins which could exist.

Fig. 28.1   Protein molecules. Proteins are long chains of amino acid molecules. There are 20 different amino acids.

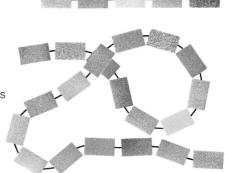

a. A single amino acid

b. A short chain of amino acids is called a polypeptide.

c. A protein molecule is made of several hundred amino acids linked in a chain. The chain coils in a particular shape for each kind of protein.

Proteins are needed for making many substances in the body

Proteins are an important part of the diet. Proteins have many different functions in the body.

The **cytoplasm** from which your cells are made contains a lot of protein dissolved in water. So proteins are needed for making new cells. Muscle cells contain an especially large amount of protein. **Cell membranes** also contain protein.

Haemoglobin, the red pigment in your red blood cells which transports oxygen, is a protein. So is **fibrinogen**, which helps in blood clotting.

Your hair and nails are made of a protein called **keratin**. Your skin is also covered with a layer of keratin. It is tough and insoluble.

The **antibodies** which help to defend you against attacks from bacteria and viruses are proteins. So are **enzymes**. Without enzymes, none of your metabolic reactions would be able to take place.

So you can see that proteins have many important roles to play in your body. When you eat food containing protein, your digestive system breaks down the protein molecules into individual amino acids. The amino acids are taken around the body in your blood and delivered to your cells. Here, the amino acids are linked together again to form whichever proteins that cell needs.

INVESTIGATION 28.1

Testing food for proteins

This test for proteins is called the **biuret test**.
1   Draw up a results chart.
2   WEAR SAFETY GLASSES. Crush or chop a sample of the food you are going to test. Put some into a test tube. Add some potassium hydroxide solution.
   Take care! This is quite a strong alkali and it can burn your skin. If you get it on your hands,

wash it off immediately with cold water.
3   Cork the test tube and shake to mix the food with the potassium hydroxide solution. Then add a little dilute copper sulphate solution. Cork and shake again.

A blue colour means there is no protein in the food. A purple colour means there is protein in the food.

Fig. 28.2   Cheese (on the left) contains protein, and gives a purple colour with the biuret test. The tube on the right shows the blue colour which indicates that no protein is present.

Vitamins are only needed in very small amounts

Vitamins are organic substances. They are only needed in very tiny amounts in your diet. They do not have any energy value at all. But without any one of them, you are likely to get extremely ill.

Vitamin A is a fat-soluble vitamin. Good sources of vitamin A include fish oil, dairy products and carrots. Vitamin A is needed to keep your skin healthy. It is also used to make the substance which helps you to see in dim light. Without vitamin A your skin becomes very dry. The cornea, the covering over the front of the eye, also gets dry. This condition is called **xerophthalmia**. You can no longer see in dim light – you suffer from **night blindness**.

Vitamin B is really lots of different vitamins. The B vitamins are all water-soluble. They are found in wheat germ, brown flour and rice, yeast extract, liver and kidney. The B vitamins help in the chemical reactions of respiration. These reactions take place in every cell in your body. They provide the cells with energy. So without vitamin B your cells run short of energy. One particular disease resulting from lack of vitamin B is beri-beri. People with **beri-beri** have little energy and very weak muscles.

Vitamin C is a water-soluble vitamin. It is found in citrus fruits and many fresh vegetables, including potatoes. But vitamin C is easily destroyed by cooking. This is one reason why you should try to eat fresh, uncooked fruit and vegetables in your diet. Vitamin C helps to keep skin strong and supple. Without it, the skin on the gums begins to crack apart and bleed. Wounds in other parts of the skin cannot heal. This disease is called **scurvy**. Sailors used to suffer from scurvy on long sea voyages when they had no fresh food to eat.

Vitamin D is a fat-soluble vitamin. It is found in fish oil, eggs and dairy products. It can also be made by your skin when sunlight falls on it. Vitamin D is needed to help your body to use calcium to make bones and teeth. Without vitamin D the bones stay soft, and bend. This is called **rickets**.

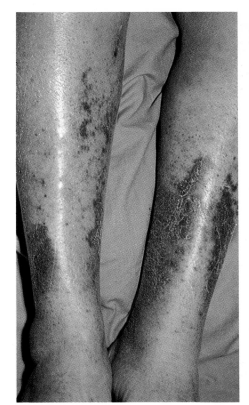

Fig. 28.3   Lack of vitamin C causes scurvy. One symptom of advanced scurvy is bleeding beneath the skin.

INVESTIGATION 28.2

Testing fruit juices for vitamin C

DCPIP is a blue dye which loses its blue colour when vitamin C is added to it. You can find out how much vitamin C a solution contains by adding it to DCPIP. The *more* vitamin C there is in the solution, the *less* of it is needed to make a certain amount of DCPIP lose its blue colour.

You will be given a solution of DCPIP and several different fruit juices. Design and carry out an experiment to find out which of the fruit juices contains the highest concentration of vitamin C.

If you were given a solution containing a known concentration of vitamin C, how could you find out the concentration of vitamin C in each of the fruit juices? Design and carry out an experiment to find out these concentrations.

EXTENSION

Fig. 28.4   This child is suffering from rickets, a disease in which the bones of growing children do not harden. It can be caused by a lack of vitamin D in the diet.

Questions

1 a Are proteins organic or inorganic substances?

b Which elements are contained in all proteins?

c How many different types of amino acids are there?

d List five foods which contain a lot of protein.

e List two foods which contain hardly any protein.

2 a Keratin and haemoglobin are two important proteins in your body. Where is each found and what does it do?

b Even if you do not eat any keratin, your body can still make it. Briefly explain why this is possible.

3 Draw up a chart to show the sources, uses and deficiency diseases for vitamins A, B, C and D.

29 A BALANCED DIET

A balanced diet is one which contains the right amount of food, with enough of all the different substances needed by the body.

Different people need different diets

Different people need different amounts of energy in their diet. Figure 27.4 on page 69 shows a few examples. The more energy a person uses up each day, the more they need in their diet. Different people also need different proportions of the seven types of food in their diet. A growing child, for example, needs plenty of protein for making new cells. An athlete needs protein for building muscles, but also plenty of carbohydrate for energy. A pregnant woman needs extra iron and calcium to build her baby's blood and bones.

A good diet is called a **balanced diet**. A balanced diet contains the right amount of energy to meet a person's needs. It also contains some of all the seven types of food – carbohydrates, fats, proteins, water, roughage, each kind of vitamin and each kind of mineral. It contains enough of all of these, but not too much of any. The right diet for you might not be the right diet for someone else. It all depends on your age, your sex and your lifestyle.

Whatever type of diet you need, there are certain things which are especially good and certain things which should be avoided.

Fresh fruit and brown bread are good for you

Fresh fruit and vegetables are a very important part of a balanced diet. They contain many vitamins and minerals. They also contain roughage. Roughage (fibre) helps to keep food moving quickly through the digestive system. This reduces the risk of several different illnesses, including bowel cancer. Brown rice and whole wheat also contain useful vitamins and roughage. So brown bread is much better for you than white.

Fig. 29.1   High-fibre foods

Vegetarian diets can be very healthy

More and more people are becoming vegetarians. Sometimes they just do not like meat. Some people think that a vegetarian diet is more healthy than one which contains meat. Other people are vegetarians because they do not like the idea of killing and eating animals. Most vegetarians will eat milk and eggs. They are sometimes called lacto-ovo vegetarians. Some vegetarians will not eat any animal products at all. They are called vegans.

A vegetarian diet can be a very healthy one. It is likely to contain plenty of roughage and to be low in saturated fats and cholesterol. But vegetarians do need to be careful to get plenty of proteins. They should eat plenty of pulses (beans, peas and lentils) which are rich in protein. Rice and other grains also contain protein. If they eat milk, eggs and cheese, these are rich in protein too. Vegetarian diets are sometimes low in certain vitamins. Vegetarians must take care to eat as wide a range of different foods as possible, to make sure they get all the amino acids, vitamins and minerals that they need.

Fig. 29.2   Vegetarian food

Too much food causes obesity

Obesity means being too fat. Obesity is caused by eating more food than you need. If the amount of energy you take in is more than you use up, the extra food is stored as fat. Being too fat is not good for you. Obese people are much more likely to suffer from heart disease and circulatory problems than people of normal weight.

The amount of food needed by different people varies widely. Even people of the same age and sex may need very different amounts of food. So do not worry if you seem to eat a lot more than your best friend! So long as you are not obviously overweight, you probably need this extra food.

Anorexia nervosa is a dangerous illness

Anorexia nervosa is a disease in which the sufferer does not eat enough food to keep them healthy. It is commonest in young people. A person suffering from anorexia nervosa does not want to eat food. If they are made to eat, they may be sick afterwards. They lose weight. Eventually, they may lose so much weight that they become ill. They may even die.

No-one is quite sure what causes anorexia nervosa. It is a psychological problem. The person may be really worried about being fat. Or they may not want to grow up and face the world with all its problems. They imagine that if they do not eat, they can avoid these problems. Anorexia can be cured. But there is no magic solution. It takes a long time and a lot of care before an anorexic person can learn to live and eat in a happy, normal way.

Fig.29.3 This mother and child in Ethiopia are suffering from a lack of food. They were forced to move away from their home because of fighting. Severe lack of food during childhood means that a person will still be small even as an adult.

Malnutrition and starvation

If you have something wrong with you which is caused by a bad diet, you are suffering from malnutrition. Malnutrition means 'bad eating'.

Malnutrition can be caused by eating too much of something. It can also be caused by not eating enough of a particular food. Children who do not get enough protein in their diet, for example, will not grow properly. In some parts of the world this is all too common. It is called **kwashiorkor**.

Starvation is not the same as malnutrition. Starvation means not getting enough food to keep you alive. Starving people do not get enough energy in their diet to balance the energy they use up. They have no fat stores to draw on, so their body begins to break down the proteins in their cells to provide energy. Children with **marasmus** suffer from a general weakness and do not grow properly due to lack of food.

Questions

1 a What is meant by a balanced diet?
  b Why is a balanced diet for one person not necessarily the right diet for another?
2 Below are listed the foods eaten in one day by a 14-year-old boy. It is not difficult to see that this is not a good diet!
- Breakfast: nothing
- Morning break: two bags of crisps, can of fizzy drink
- Lunch: beefburger, chips, baked beans, can of fizzy drink, chocolate
- Tea: two cups of tea, each with two spoonfuls of sugar; piece of cake, three chocolate biscuits
- Supper: fish and chips, can of fizzy drink, ice cream

  a Explain, with *reasons*, what is wrong with this diet.
  b Suggest some changes which the boy could make in this diet, without giving up the things that he really likes eating.
3 Read the following passage, and then answer the questions.

Diet and intelligence

A lot of people's diets consist largely of processed food. Children come to school without having eaten any breakfast. They eat crisps and chocolate at break-time and choose cooked, fatty foods at lunchtime. Their diet may contain almost no fresh food.

A science teacher in a comprehensive school in Wales has investigated the diets of some of the children in his school. He found that many of them were not getting enough of up to ten different vitamins and minerals. He wondered if this was affecting their success in school.

In 1986 he gave all children in the second year at school a mental test and recorded the results. For the rest of the year, half of these children were given vitamin pills. The other half were also given a pill, but without any vitamins in it. They did not know which was which. At the end of the school year all the pupils were tested again. On many of the tests, there was no difference between the children who had taken extra vitamins and those who had not. But on one sort of intelligence test, the children who had had vitamin pills did much better than they had before. Other similar tests have been conducted in other parts of the world, with similar results. Does this mean that all children should take vitamin pills? Probably not. But it does mean that we should think carefully about what we eat, and make sure that our diet contains plenty of vitamins.

1 What is meant by 'processed foods'? Why are they likely to contain less vitamins than fresh foods?
2 Why did the science teacher decide to try giving children extra vitamins?
3 Why were some children given 'dummy' pills?
4 What does this experiment suggest about the effect of lack of vitamins on intelligence?

30 THE HUMAN DIGESTIVE SYSTEM

The digestive system is made up of the alimentary canal and glands which secrete juices into it.

The alimentary canal is a tube leading from mouth to anus

Food goes into you through your mouth. Eventually, solid remains emerge at the other end as faeces. What happens to the food in between? Food travels through your body along your **alimentary canal**. This a tube which begins at the mouth and ends at the anus. The tube is continuous. It is wide in some parts and narrow in others. It bends back on itself in places but is basically just a single tube running right through your body.

Fig. 30.1   The human alimentary canal. The alimentary canal is the tube along which food passes. The canal, plus the other organs which secrete liquids into it, such as the liver, make up the digestive system.

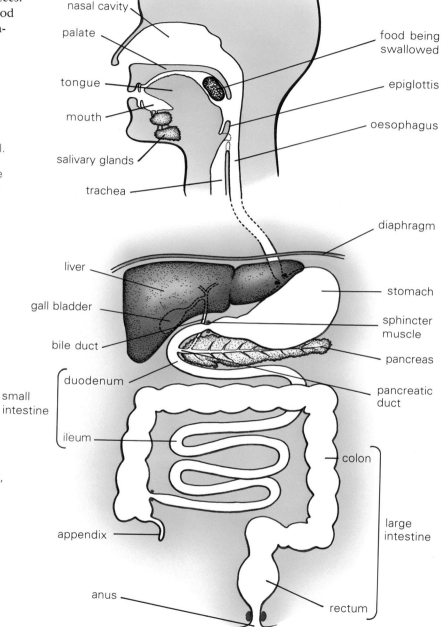

food is moving this way

longitudinal muscles

lumen - the space inside the tube

circular muscles contract, squeezing the food forwards

circular muscles relax, allowing the tube to open wider

food

Fig. 30.2   Peristalsis. Muscles in the wall of the alimentary canal contract in waves, pushing food along.

The walls of the alimentary canal contain muscles

All along the alimentary canal there are strong muscles in the walls. These muscles push the food along. You can see this happening in your oesophagus when you swallow. The rippling movements of the muscles are called **peristalsis**. Peristalsis takes place all along your alimentary canal. The muscles work best when you have plenty of fibre in your diet. A lack of fibre can cause constipation, when the muscles do not work so well and the food stops moving along.

Mucus stops food and enzymes damaging the walls of your alimentary canal

The walls of your alimentary canal are made up of soft, living cells. Inside your alimentary canal is a mixture of all sorts of food – some of it quite hard and rough – and enzymes. The living cells must be protected from damage. So scattered amongst them, are goblet cells. These make mucus. The mucus covers the inside of the alimentary canal with a slimy layer, over which the partly digested food can easily slide. And the enzymes inside the alimentary canal cannot get at the living cells and damage them.

The stomach wall needs special protection because the stomach contains hydrochloric acid. This acid helps to kill bacteria in the food. Normally the stomach wall is well protected by its layer of mucus. But sometimes the amount of acid is too great and it begins to digest the stomach wall. This is painful and is called a **stomach ulcer**. The acid may also damage the wall of the next part of the canal – the **duodenum**. This is called a **duodenal ulcer**. If the hole goes right through, the contents of the alimentary canal can leak out. This is called a **perforated ulcer**. It is exceedingly painful and dangerous if not quickly treated.

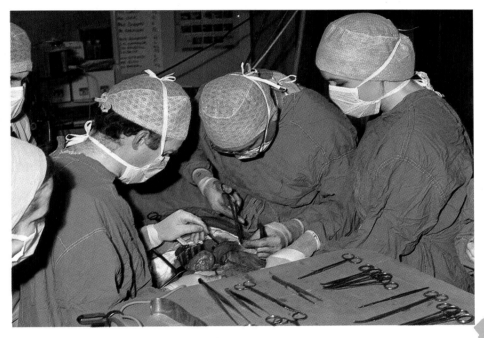

Rings of muscle can close off regions of the alimentary canal

At various places along the alimentary canal there are rings of muscle called **sphincter muscles**. These can contract to squeeze the tube closed. Sphincter muscles at the top and bottom of the stomach close to hold food inside the stomach while it is churned up with enzymes and hydrochloric acid. It may be held there for several hours. Sometimes the sphincter muscles do not work as well as they should. Acid food can then get squeezed out of the top of the stomach into the oesophagus. The acid burns the wall of the oesophagus, which hurts. This is called **heartburn**.

There is also a sphincter muscle right at the end of the alimentary canal. This is the anal sphincter. It stays closed most of the time. It opens to allow faeces to pass out of the rectum.

The liver and pancreas make fluids which help to digest food

The alimentary canal is not the only part of your body which helps with digestion. There are also several glands which pour liquids into the canal. These glands and the alimentary canal make up your **digestive system**.

The largest gland is the **liver**. The liver has many functions besides digestion. But it does help in digestion by producing **bile**. The bile is stored in a small sac inside the liver called the **gall bladder**. A tube called the **bile duct** carries the bile from the gall bladder into the duodenum. It is squirted on to the food as it emerges from the stomach. Bile helps to digest fats.

On the left-hand side of your body, just under your stomach, is a soft, creamy coloured gland called the **pancreas**. Like the liver the pancreas has other functions beside digestion. But most of the cells in the pancreas produce a liquid called **pancreatic juice**. The juice flows along a tube called the **pancreatic duct**. This, like the bile duct, opens into the duodenum. Pancreatic juice contains enzymes which help to digest proteins, fats and carbohydrates.

Fig. 30.3 An operation being performed on the alimentary canal.

Questions

1 a List, in order, the parts of the alimentary canal through which food passes after you have eaten it.
b What is peristalsis?
c Why does the wall of the alimentary canal contain goblet cells?

2 a What are sphincter muscles?
b Name two places in the alimentary canal where sphincter muscles are found.

31 CATALYSTS

Catalysts are substances which speed up chemical reactions without being changed themselves.

Catalysts speed up reactions without being changed themselves

One way of making oxygen in the laboratory is by the decomposition of hydrogen peroxide, H_2O_2.

hydrogen peroxide $\longrightarrow$ water + oxygen

$2H_2O_2(aq) \longrightarrow 2H_2O(l) + O_2(g)$

Under normal conditions, this reaction is very slow. It can be speeded up by using more concentrated hydrogen peroxide, or by heating it. But a much easier way of speeding it up is to add **manganese (IV) oxide**, MnO_2. Manganese (IV) oxide is a fine, black powder. If you add it to hydrogen peroxide solution – even if it is cold and dilute – the hydrogen peroxide starts to decompose rapidly. Surprisingly, the manganese (IV) oxide is not used up. When the reaction finishes, the black powder is still there.

Manganese (IV) oxide is an example of a **catalyst**. A catalyst is **a substance which speeds up a chemical reaction without being changed or used up.**

Catalysts are important in industry

Catalysts are very important to chemical manufacturers. They allow more product to be made in a given length of time. They are not used up, so they do not have to be continually added to the reactants. But they do have to be cleaned every now and then. This is because the activity of a catalyst involves its surface. Dirt or impurities on a catalyst's surface will stop it acting as efficiently as it should. Industry uses many different catalysts to speed up the reactions it relies on.

Fig. 31.2 Biological washing powders contain enzymes which break down stains such as coffee, egg, blood or sweat.

Biological catalysts are called enzymes

Living organisms have hundreds of different chemical reactions going on inside them. Some of these reactions need to happen quickly. The reactions could be speeded up by heating the reactants. But living cells are rapidly killed if their temperature goes too high.

Fig. 31.1 The conical flask contains hydrogen peroxide solution. Without a catalyst nothing happens. But when a small pinch of manganese (IV) oxide is added, the hydrogen peroxide rapidly decomposes to water and oxygen. The manganese (IV) oxide is not used up in this reaction.

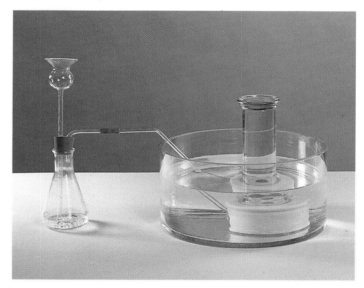

So living organisms use catalysts to speed up their reactions. These catalysts are called **enzymes**. Each different reaction happening in a living organism has a different enzyme catalysing it. So there are hundreds of different kinds of enzyme.

Enzymes are proteins and consist of very large molecules. These molecules have special shapes which are important to their ability to act as catalysts. If enzymes are heated above 45°C, their molecules lose their shapes, and so they don't work well as catalysts at higher temperatures.

Catalysing the decomposition of hydrogen peroxide with an enzyme

You have seen how hydrogen peroxide can be made to decompose quickly by using manganese (IV) oxide as a catalyst. There is also a biological catalyst which will speed up this reaction. It is called **catalase**. Catalase is found in many different kinds of cell. You can find it in apples, yeast, meat (muscle cells) – almost anything! One of the places where there is an especially large amount of catalase is in liver.

Catalase is needed in living cells because hydrogen peroxide is poisonous. Hydrogen peroxide is thought to be made as a by-product of several reactions in cells. It must be decomposed instantly, before it can do any damage. This is what catalase does.

1 Read through this experiment and then design and draw up a results chart.

2 Measure out 20 cm³ of hydrogen peroxide into each of four boiling tubes.

3 Cut four small pieces of fresh liver. They must all be of the same size, around 0.5 cm².

4 Cook two of the pieces of liver in boiling water for about 5 min. Remove them and cool.

5 Grind one raw and one cooked piece of liver to a paste. Keep them separate from one another.

You now have four samples of liver – whole raw, ground raw, whole cooked and ground cooked.

Make sure that you are thoroughly organised before you go any further – things will happen quickly!

6 Start a stopclock. Put your four samples of liver into the four tubes of hydrogen peroxide solution. Try to do them all at the same time. After 2 min, measure the height of the froth in the boiling tube, and record it in your results chart.

7 Light and then blow out a splint.

Push the glowing splint through the froth in one of the tubes, and record what happens.

Questions

1 Write a word equation, and a balanced molecular equation, for the reaction which happened in your boiling tubes.

2 The liver contained a catalyst. What is the name of this catalyst? What type of catalyst is it?

3 Why does liver contain this catalyst?

4 Which type of liver made the reaction happen fastest? Explain why you think this is.

5 Which type of liver was least effective in speeding up the reaction? Explain why you think this is.

Questions

1 This question is about the decomposition of hydrogen peroxide to water and oxygen.

a Give two ways in which the decomposition of hydrogen peroxide could be speeded up.

b Give three ways in which the decomposition of hydrogen peroxide could be slowed down.

c Manganese (IV) oxide acts as a catalyst in this reaction. How could you prove that the manganese (IV) oxide is not used up in the reaction flask?

d Is manganese (IV) oxide
i a reactant?
ii a product in this reaction?

e Do you think that manganese (IV) oxide would be a better catalyst in lump form, or in powder form? Explain your answer.

2 New cars must by law have catalysts fitted into their exhaust systems.

a Why do you think that this is done?

b Find out why using leaded petrol prevents such catalysts being used.

3 Enzymes are biological catalysts. All enzymes are proteins. Protein molecules are easily destroyed by high temperatures.

The graph below shows how a particular biological reaction is affected by temperature. The reaction is catalysed by an enzyme.

a At which temperatures did the reaction take place most slowly?

b At which temperature did the reaction take place most quickly?

c What happened to the reaction as the temperature was raised from 10 °C to 20 °C?

d What do you think began to happen to the enzyme at 45 °C?

e Explain why the reaction got slower as the temperature was raised from 45 °C to 60 °C.

f Human body temperature is normally around 37 °C. If you are very ill, your temperature can go up to 40 °C. Why is this dangerous?

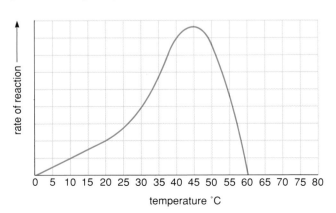

77

32 DIGESTION

Large food molecules must be broken down to small ones before they can get into your bloodstream. This is called digestion.

Digestion means breaking down large food molecules into small ones

The walls of the alimentary canal are made up of living cells. Food molecules must pass through these living cells to get into the blood vessels and be taken around the body. Only small molecules can get through the walls of the alimentary canal and into the bloodstream. Water molecules, vitamin molecules and mineral ions are all small enough to get through. But much of the food that you eat is made up of large molecules. These large molecules must be broken down to small ones before they can be absorbed. The process of breaking down large food molecules to small ones is called **digestion**.

Enzymes catalyse the breakdown of large food molecules

The breakdown of large food molecules to small ones is a chemical reaction. Like all reactions which take place in living things, the reactions of digestion are catalysed by enzymes. The enzymes which help in digestion have names ending with 'ase'. Enzymes which catalyse the digestion of carbohydrates are called **carbohydrases**. Enzymes which catalyse the digestion of proteins are called **proteases**. Enzymes which catalyse the digestion of fats are called **lipases**. 'Lipid' is another word for 'fat'.

Like all enzymes, digestive enzymes will only work well at particular temperatures and pH. All of your digestive enzymes have an optimum temperature of around 37–40 °C. But their optimum pHs vary. **Amylase**, a carbohydrase found in your saliva, works best in slightly alkaline conditions at a pH of about 7.5. **Pepsin**, a protease in your stomach, needs acidic conditions around pH 2. And the enzymes in your duodenum and ileum need slightly alkaline conditions. This is provided by sodium hydrogencarbonate, an alkali secreted in bile and pancreatic juice.

Fig. 32.1 How mammals deal with food

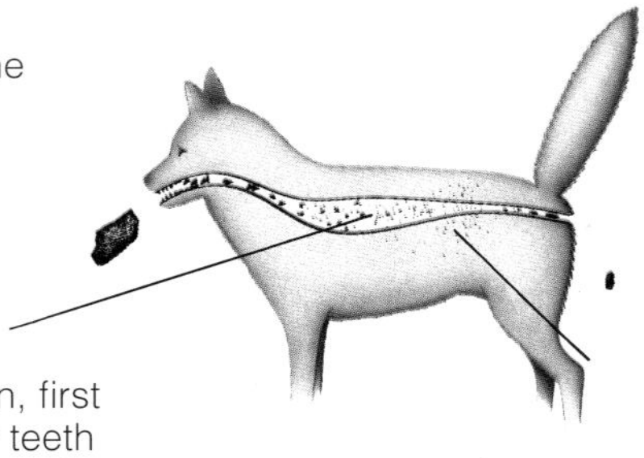

1. Ingestion.
Food is taken into the alimentary canal.

2. Digestion.
Food is broken down, first into small pieces by teeth and muscles, and then into small molecules by enzymes.

4. Egestion.
Any food which could not be broken down into small molecules is passed out of the body.

3. Absorption.
The small molecules pass out of the alimentary canal into the blood, which takes them all around the body.

INVESTIGATION 32.1

The absorption of carbohydrates from a model gut

Visking tubing, like the walls of your digestive system, will only let small molecules pass through it. You are going to give two pieces of visking tubing a 'meal' and see what happens.

1. Take two pieces of visking tubing. Wet them and open them out into tubes. Pushing a pencil inside may help. Tie one end of each, very tightly.
2. Three-quarters fill one piece of tubing with starch solution. Three-quarters fill the other piece with glucose solution. These are the 'meals'.
3. Tie the tops of both pieces of tubing tightly. Rinse them both to remove any spilt starch or glucose solution from their outsides.
4. Put each 'gut' into a beaker. Curl them up to lie in the bottom of their beakers. Pour in enough warm water just to cover each of them. Leave them for at least half an hour — longer if you can.
5. Now take samples of the water in each beaker. Test each sample for starch, and record your results. Test each sample for sugar and record your results.

Questions

1. Which part of your apparatus represented:
   a. the wall of the digestive system
   b. the blood?
2. Did you find starch in the water in either beaker? Explain your findings.
3. Did you find sugar in the water in either beaker? Explain your findings.
4. Why did you use *warm* water to cover your pieces of tubing?
5. Why is it best to use only enough water just to cover the pieces of tubing?
6. Starch molecules are made of long strings of glucose molecules, joined in a chain. What does this investigation suggest must happen to starch molecules before they can be absorbed into your blood from your digestive system?

Carbohydrate is digested in the mouth and small intestine

The main types of carbohydrate which you eat are cellulose, starch and sucrose. You cannot digest cellulose at all. Its large molecules cannot be broken down in your digestive system so you cannot absorb them. They pass straight through as fibre and leave your body in the faeces.

Starch, though, is easily digested. The process begins in your mouth. Saliva contains an enzyme called **amylase**, which begins to break down starch to maltose. You do not usually keep food in your mouth for long enough for your amylase to finish digesting any starch in it. When the food is swallowed and enters the stomach the amylase stops working. This is because it cannot work in acid conditions. So no carbohydrate digestion takes place in the stomach.

But when the food leaves the stomach carbohydrate digestion continues. Pancreatic juice flowing into the duodenum contains more amylase to finish changing starch into maltose. Another enzyme, called **maltase**, is found a little further along, in the ileum. Maltase digests maltose, breaking it up into glucose molecules. These are small enough to be absorbed through the ileum wall.

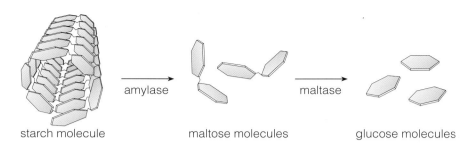
Fig. 32.2 Digestion of carbohydrates

starch molecule   amylase   maltose molecules   maltase   glucose molecules

Protein is digested in the stomach and small intestine

Large protein molecules are digested by proteases. The first time a mouthful of food meets a protease enzyme is when it reaches your stomach. Here the protease pepsin begins to break down the long protein molecules into shorter ones called **polypeptides**.

After a time in the stomach food is allowed through into the duodenum. Pancreatic juice squirts out on to it from the pancreatic duct. This contains a protease called trypsin. **Trypsin** begins to break down the polypeptides into even shorter chains.

The food quickly moves on into the ileum. Enzymes on the walls of the ileum finish breaking down the polypeptides into individual **amino acids**. The amino acid molecules are small enough to get through the wall of the ileum and into the blood capillaries.

Fats are digested in the small intestine

Fats are more difficult to digest than proteins or carbohydrates. This is because they are not soluble in water. They form globules into which enzymes cannot penetrate.

So before enzymes can digest fats the fat globules must be broken up. This is done by **bile salts**. Bile salts are detergent-like substances contained in bile. They emulsify fats, breaking up big globules into very tiny ones. The tiny globules mix in with the digestive juices and can be attacked by enzymes.

The enzyme which digests fats is called **lipase**. There is lipase in pancreatic juice and also on the walls of the ileum. So all fat digestion happens in the small intestine. Lipase breaks up fat molecules into fatty acids and glycerol. These are then absorbed through the walls of the ileum.

Fig. 32.3 Digestion of proteins

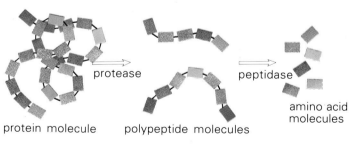

protein molecule   protease   polypeptide molecules   peptidase   amino acid molecules

Fig. 32.4 Digestion of fat

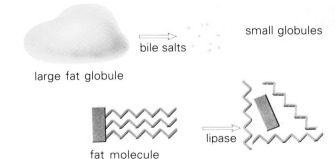

large fat globule   bile salts   small globules

fat molecule   lipase   fatty acid and glycerol molecules

Questions

1 Copy the following chart. In the first three columns, put a tick in the correct line or lines. In the last column write 'acidic' or 'alkaline' in each line.

	carbohydrate digested	protein digested	fat digested	acidic or alkaline
mouth				
stomach				
duodenum				
ileum				

2 a Why do water, vitamins and minerals not need digesting?

b What type of food does lipase digest?

c Why is this type of food especially difficult to digest?

d How does bile help in the digestion of this type of food?

Teeth and muscles help in mechanical digestion

Digestion is the breaking up of large food molecules into smaller ones, so that they can be absorbed through the walls of the alimentary canal. The reactions of digestion are speeded up by enzymes which catalyse the reactions.

The reactions are also speeded up by teeth and muscles. Teeth break up large particles of food increasing their surface area. This allows enzymes to come into contact with the food molecules more quickly. The reactions of digestion are therefore speeded up. Stomach muscles have a similar effect. When your stomach contains food, the muscles in its walls make churning movements. This mixes the food with the enzymes and acid. It also helps to break down lumps of food. The food becomes a liquid mass called **chyme**.

Teeth contain living cells

Teeth are alive. They contain living cells. These cells are supplied with food and oxygen by blood vessels. The blood vessels and also nerves are found in a soft, central area in the tooth. This is called the **pulp cavity**.

Surrounding the pulp cavity is a layer of bone-like material. It is called **dentine**. Dentine, like bone, contains living cells. The cells are embedded in a background material, or **matrix**, containing calcium salts. These make the dentine hard.

The dentine is covered by an even harder material called **enamel**. Enamel is the hardest substance in your body. It is very difficult to scratch the surface of enamel. But it can be cracked and it can be dissolved by acids. Only the part of the tooth which shows above the gum is covered by enamel. This part is called the **crown** of the tooth.

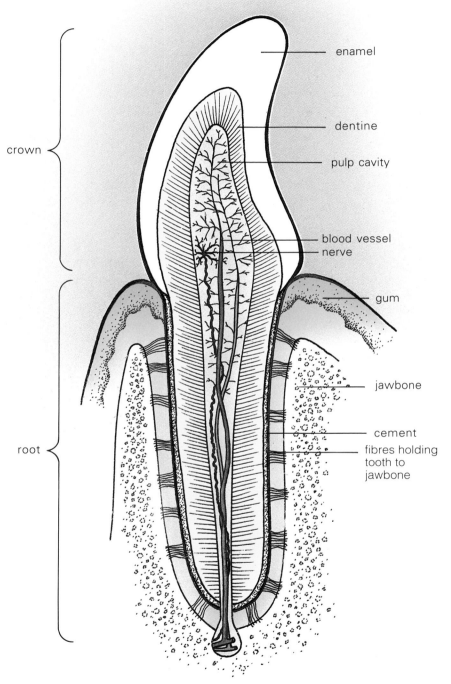

Fig. 33.1 Vertical section through a human incisor

enamel

dentine

pulp cavity

blood vessel
nerve

gum

jawbone

cement
fibres holding tooth to jawbone

crown

root

The part which is buried in the gum and jaw bone is called the **root**. The root is covered by **cement**. Cement, like enamel, is very hard.

Connecting the root to the jaw bone are thousands of **fibres**. These are slightly stretchy. If you bite on something very hard, or fall and bang a tooth, these fibres can give a little. They allow your tooth to move slightly without damaging anything.

Tooth decay is caused by acids

Enamel is the hardest substance in your body. It forms an excellent protective covering over your teeth. But it is easily damaged by acids. Acids cause tooth decay. Acids are formed on your teeth by bacteria. Everyone has bacteria living in their mouth. They are not normally harmful. But if you leave sugary foods on your teeth the bacteria will feed on them. The bacteria form a sticky covering called **plaque** on your teeth. As they feed on the sugar, the bacteria produce acid. The acid dissolves the enamel.

If you have plenty of fluoride in your body your teeth are better able to resist this attack by acid. Fluoride toothpastes help a lot. Another way of getting fluoride is in drinking water.

But if the acid *does* get through the enamel the decay spreads quickly. Dentine is much softer than enamel, so the acid dissolves it faster. The tooth may begin to be painful now. Dentine contains living cells, and they are sensitive.

Gum disease is also caused by bacteria

Bacteria often collect along the edges of your teeth where they meet the gum. These bacteria may work their way down between the tooth and the

Fig. 33.2 Tooth decay

1. Bacteria and food are trapped in a groove on or between teeth. The bacteria break down the food, releasing acids. The acids begin to dissolve the enamel.

2. When the acid breaks through to the dentine, the decay spreads faster. Dentine is softer than enamel, and contains living cells.

3. If the decay is not treated, it will probably reach the pulp cavity. This is very painful.

4. Once into the pulp cavity, bacteria can get into the blood vessels. They may cause an infection at the base of the tooth. An abscess forms, which fills with pus.

gum. They can damage the gum and the fibres holding the tooth in position. Over a long period of time the tooth may become loose and may even fall out.

Brushing teeth regularly to remove bacteria from your teeth can help to prevent tooth decay and also gum disease. It is best to use fluoride toothpaste. A regular visit to a dentist can also help to spot problems early so that something can be done about them before it is too late. Making sure that your teeth are not covered with sugar for long periods of time will also help to ensure that you do not lose teeth.

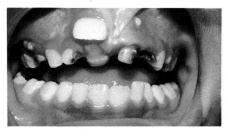

Fig. 33.3 This eight-year-old has very bad tooth decay in his upper jaw. The large tooth at the top is an adult incisor coming through, but it is growing crookedly because of the decay.

Untreated decay may cause an abcess to form

A decaying tooth can be treated with a **filling**. A dentist can drill away all the decayed part, and replace it with a filling material. But if this is not done the decay may spread to the pulp cavity. Bacteria can now get from the surface of the tooth right into the blood vessels and nerves. The tooth becomes very painful. If the bacteria infect it badly, an **abscess** may form. This is an extremely painful swelling, full of bacteria. White blood cells fight the bacteria. The mixture of living and dead white cells and bacteria is called **pus**.

Dentists will not normally take out an abscessed tooth, even though it is very painful. They are worried that if they pull the tooth out the bacteria in the abscess may get into your blood. If this happens they may make you very ill indeed. Instead, the dentist will prescribe antibiotics to kill the bacteria. When the bacteria in the abscess are killed the tooth can safely be removed.

INVESTIGATION 33.1

Human teeth

1   Use a mirror to look at your own teeth. Identify your **incisors, canines, premolars** and **molars**. Count and record how many of each you have on your top jaw. Repeat for your bottom jaw.

2   The full number of teeth in an adult human is 32. The last four teeth to appear are the back molars. They are sometimes called wisdom teeth. Do you have your wisdom teeth yet? Do you have any other teeth missing?

3   Think of how you use your teeth when you eat an apple. (Better still, eat an apple and think hard about how you are using your teeth.) Describe how you use each of your four kinds of teeth.

4   Make two copies of the diagram below. One is for the top jaw, and the other for the lower jaw. Look again at your own teeth. If you are missing any of the teeth on your diagram shade them in. If any of your teeth have fillings put a cross on those teeth on the diagram.

5   Collect the class results for question 4. You will need to design a results chart to do this. Decide on a good way of displaying these results as a graph or chart.

6   Do any particular teeth tend to be missing in your class? If so, can you suggest why this might be?

7   Do any particular teeth in your class tend to have fillings? If so, can you suggest why this might be?

Fig. 33.4

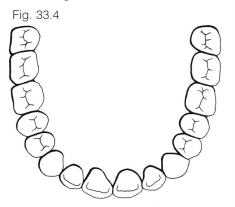

34 ABSORBING FOOD

Food molecules move through the walls of the digestive system into the blood. This is called absorption.

Small food molecules are absorbed in the ileum

By the time that food reaches the ileum, digestion is almost complete. Protein molecules have been broken down to amino acids. Starch molecules have been broken down to glucose. Fats have been broken down to fatty acids and glycerol.

These small molecules can now get through the walls of the digestive system into the blood. This is **absorption**. Absorption of digested food happens in the ileum.

Fig. 34.1 A villus. There are thousands upon thousands of these lining your small intestine. They are about 1 mm tall. They contain muscles which shorten and lengthen them rhythmically during digestion, helping to bring their surfaces into contact with fresh supplies of food.

The inside of the ileum has a very large surface area

The ileum is the longest part of your alimentary canal. It may be 5 m long. So it takes a long time for food to pass through it. This gives plenty of time for food to be absorbed into the blood. The ileum is also one of the narrowest parts of the alimentary canal. So food inside it is always quite near to the walls. This makes it easier for the food molecules to pass through the walls into the blood.

The inner surface of the ileum is thrown into folds. These folds increase the surface area. The larger the surface area, the faster absorption can take place. On the folds are thousands of finger-like projections, called **villi**. Villi are about 1 mm high. The villi also help to increase the surface area of the inside of the ileum. Even the villi have little projections on them, called microvilli!

Inside each villus is a blood capillary. The blood capillary absorbs amino acids and glucose. It leads into the **hepatic portal vein**. This vein takes the absorbed food to the liver. Each villus also contains a lacteal. This is a branch of the lymphatic system. The lacteal absorbs fatty acids and glycerol. It leads into a larger lymph vessel which empties its contents into a vein near the heart.

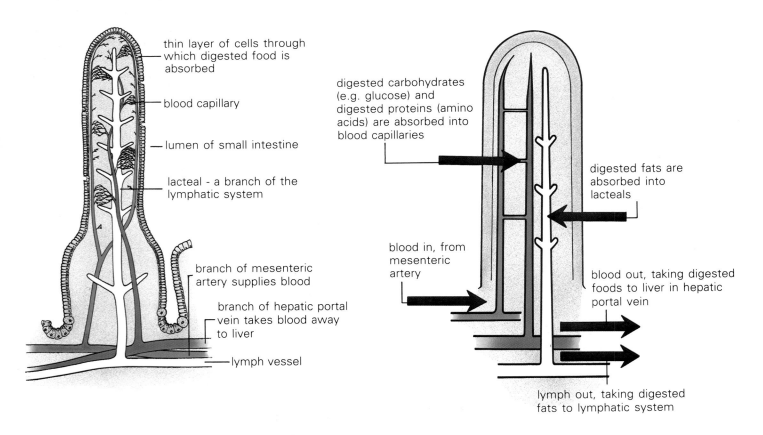

thin layer of cells through which digested food is absorbed

blood capillary

lumen of small intestine

lacteal - a branch of the lymphatic system

branch of mesenteric artery supplies blood

branch of hepatic portal vein takes blood away to liver

lymph vessel

digested carbohydrates (e.g. glucose) and digested proteins (amino acids) are absorbed into blood capillaries

digested fats are absorbed into lacteals

blood in, from mesenteric artery

blood out, taking digested foods to liver in hepatic portal vein

lymph out, taking digested fats to lymphatic system

The colon absorbs water and inorganic ions

When the digested food has been absorbed in the ileum, there is still quite a lot left inside the alimentary canal. This includes water, inorganic (mineral) ions, indigestible food such as cellulose, bacteria, mucus from the lining of the digestive system, and old cells which have worn away from its surface. This mixture passes on into the colon.

In the colon, water is absorbed from the food. The colon also absorbs inorganic ions such as sodium and chloride.

The contents of the colon move on into the rectum. Here they are formed into **faeces**. There is a muscle at the anus called the anal sphincter. Normally this is contracted. When the anal sphincter muscle relaxes, the faeces pass out through the anus.

The food absorbed in the ileum is taken to the liver

The carbohydrates and amino acids that are absorbed into the blood capillaries in the ileum, dissolve in the blood plasma. They are taken in the hepatic portal vein to the liver.

One of the functions of the liver is to regulate (control) the amounts of carbohydrate and amino acids which are allowed into the bloodstream. If you have eaten a meal containing a large amount of carbohydrate, a large amount of glucose will arrive at the liver in the hepatic portal vein. The liver will convert some of this glucose into a polysaccharide called **glycogen**. The glycogen is stored in the liver. Only the right amount of glucose will be allowed out of the liver to be delivered to the body cells.

In the same way, the liver will only allow the right amount of amino acids to be carried to the body cells in the blood. Any extra ones are changed into **urea**. The urea is passed into the blood and taken to the kidneys to be excreted.

Fig. 34.2 A child being given a mixture of glucose, salt and water. This is called 'oral rehydration'. It is a very effective and simple way of replacing fluid lost through illnesses such as diarrhoea.

Assimilation is the use of absorbed food by body cells

The food absorbed by the ileum is eventually used by various cells in the body. The use of this food is called **assimilation**.

Carbohydrate is carried in the blood in the form of **glucose**. Cells take up glucose through their cell surface membranes. They then use the glucose for respiration to produce energy. All cells need a constant supply of glucose.

Some cells can store glucose. They convert it into the polysaccharide **glycogen**. Muscle cells and liver cells are two examples of cells which do this. Excess carbohydrate will be converted into **fat**. This is stored in several places in the body. Much of it is stored under the skin.

Amino acids are also carried to the cells by the blood. They are taken up by the cells through their cell surface membranes and used for building proteins. The DNA in the nucleus of each cell gives instructions about the order in which the amino acids should be joined together. Different orders of amino acids make different proteins. Each cell only follows some of the DNA instructions so each cell only makes certain proteins. Cells in your salivary glands, for example, make the protein amylase. Cells in your hair follicles make the protein keratin.

Questions

1 List the features of the ileum which make it good at absorbing digested food.
2 Match each of the following parts of the alimentary canal with its functions:

Parts:
mouth, oesophagus, stomach, duodenum, ileum, colon, rectum.

Functions:
- passes food to stomach
- absorbs digested food
- begins the digestion of starch by amylase
- absorbs water
- produces hydrochloric acid
- forms undigested food material into faeces
- continues the digestion of starch by amylase
- receives secretions from the gall bladder and pancreas
- begins the digestion of protein by proteases

Questions

1 Read the following passage, and then answer the questions.

Gastric secretion in humans

The stomach walls secrete a liquid called gastric juice. Gastric juice contains water, hydrochloric acid and the protease pepsin.

Some of the earliest studies on the secretion of gastric juice were performed on people who had been wounded. One of the most famous was Alexis St. Martin, who was wounded by duck shot which made a hole into his stomach in about 1825. The hole never completely closed so that the contents and behaviour of his stomach could be investigated. Another famous patient was an American boy called Tom. Tom swallowed boiling hot clam chowder when he was nine years old, damaging his oesophagus so badly that it closed right over. A hole had to be made directly into his stomach so that he could be fed.

Studies on these people, and more recent experiments, have shown that the secretion of gastric juices depends on all sorts of different factors. It is not surprising that gastric secretion speeds up when a person smells, sees or tastes food. The gastric juices are produced so that they are ready to digest the expected food when it arrives. The presence of food in the stomach also causes gastric juice to be secreted. Food containing protein has a greater effect than pure fat or carbohydrate.

It was also found that gastric juices are secreted when someone is excited or angry. This is thought to be a possible cause of stomach ulcers. In contrast, a depressed, frightened person has very little gastric secretion. Another factor which reduces the secretion of gastric juices is the presence of food in the duodenum.

a What is gastric juice?

b What is 'secretion'?

c In what way did Alexis St. Martin's and Tom's injuries enable research to be done on gastric secretion?

d List three factors which speed up the rate of gastric secretion.

e Why is it sensible for protein-containing foods to have the greatest effect on gastric secretion?

f It is well-known that people who suffer from stress are more likely to suffer from stomach and duodenal ulcers. Explain why this might be.

g Why is it useful for the presence of food in the duodenum to reduce gastric secretion?

2 The following information appeared on the lid of an ice-cream carton.

Ingredients: milk, double cream, sugar, eggs, emulsifier (E471), stabilisers (guar gum, locust bean gum), natural flavouring, malt extract, natural colour (betanin).

Nutritional information;

	typical values per 100 g:
Energy	479 kJ
Protein:	2.1 g
Carbohydrate:	12.7 g
Fat:	6.4 g

a What percentage by weight of the ice cream is protein?

b Which ingredients in the ice cream do you think provide this protein?

c What percentage by weight of the ice cream is probably water?

d A boy had a 250 g serving of ice cream. How much fat did he eat?

e Which ingredients in the ice cream do you think provide this fat?

f The boy needs about 12 000 kJ each day. How much ice cream would he need to eat to provide this much energy?

g Why would this not provide a balanced diet?

h What do you think is the purpose of the emulsifier in the ice cream?

3 A sample of food was tested to find out which food types it contained. The results of the tests are given below.

Test	Colour obtained
A sugar test	blue
B fat test	translucent mark which disappeared when dried
C protein test	purple

a Which food types were present in this food sample?

b What food could it have been? Choose from: lettuce, beef, egg white, sultana, butter.

c Which test would involve heating the food?

d What reagents would be used for Test C?

4 Explain why:

a Taking milk of magnesia tablets, which contain magnesium hydroxide, can help in relieving the pain of indigestion.

b People suffering from diarrhoea should drink plenty of liquid, preferably containing some sugar and salt.

c The lining of the ileum is covered with thousands of villi.

d Both fungi and animals are described as being heterotrophic.

e Lack of iron in your diet makes you tired and listless.

f You should try not to eat too much animal fat.

g Vegetables should not be overcooked.

REPRODUCTION

35 ASEXUAL REPRODUCTION

Every species of living organism is able to reproduce. Asexual reproduction produces new organisms just like their parent.

Reproduction is a characteristic of all living things

One feature of living things which makes them different from non-living things, is that they can **reproduce.** All living things eventually die, perhaps just from 'old age', or perhaps because they are killed by disease or predators. Reproduction replaces these deaths, so that the species does not die out.

Every kind of organism has its own kind of reproduction. Humans use **sexual reproduction.** Almost all animals, and many plants, use sexual reproduction. But some plants, a few animals, and many simple organisms, use **asexual reproduction**. Some use both!

Asexual reproduction is common in plants

Many plants can reproduce just by growing new plants on the old one. You may have seen a spider plant, with many young spider plants hanging all around it. If you plant one of these, it will grow into a new plant, and may eventually produce young spider plants itself. This is an example of **asexual reproduction.** A single organism grows new organisms from its body.

Many plants can do this. Strawberry plants, for example, grow long stems, at the end of which young plants grow and root. If you grow cacti or succulents in your house, you can often grow new plants just by breaking a piece off an old one and planting it. Gardeners grow new plants by taking **cuttings** from old ones. A cutting is a piece of stem or root, cut from a growing plant. The cutting is put into soil. After a while, it will grow roots, and become a new plant.

Fig. 35.1 Spider plants can reproduce asexually.

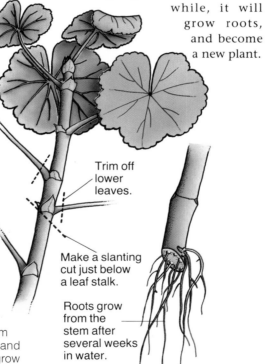

Trim off lower leaves.

Make a slanting cut just below a leaf stalk.

Roots grow from the stem after several weeks in water.

Fig. 35.2 Growing a geranium cutting. If you cut and trim a geranium shoot, as shown by the dotted lines, and then stand the shoot in water, it will grow roots. This is a type of asexual reproduction. The new plant will be just like its parent.

Fig. 35.3 Commercial producers of pot plants use asexual reproduction to ensure that all their plants are as similar as possible. Although these cyclamen vary slightly in shape and size, their leaf shape and pattern, flower colour and flower size are all very alike. Each plant has exactly the same genes. Organisms like this, all with an identical genetic make-up, are sometimes called **clones**.

Asexual reproduction makes new organisms just like the parent

The new plants produced by asexual reproduction are just like their parent. If you take a cutting from a geranium with pink flowers, the cutting will grow into a geranium which has pink flowers. This is because the cells of the cutting are exactly like the cells of the parent. They contain exactly the same **genes**. Genes are found on the **chromosomes** in the nucleus of a cell. They give instructions about the way in which the cell behaves. Asexual reproduction produces new organisms with the same genes as the parent. These genetically identical organisms are called **clones**.

Mitosis makes new cells identical to the parent cell

When a cell divides into two, the **chromosomes** in the nucleus must be shared out between the two new cells. The chromosomes carry the genes, which give instructions about what sort of organism the new cells will grow into.

When a plant reproduces asexually, some of its cells divide to make new cells. These cells will themselves divide, to make the hundreds of thousands of cells in the new organism. Each of these cell divisions is done in such a way that the new cells have exactly the same number and kind of chromosomes as their parent cell. This kind of cell division is called **mitosis**.

So all the cells have identical instructions. They will grow into very similar plants, provided the conditions under which they are grown are similar.

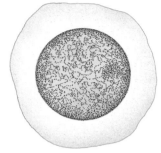

1 Before the cell divides, the chromosomes in the nucleus are very difficult to see because they are very long and thin.

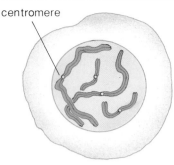

centromere

2 The chromosomes get much shorter and fatter, so they can now be seen with a light microscope. Each chromosome is made up of two threads joined by a centromere.

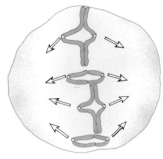

3 The chromosomes line up along the centre of the cell. Their two threads split apart, and move to opposite ends of the cell.

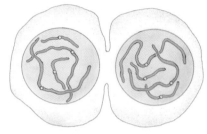

4 The threads make two groups and a nuclear membrane forms round each group. The cell splits in two. Later each thread will make an exact copy of itself to form chromosomes made of two threads again.

Fig. 35.4   Mitosis. This is the usual way in which a cell divides into two. Two new cells are made from one old one. The new cells have exactly the same kind and number of chromosomes as the parent cell.

Micropropagation is used commercially

Taking cuttings is an excellent way of getting many new, almost identical plants from one parent. Another method is to use **micropropagation**. A growing point is taken from the tip of a plant. The cells are separated from each other. They are placed on a jelly, in which there are hormones that make the cells divide to form a small group of cells. This small group of cells grows roots, forming a plantlet. This tiny plantlet is then moved to a different jelly, with different hormones that encourage it to grow shoots. Using this technique, many hundreds of plants can be propagated from just one parent.

Bacteria reproduce asexually

Green plants are not the only organisms which reproduce asexually. Asexual reproduction is very common in simple organisms, such as bacteria and protoctista.

Bacteria are single-celled organisms. When the cell gets to a certain size, it splits into two. The two small cells grow, and then divide again into four, and so on. This can happen very fast. *Salmonella* bacteria can divide once every twenty minutes if they are in warm food.

Fig. 35.5   The tiny plants growing on the jelly in this dish have developed from small groups of cells taken from a 'parent' plant. The technique is called micropropagation or tissue culture. Can you suggest why it has these names?

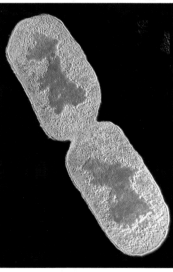

Fig. 35.6   A bacterium divides into two. This type of bacterium lives in the human gut, where it is normally quite harmless. The red area shows the chromosome made of DNA. It was copied inside the parent cell before division took place, so that each daughter cell gets a perfect copy of the chromosome from the parent cell. Magnification: x 37 500.

36 SEXUAL REPRODUCTION

A male sex cell fuses with a female one in the process of fertilisation, forming a zygote. This is sexual reproduction.

Sexual reproduction involves gametes and fertilisation

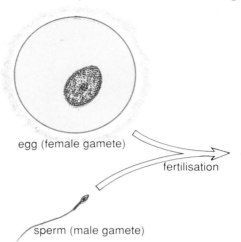

Fig. 36.1   In sexual reproduction, two gametes fuse together to form a zygote.

egg (female gamete)

fertilisation

sperm (male gamete)

zygote

growth

embryo

In asexual reproduction, a single organism grows new organisms from itself, or it splits into two. But many organisms produce special cells for reproduction. These special cells are called **sex cells** or **gametes.** In humans, the gametes are eggs and sperms.

The gametes fuse together in a process called **fertilisation.** Two gametes become a single cell, which is called a **zygote.** The zygote divides over and over again, to produce a young organism.

This method of reproduction is called **sexual reproduction.** It involves gametes, fertilisation and zygotes. None of these are involved in asexual reproduction.

vacuole, containing enzymes

nucleus, containing chromosomes

length 0.05 mm

tail

Fig. 36.2   A sperm

Male gametes can move

Most species of sexually reproducing organisms have two kinds of gametes. Humans, for example, have sperms and eggs. The two types of gametes are **male** and **female.** Male gametes move actively to find the female gametes. Female gametes usually move very little, if at all.

Figure 36.2 shows a human sperm. It is a single cell. Sperms are very small cells. Most of the cell is taken up by the nucleus. The nucleus contains the chromosomes.

The rest of the cell is for swimming. The long tail can lash back and forth, propelling the streamlined sperm cell forwards.

At the tip of the sperm's head is a vacuole containing enzymes. These will help the sperm to digest its way into an egg if it finds one.

Eggs are much larger than sperms

An egg, like a sperm, is a single cell. But egg cells are much larger than sperm cells. There are two main reasons for this. One is that eggs contain food stores, to supply energy and materials for the growth of the young organism, if the egg is fertilised. These food stores are often called **yolk.** Another reason is that eggs do not need to move actively, so it does not matter if they are large and bulky. Sperms need to be small and mobile.

A human egg is about the size of a full stop. Like a sperm cell, it has a nucleus containing chromosomes. Its cytoplasm contains yolk.

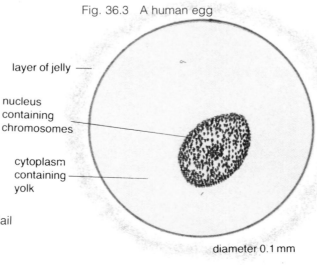

Fig. 36.3   A human egg

layer of jelly

nucleus containing chromosomes

cytoplasm containing yolk

diameter 0.1 mm

Gametes have only half the normal number of chromosomes

In the nucleus of every cell in your body, there are 46 chromosomes. Chromosomes are long threads of a chemical called DNA. The DNA carries coded instructions called **genes**, which tell the cell what sort of substances to make. The code tells the cell what to do, and how to grow. Your chromosomes and the genes which they carry make you a person rather than a mouse or a plant. They also influence all sorts of other things about you, such as your sex, height, the colour of your hair, and so on.

You began life as a single cell – a zygote. This single cell had 46 chromosomes. It divided over and over again to produce millions of cells, all with 46 chromosomes. This mass of cells is you.

The 46 chromosomes in the zygote came from the sperm and egg which fused together to form it. Both the sperm and the egg had 23 chromosomes. All gametes must have only half of the full number of chromosomes. When they fuse together, they form a zygote with the full number of chromosomes.

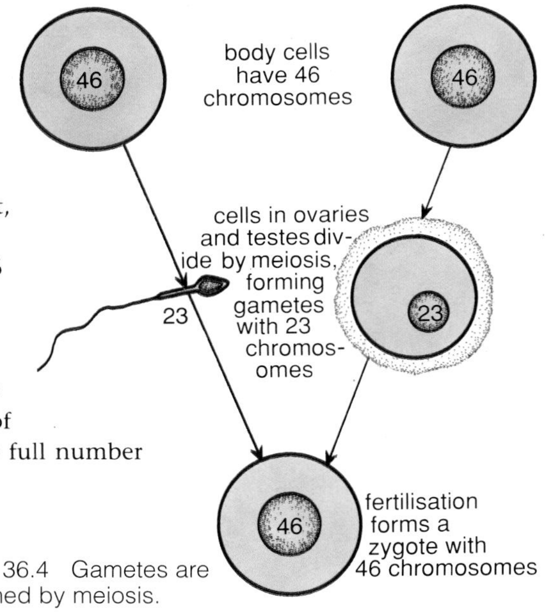

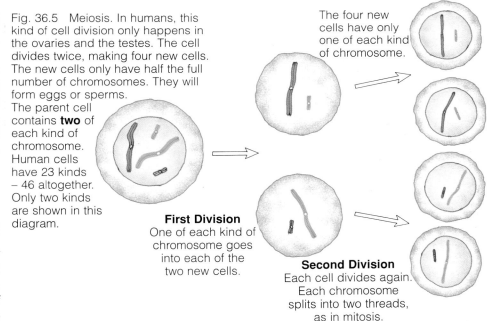

Fig. 36.4 Gametes are formed by meiosis.

body cells have 46 chromosomes

cells in ovaries and testes divide by meiosis, forming gametes with 23 chromosomes

fertilisation forms a zygote with 46 chromosomes

Haploid and diploid cells

The 46 chromosomes in a human cell can be arranged in pairs. You can see a photograph of human chromosomes arranged like this on page 156. In each cell, there are 23 kinds of chromosomes, two of each kind. A cell containing two of each kind of chromosome is called a **diploid** cell. All your cells are diploid.

Gametes such as sperms and eggs only contain one of each kind of chromosome. So human gametes contain 23 chromosomes. Cells which contain one of each kind of chromosome, are called **haploid** cells. All gametes are haploid cells.

Meiosis forms haploid cells from diploid cells

Gametes are formed when ordinary body cells divide. A special kind of cell division called **meiosis** is needed. Meiosis shares out the pairs of chromosomes from the diploid cell, so that the new cells each get one of each pair. In humans, meiosis shares out the 46 chromosomes in a diploid cell, to make gametes with 23 chromosomes each. The cells formed by meiosis are genetically different from each other, so meiosis produces **variation**. You can read more about this in Topic 67.

Meiosis is not a very common kind of cell division. In humans, it only happens in the **ovaries**, where eggs are made, and in the **testes**, where sperms are made.

Fig. 36.5 Meiosis. In humans, this kind of cell division only happens in the ovaries and the testes. The cell divides twice, making four new cells. The new cells only have half the full number of chromosomes. They will form eggs or sperms. The parent cell contains **two** of each kind of chromosome. Human cells have 23 kinds – 46 altogether. Only two kinds are shown in this diagram.

The four new cells have only one of each kind of chromosome.

First Division
One of each kind of chromosome goes into each of the two new cells.

Second Division
Each cell divides again. Each chromosome splits into two threads, as in mitosis.

― EXTENSION ―

Questions

1 How does the process of asexual reproduction differ from that of sexual reproduction?
2 Explain exactly what you understand by the words:
   a gamete   d haploid
   b fertilisation   e diploid
   c zygote
3 A sperm cell is a very specialised cell, adapted to fertilise an egg and form a zygote. Discuss the features of a human sperm cell which enable it to perform this function efficiently.

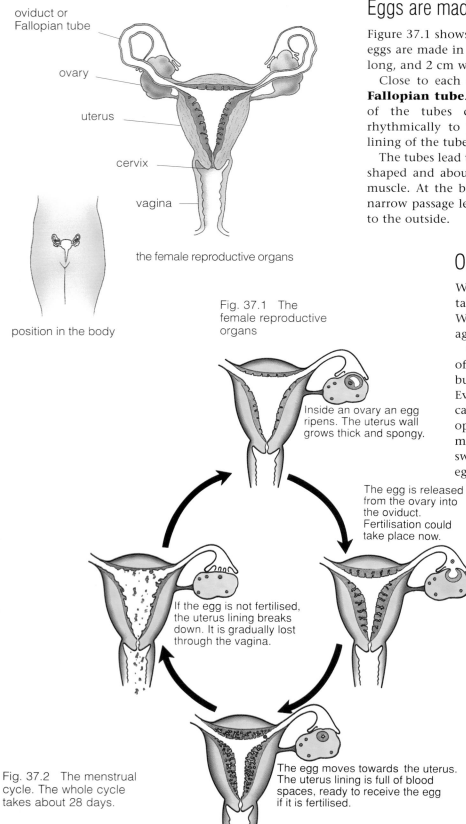

oviduct or Fallopian tube

ovary

uterus

cervix

vagina

the female reproductive organs

position in the body

Fig. 37.1 The female reproductive organs

Inside an ovary an egg ripens. The uterus wall grows thick and spongy.

The egg is released from the ovary into the oviduct. Fertilisation could take place now.

If the egg is not fertilised, the uterus lining breaks down. It is gradually lost through the vagina.

The egg moves towards the uterus. The uterus lining is full of blood spaces, ready to receive the egg if it is fertilised.

Fig. 37.2 The menstrual cycle. The whole cycle takes about 28 days.

Eggs are made in the ovaries

Figure 37.1 shows the reproductive organs of a woman. The eggs are made in the two ovaries. Each ovary is about 3 cm long, and 2 cm wide.

Close to each ovary is the opening of the **oviduct** or **Fallopian tube**. Each tube is about 10 cm long. The walls of the tubes contain muscles, which can contract rhythmically to produce rippling movements. The inner lining of the tubes is made of cells covered with **cilia**.

The tubes lead to the womb, or **uterus**. The uterus is pear shaped and about 8 cm long. It has thick walls, made of muscle. At the base of the uterus is the **cervix**. This is a narrow passage leading into the **vagina**. The vagina opens to the outside.

One egg is released each month

When a girl is born, her ovaries already contain many thousands of immature eggs. When she reaches about 12 to 14 years of age, some of these eggs begin to mature.

Once every 28 days one of the eggs in one of the ovaries moves to the edge. It forms a bump pushing outwards from the ovary. Eventually, it bursts out. This process is called **ovulation**. The egg is caught in the opening of the oviduct. The rippling movements of the muscles in the oviduct, and the sweeping movements of the cilia, carry the egg very slowly towards the uterus.

If the egg is not fertilised, then menstruation occurs

The egg continues slowly onwards towards the uterus. If it is not fertilised, it only lives for about one day. So it does not even get as far as the uterus before it dies. It simply disintegrates.

Each time an egg is released from an ovary, the uterus prepares itself, just in case the egg is fertilised. Its lining becomes thick, soft and full of blood capillaries. But if the egg is not fertilised, this lining is no longer needed. It slowly breaks down and is gradually lost from the body through the vagina, over a period of about three to six days. This is called **menstruation**.

These events are controlled by hormones. You can read more about these hormones in Topic 83.

Sperms are made in the testes

Figure 37.3 shows the reproductive organs of a man. The sperms are made in the testes. The testes are inside the **scrotum**. They are here, rather than deep inside the body, because sperm production is very sensitive to temperature. The temperature of the scrotum is about 2 °C lower than inside the body.

Each testis is made up of hundreds of tiny tubes, called **seminiferous tubules.** This is where the sperms are made. Each tube is about 70cm long, but the tubes are so narrow, and are coiled up so tightly, that they fit into a very small space.

The tubules all lead into the **epididymis.** This contains a single tube, looped round and round. The sperms all go into this tube from the testis. The tube then leads into the **sperm duct,** or **vas deferens**. The sperm ducts from each testis lead upwards, looping round behind the bladder. They join together just below the bladder. The tube is now called the **urethra**. It runs down through the penis, and opens to the outside.

Questions

1 Write a brief description of the functions of each of the following:
   a ovary   **d** sperm duct
   b oviduct   **e** seminal vesicle
   c testis   **f** prostate gland.
2 Why:
   a is the lining of each oviduct covered with ciliated cells?
   b does menstruation occur?
   c are the testes outside the body in the scrotum?
   d do the seminal vesicles secrete a fluid containing fructose?

Glands make a liquid for the sperms to swim in

In a woman, only one egg is released each month. But in a man, sperms are made all the time. About two billion sperms are made each day! If mating does not occur, many of these sperms are lost. They can be broken down in the epididymis.

When sperms are first made, they cannot swim. As they make their long journey from the testis to the urethra, they gradually mature, and become able to lash their tails. Two glands help them to do this. Firstly the **seminal vesicles** make a fluid containing a sugar called fructose, which provides energy for the sperms. Secondly the **prostate gland** makes a fluid containing citric acid, which the sperms also use as an energy source. These glands empty their fluids onto the sperms as they pass by.

The final mixture of sperms and these fluids is called semen.

Fig. 37.3   The male reproductive organs

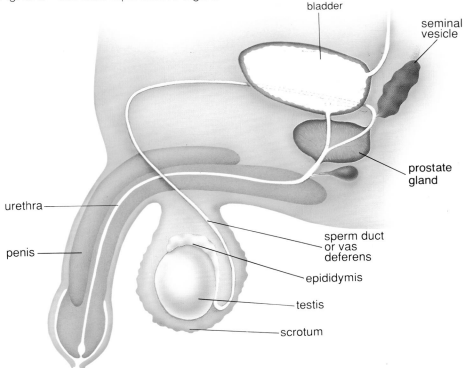

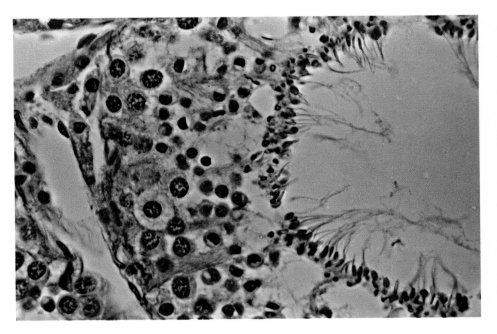

Fig. 37.4   A section across a seminiferous tubule inside a mammal's testis, magnified about 1500 times. You can see the sperms lying in a ring with their tails pointing into the middle of the tubule. They have developed from cells on the edge of the tubule which divide and move gradually towards the centre as they develop into sperms.

Humans, like all mammals, have internal fertilisation. Fertilisation happens high in the oviduct.

Fertilisation takes place in the oviduct

A human egg will not begin to develop into a baby unless it is fertilised by a sperm. In humans, as in all mammals, fertilisation takes place inside the female's body. This is called **internal fertilisation**.

When a man is sexually excited, his penis becomes erect. The penis can then be placed inside the woman's vagina. Touch receptors in the penis stimulate muscles around the sperm ducts and urethra to contract rhythmically. This pushes semen out of the urethra, and into the vagina. This is called **ejaculation**. The semen is left high in the vagina, near the cervix.

A single ejaculation may leave 200 million sperms in the vagina. They now have to swim the rest of the way to the egg. They swim up through the cervix and the uterus, into the oviduct. This can take as little as 30 minutes. But only a few hundred of them will ever arrive in the oviduct. The rest die.

If there is an egg in the oviduct, the sperms cluster round it. After a short while, one of them makes contact with the egg's cell surface membrane. The membranes of the egg and the sperm fuse together. Almost instantly, the egg's membrane changes, so that no more sperms can fuse with it.

The head of the successful sperm then enters the egg. The nucleus of the sperm and the nucleus of the egg fuse together. This is fertilisation.

Fig. 38.1   The path taken by sperms to an egg

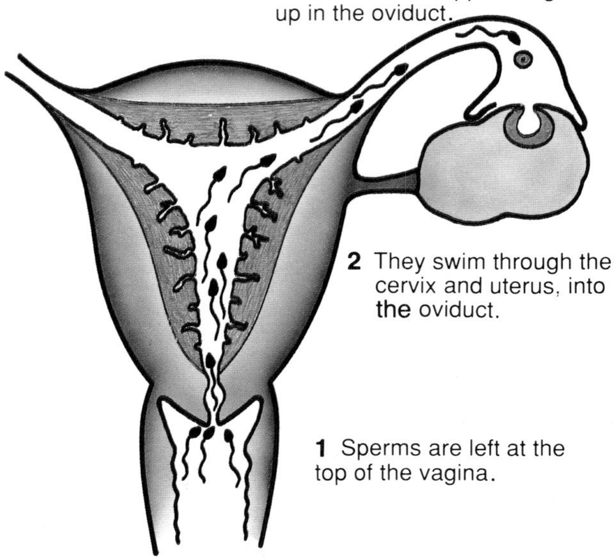

3 Fertilisation happens high up in the oviduct.

2 They swim through the cervix and uterus, into the oviduct.

1 Sperms are left at the top of the vagina.

Fig. 38.2   Fertilisation

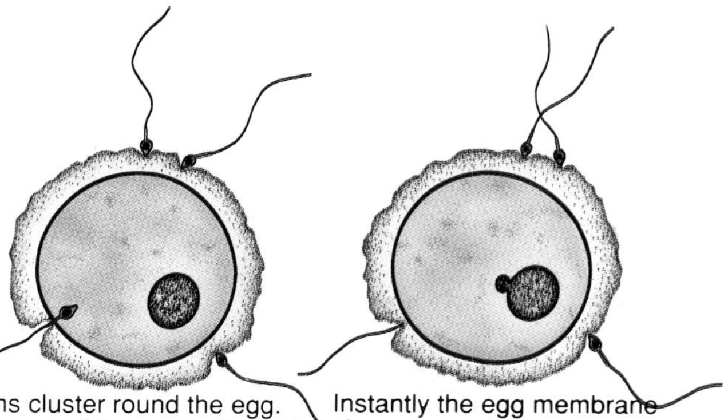

The sperms cluster round the egg. Eventually, one of them gets through the egg membrane.

Instantly the egg membrane changes, so that no more sperms can get in. The nucleus of the successful sperm fuses with the nucleus of the egg.

Fig. 38.3   Implantation

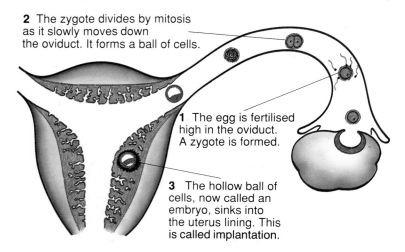

2 The zygote divides by mitosis as it slowly moves down the oviduct. It forms a ball of cells.

1 The egg is fertilised high in the oviduct. A zygote is formed.

3 The hollow ball of cells, now called an embryo, sinks into the uterus lining. This is called implantation.

The zygote implants into the uterus wall

When the sperm and the egg fuse together, they form a cell known as a **zygote**. The zygote moves slowly along the oviduct towards the uterus. It is carried along by the movements of the muscles in the oviduct walls, and by the cilia. As it travels along, it divides again and again to form a ball of cells.

It takes about seven days for the ball of cells to reach the uterus. During this time, the cells feed on the yolk from the egg. The ball of cells is very tiny, only a little larger than the egg from which it has developed.

The inner lining of the uterus becomes thick, spongy, and well supplied with blood capillaries. The ball of cells sinks into it, burying itself completely in the uterus lining. This process is called **implantation**.

The placenta is the embryo's life support system

The ball of cells is now called an **embryo**. The cells continue to divide, gradually beginning to arrange themselves to form a small human being. It takes eleven weeks before all the embryo's organs have developed. When this has happened it is called a **fetus**.

Once the embryo has implanted into the uterus, it can begin to feed from its mother's blood. It does this through the **placenta**. The placenta grows partly from the embryo, and partly from the mother. It is a flattened circular disc, which fits closely into the wall of the uterus. On the embryo's side, there are thousands of tiny folds called **villi**. On the mother's side, there are blood spaces. The blood in these spaces surrounds the villi.

Inside the villi, there are many blood capillaries belonging to the embryo. Food substances, such as glucose and amino acids, can pass from the mother's blood into these capillaries, and so can oxygen. Waste materials, such as carbon dioxide and urea, can pass from the embryo's blood into the mother's blood.

The embryo's blood capillaries in the villi all connect up to the **umbilical artery** and **umbilical vein**. These run inside the **umbilical cord**, which connects the embryo to the placenta. The umbilical artery carries blood from the embryo to the placenta. The umbilical vein carries blood from the placenta to the embryo.

The large surface area of the villi in the placenta helps to speed up the transfer of substances between the mother and the embryo.

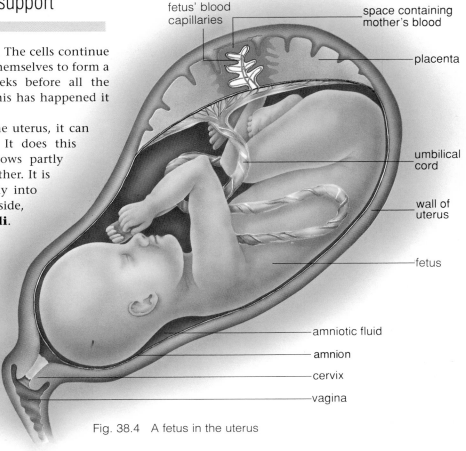

Fig. 38.4   A fetus in the uterus

fetus' blood capillaries
space containing mother's blood
placenta
umbilical cord
wall of uterus
fetus
amniotic fluid
amnion
cervix
vagina

Many substances can cross the placenta

Food, oxygen and waste materials are not the only substances which can cross the placenta. Harmful substances, such as bacteria, viruses and drugs can also pass from the mother's blood into the blood of her fetus. Carbon monoxide, from cigarette smoke, passes easily into the blood of the fetus.

Useful substances can cross the placenta, too. These include antibodies, which can help to protect the fetus from disease. The antibodies stay in a baby's blood for some time after it is born, helping to protect it from infection in the first few weeks of its life.

The amniotic fluid acts as a shock absorber

The growing fetus is surrounded by a bag called the **amnion**. The amnion makes a liquid called **amniotic fluid**, which completely surrounds the fetus.

The amniotic fluid provides a perfect environment for the fetus. It supports the fetus, absorbing any bumps and bangs, and the fetus can move around freely in it.

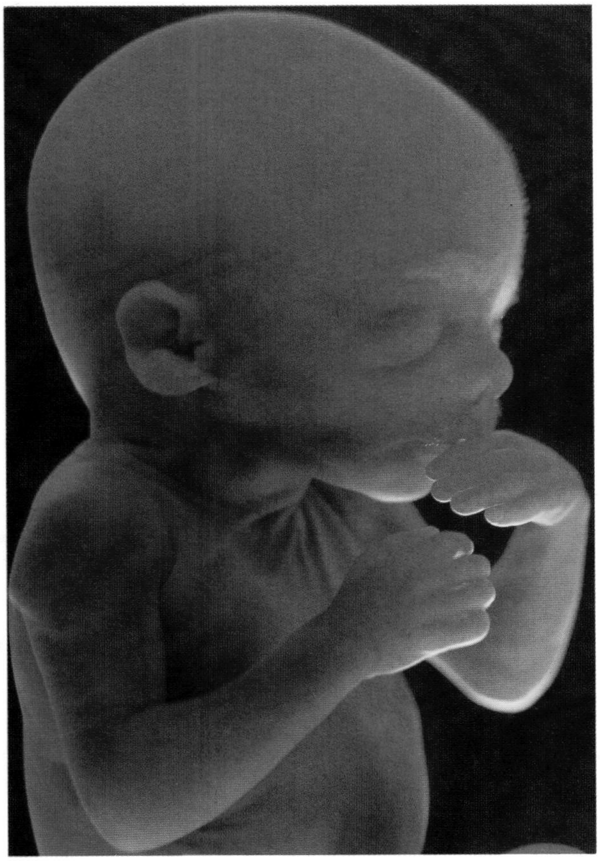

Fig. 38.5   A human fetus at around five months old

39 PREGNANCY AND BIRTH

Pregnancy causes many changes in a woman's body, and she must take care of herself and her growing child.

A pregnant woman needs to care for herself and her baby

The time between fertilisation and birth is called the **gestation period.** In humans, this is about nine months or forty weeks. During this time, the mother's body undergoes many changes.

As the embryo grows inside the mother's uterus, her blood system adapts to the extra demands being made on it. The heart gradually increases the amount of blood which it pumps per minute. By half way through the pregnancy, the heart will probably be pumping an extra $1.5\,dm^3$ of blood every minute.

A woman gains about 12.5 kg of body weight during pregnancy. This is partly due to the weight of the uterus, the placenta, the amniotic fluid and the embryo but about 3.5 kg is due to extra fat stores which her body accumulates.

So a pregnant woman's heart beats faster, and the weight she has to carry around is greater, than when she was not pregnant. She therefore uses more energy. A pregnant woman needs to eat more food than a woman who is not pregnant. She will probably need an extra 1.5 MJ per day.

Fig. 39.1   Swimming is excellent exercise for pregnant women, as it exercises a wide variety of muscles, without putting too much strain on any of them.

A good diet and exercise are very important during pregnancy

It is always important to eat a good diet, but it is especially important during pregnancy. The baby's developing bones and teeth require a lot of **calcium**. So the mother should try to include calcium-rich foods, such as milk, in her diet. Extra **iron** is also needed to make haemoglobin for the baby's blood, and for the mother's extra blood. Even a good diet cannot always supply all the iron which is needed, so pregnant women often take iron tablets.

Exercise is also important. It keeps the lungs and heart in good working order and strengthens muscles, which will be needed during the birth. Exercise also helps to keep the mother feeling fit and well. But strenuous exercise is not a good idea in pregnancy. A good exercise for pregnant women is swimming. Antenatal clinics also teach special exercises which help to strengthen the muscles used during birth.

Pregnant women should not take drugs

There are several things which a pregnant woman should avoid. One of them is smoking. Cigarette smoke contains many harmful substances which can cross the placenta and get into the baby's blood. **Carbon monoxide** combines with the haemoglobin in the baby's red blood cells. This stops the haemoglobin from carrying oxygen. So a baby whose mother smokes during pregnancy may not get as much oxygen as it needs, while it is in the uterus. It may be smaller at birth, and more likely to get infections, than other babies.

Alcohol should also be avoided during pregnancy. It easily crosses the placenta into the baby's blood. Alcohol can affect the developing brain. Babies born to mothers who regularly drink a lot of alcohol can be very ill indeed.

Many **drugs** can also harm the growing baby. Doctors are very careful when they prescribe drugs to a pregnant woman. All addictive drugs, such as heroin, are very dangerous to an unborn child. The baby may become addicted to them before it is born.

Birth takes place after nine months

Towards the end of pregnancy, the baby usually turns round so that it is lying head down in the uterus. The head lies over the cervix.

Birth begins with gentle, rhythmic contractions of the strong muscles in the uterus wall. The mother may not feel these at first, but they gradually get stronger and more frequent. They begin to feel like cramps, and are called **labour pains**. The muscle contractions gradually pull the cervix open. This stage of labour is the longest. It can take several hours. During this stage, the mother can walk about or relax. If she has been to antenatal classes, she will have been taught breathing exercises to help her to relax during the contractions.

When the opening of the cervix is about 10 cm wide, the muscles begin to contract in a different way. Now they push downwards, pushing the baby down through the cervix and vagina. The mother can help with this stage, pushing downwards in time with the contractions of the uterus. This stage usually only takes about three quarters of an hour.

Once the baby's head is through the vagina, the rest of its body slides out quite quickly. It is still attached to the uterus by the umbilical cord. A midwife will cut the cord after clamping it tightly to stop any infection getting in. This is absolutely painless, because the cord contains no nerves.

A little while later, the placenta falls away from the uterus wall, and passes out through the vagina. The placenta is often called the **afterbirth.**

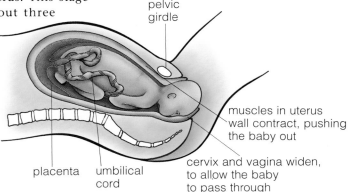

pelvic girdle

muscles in uterus wall contract, pushing the baby out

cervix and vagina widen, to allow the baby to pass through

placenta

umbilical cord

Fig. 39.2 Birth

Fig. 39.3 This baby girl was born just seconds ago. The umbilical cord is still attached to the mother, and will now be tied and cut.

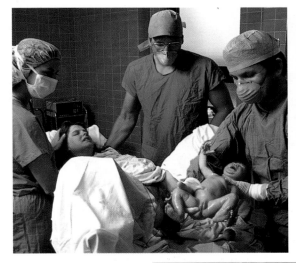

Fig. 39.4 A mother feeding her newborn daughter. Breast feeding is better than bottle feeding because the milk supply arrives at just the right temperature, with no harmful bacteria and with the mother's antibodies to help to protect the baby until its own immune system begins to operate. And it's free!

Newborn babies need special care

Being born must be rather a shock! The baby has spent nine months floating in warm fluid, cushioned from bumps and bangs. It has been supplied with oxygen and food directly from its mother's blood. Suddenly, it finds itself in the air. It has to breathe and feed for itself for the first time in its life.

Newborn babies usually begin breathing very shortly after they are born. They need to be kept warm, as their small bodies can easily lose heat.

Very small, ill babies may be unable to keep themselves warm, even in a warm room. These babies may need to be cared for in an **incubator** until they are well enough to sleep in a cot. An incubator provides a thermostatically controlled temperature, to keep the baby warm.

Fig. 39.5 This tiny 12-hour old baby was born 13 weeks premature. The warmth and humidity inside the incubator can be adjusted to just the right levels. Premature babies often have difficulty in breathing, and this one is breathing with the aid of a respirator.

40 GROWTH AND DEVELOPMENT

Humans grow until they are about 20 years old. Growth and development take place together.

Growth and development take place together

Growth is a permanent, irreversible increase in size. When an organism grows, its cells divide many times by mitosis. You began as one cell. This cell divided to make more cells, and these cells later divided to make even more cells. Your body is now made up of millions of cells, all of which originally came from this one cell. All the cells are genetically identical, because they were all produced by mitosis.

But a human being does not simply get bigger as it grows. It also changes. When a baby is born, it needs a great deal of care. It cannot feed itself. It cannot walk. As it grows, changes gradually take place in its body, so that it becomes more independent. Eventually it becomes able to reproduce. These changes are called **development**.

Fig. 40.1 A family in Sudan. What visible differences are there between the youngest and oldest members of this family? Do the changes which cause these differences take place gradually or suddenly?

There are many ways of measuring growth

A simple way of measuring how fast a child is growing is to measure its height. The child's height can be measured at about the same time each year, and a graph drawn. Another way is to measure weight. This is just as quick and easy to do. Which method do you think is the best?

Scientists measuring the growth of plants may use another method. Just measuring the height of a plant does not always tell you all that you want to know, because a lot of the plant may be underground. If you want to include the plant's roots in your measurements, you will need to uproot the plant, wash

any soil off it, and then weigh it.

The trouble with this method is that, even if you replant the plant in the soil, it will have been disturbed. It will not grow normally. So, if you use this method, you will need to use lots of plants. You could, for example, plant 100 plants, and pull one up every day to weigh. If all your plants were of the same kind, and were treated in the same way, then your results would still be quite accurate. Better still, you could have 300 plants, and pull three up every day. Then you could work out an average.

An even better method is to measure

the **dry weight** of your plants. When you have pulled up the plant and washed off the soil, you put the plant into a cool oven. You leave it there until all the water in it has evaporated. All that remains is the 'dry' material which the plant contained.

The amount of water that plants contain varies tremendously, depending on weather and soil conditions. When you measure dry weight, you know that any differences in weight are not just due to these temporary fluctuations in the amount of water.

Adolescence is the change of a child into an adult

If you draw a growth curve (a graph of size against time) for a human, you will notice that there is a growth spurt around the ages of 11 to 15. At the same time, important changes take place in both boys and girls. This time in a person's life is called **adolescence**.

The changes which occur at adolescence are controlled by **hormones**. In girls, the hormone is **oestrogen**. In boys, the hormone is **testosterone**. In girls, the breasts begin to develop, and menstruation begins. In boys, the testes and penis grow larger, and the voice breaks.

In both boys and girls, pubic hair begins to grow, and hair also grows under the arms. The action of sweat and sebaceous glands increases. Many young people suffer from acne at this time, because of changes in the behaviour of the glands in their skin.

Adolescence is also a time of change in a person's way of thinking. People tend to become more self-conscious and to develop intellectually. This is often the time in a person's life when their brain has the greatest capacity for learning. But it can also be a time when a person feels quite insecure, as they adjust to all these big changes in their lives.

Adolescence tends to begin a year or two earlier in girls than in boys. It is not possible to say how long it lasts, but probably most people would feel they were fully adult by the age of eighteen.

Fig. 40.3 Bamboos growing in Bali. Bamboos are giant grasses. Some of them can grow up to 91 cm in one day, and to a maximum height of 37 m. How could you measure the rate of growth of a bamboo plant?

Fig. 40.2 Most crabs have a hard, protective outer skeleton, which has to be moulted at intervals as they grow. But hermit crabs have softer bodies, and live in mollusc shells for protection. This one has grown out of its temporary home, and is considering a move into more generous accommodation.

Questions

Age (years)	Height (cm) male	Height (cm) female
0	53	53
1	61	61
2	71	71
3	89	87
4	96	92
5	100	96
6	105	101
7	110	106
8	114	110
9	118	114
10	121	119
11	125	127
12	129	133
13	132	136
14	136	139
15	143	144
16	150	150
17	155	155
18	163	158
19	170	161
20	173	164
21	175	164
22	175	164
23	175	164
24	175	164

1   Explain the difference between growth and development.

2 a The chart on the left shows the heights of a human male and a human female for the first 24 years of their lives. Use these data to plot two line graphs, on the same pair of axes.

 b At what ages do you think adolescence occurred in:
  i   the female?   ii the male?
  Give reasons for your answers.

 c What is the average growth rate per year for the male, between the ages of 9 and 17?

 d What is the average growth rate per year for the female, between the ages of 9 and 17?

3 a Briefly describe a suitable method for measuring the growth of each of the following:
  i   a mouse
  ii an oak tree
  iii a caterpillar
  iv sunflower seedlings.

 b Describe, in detail, how you would measure the growth of sunflower seedlings from germination until the adult plants die. Give full details of the number of plants you would use, how you would grow them, what you would measure and when and how you would display your results.

41 BIRTH CONTROL

The human population is rising at an alarming rate. Adults who become parents when they do not want children can be very unhappy. Birth control helps to prevent this problem.

Birth control is the prevention of unwanted pregnancies

Having a baby is a major event in a person's life. A new person is brought into the world. Despite all the extra responsibilities and sleepless nights, this can be a wonderful experience for the parents, especially if they want to have children.

But many children are born who are not wanted by their natural parents. An unwanted child can be very unhappy. If parents have not planned to have a child, they will probably find it very difficult to cope with the big changes that a baby will make in their lives.

Sometimes, people can't have children, even though they want them. They may adopt children. Some children, whose natural parents are unable to care for them, may be adopted. An adopted child is a wanted child.

The population of humans on the Earth is rising fast. It is very important that we try to slow down this increase by keeping down the number of births. Birth control does just this. Birth control is the prevention of unwanted pregnancies. Birth control can help to make sure that every child that is born is a wanted child, and can also help to keep the human population at a reasonable level.

Only one sperm is needed to fertilise an egg

When a girl reaches adolescence, she begins to release an egg from her ovaries once a month. If a single sperm reaches an egg in the oviduct, then pregnancy may result.

The safest way to make sure that this does not happen is to avoid sexual intercourse. Even a very small amount of semen deposited near the vagina may be enough to fertilise an egg. If a woman does not want to become pregnant, then the safest thing she can do is to make sure that no sperm has any chance of getting into her vagina.

The rhythm method

One way of cutting down the risk of pregnancy is to work out when an egg is most likely to be in the oviduct and to avoid sexual intercourse around this time. A woman is then less likely to become pregnant.

If a woman has a regular, 28 day menstrual cycle, then an egg is most likely to be released on day 14 of this cycle. If she avoids sex for several days on either side of this, then she probably will not get pregnant.

The big problem with this method is that many women do not have regular menstrual cycles. Even women who do have regular cycles may find that their cycles are changed if something different happens in their lives, like going on holiday or being ill. So it is not easy to predict just when the egg will be in the oviduct. A woman can get a little more information by taking her temperature every day. Body temperature rises by about 0.5°C just after the egg is released. But even this is not absolutely reliable, because such a small temperature rise might be caused by other things, too.

So this method is useful for cutting down the risk of pregnancy without using any contraceptive devices or creams, but it is not a reliable method.

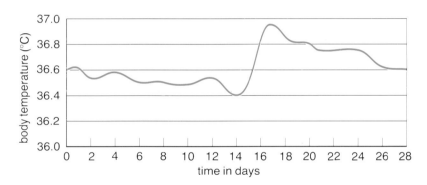

Fig. 41.1   Temperature changes during the menstrual cycle. Release of an egg on day 14 is accompanied by a small rise in body temperature.

Fig. 41.2   How to put on a condom. The air should be squeezed out of the end to catch the semen.

Condoms help to prevent the spread of sexually transmitted diseases

A **condom** is a sheath which is pulled over the erect penis. When semen is ejaculated from the penis, it is trapped in the sheath. If the sheath is put on and removed carefully, then the semen cannot escape, and come into contact with the woman's body.

A condom is an example of a **barrier method** of birth control. It acts as a barrier between the sperm and the egg. The woman can also put some **spermicidal cream** inside her vagina, which will kill any sperm which do escape.

Used properly, a condom is an excellent method of preventing pregnancy. It also has another big advantage. It stops bacteria and viruses passing between the woman's vagina and the man's penis, in either direction. So condoms are a very good way of slowing down the spread of AIDS and other sexually transmitted diseases.

The cap must be fitted by a doctor

Another barrier method for preventing pregnancy is the **cap** or **diaphragm.** This is a flexible piece of rubber with a springy edge. Its edges are squeezed together before it is put into the vagina, so that it opens out to sit over the opening to the cervix. If any sperms are released into the vagina, they cannot get past the cap, and so cannot fertilise an egg. Spermicidal cream around the edge of the cap makes even more sure that the sperms cannot get through.

It is very important that the cap fits properly. Women's cervices are different sizes, so the cap needs to be fitted by a doctor in the first place. But once a woman has been fitted with a cap, she can take it out and put it in herself.

The cap does not help to prevent infection being passed between a man and a woman, but it is effective at preventing pregnancy.

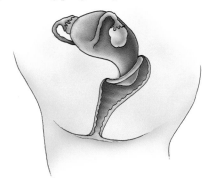

Fig. 41.3 The cap fits over the cervix, preventing sperms from getting into the uterus.

Intra-uterine devices prevent implantation

An intra-uterine device, or IUD, is a small piece of metal or plastic. It is bent into a coil, and fitted inside the uterus. It must be fitted by a trained person, and is left in all the time, until the woman wishes to have children.

IUDs probably prevent pregnancy by stopping fertilised eggs from implanting into the uterus. They are very effective

The pill contains hormones which stop eggs being released

The contraceptive pill contains the hormone **progesterone** and sometimes **oestrogen** as well. These hormones stop the ovaries from releasing eggs. As there is no egg in the oviduct, it is impossible for fertilisation to occur.

The pill has to be taken every day without fail, to keep the hormone level high enough. If even one day is missed, then an egg may be released. Usually, a woman stops taking the pill for seven days each month. During this time, she will have a period.

The pill can only be obtained on prescription from a doctor. This is because it can have side effects, so a woman on the pill needs to have regular check-ups by her own doctor, or at a family planning clinic.

The pill is a very reliable method of birth control. But it gives no protection against the transfer of sexually transmitted diseases between a man and a woman. Most doctors will not advise a woman to go on taking the pill for twenty or thirty years, because of possible harmful side effects.

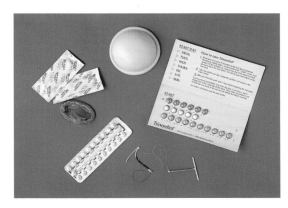

Fig. 41.4 A variety of contraceptives. Beginning at the top and working clockwise: a diaphragm, pills, intra-uterine devices, pills and condoms. Which of these would give some protection from the transmission of diseases such as AIDS?

at this. But they are not usually recommended for people who have not already had children. Some women find them uncomfortable, and there is a slight risk of developing infection in the uterus. IUDs also give no protection against the transfer of infections between a man and a woman.

Sterilisation cannot usually be reversed

When a couple have had all the children they want, one of them may choose to be **sterilised**.

The operation is a simple one. In a man, the sperm tubes leading from the testes to the penis are cut, so that the sperms cannot reach the penis. The seminal vesicles and prostate glands behave as normal, so semen is still produced but it contains no sperms.

In a woman, the Fallopian tubes are cut, so that there is no way a sperm can reach the eggs. The woman still produces an egg each month, and she still has periods as usual.

Sterilisation is an excellent way of preventing pregnancy. There are no side effects, and it is a very safe method. But it is not a method for young people,

because it is usually permanent. It is not usually possible to join the tubes together again. So sterilisation is mostly used by people who have completed their family, and will never want to have any more children.

Question

1 Draw up a table summarising the different methods of birth control.

You will need four columns. The first column will be for the names of the methods. Include: avoiding sexual intercourse, the rhythm method, condoms, the cap, the pill, IUDs and sterilisation.

The second column will be for a brief description of how the methods work. The third and fourth columns will be for an explanation of the advantages and disadvantages of each method. Think about ease of use, how good the method is at preventing pregnancy and whether it helps to stop the spread of infection. Remember too, that many people live in parts of the world where medical help is not easy to obtain, and where hygiene is not always very good.

Help can be given to people who want to have children but are not able to do so easily. Farmers may also wish to increase the fertility of their animals.

Using hormones can increase egg production

Every year, thousands of couples are disappointed that they cannot have a baby. One in ten women do not manage to become pregnant within a year of trying to start a family.

Very often, there is no real problem, and the woman does eventually get pregnant and have a child. But sometimes help is needed. It may be that there is something wrong with the man's sperms. Or it might be that the woman is not producing eggs, or that the sperms cannot reach the eggs because of a blockage in the Fallopian tubes.

If a woman is not producing eggs, then a course of hormone treatment may help her. The hormones stimulate the woman's ovaries to produce **oestrogen**, which causes eggs to ripen and be released. The dose of the hormones must be carefully controlled. If the dose is too high, then a lot of eggs may be released at once. The woman could then have triplets, quads or even more babies at once!

Fig. 42.1   The use of hormones to increase a woman's fertility sometimes results in a multiple birth.

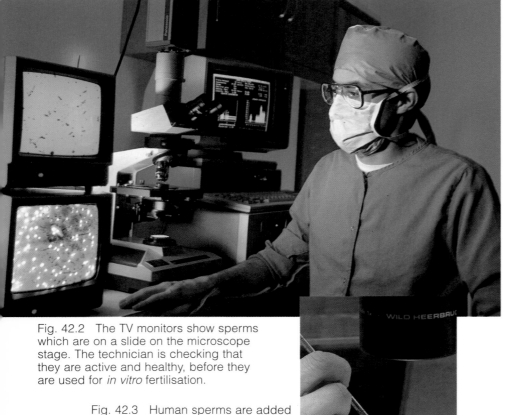

Fig. 42.2   The TV monitors show sperms which are on a slide on the microscope stage. The technician is checking that they are active and healthy, before they are used for *in vitro* fertilisation.

Fig. 42.3   Human sperms are added to human eggs in a petri dish. This process takes place in a special dust-free cabinet, and everything must be spotlessly clean. The process is watched through the microscope to check if fertilisation is successful.

Damaged Fallopian tubes can prevent sperms reaching eggs

Another cause of infertility is a blockage in the Fallopian tubes. Although eggs are being released, sperms cannot reach them. Sometimes, the blockage can be cleared by surgery. The woman can then become pregnant in the normal way.

If the tube cannot be successfully unblocked, then **in vitro fertilisation** can be tried. A baby begun in this way is often called a **test tube baby.**

The woman is first given a course of hormones to make her produce a lot of eggs. The eggs are taken from her body, and put into warm fluid in a test tube or dish, in a hospital laboratory. Some of her partner's sperms are added to the dish. The sperms fertilise the eggs. Zygotes are formed, which divide to form tiny human embryos.

The embryos are kept in the dish for one to two days. They are kept at 37°C, the temperature of the human body. If after this time, the embryos seem healthy, they can be placed inside the woman's uterus. Usually, three are put in, in case one or two do not develop. The embryos implant into the uterus lining, and develop in the normal way.

Read the following passage, and then answer the questions at the end.

Beefing up dairy herds

Cattle are farmed in Britain for two main reasons. Some are dairy cattle, which produce milk. Breeds such as Friesians have been bred for this purpose over many years. They convert a lot of the food they eat into milk. Dairy cows continue to produce milk for many years.

Other cattle are bred for beef production. They convert the food they eat into muscle, which we eat as meat. Beef cattle tend to be larger and heavier than dairy cattle. Beef cattle grow quickly for the first year or so of their lives, converting food into muscle very efficiently. After that, they do not grow much at all.

Not many pure-bred beef cattle are produced in Britain. Most breeding cows (female cattle) are dairy cows. To produce beef cattle, the dairy cows are fertilised with sperm from beef bulls. The calves which are born are cross-bred calves, with some of the characteristics of both their parents. Although they will produce more and better meat than dairy calves, it will not be as good as the meat from a pure-bred beef calf.

Some farmers are now beginning to get round this problem by using a test tube fertilisation technique, and embryo transfer. Eggs are taken from beef cows which have been slaughtered for meat. They are taken to a laboratory, where they are fertilised with sperm taken from a beef bull. The fertilised eggs are kept in warm, moist conditions, as close to the conditions inside a cow's womb as possible. They develop into a tiny ball of cells — an embryo. If the embryos are not to be used immediately, they can be frozen in liquid nitrogen, and stored for a very long time.

The embryos are taken to dairy farms. They are placed inside the wombs of dairy cows. Each cow receives two embryos. In some cows, both embryos will develop. Some, though, will give birth to just one calf.

In this way, a dairy cow can give birth to a pure-bred beef calf.

1 Explain the differences between beef and dairy cattle.
2 Are dairy cows always fertilised with sperm from beef bulls? Explain your answer.
3 What is meant by 'pure-bred beef cattle' (third paragraph)?
4 In the test tube fertilisation technique described in the passage, why does fertilisation have to take place in a laboratory, not in the cow?
5 Describe what happens to the eggs after they have been fertilised.
6 Why do you think each cow receives two embryos?
7 Read the first two paragraphs again. Can you suggest why farmers prefer to use dairy cows for breeding, rather than beef cows? (Think about the amount of money the farmer has to spend on feed for his cattle, and the return the farmer gets on expenses.)
8 Explain why farmers will find the test tube fertilisation technique described above useful. What effects might it have on cattle farming in Britain?
9 What are your views on the use of such techniques as test tube fertilisation and embryo transfer? Do you think there should be strict rules governing their use? If so, what do you think these rules should be?

Fig. 42.4   The techniques of test tube fertilisation and embryo transfer have allowed the black and white dairy cows to give birth to calves of a different, beef-producing, breed.

Fig. 42.5   An embryo at the stage at which it can be transferred to the womb of a cow. At this stage, it is just a tiny ball of cells about 0.1 mm across.

Flowers are used for sexual reproduction. Many flowers make both male and female gametes. The male gametes are inside the pollen grains. The female gametes are inside the ovules.

Male and female gametes are made inside flowers

Many plants can reproduce sexually. They do this by means of flowers. Figure 43.1 shows a section through a flower. The parts shown on this diagram are found in most flowers, although they may be different shapes and sizes, and they may occur in different numbers.

Many flowers make both male and female gametes. They are **hermaphrodite.** The male gametes are made in the **anthers.** Here, **pollen grains** are produced. The male gametes are found inside the pollen grains.

The female gametes are made in the **ovaries.** Inside each ovary are one or more **ovules.** The female gametes are found inside the ovules.

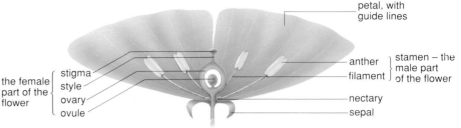

Fig. 43.1 A flower cut in half

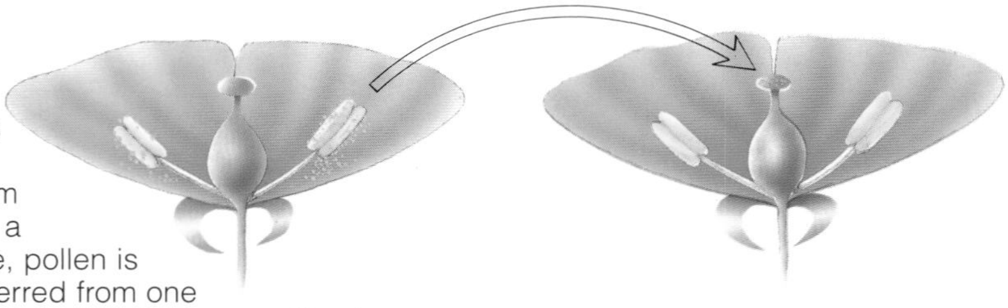

Fig. 43.2 Pollination is the transfer of pollen from an anther to a stigma. Here, pollen is being transferred from one flower to another. This is cross-pollination. Some flowers use self-pollination, transferring pollen from their own anther to their own stigma.

INVESTIGATION 43.1

Investigating the structure of a flower

You are going to take a flower apart, working from the outside inwards. Save all the parts, to stick onto a sheet of paper and keep. Arrange the parts carefully, name them, and label them.

1 Find the **sepals** on the outside of the flower. They are often green, but some flowers have brightly coloured sepals. How many are there? What do you think their function is? (Look at a flower which has not opened yet to help you to answer this question.) Remove the sepals carefully.

2 The next layer is made up of the **petals.** Take them off. How many are there? What is their function? How are they adapted to perform this function?

3 You may be able to find **nectaries** on the stalk, where the petals were attached. Do you have nectaries on your flower? Exactly where are they? What do they contain? What is their function?

4 Find the **stamens** on the remains of your flower. These are the male part of the flower. How many stamens are there? Is there pollen on them? What colour is it? Each stamen is made up of an **anther** and a **filament**. Draw one stamen, and label it. Remove the stamens.

5 Now all that is left is the female part of the flower. There will be one or more **ovaries.** Each ovary has a **style** and a **stigma** on top. Draw one ovary with its style and stigma, and label it. What is the function of the stigma? How is it adapted to carry out this function?

6 Cut an ovary in half. Inside it are the **ovules.** How many ovules are there in the ovary? About how big is each ovule?

Pollination carries male gametes towards female gametes

Plants cannot move actively. A male plant, or the male part of a plant, cannot move towards a female plant to fertilise it. So plants use insects or the wind to carry their male gametes towards the female gametes.

The male gametes are safely packed inside pollen grains. The gametes are surrounded by a tough, protective coat, which stops them from drying out. This is very important, because the male gametes must travel through the air to get to the female gametes.

The female gametes are inside the ovules. Each ovule contains one female gamete. The ovules are inside the ovaries in the flower. So, for fertilisation to occur, the male gametes inside the pollen grains must be brought to the ovaries.

Pollen grains are made in the anthers. They are carried from the anthers by insects, or by the wind. The pollen grains are carried to the stigma of either the same flower, or a different flower of the same kind. This is called **pollination.**

Insect-pollinated flowers are often brightly coloured

Not even an insect will do something for nothing! Plants which use insects to transfer their pollen must give the insects something in reward. The rewards they offer are **nectar**, and **pollen** itself.

Insect-pollinated flowers usually produce nectar. This is a concentrated sugar solution, made for insects to feed on. The flowers may be brightly coloured, to advertise themselves to insects. Flowers may also have a strong scent to attract insects. When the insects arrive at the flower, they search for the nectar. This is usually at the base of the flower, so that the insect must push past the anthers to reach its reward. Pollen from the anthers is rubbed onto the insect's back.

If an insect has found nectar in one flower, it will continue to visit other flowers of the same kind. As it pushes down into the next flower to reach the nectar, some of the pollen on its back will rub onto the flower's stigma. The second flower has been pollinated.

Many insects, including honey-bees, also feed on pollen. Honey-bees collect pollen to take back to the hive, for feeding their larvae. As they collect and transport the pollen, moving from flower to flower, some will rub off on stigmas. Flowers make lots of extra pollen to allow for the pollen which bees collect and take away. It is worth it to them, to make sure that they are successfully pollinated.

Fig. 43.3 Poppies are insect-pollinated flowers. Their bright colours attract insects which carry pollen from the anther of one flower to the stigma of another.

Fig. 43.4 Hazel trees have wind-pollinated flowers. Many male flowers are grouped together to form catkins. They produce enormous quantities of pollen; the pollen falls like clouds of dust into the air, when the wind blows or when something brushes against the catkins. The female flowers, which cannot be seen here, are smaller. They have large stigmas to catch pollen blowing in the wind.

Wind-pollinated flowers have long anthers and stigmas

Many flowers, including grasses, rely on the wind to carry their pollen from one flower to another. They do not need to produce nectar, or to have brightly coloured or strongly scented flowers. Many wind-pollinated flowers are brown or green.

The anthers of these flowers tend to dangle out of the flower, where the wind can catch them. The filaments are very flexible, so that the anther shakes in the wind. The pollen grains tend to be very small and light, so that they can float long distances on the wind. It is this sort of pollen which is most likely to cause hay fever in sensitive people.

The stigmas also dangle outside the flower, so that they can catch pollen as it drifts by. They are often large and feathery, to increase their surface areas.

INVESTIGATION 43.2

Comparing an insect-pollinated and a wind-pollinated flower

Look very carefully at your two flowers; search for differences between them. Make sure you can identify all the different parts on each flower. You may need to take the flowers apart, but do not do this until you are sure you have seen all you need to see while they are intact!

Decide how you will record your observations. You may want to use a comparison chart. Labelled drawings are also a good idea.

Try to explain each difference you find. For example, you will probably find that your insect-pollinated flower is brightly coloured, whereas the wind-pollinated flower is dull. This is because the insect-pollinated flower needs to attract insects, but the wind-pollinated flower does not.

After fertilisation, the ovule becomes a seed, and the ovary becomes a fruit. Fruits help to disperse seeds. Seeds will only germinate when conditions are good for plant growth.

Fertilisation happens inside the ovules

Pollination carries pollen from the anther, where it was made, to the stigma. The male gamete now has to find its way to the female gamete.

The stigma makes a liquid, containing sugar. If the stigma belongs to the right species of flower, the pollen grain responds to this liquid by beginning to grow a tube. The tube grows out of the grain, and down through the style towards the ovules in the ovary. It secretes enzymes which digest a pathway for it through the style.

The tube grows all the way to one of the ovules. The male gamete leaves the pollen grain, and makes its way along the tube. When it reaches the ovule, it goes inside, and fuses with the female gamete. Fertilisation has taken place. A zygote is formed.

After fertilisation, the ovule becomes a seed

Once the ovules in a flower have been fertilised, many changes take place. The petals, sepals and stamens are no longer needed. They wither and fall away. Often, the style and stigma are lost too. All that remains is the ovary, containing the fertilised ovules.

Each fertilised ovule contains a zygote. The zygote begins to divide, to form an **embryo plant**. After a few days, the beginnings of the root and shoot systems can be seen. The embryo root system is called the **radicle**, and the embryo shoot system is called the **plumule**. The embryo also contains one or two seed leaves, or **cotyledons.** The cotyledons often take food from the parent plant, which they store away for future use.

The ovule, which contains this embryo plant, is now called a **seed**. It grows a tough, protective coat, called a **testa**.

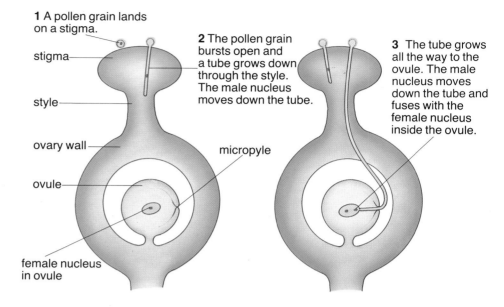

1 A pollen grain lands on a stigma.

stigma

style

ovary wall

ovule

female nucleus in ovule

2 The pollen grain bursts open and a tube grows down through the style. The male nucleus moves down the tube.

micropyle

3 The tube grows all the way to the ovule. The male nucleus moves down the tube and fuses with the female nucleus inside the ovule.

Fig. 44.1   Fertilisation in a flower

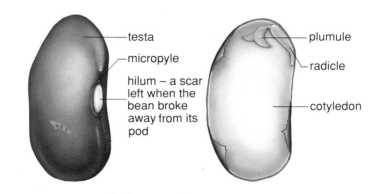

testa

micropyle

hilum – a scar left when the bean broke away from its pod

plumule

radicle

cotyledon

Fig. 44.2   The structure of a bean seed

INVESTIGATION 44.1

Investigating the structure of a seed

1 Make a labelled diagram of your seed. You should be able to see the testa, and a scar where the seed has been broken away from the fruit. You may also be able to see a very small hole near this scar. The hole is called the **micropyle**. What sort of fruit do you think contained your seed?

2 Peel away the testa. Find the two cotyledons. What is their function? Gently pull the cotyledons apart, and look for the rest of the embryo plant. Find the radicle and the plumule. Draw the whole embryo plant, and label it.

The ovary becomes a fruit

The ovary itself also changes. It becomes a **fruit.** Some ovaries become sweet and juicy, forming edible fruits like apples and oranges. Sometimes they become hard and woody, forming the shells of nuts. Sometimes they may grow wings, as in sycamore fruits.

Ovaries become fruits for two reasons. The first is to protect the seeds they contain. The second is to help the seeds to be spread, or **dispersed**, to new areas.

Sweet, fleshy fruits are attractive to animals — including humans. The animals may carry these fruits away to eat them, and drop the inedible pips (the seeds) in new places. Or animals may eat the whole fruit, including the seeds, as humans usually do with tomatoes. The seeds pass right through the digestive system, and pass out undigested in the faeces. Again, the seeds will end up in a new place.

Fruits such as sycamore can be carried on the wind. Some very light fruits, such as dandelion 'parachutes', may be carried very long distances before dropping down to the ground.

It may surprise you that all these things are called fruits. A fruit is an ovary after fertilisation. A fruit contains seeds. So not only oranges and blackcurrants are fruits, but also things such as cucumbers, pea pods and walnuts.

Seeds usually stay dormant for a while

When fertilisation happens inside an ovule, the embryo grows quickly. A radicle, plumule and cotyledons are formed. The testa develops. But usually this is as far as it goes for a while. The seed stays like this for some time. It goes into a resting stage. It is said to be **dormant**.

There are several good reasons for seeds to stay dormant for a few months. In countries where there are distinct seasons, such as Britain, many seeds are produced at the end of the summer. If they grew into new plants immediately, the plants might be killed during winter. By waiting until spring, the new plants stand a better chance of survival.

Another reason is that dormancy gives time for the seeds to be dispersed to new areas. Unlike animals, plants cannot just get up and walk to a new place if they find themselves overcrowded. Seeds need to be carried away from their parent by animals, water, or the wind, if they are to find a space of their own in which to grow.

Fig. 44.3   Fruits. Working clockwise from the apple they are: love-in-the-mist, hawthorn, old man's beard (wild clematis), peas, and maple. How do you think the seeds in each fruit are dispersed? How is each fruit adapted to help the seeds to be dispersed?

INVESTIGATION 44.2

What conditions do mustard seeds need for germination?

You will be provided with some mustard seeds. These are quite small seeds which germinate quickly if conditions are right.
1 Design and carry out an experiment to find out what conditions these seeds need for germination. Get your design checked before you set up your experiment.
2 When you have finished your experiment, design a second experiment to investigate one of the conditions in more detail. For example, you may find that mustard seeds germinate better in warm temperatures than in cold ones. But exactly what temperature produces the best germination rate?

Seeds germinate when conditions are good for plant growth

Many kinds of seeds can lie dormant for long periods of time before they germinate. They can wait for years, if necessary, until the conditions for germination become right.

If you do Investigation 44.2, you will find out what conditions mustard seeds need for germination. Not all plants need exactly the same kind of conditions.

When a seed germinates, it begins by taking in water. The water dissolves enzymes in the cotyledons. The enzymes digest the stored food, and make it soluble. The soluble food then diffuses to the radicle and plumule, allowing them to grow.

The radicle grows first. It pushes down into the soil, and begins to absorb water and minerals. The plumule pushes upwards. When it breaks out above the soil, into the light, it becomes green and begins to photosynthesise. Until now, the growing seed was relying on its food stores, but now it can make its own food.

1 Read the following passage, and then answer the questions.

Reproduction in water and on land

All sexually reproducing organisms have to solve the problem of getting male and female gametes together. In water, this is not too difficult. The male gametes can swim through the water to find the female gametes. If the male and female organisms are quite close together, the male gametes have a reasonable chance of finding a female gamete.

Fish such as herrings, for example, collect together in huge groups. The females release hundreds of thousands of eggs into the sea. The males then release sperms. Thousands of eggs and sperms are lost in this way. Some eggs are eaten by other fish, and some are just not fertilised. But this method obviously works, as plenty of young fish are produced.

Frogs have improved the method slightly. The male frog clings tightly to the female's back when she is ready to lay her eggs. She finds a suitable place in a pond, and lays large groups of eggs called spawn. As she lays them, he is in a perfect position to release sperms over them. The sperms have a good chance of finding the eggs and most of the eggs are fertilised.

Land-living, or terrestrial, animals have more of a problem. Sperms cannot swim through air, so most land animals use internal fertilisation. The male animal introduces his sperms into the female's body. The sperms are kept moist throughout their journey to the female gamete. This method also improves the chances of a male gamete meeting a female one. So internal fertilisation wastes fewer eggs and sperms than the external fertilisation used by many aquatic animals.

a What is meant by
  i aquatic?
  ii terrestrial?
b Explain the difference between external and internal fertilisation.
c Why do most land-living animals use internal fertilisation?
d What other advantage does internal fertilisation have over external fertilisation?
e Why do you think a female fish produces thousands of eggs each year, whereas most mammals produce fewer than 30?

2 Read the following passage, and then answer the questions.

Cigarette smoking in pregnancy

Cigarette smoke contains harmful substances. Many of these, such as the gas carbon monoxide, are absorbed into the mother's blood, and cross the placenta into the baby's blood.

Several groups of scientists have collected information about the effects of cigarette smoking during pregnancy on mothers and their babies.

One group looked at the numbers of babies which died before or just after birth. They found that, in their sample, for every thousand mothers between 20 and 24 years old who did not smoke, six babies were lost. Smokers in the same age group lost nine babies per thousand. Non-smoking mothers between 25 and 34 years old lost seven babies per thousand, compared with ten per thousand in smoking mothers. Mothers over 35 years old who smoked lost 12 babies per thousand, while non-smoking mothers in this age group lost nine babies per thousand.

Another group of scientists looked at the length of pregnancy in smoking and non-smoking mothers. The normal length of pregnancy is 42 weeks. The scientists found that 1.00% of mothers who smoked heavily gave birth at 24 weeks, whereas only 0.36% of non-smoking mothers did so. At 30 weeks, the figures were 1.20% for smokers, and 0.46% for non-smokers. At 36 weeks, 1.80% of smokers gave birth, and 0.90% of smokers.

a Draw up two charts to show this information clearly.
b Summarise the effects of smoking during pregnancy on the likelihood of a baby dying just before or just after birth.
c Summarise the effects of smoking during pregnancy on the likelihood of a baby being born early.

3 Draw two columns in your book. Head one of them 'Asexual Reproduction', and the other 'Sexual Reproduction'. Copy each of the following statements into the correct column. One of them needs to be written in both columns.

a gametes involved
b gametes not involved
c always only one parent
d sometimes only one parent, often two parents
e young genetically identical with parent
f young genetically different from each other, and from parent or parents
g fertilisation involved
h fertilisation not involved
i used by mammals
j used by plants

4 The table shows the dry mass of a bean seed before, during and after germination. The bean seed was planted on day 0.

Time (days)	Dry mass of bean plant (g)
0	1.4
5	0.7
10	1.3
15	4.2
20	7.4
25	13.6
30	27.0
35	32.3
40	40.1
45	50.7
50	62.3

a Use these figures to draw a growth curve for the bean plant.
b What is meant by 'dry mass'?
c How would these results have been collected?
d Why does the dry mass of the bean decrease between day 0 and day 5?
e The rate of growth of the bean is not steady. Suggest three reasons why this might be so.

ORGANISMS IN THEIR ENVIRONMENT

45 ECOLOGY

Ecology is the study of living organisms in their environment.

A habitat contains a community of living things

The **habitat** of a living organism is the place where it lives. Some examples of habitats are a pond, a hedgerow around the school grounds, a rocky seashore. A wide variety of living things are found in a habitat. All the living things in a habitat are called a **community**. A community is made up of many different species of animals, plants, fungi, bacteria and protoctista.

Fig. 45.1 This rock pool community is made up of various seaweeds, a sea slug, mussels, snakelocks, anemones, winkles, a shore crab and limpets.

An organism's niche is its role in the community

Fig. 45.2 A pond is a **habitat** for many kinds of organisms. The pond and the organisms make up an **ecosystem.** All the organisms together make up the pond **community**. All the organisms of one kind are a **population**.

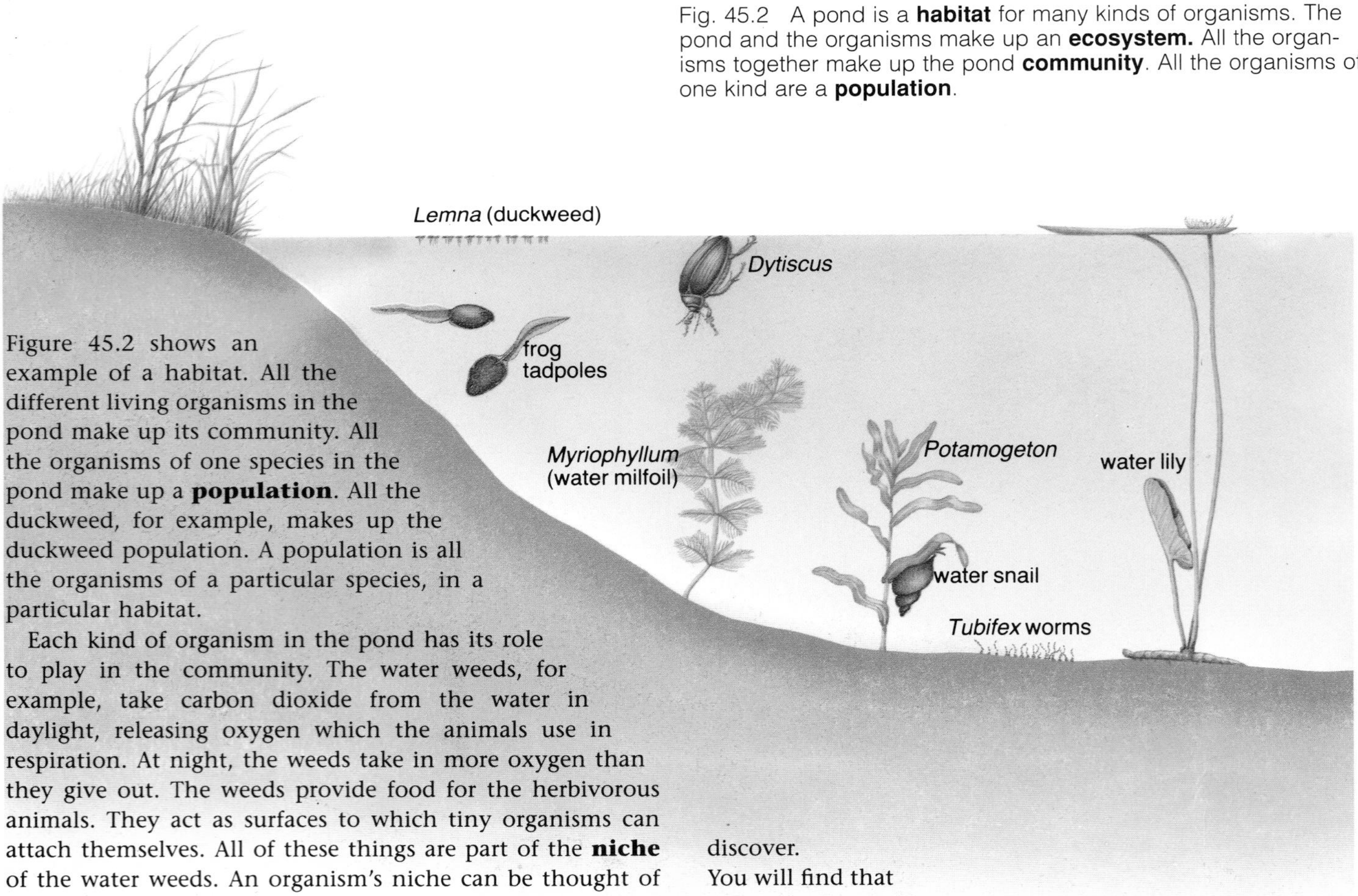

Lemna (duckweed)

Dytiscus

frog tadpoles

Myriophyllum (water milfoil)

Potamogeton

water lily

water snail

Tubifex worms

Figure 45.2 shows an example of a habitat. All the different living organisms in the pond make up its community. All the organisms of one species in the pond make up a **population**. All the duckweed, for example, makes up the duckweed population. A population is all the organisms of a particular species, in a particular habitat.

Each kind of organism in the pond has its role to play in the community. The water weeds, for example, take carbon dioxide from the water in daylight, releasing oxygen which the animals use in respiration. At night, the weeds take in more oxygen than they give out. The weeds provide food for the herbivorous animals. They act as surfaces to which tiny organisms can attach themselves. All of these things are part of the **niche** of the water weeds. An organism's niche can be thought of as its 'profession' in the community in which it lives.

Each kind of organism in a community has a different niche. Niches of different species can overlap, but are never identical. If you make a detailed study of a habitat, you may be able to find out quite a lot about some of the species you discover.

You will find that different kinds of plants, for example, live in slightly different places, reproduce in slightly different ways, and provide food for different kinds of animals. Each species has its own particular niche.

108

An ecosystem is made up of interacting living and non-living things

The pond in Figure 45.2 does not contain living things only. It also contains mud, stones, water, and gases dissolved in the water. These non-living parts of the pond affect the living organisms in it. They are part of the pond **ecosystem**.

An ecosystem consists of a community and its environment. The living organisms affect each other. They affect their environment, and are affected by their environment. An ecosystem consists of both living and non-living things.

Although a pond is an example of an ecosystem, you can also think of ecosystems on a much larger scale. The whole of the Earth is one big ecosystem!

Organisms are adapted to live in their environment

Each species of organism has a particular type of habitat in which it is adapted to live. Limpets, for example, are adapted to live on rocky shores where they are covered by the tide for part of the day. Their shell protects them from predators and stops them from drying out when the tide is out. Their strong muscular foot clamps them tightly to the rock so that they are not dislodged by waves. They have a rasping tongue which scrapes algae off the rocks when the tide covers them.

The factors which affect a living organism can be divided into **physical factors** and **biotic factors**. Physical factors are non-living ones. In the case of the limpet, some of the most important physical factors are the tide which repeatedly covers and uncovers it, the waves which splash against it, the rock on which it lives, and the temperature of the air and water around it. The biotic factors are the other limpets around it (which might take up space or eat food it might have used), the algae which it eats, and predators which try to eat it.

The adaptations of the limpet enable it to live successfully in its environment and to cope with the environmental factors which affect it. The factors are different in different places, so organisms need different adaptations to be able to live there. A limpet would not survive long in an oak wood, or even on a sandy sea shore.

Fig. 45.3 Rain forests are some of the most complex ecosystems in the world. This one is in the Monteverde Cloud Forest Reserve in Costa Rica.

Fig. 45.4 The limpet, *Patella*, is adapted to live successfully on a rocky shore.

Tentacles are sensitive to touch and chemicals, helping the limpet to find food and avoid predators. A simple eye is also present near the base of each tentacle.

The shell prevents the limpet from drying out when the tide is out. The shape of the shell reduces damage by wave action.

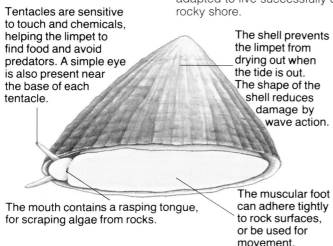

The mouth contains a rasping tongue, for scraping algae from rocks.

The muscular foot can adhere tightly to rock surfaces, or be used for movement.

Question

1 Write definitions of:
   a habitat
   b community
   c niche
   d population
   e ecosystem
   f physical factors
   g biotic factors.

Keys can help you to identify organisms

One of the first things you will want to do when studying a habitat is to find out what lives there. Often, just walking round and looking will enable you to find many different species, especially the larger ones. Plants, in particular, are easily seen.

But many of the animals need hunting for more carefully. Small mammals like voles can be trapped carefully and then released. Larger mammals like foxes may leave droppings and paw prints. Small soil-dwelling animals can be seen by using the apparatus shown in Figure 46.1.

Once you have found an organism, you will need to identify it. Unless you have someone with you who knows all the animals and plants, you will need to use books. Pictures in identification books are a quick and easy way to identify many plants and animals. But sometimes, to be absolutely sure of your identification, you will need to use a key. Many keys use quite small features,

which are awkward and difficult to see. So keys take much longer to use than a picture book. But if you have a good memory, you will only need to use the key once for each kind of organism. The next time you meet it, you will know what it is without having to look it up.

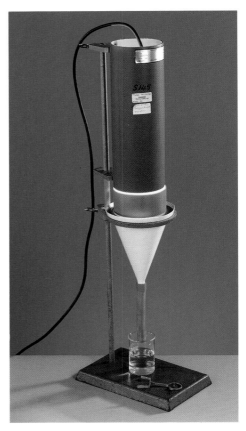

Fig. 46.1 A Tullgren funnel can be used to extract and collect small animals from soil. The soil sample is placed on a piece of wire mesh at the top of a funnel and a light is shone onto it. The heat and light drive the animals downwards. They fall through the funnel and tube, and are collected in alcohol. This kills and preserves them. If they were not killed, the predators would eat the other animals.

Fig. 46.2 Using a quadrat to record the different kinds of plants growing on a lawn.

Quadrats are used for sampling

When studying a habitat, you will probably want to find out how many of each kind of organism lives there. Unless the habitat is tiny, it will be impossible to count every individual animal and plant. Instead, you can count individuals in just a part of the habitat.

It is important that the part you sample should be representative of the whole habitat. The best way to do this is to take **random samples**. If you choose which parts to sample, you might unconsciously choose the easy parts or the most interesting parts.

On land, **quadrats** are often used for random sampling. A quadrat is a square frame, often with sides 0.5 m long. It is placed randomly on the ground, either by throwing, or by using random numbers as coordinates which you then pace out. (You can get printed tables of random numbers or use a calculator which can generate them.) Then you can estimate the numbers of different kinds of organisms inside the quadrat. If they are large and easy to see, like limpets, you could just **count** them. If it is difficult to decide where one finishes and another one starts, like grass plants, you could estimate what **percentage** of the ground inside the quadrat is covered by each species. You record the numbers, or percentage cover, of each species in your quadrat. Then you do it again several times, placing the quadrat randomly each time.

Quadrats are not much use in a pond. **Nets** are a better way of sampling the water. Again, you must try to place the net randomly. It is also important to try to sweep the net through the water in the same way each time and for the same length of time. Then you know that all your samples are roughly equivalent to each other. Nets can also be swept through grass to catch insects.

Mark–release–recapture can estimate populations of mobile organisms

Neither quadrats nor sweep nets would be of any use in estimating the population of mice in a hedgerow or woodlice under a log. A technique which you can use for mobile animals is called the **mark–release–recapture** technique.

You begin by catching as many of the animals as possible. Special traps can be used for small mammals. Fingers and a dish are good enough for woodlice or snails. Nets will catch water boatmen. Then count and mark all your captured animals. The method of marking must not harm the animal in any way, so choose it carefully. Mice can be marked by clipping a small piece of fur from their back. Snails, woodlice and water boatmen can be marked with a tiny dot of waterproof paint.

Release all your marked animals. Give them time to move around and get thoroughly mixed in with the rest of the population. Then, once again, capture as many as you can. Count the total number which you catch, and the number of these which are marked.

You can then calculate the approximate number of organisms in the population using this equation:

number in population =

$$\frac{\text{total number caught 1st time} \times \text{total number caught 2nd time}}{\text{number of marked animals caught the 2nd time}}$$

Questions

1 A student made a study of a rectangular pond in a school's grounds. The pond was 5 m long, 4 m wide and 1 m deep, with straight sides.

a What is the total surface area of the pond?

b What is the total volume of the pond?

The student decided to measure the size of the water boatman population in the pond, using a small dustbin with no bottom. The bin had a diameter of 50 cm. The student put the bin firmly on the bottom of the pond and then used a net to catch all the water boatmen trapped inside it. (The bin was tall enough to reach above the water surface.) There were 19 water boatmen in the bin. The student did this twice more, catching ten water boatmen the second time, and one the third time.

c What volume of water was trapped inside the dustbin each time?

d What was the average number of water boatmen in this volume of water?

e If the water boatmen were distributed evenly in the pond, calculate the probable population in the whole pond.

f Suggest several reasons why this number might not be accurate.

g Describe another possible method for calculating the water boatman population.

2 a Use the key below to identify the leaves A to E in Figure 46.3.

───── *EXTENSION* ─────

b Leaf F is a cherry leaf. Modify the key so that this leaf can also be identified from it.

1	Leaf stalk present	go to 2
	Leaf stalk absent or very small	oak
2	Leaf palmate (divided into fingers)	go to 3
	Leaf not palmate	go to 4
3	Distinct, elongated points	maple
	Points not elongated	sycamore
4	Leaf margin (edge) smooth	eucalyptus
	Leaf margin serrated (jagged)	rose

Fig. 46.3

INVESTIGATION 46.1

Identifying and counting organisms in a habitat

1 Look carefully around the habitat you are studying. Use help, books and keys to identify as many as possible of the animals, plants and fungi you find. Make a list of them.

2 Use appropriate methods to find some of the less obvious organisms in your habitat – e.g. looking for tracks, droppings or burrows; using a Tullgren funnel; making a microscopic examination of water samples, and so on.

3 Choose appropriate methods to find out the relative sizes of the populations of some of the organisms in the habitat. You could count them, use quadrats, nets, or the mark–release–recapture technique.

Questions

1 Explain why you chose your particular methods in steps 2 and 3 in this investigation.

2 How accurate do you think your findings are? Did you find all the species that are there? Are you sure all your identifications are correct? How accurate are your estimates of population sizes? What could you do to increase the accuracy of your results?

───── *EXTENSION* ─────

3 You have made your study at a particular time of year. Choose a different season and suggest what differences you might find. Give reasons for your suggestions. (If possible, repeat your study during this second season and see how accurate your predictions were.)

Classification makes identification easier

Humans love to classify things. Putting things into groups makes it easier for us to understand them. When we have thousands of different objects to deal with, classifying them helps us to put them into some sort of order. It also helps us to identify a new object, by deciding which group it fits into. If you find an animal you have never met before, you can at least decide whether it is an insect or a mammal even if you do not know precisely what it is.

Carl Linnaeus was the first person to attempt a thorough classification of living organisms. He was a Swedish botanist who lived from 1707 to 1778. He classified living things according to similarities in their structure. He gave each kind of organism a two-part Latin name. We still use this system today.

Fig. 47.1 Carl Linnaeus

Homologous structures are used in classification

Living things are thought to have **evolved** over thousands of millions of years. First, very simple single-celled organisms appeared. Gradually, some of them changed, or evolved, into more complex organisms. Mammals, the group to which humans belong, first appeared about 250 000 000 years ago.

Biologists classify living things according to how closely they are thought to be related. Mammals and birds, for example, are thought to have evolved from reptiles, so mammals, birds and reptiles are put into the same group.

Various kinds of clues can be used to work out these relationships. Perhaps the most useful are similarities in structure. Mammals, birds, reptiles and amphibians all have a backbone, and five-fingered or **pentadactyl** limbs. So it looks as though they all evolved from the same group of ancestors, and are quite closely related.

Features like the backbone and

Groups range from kingdom to species

There are various sizes of groups into which living things are put. The largest group is the **kingdom**. All living organisms are divided into five kingdoms – bacteria, protoctista, fungi, plants and animals. Each of these groups contains thousands and thousands of different organisms.

Each kingdom is further divided into **phyla**. The Animal Kingdom, for example, has many phyla, including molluscs, annelids and chordates – the group to which you belong. Phyla are divided into **classes**, then **orders**, then **families**, then **genera**, and finally **species**. Table 47.1 shows how this system can be used to classify a horse.

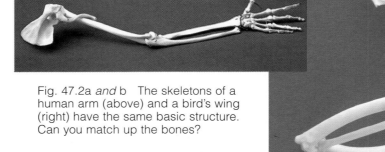
Fig. 47.2a *and* b The skeletons of a human arm (above) and a bird's wing (right) have the same basic structure. Can you match up the bones?

pentadactyl limbs are called **homologous structures**. Homologous structures are ones which are built to the same design, but with variations because of differences in the way they are used. Your arm and a bird's wing, for example, are homologous structures. They are used for very different purposes, but have the same basic bone structure. They show that you and a bird are really quite closely related.

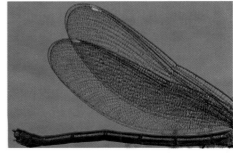
Fig. 47.2c An insect's wing is a completely different structure. It is made from outgrowths of the insect's external skeleton, supported by hollow veins. So, although both insects and birds have wings, they are not closely related.

Table 47.1 Classifying a horse

Kingdom	*Animalia*	organisms whose cells do not have cell walls, and are made of many cells
Phylum	*Chordata*	animals with a stiffening rod along their back, and often with a backbone
Class	*Mammals*	chordates with fur
Order	*Perissodactyla*	mammals with hooves, with an odd number of toes - includes tapirs, rhinoceroses and horses
Family	*Equidae*	horses and zebras
Genus	*Equus*	horses
Species	*caballus*	the domestic horse

Latin name – *Equus caballus*

Fig. 47.3 All of these animals are mammals belonging to the order Primates. Primates are adapted to be tree-dwelling animals, with grasping hands and feet, and often with nails instead of claws. Sight is a very important sense. The brain is larger in proportion to body size than in most other mammals.

a Tree shrews are the most primitive primates.

b Lemurs, such as this ring-tailed lemur, are long-tailed primates found only in Madagascar. They have large eyes, which face forward in many species.

d The group of primates most similar to humans is the apes, which includes chimpanzees, gorillas, gibbons and orangutans. Chimpanzees live in groups with elaborate social structures. They spend a lot of time on the ground. They are very intelligent, and can use simple tools.

e Humans are primates with especially well developed brains. Their upright stance has left their hands free to use tools. Complex social organisation, and communication through language means that humans can learn from each other, passing new skills to new generations.

Each organism is given a Latin name

When Linnaeus classified living organisms, the language which was most widely understood in the scientific world was Latin. So Linnaeus used Latin when he named things. We still use Latin for this today. Although no-one speaks Latin any more, it is good for each organism to have a name which is the same all over the world. The name *Equus caballus* means 'horse' to all scientists, whatever language they speak. Many organisms do not have common names, only Latin ones.

The Latin name of an organism is the name of its genus and the name of its species. The name of its genus must always be given a capital letter, and the name of its species a small one. Because the name is in Latin, not English, you should underline it or write it in *italics*.

This system of naming living things is called the **binomial system**. Binomial means 'two names'.

c Monkeys tend to be social animals. They are very agile, and have forward-facing eyes, which help them to judge distances when leaping in trees.

Questions

1 The Latin name for the human species is *Homo sapiens*. Using information from these two pages, classify yourself in the same way as has been done for a horse in Table 47.1.

2 What other animals belong in your order? What features do you share with them? What differences are there between you and them?

113

Bacteria have no nuclei

The commonest kind of organisms in almost any ecosystem are **bacteria**. They are very small so you will not easily be able to see them even with a good microscope. But if you try Investigation 48.1, you can grow colonies of bacteria, which are easily visible to the naked eye.

The cells of bacteria are different from animal and plant cells. Bacterial cells are **prokaryotic** cells. The most important difference between prokaryotic cells and other cells is that prokaryotic cells have no nucleus. The DNA of a bacterium lies loose in the cytoplasm, and is not protected by a nuclear membrane. Bacteria are mostly single-celled organisms. Their cells are much smaller than animal or plant cells.

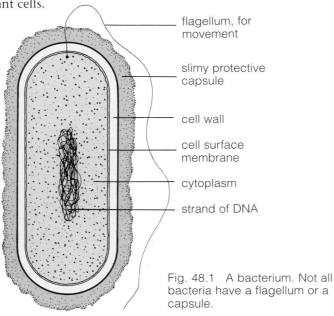

flagellum, for movement

slimy protective capsule

cell wall

cell surface membrane

cytoplasm

strand of DNA

Fig. 48.1   A bacterium. Not all bacteria have a flagellum or a capsule.

Protoctista are single-celled organisms with nuclei

Protoctista are simple organisms with nuclei. They include **protozoa** and **algae**. Many protoctista are made of just one cell. The cells of single-celled protoctista are larger than those of bacteria, so you can see them quite easily with a microscope. If you look at a sample of pond water, particularly if there are rotting leaves in it, you will see several kinds of protoctista. Some of them are animal-like, swimming round actively hunting for food. They are called protozoa. They eat smaller protoctista or bacteria. Others are plant-like, drifting or swimming through the water, keeping close to the surface so that their chlorophyll can trap sunlight for photosynthesis. They are called algae. Some algae, such as seaweeds, are made up of many cells.

Bacteria feed in many different ways

Bacteria feed in many different ways. Some bacteria have chlorophyll and can **photosynthesise**. Their chlorophyll is not the same as the chlorophyll in plants, and it is not found inside chloroplasts.

Other bacteria feed on organic material by secreting enzymes onto it. The enzymes digest the food, breaking down large molecules to small ones. The small soluble molecules then diffuse into the bacterium's cell. This method of feeding is called **saprotrophic nutrition.**

Saprotrophic bacteria have several important roles in any ecosystem. They break down dead plants and animals, animal faeces and other waste material. They are **decomposers**. Without them, the nutrients in bodies and waste would not be able to return to other organisms in the ecosystem. These bacteria are very important in the carbon and nitrogen cycles.

But saprotrophic bacteria can be a nuisance, too. They will feed on human food, digesting it and making it go bad. They may reproduce so much on the food that, when you eat it, you get a large mouthful of bacteria and their waste products as well as food. This can make you very ill. Bacteria which do this include *Salmonella* and *Campylobacter*.

We make use of many kinds of saprotrophic bacteria. The bacterium *Lactobacillus* feeds on milk, turning it into yoghurt. These bacteria do not produce harmful waste products, so we can eat them with no problems. Bacteria are also used in making cheese. The treatment of sewage uses bacteria which break down harmful substances in the sewage into less harmful ones.

Several different kinds of bacteria live on or in your body. Most of these are harmless, but a few can make you ill. These are called **pathogenic bacteria**. It is often their waste products, pouring into your blood stream, which make you ill.

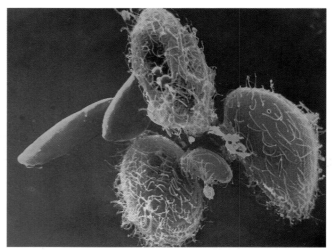

Fig. 48.2   Some protoctista are covered with hair-like cilia, which beat in the water to produce movement.

Growing bacteria

If you have done Investigations 45.1 and 46.1, you may feel that you know quite a lot about the things which live in the ecosystem you are studying. But you have not yet met some of the most numerous and important ones – the bacteria. Bacteria have many very important roles to play in an ecosystem, and exist in huge numbers.

1 Take a sterile Petri dish, containing a layer of sterile agar jelly. ('Sterile' means containing no life. The dish and jelly will have been treated to kill any micro-organisms on them.) Agar jelly provides a good place for bacteria and small fungi to grow, and contains all the food they need.

2 Take a small sample of some material from the ecosystem you are studying. It could be water, soil, rotting leaves, tree bark – almost anything you like. If necessary, shake a little of your chosen material in a bottle of sterile water.

3 Use a sterile pipette or loop to spread some of the material onto the surface of the agar jelly. Take care not to breathe on it, or to touch the inside of the dish or its lid, or to leave the dish open for long – you do not want bacteria from yourself or from the air to get in. Put the lid back on quickly.

4 Seal the lid to the base of the dish with two small strips of Sellotape. Label the dish with the date and the source of the sample.

5 Leave the dish at room temperature, upside-down so that no droplets of moisture drop onto the surface of the jelly. After a few days, inspect it to see what has grown on the jelly.

Questions

1 Why is it important that all the equipment you use should be sterile? Find out how it was sterilised.

2 Each colony on the jelly may have grown from a single bacterium or fungus. Can you see individual colonies? If so, how many are there? Use Figure 48.4 to identify which ones are bacteria and which are fungi.

3 It is possible to use this method to estimate the number of bacteria in a certain volume of soil. Describe exactly what you would need to do to find this out.

— EXTENSION—

Fungi are all saprotrophic

Fungi include the familiar mushrooms and toadstools. These structures grow from a mass of underground threads called **hyphae**.

Hyphae, like plant cells, have cell walls. They also have nuclei. But they never have chlorophyll, so fungi cannot photosynthesise. All fungi are saprotrophs.

Fungi play a similar role in an ecosystem to saprotrophic bacteria. They are decomposers. Some of them, also like saprotrophic bacteria, can rot human food. A very few, such as the ringworm fungus and athlete's foot, can cause disease.

Quite a few fungi are very useful to humans. Mushrooms and many other fungi are edible. Fungi are used in making cheese. Some fungi, for example the blue mould *Penicillium*, make substances which kill bacteria. These substances are called **antibiotics**, and their discovery revolutionised the treatment of disease.

Yeast is a rather unusual single-celled fungus. It is used in making bread, beer and wine.

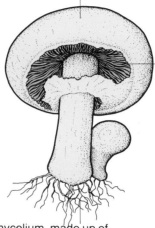

cap

gills, where spores are produced for reproduction

mycelium, made up of threads called hyphae – the hyphae secrete enzymes into the soil, digesting organic matter which is then absorbed

Fig. 48.3   A field mushroom

Fig. 48.4   Fungi and bacteria growing on agar jelly in a Petri dish. The large furry area on the right is a fungus. All the other colonies are bacteria.

Classification summary

Kingdom Prokaryota Single-celled organisms with no nuclei. Includes bacteria. Cells are much smaller than in any of the other kingdoms.

Kingdom Protoctista Simple organisms with nuclei. Most live in water. May have chlorophyll, like plant cells, or not, like animal cells. Examples: *Amoeba*, *Fucus*.

Kingdom Fungi Many-celled (multicellular) organisms with cell walls but no chlorophyll. Often made up of hyphae. All are saprotrophic. Examples: *Mucor*, *Saccharomyces* (yeast).

Plants photosynthesise. Plants are producers of food.

Plants are multicellular and photosynthetic

The plant kingdom is made up of many-celled organisms which can photosynthesise. Plants have cells with nuclei, cell walls and chloroplasts.

The most familiar plants are the large ones which we see around us all the time – grass, flowers, and trees. These mostly belong to the phylum **Angiospermophyta**. They are the most highly evolved group of plants.

But there are many other groups of plants. One which you will probably come across as you study an ecosystem is the group containing the mosses and liverworts. They belong to the phylum **Bryophyta**. These are all small plants, with tiny single-celled rootlets, and simple stems and leaves. They do not have flowers, but reproduce by spores. Quite closely related to them are the ferns and horsetails, phylum **Filicinophyta** and **Sphenophyta**. They tend to be larger than bryophytes and have proper roots. They, too, reproduce with spores and do not have flowers.

Plants are producers

All plants photosynthesise. They take inorganic substances from the air and soil, and make organic substances from them. They make organic food which other organisms can eat. All the saprotrophs and animals in an ecosystem rely on the food which plants make. So plants are called the **producers** of an ecosystem, because they produce the food which supports all the other organisms in the system.

Phylum Bryophyta

Fig. 49.1   Moss growing in woodland in the Lake District

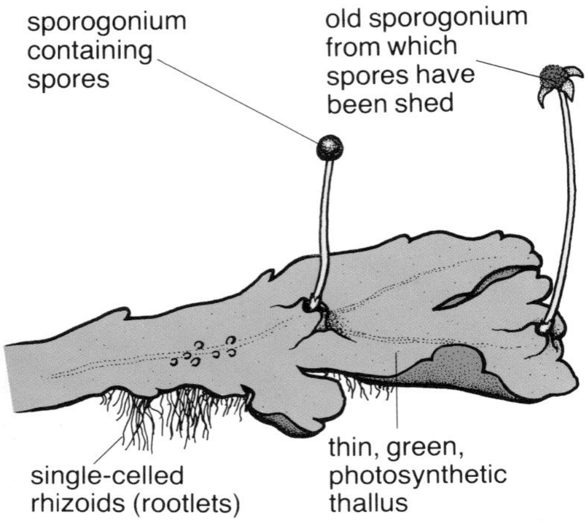

sporogonium containing spores

old sporogonium from which spores have been shed

single-celled rhizoids (rootlets)

thin, green, photosynthetic thallus

Fig. 49.2   A liverwort

Phylum Sphenophyta

Fig. 49.3   Great horsetail, *Equisetum telmateia*

Phylum Filicinophyta

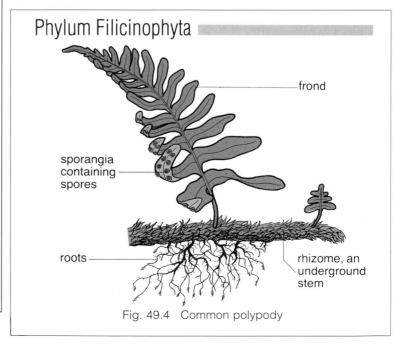

frond

sporangia containing spores

roots

rhizome, an underground stem

Fig. 49.4   Common polypody

Phylum Coniferophyta

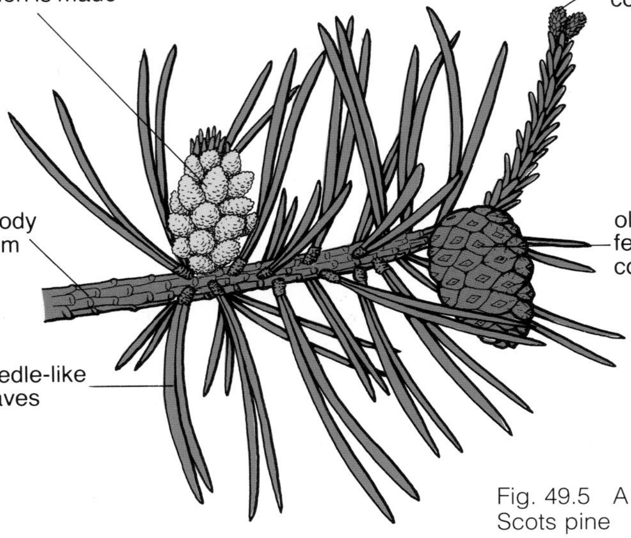

group of male cones, where pollen is made

young female cone

woody stem

older female cone

needle-like leaves

Fig. 49.5   A branch of Scots pine

Fig. 49.6   Giant redwoods, *Sequoiadendron giganteum*, are conifers. These are in the Sequoia National Park in California.

Phylum Angiospermophyta

flower

leaf

bulb

roots

Fig. 49.7   A snowdrop

Fig. 49.8   Horse chestnut trees, *Aesculus hippocastranum*, are flowering plants.

Classification summary

Kingdom Plantae
Many-celled organisms, whose cells have cell walls and chloroplasts. They all contain chlorophyll, and photosynthesise.

Phylum Bryophyta Mosses and liverworts. Small plants with single-celled rootlets, with simple leaves. Have no flowers, reproduce by spores. Most live in damp, shady places. Examples: the moss *Funaria*, and the liverwort *Marchantia*.

Phylum Sphenophyta Horsetails. Have no flowers, reproduce by spores, which are produced in cones. Leaves arranged in whorls around the stem. Example: the horsetail *Equisetum*.

Phylum Filicinophyta Ferns. Have no flowers, reproduce by spores. Leaves are fronds, which are coiled when in bud. Spores are produced in structures called sori, on the fronds. Example: the male fern *Dryopteris*.

Phylum Coniferophyta Conifers. Often tree-sized plants, with no flowers. They produce seeds in cones. Example: pine trees, *Pinus*.

Phylum Angiospermophyta Flowering plants. They produce seeds, inside fruits. Examples: the horse chestnut *Aesculus*, and the strawberry plant, *Fragaria*.

Invertebrates are animals without backbones. They include many different phyla.

There are many different phyla of invertebrates

The words 'vertebrate' and 'invertebrate' are very commonly used. Everyone knows that vertebrates are animals with backbones, and that invertebrates are animals without backbones. But the invertebrates contain many different phyla, many of them only quite distantly related. Perhaps it is because we have backbones that we tend to lump together all the animals which don't.

Only some of the more obvious and common invertebrate phyla are mentioned on these four pages.

Jellyfish belong to the phylum Cnidaria

If you look around on almost any rocky shore, you will find sea anemones. These soft-bodied animals, with a ring of tentacles around their mouth, belong to the phylum Cnidaria. Jellyfish also belong in this phylum. All cnidarians live in water.

Cnidarians are carnivorous animals. They trap prey in their tentacles, push it inside their mouths, and digest it. Many feed on microscopic animals, but some eat quite large fish.

One group of cnidarians make hard skeletons around their soft bodies. These are the **corals**. They form the basis of the enormously varied communities of animals found on and around coral reefs. These cnidarians have microscopic algae living inside their bodies. The algae photosynthesise. They are the producers of the coral reef.

Phylum Cnidaria

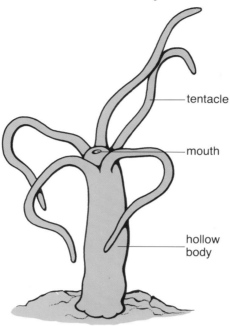

Fig. 50.1   Hydra

tentacle

mouth

hollow body

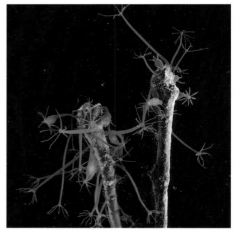

Fig. 50.2   *Hydra* is a small, freshwater cnidarian, quite common in ponds and streams in Britain. It traps tiny animals with its tentacles.

Fig. 50.3   Corals are cnidarians. They have the usual soft, cnidarian body, but it is surrounded by a skeleton of calcium compounds, which can build up into coral reefs. The corals in this picture are in the Red Sea.

Earthworms are annelids

The phylum Annelida is made up of the worms with rings round their bodies. Earthworms belong to this phylum. Annelids live in water or in damp places.

Earthworms feed on dead and decaying leaves. They are very important in many ecosystems, as they help to improve the soil for plant growth. They drag leaves into their burrows, where the leaves decay to form humus. Their faeces contain digested organic material which also helps to form humus. Their burrows let air into the soil and provide drainage.

Other annelids are carnivores, actively hunting among rocks and seaweeds on the seashore and in shallow water. Some, such as leeches, are parasites.

Phylum Mollusca

Phylum Annelida

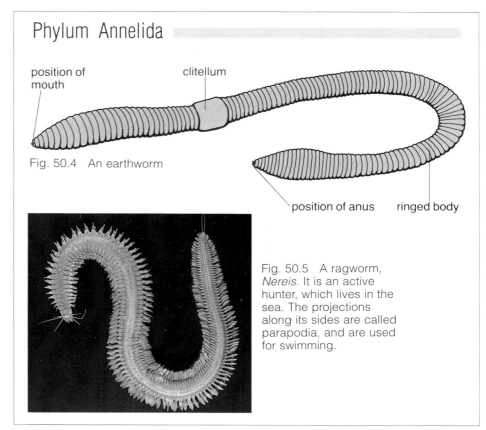

position of mouth

clitellum

position of anus   ringed body

Fig. 50.4   An earthworm

Fig. 50.5   A ragworm, *Nereis*. It is an active hunter, which lives in the sea. The projections along its sides are called parapodia, and are used for swimming.

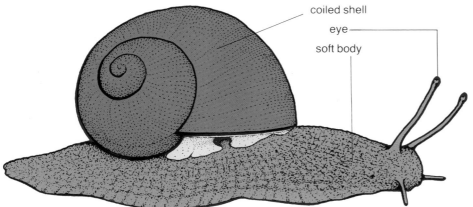

coiled shell

eye

soft body

Fig. 50.6   A garden snail

Slugs and snails belong to the phylum Mollusca

Molluscs are soft-bodied animals, often with a shell. Many of them, such as mussels and limpets, live in or near water. Mussels are filter feeders, sucking water through the opening of their shell and filtering out anything edible from it. Limpets are grazers, scraping their rough 'tongue' over the surfaces of rocks.

Squids, octopuses and cuttlefish are also molluscs. So are slugs and snails. Some slugs and snails live in water, but many live on land. Most of them are herbivores. A few, such as dog whelks, are carnivores.

Fig. 50.7   Common mussels, *Mytilus edulis*. Water is sucked in through the open shell, and then passed over the gills which filter out food.

Fig. 50.8   An Australian squid, *Euprymna tasmania*. Squid are carnivores. They are able to change their colour very rapidly, either for camouflage or as signals to other squid.

The arthropods are the largest group of animals

If you judge success by sheer numbers, then the phylum Arthropoda wins by a long margin. The arthropods are invertebrates with jointed legs. Arthropods have an exoskeleton, often hardened with calcium.

There are several groups of arthropods. The class **Myriapoda** contains the millipedes and centipedes. Class **Arachnida** contains spiders and scorpions. Class **Crustacea** contains lobsters, crabs and woodlice. Class **Insecta** is the insects.

Arthropods can fill many different niches in an ecosystem. They may be herbivores, detritus (dead organic material) feeders, carnivores or parasites. Arthropods can be found in all parts of the world – on land, in water, in the air, in deserts, and even in the Arctic and Antarctic.

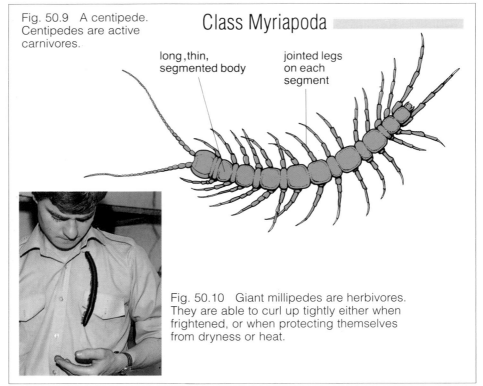

Class Myriapoda

Fig. 50.9 A centipede. Centipedes are active carnivores.

long, thin, segmented body

jointed legs on each segment

Fig. 50.10 Giant millipedes are herbivores. They are able to curl up tightly either when frightened, or when protecting themselves from dryness or heat.

Class Arachnida

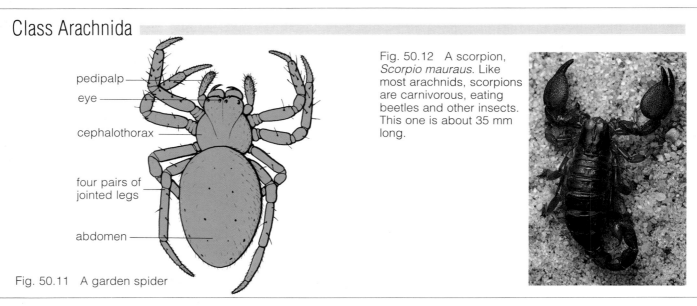

pedipalp

eye

cephalothorax

four pairs of jointed legs

abdomen

Fig. 50.11 A garden spider

Fig. 50.12 A scorpion, *Scorpio mauraus*. Like most arachnids, scorpions are carnivorous, eating beetles and other insects. This one is about 35 mm long.

Class Crustacea

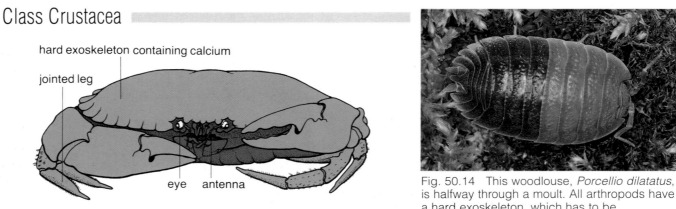

hard exoskeleton containing calcium

jointed leg

eye   antenna

Fig. 50.13 A crab

Fig. 50.14 This woodlouse, *Porcellio dilatatus*, is halfway through a moult. All arthropods have a hard exoskeleton, which has to be periodically shed and replaced as its owner grows inside it.

Class Insecta

Fig. 50.15 A Large White butterfly

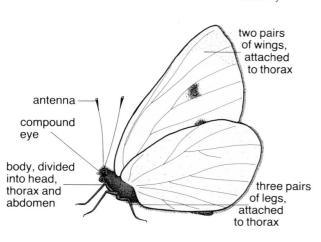

two pairs of wings, attached to thorax

antenna

compound eye

body, divided into head, thorax and abdomen

three pairs of legs, attached to thorax

Fig. 50.16 Both ladybirds, and the greenfly on which they feed, are insects. Greenfly are slightly unusual insects, because many do not have wings. If you want to spray your roses to get rid of greenfly, make sure you choose a spray which doesn't kill the ladybirds as well. Better still, let the ladybirds remove the greenfly for you.

Fig. 50.17 A woodworm beetle, *Anobium punctatum*, crawling out from the piece of wood in which it has spent its life as a larva. Its large, compound eyes and six legs are typical of insects. Its first pair of wings are hard wingcases; underneath is a pair of proper wings.

Classification summary

Kingdom Animalia Many-celled organisms, whose cells have no cell walls or chloroplasts. They feed on organic food originally made by plants.

Phylum Cnidaria Sea anemones, jellyfish and corals. They have soft bodies, with a ring of tentacles surrounding a mouth. This is the only opening to the digestive system – waste food goes out the same way it went in. Examples: the beadlet anemone, *Actinia*, and the tiny fresh-water animal, *Hydra*.

Phylum Mollusca Slugs, snails, limpets, octopuses. Soft-bodied animals, often with a shell. Their bodies are not divided into segments. Examples: the garden snail, *Helix*, and the cuttlefish, *Sepia*.

Phylum Annelida Worms with ringed segmented bodies. They have no legs but many have stiff bristles called chaetae which help in movement. Examples: the common earthworm, *Lumbricus*, and the carnivorous marine ragworm, *Nereis*.

Phylum Arthropoda Animals with hard exoskeletons, segmented bodies, and jointed legs.

Class Myriapoda Millipedes and centipedes. They have long bodies, clearly divided into rings, with a pair of legs on each segment. Example: the centipede, *Lithobius*.

Class Crustacea Crabs, lobsters and woodlice. They have very hard exoskeletons which contain calcium. Example: the crab, *Cancer*.

Class Arachnida Spiders and scorpions. They have eight jointed legs. Example: the garden spider, *Areneus*.

Class Insecta Insects. They have six jointed legs and a body divided into head, thorax and abdomen. Many have two pairs of wings. Examples: the house fly, *Musca*, and the ladybird, *Adalia*.

51 VERTEBRATES

Vertebrates include fish, amphibians, reptiles, birds and mammals.

Vertebrates belong to the phylum Chordata

Vertebrates are animals with backbones. They belong to the phylum Chordata. The chordates are animals with a stiffening rod along their backs. Some chordates, such as sea-squirts, have this rod only during the early stages of their life. In vertebrates, the rod is replaced by a backbone made of cartilage or bone.

Class Pisces

Fig. 51.1 These sardines are in the sea off the Galapagos Islands, in the Pacific Ocean. It is thought that keeping together in a group, or shoal, makes it more difficult for an individual fish to be singled out by a predator.

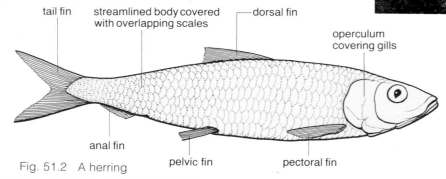

tail fin — streamlined body covered with overlapping scales — dorsal fin

operculum covering gills

anal fin — pelvic fin — pectoral fin

Fig. 51.2   A herring

Fish belong to the class Pisces

Fish are all aquatic animals, apart from a few kinds like lungfish which can spend quite long periods on land. Gas exchange takes place through gills, and they have bodies covered with scales. Fins help to stabilise them in the water.

Amphibians must reproduce in water

The class Amphibia contains frogs, toads, salamanders and newts. These animals have smooth, moist skins with no scales. The adults may live on land, but they always have to go back to the water to breed. They lay their eggs in water, where they hatch into tadpoles. The tadpoles undergo a dramatic change, called metamorphosis, when they become adults.

Class Amphibia

smooth, moist skin   eardrum

Fig. 51.3   A frog

Fig. 51.4   A fire salamander, *Salamandra salamandra*. Its smooth skin gives away that it is an amphibian, not a reptile. This is a land animal, but its tadpoles live in water.

Reptiles lay eggs with rubbery shells

Reptiles have tough scales all over their bodies. They may live in water, like turtles and crocodiles, or on land, like many lizards and snakes. Their rubbery-shelled eggs are always laid on land.

Class Reptilia

Fig. 51.5 This snapping turtle, *Chelydra serpentina*, is a typical reptile, with hard, dry, scaly skin.

Birds belong to the class Aves

Birds, like mammals, can keep their body temperature constant. They are homeothermic. Their covering of feathers helps them to keep warm. Some parts of their body, usually the lower parts of their legs, are covered with scales instead of feathers. They lay eggs with hard shells. All birds have beaks, and all have two wings, though not all of them can use their wings for flight.

Mammals have hair

Any vertebrate with hair is a mammal. Mammals are homeothermic. Their young develop inside their bodies, attached to their mother through an umbilical cord and placenta. After birth, the young are cared for by their parents, and fed on milk from the mother's mammary glands.

Class Aves

Fig. 51.6 Birds have adapted to living almost everywhere in the world. These birds are greater flamingos, *Phoenicopterus ruber*, from Saudi Arabia. They feed in salty lakes, dragging their downcurved beaks through the water and filtering out anything edible.

Fig. 51.7 The violet-eared hummingbird, *Colibri thallassinus*, feeds on nectar. Hovering like this requires great coordination and energy. The wings of some hummingbirds can beat at 90 beats per second.

Class Mammalia

Fig. 51.8 All mammals suckle their young. The care given to the young, as they develop inside the mother's body, and also after they are born, means that young mammals have a better chance of survival than most other vertebrates.

Classification summary

Phylum Chordata Animals with a stiffening rod along their back. Many have backbones of cartilage or bone.

Class Pisces Fish. Have scales, gills, and fins. Aquatic. Example: the herring, *Clupea*.

Class Amphibia Amphibians. Have smooth skins. Four legs. Lay soft eggs in water, from which tadpoles hatch. Tadpoles have gills, which are usually lost when they metamorphose into adults. Adults have lungs. Example: the common frog, *Rana*.

Class Reptilia Reptiles. Have scaly skins. Four legs. Lay rubbery-shelled eggs on land. Gas exchange takes place through lungs. Example: the lizard, *Lacerta*.

Class Aves Birds. Have feathers, some scales and a beak. Four limbs, of which two are wings. Lay hard-shelled eggs on land. They are homeothermic. Example: the wren, *Troglodytes*.

Class Mammalia Mammals. Have hair and four legs. Young develop inside mother, feeding through the placenta. Milk is produced from mammary glands. They are homeothermic. Example: the short-tailed vole, *Microtus*.

Energy enters an ecosystem as sunlight, and is transferred to chemical energy by photosynthesis.

Food is a chemical energy store

All living things need energy. You need energy for movement, for driving the metabolic reactions inside your cells, and for keeping warm.

You get your energy from the food you eat. All living things get their energy from **organic food**. Food contains a store of chemical energy. Living cells are able to transfer this chemical energy into other forms, such as movement energy and heat energy.

The food is made by plants. Plants use light energy from sunlight to make organic substances like carbohydrates, fats and proteins. They transfer light energy from sunlight into chemical energy in food. This process is called photosynthesis.

Energy flows along food chains

Within an ecosystem, organisms eat other organisms, and in turn are eaten themselves. Figure 52.1 shows an example of how this might happen in a hedgerow ecosystem. It is called a **food chain**.

The arrows in a food chain show how energy is transferred from one organism to another. When a rabbit eats grass, energy is transferred from the grass to the rabbit. The arrows in a food chain represent energy flow along the chain.

Usually there are many food chains in an ecosystem. They all interact with one another. A diagram showing this is called a **food web**.

Every food chain begins with the Sun. The next link is a green plant. Plants make or produce the food for the rest of the chain, so they are called **producers**. Animals eat or consume this food, so they are **consumers**. An animal which eats a plant – a herbivore – is a **primary consumer**. An animal which eats a primary consumer is a **secondary consumer**, and so on. An animal which regularly eats both plants and animals is an **omnivore**. Organisms which feed by breaking down dead bodies or waste material are called **decomposers**. Many fungi and bacteria are decomposers.

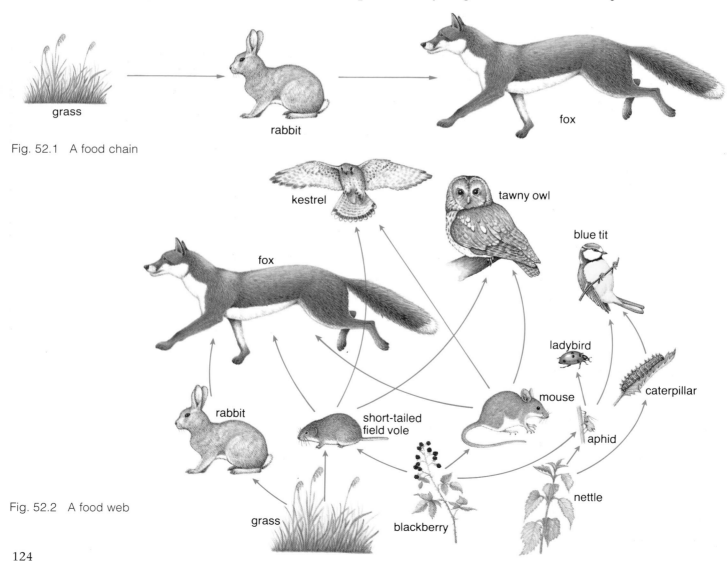

grass

rabbit

fox

Fig. 52.1 A food chain

kestrel

tawny owl

blue tit

fox

ladybird

mouse

caterpillar

rabbit

short-tailed field vole

aphid

nettle

Fig. 52.2 A food web

grass

blackberry

Energy is wasted along a food chain

Whenever energy is transferred from one organism to another, some is wasted. Imagine a field of grass being eaten by rabbits. Some of the grass is eaten and digested by the rabbits, absorbed into their bodies, and used in their cells. But a lot of the grass they eat is not digested. It passes out of their bodies in their faeces. And the rabbits will not eat all of the grass. Some of it will be trampled. Some might become old, tough and inedible. Nowhere near all the stored chemical energy in the grass will be passed on to the rabbits.

More energy will be wasted as the chemical energy in the grass is transferred into other forms of energy inside the rabbits' bodies. A lot will be transferred into heat energy, which is given out from the rabbit to the air around it. The total chemical energy that ends up stored in the rabbits' bodies will be nowhere near as much as the total chemical energy which was stored in the grass.

At every step in a food chain, energy is transferred as heat to the surroundings. The amount of energy arriving in a useful form at the end of a chain is only a small fraction of the amount of energy at the beginning.

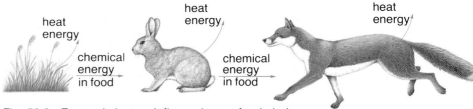

Fig. 52.3   Energy is lost as it flows along a food chain.

Pyramids of numbers represent population sizes

Look back at the food chain in Figure 52.1. If you were able to count the numbers of grass plants, rabbits and foxes in an ecosystem, you would find that the number of plants was much higher than the number of rabbits, which was much higher than the number of foxes. Figure 52.4a shows this in a diagram called a **pyramid of numbers**.

The area of each block in this pyramid represents the number of organisms at that step in the food chain. Each step in the pyramid is called a **trophic level**.

Numbers of organisms decrease along a food chain because the available energy decreases. The longer the food chain, the more energy is lost. Food chains rarely have more than five links. There would not be enough energy left to support a population of fifth consumers at the end.

a a pyramid of numbers

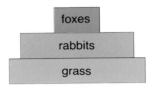

b a pyramid of numbers

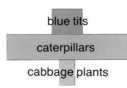

c a pyramid of biomass

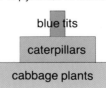

Fig. 52.4

INVESTIGATION 52.1

Working out food chains

1 Look back at the list you made in Investigation 46.1 of the organisms in the ecosystem you are studying. Use help, your own observations and books to find out what some of them eat.

2 Draw up a food web for your ecosystem. Don't forget to include the decomposers. Don't worry if you cannot include every organism.

Questions

1 Which organisms in your ecosystem do you estimate have the largest populations? Can you suggests reasons for this, in terms of energy flow?

2 Which organisms are rare in your ecosystem? Suggest reasons for this.

3 Choose a short food chain within your food web. Use appropriate methods to measure the populations of the organisms in the web. (You may already have done this in Investigation 46.1.) Draw a pyramid of numbers for this food chain. Remember that the area of the boxes in the pyramid represents the numbers of organisms.

— EXTENSION —

Pyramids of biomass show the amount of living material

Figure 52.4b also shows a pyramid of numbers. It is an odd shape because the primary consumers, caterpillars, are much smaller than the producer, the cabbage plant. A much better way of showing this information is to draw a **pyramid of biomass**. 'Biomass' is the mass of living material. A pyramid of biomass shows the amount of living material at each trophic level.

Questions

1 a In what form does energy enter an ecosystem?

b In what form does energy enter you?

c What is the name of the reaction occurring inside all of your cells, which transfers chemical energy in digested food into useful energy for your cells?

d Why is there less energy available for carnivores than for herbivores?

2 It has been suggested that a move towards vegetarianism would allow the Earth's limited food supplies to feed more people. Do you think this is true? Discuss the possibility of such a change taking place, and any problems which would be associated with it.

— EXTENSION —

125

53 THE CARBON CYCLE

Carbon dioxide is taken from the air by green plants, and put back into the air by all living organisms and by burning.

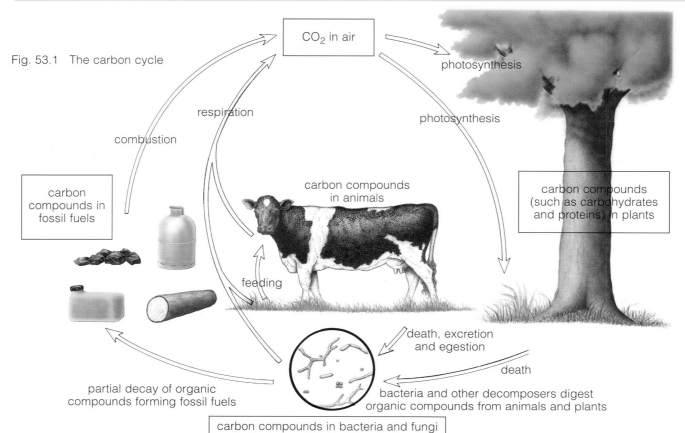

Fig. 53.1   The carbon cycle

CO$_2$ in air

photosynthesis

respiration

photosynthesis

combustion

carbon compounds in fossil fuels

carbon compounds in animals

carbon compounds (such as carbohydrates and proteins) in plants

feeding

death, excretion and egestion

death

partial decay of organic compounds forming fossil fuels

bacteria and other decomposers digest organic compounds from animals and plants

carbon compounds in bacteria and fungi

Carbon atoms are cycled

Many of the molecules from which living organisms are made contain carbon atoms. Carbohydrates, fats and proteins all contain carbon atoms. These carbon atoms are passed from one organism to another, into the atmosphere and into the soil. The possible pathways a carbon atom could take are shown in Figure 53.1. This is called the **carbon cycle**.

Photosynthesis uses up carbon dioxide

Only about 0.04 % of the air is carbon dioxide. Plants use carbon dioxide from the air when they photosynthesise. They use it to make food. The carbon from the carbon dioxide becomes part of the food molecules. Plants can only photosynthesise during daylight, because photosynthesis needs energy from sunlight.

Respiration produces carbon dioxide

All livings things need energy. They get their energy from food. When the energy is released from food, carbon dioxide is produced. This is where the carbon dioxide which you breathe out comes from.

All living things respire. So all living things produce carbon dioxide. Even plants produce carbon dioxide. They do it all the time. But during the day, they use it up in photosynthesis faster than they make it in respiration. So in the daytime plants take in carbon dioxide. At night they give it out.

Decomposers release carbon dioxide

Dead plants and animals contain a lot of carbon. So do their waste materials, such as urine, faeces and fallen leaves. All of these substances can be used as food by **decomposers**, such as bacteria and fungi. The decomposers break down the molecules in the dead bodies and waste materials, and use them to build their own bodies. They use some of the molecules for respiration. When they do this, they release carbon dioxide.

Burning produces carbon dioxide

When things burn, they react with oxygen in the air. The fuels which we burn all contain carbon. The carbon reacts with oxygen in the air to form carbon dioxide.

How did the carbon get into the fuels? Fossil fuels, such as coal, oil and gas, were formed from plants and bacteria. The plants took carbon dioxide from the air. So the fuels contain carbon.

The enhanced greenhouse effect and global warming

Carbon dioxide in the air behaves rather like the glass of a greenhouse. It lets the Sun's rays through on to the surface of the Earth. Some of these rays heat the Earth's surface. Some of this heat escapes from the Earth and goes back into space. But the carbon dioxide in the atmosphere traps some of the heat and stops it escaping. This is called the **greenhouse effect**. Without the carbon dioxide, the Earth would lose much more heat and would be much colder than it is. Earth would be a frozen, lifeless planet.

Photosynthesis takes carbon dioxide out of the air. Respiration and burning put carbon dioxide into the air. These processes balance each other, so the amount of carbon dioxide in the air stays approximately the same.

But humans may now be upsetting the balance. We burn more and more fossil fuels. We also cut down and burn growing trees. This releases extra carbon dioxide into the air, which increases the greenhouse effect. As a result, the Earth may be getting warmer. This is called **global warming**.

Carbon dioxide is not the only gas which acts like a blanket around the Earth. **Methane** has a similar effect. Although there is much less methane in the atmosphere than carbon dioxide, the amounts are increasing and its effect on global warming is significant. Methane is produced in especially large amounts by cattle, by termites, and sometimes from the mud in paddy fields where rice is grown.

Does global warming matter? We do not know to what extent global warming will happen, or exactly what its effects will be. If it does happen, then it will change weather patterns on the Earth. Some places will become drier, while others will become wetter. Global warming may cause a lot of ice at the poles to become liquid water, which would increase sea levels. This could flood many major cities.

some energy is reradiated
from the Earth's surface

some radiation escapes
back into space

radiation from Sun
reaches Earth

some radiation is reflected or absorbed
by greenhouse gases

Fig. 53.2 The greenhouse effect. Radiation from the Sun passes through the atmosphere on to the Earth's surface. Here, some is reflected, while some is absorbed and reradiated as heat. Some of this reradiated energy escapes into space, but some is retained in the atmosphere. Gases such as carbon dioxide, ozone and methane increase the amount of energy retained. This warms the Earth.

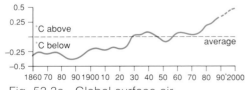

Fig. 53.3a Global surface air temperatures.
The horizontal dotted line shows the average air temperature on the Earth's surface. It is calculated from all the measurements taken, all over the world, between 1950 and 1979.

Eight of the nine warmest years this century have occurred in the 1980s. In 1988, the global average temperature was 0.34 °C above the long-term average. We do not know whether this has been caused by increased CO_2 emissions, or whether there is some other natural cause.

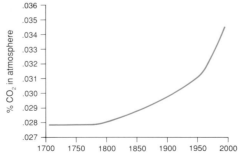

b Atmosphere carbon dioxide levels. In recent years the CO_2 level has begun to rise much more steeply than before. The levels of carbon dioxide in the 18th and 19th centuries have been measured from bubbles of air trapped in ice at the Poles.

Questions

1 a What is the percentage of carbon dioxide in the atmosphere?

b Which process removes carbon dioxide from the atmosphere?

c Which processes return carbon dioxide to the atmosphere?

2 Discuss the causes, and possible results, of the enhanced greenhouse effect. What do you think that humans can do to keep the damage to a minimum?

EXTENSION

54 THE WATER CYCLE

Water moves in a continuous cycle from the land and sea into the atmosphere and back again. Human activities can disrupt the balance of this cycle, and cause drought and flooding.

Water evaporates from land and sea

A very large part of the Earth's surface is covered with liquid water. Some of this water evaporates. It goes into the air as water vapour. Water also evaporates from plants' leaves. This process is called **transpiration**. Transpiration is an extremely important way of putting water vapour into the air.

Water vapour condenses as it goes into the atmosphere

When water evaporates into the air, it is in the form of a gas. You cannot see it. But as it rises, the gas cools. When it is cool enough, it changes from a gas into a liquid. This process is called **condensation**. The liquid water forms tiny droplets. They form clouds. Sometimes, if it is cold enough, the water will form tiny ice particles in the cloud.

Water falls from clouds as rain, hail or snow

Eventually, the droplets in the cloud become so large that they fall to the ground. This is called **precipitation**. Precipitation may fall as rain, hail or snow. Some of the water falls on to land. It may sink into the soil, where it will eventually find its way into streams and rivers. These flow into lakes or the sea. The water can evaporate from the surfaces of any of these bodies of water. Some of the water which falls on to land will be taken up by plant roots. It travels up through the plant, and is lost to the air by transpiration.

Deforestation can cause soil erosion and flooding

Trees are very important to the water cycle. But in many parts of the world people have cut trees down. If this is done on a large scale, it is called **deforestation**.

Deforestation happens because people want the land for growing crops, keeping animals such as cattle, and for building roads and houses. They may also want to use the wood for building, making tools and making furniture. In Europe, huge areas of woodland were cut down long ago. Today, deforestation is happening most rapidly in tropical rain forests, such as those in Brazil and some parts of south east Asia.

If there are trees where the rain falls, much of the rain hits the trees before it hits the ground. If there are no trees or other plants, the rain falls directly on to the ground. This can damage the soil. It presses the top layer of soil tightly together. So as more rain falls, it cannot sink into the soil. It runs over the surface. As it does this, it wears away the soil. The soil is carried along with the water, into streams and rivers. Plant roots also help to stop soil washing away when it rains. The roots bind the soil together. Tree roots are especially good at this, as they go very deep into

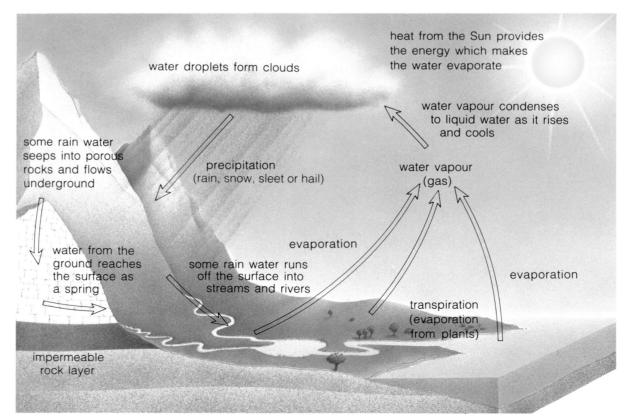

Fig. 54.1 The water cycle

the soil. Without trees, soil easily washes away.

This **soil erosion** is damaging in two ways. Firstly, it means that soil is lost from the land. Soil takes hundreds or thousands of years to form. If it is lost like this, it is very difficult to replace. Secondly, the soil fills up the streams and rivers. When it rains, the water cannot flow so easily in them. The water overflows from the riverbed. This can cause very serious flooding.

Fig. 54.3 Bangladesh has suffered very serious flooding in recent years. This is thought to have been caused by removal of trees from the hills on which rain falls. The water runs off the bare hillsides into rivers, carrying mud which fills the riverbeds and makes them overflow.

Fig. 54.2 Water running over bare ground washes away the soil. Tree roots help to stop this happening. This erosion has happened because prospectors for gold have cut down many trees in a rain forest, allowing rain to wash away the river banks.

Fig. 54.4 Overgrazing in dry scrubland in Sahel, Nigeria, is turning the area into a desert. There are too many animals and these destroy the vegetation by grazing and trampling, leaving the soil open to erosion, and reducing the amount of moisture in the already dry air. Humans also cut down trees to use for fuel. Little can now be grown on this land, but careful farming practices, which look after the soil, can provide food for large numbers of people from a small area of land.

Lack of trees reduces evaporation

Lack of trees does not only cause soil erosion and flooding. It can also cause droughts. If there are plenty of trees, they soak up a lot of the rain water through their roots. The water then evaporates from their leaves in the process of transpiration. This keeps the air moist. Clouds can form, and more rain can fall.

But if there are no trees, the rain which falls runs directly into rivers. Not very much will evaporate into the air. The air becomes dry. Clouds do not form and less rain falls.

Questions

1   Discuss the ways in which human activities can disrupt the water cycle. What damage might this cause to humans and other living organisms? What can be done to prevent this damage?

EXTENSION

129

55 ACID RAIN

Acid rain is caused when sulphur dioxide and nitrogen oxide gases are released into the air. They dissolve in water droplets, and fall to earth as rain or snow.

Sulphur dioxide is emitted when fossil fuels are burnt

Fossil fuels, such as coal, natural gas and oil, contain sulphur. When they are burnt, the sulphur combines with oxygen. It forms sulphur dioxide. The sulphur dioxide is given off as a gas.

Sulphur dioxide is an unpleasant gas. It damages living things. Humans who breathe in a lot of sulphur dioxide over a long period of time have an increased risk of suffering from colds, bronchitis and asthma. Sulphur dioxide can kill plant leaves. It may completely kill the plant.

Fig. 55.1 The upper branches of this tree may have been killed by acid rain.

INVESTIGATION 55.1

The effect of sulphur dioxide on plants

Sodium metabisulphite solution gives off sulphur dioxide. You are going to test its effect on two kinds of important crop plants.

1 Fill four containers with damp compost. Press the compost down firmly, but not too hard. Make the tops level.
2 Put barley seeds on to the compost in two containers. Spread them out evenly. Put maize seeds on to the compost in the other two containers.
3 Cover all the seeds with enough compost to hide them completely. Label all four containers.
4 Leave the containers in a warm place until most of the seeds have germinated. Keep them well watered.
5 When the shoots of barley and maize are about 3-5 cm tall,

make labelled diagrams of each of the four sets of seedlings.
6 Now take four small containers, such as watch glasses. Into two of them place a piece of cotton wool soaked in sodium metabisulphite solution. (TAKE CARE. Do not get it on your hands.) In the other two, place a piece of cotton wool soaked in water.
7 Place each container of seedlings in a large plastic bag, with one of the watch glasses. You should have one of your groups of barley seedlings with a container of sodium metabisulphite solution and one with a container of water. Do the same with the maize seedlings. Tie the plastic bags tightly, so that no air can get in or out.
8 Make labelled diagrams of each of your four sets of seedlings about

30 min after putting them into their bags, and again after one or two days.

Questions

1 Why were some seedlings enclosed with sodium metabisulphite solution, and some with water?
2 Were both types of plant affected in the same way by sulphur dioxide? Explain what these effects were, and any differences between the maize and barley seedlings.

Sulphur dioxide and nitrogen oxides form acid rain

Sulphur dioxide dissolves in water to form an acid solution. Nitrogen oxides, which are produced when nitrogen and oxygen from the air react inside internal combustion engines, also form an acid solution when they dissolve. Sulphur dioxide and nitrogen oxides are carried high into the air. Here, they dissolve in water droplets in clouds. They make the water droplets acid. The clouds may be carried many miles before they drop their water. It falls as acid rain or snow.

Acid rain damages trees and aquatic animals

Acid rain can damage trees. Acid rain washes important minerals, such as calcium and magnesium, out of the soil. Acid rain falling on thin soils, such as those in the mountains of Scandinavia, can kill huge areas of forest.

As the acid water runs through the soil, it washes out aluminium ions. The aluminium runs into rivers and lakes. Aluminium is very toxic to fish. Some acid rivers and lakes now contain hardly any fish.

Acid rain damages buildings

Acid rain can also damage buildings. The acid reacts with carbonates in limestone. The limestone dissolves, so that the stone gradually crumbles away.

Fig. 55.2 Stonework in Lincoln Cathedral

What is the major cause of acid rain?

Normal rain is slightly acid anyway. This is because carbon dioxide in the air dissolves in rain drops to form carbonic acid. Carbonic acid is a very weak acid. So even ordinary rain has a pH a little below 7.

But the large amount of sulphur dioxide and nitrogen oxides which we are now releasing into the air are making rain much more acid than this. We are damaging plants, animals and buildings. Something must be done to stop this getting any worse.

Scientists are still not sure about the most important cause of acid rain. Is it power stations burning coal? Certainly these are very important. Large amounts of sulphur dioxide are released from these power stations. Many of them are now beginning to remove the sulphur dioxide from the smoke they produce, so that it does not go into the air. But this is expensive and means that we will have to pay more for the electricity they make. Or are cars the most important producers of acid rain? Car exhaust fumes contain nitrogen oxides. Since 1956 the amounts of sulphur dioxide emitted by coal burning have gone down. But the acid rain problem has got worse! Over this time the numbers of cars on the roads has increased enormously. So it looks as though cars are as much to blame as coal-burning factories and power stations.

Combustion of fossil fuels, for example oil or coal in power stations, releases sulphur dioxide into the air. Nitrogen oxides are released in vehicle exhaust fumes. The sulphur and nitrogen oxides dissolve in water droplets in clouds, making them acidic. They may be carried for hundreds of kilometres.

Plants may be damaged when acid rain falls on them. Acidification of the soil allows toxic elements to dissolve, and be washed into streams, rivers and lakes. Fish and other aquatic organisms may be killed.

Fig. 55.3 Acid rain

Questions

1 a How is sulphur dioxide produced?
  b What damage can be done by sulphur dioxide gas?
  c What is produced when sulphur dioxide dissolves in water?
2 Both sulphur dioxide and nitrogen oxides contribute to the formation of acid rain.
  a What are the major sources of these two gases?
  b Describe the kind of damage which can be done by acid rain.
  c Is normal rain neutral, acidic or alkaline? Explain your answer.
  d What do you think could be done to reduce the damage caused by acid rain?

56 OZONE

The layer of ozone in the atmosphere, high above the Earth's surface, protects us from ultraviolet light.

Ozone is found in the atmosphere

Ozone is a gas. Whereas oxygen gas has two oxygen atoms in its molecules, ozone has three. The molecular formula for ozone is O_3.

Ozone is formed from oxygen. Quite a lot of ozone is formed near the ground. For example, ozone is produced when sunlight interacts with nitrogen oxides from vehicle exhaust fumes. This ozone may contribute to the formation of smog over cities where there is a lot of traffic.

So high concentrations of ozone in the air near ground level are not good for us. But high above us, between 20 km and 35 km above the ground, there is an area where large concentrations of ozone occur naturally. This high-level ozone, up in the stratosphere, is called the **ozone layer**. It is very important to all living things on Earth.

Ultraviolet light damages cells

Various forms of electromagnetic radiation reach the Earth from the Sun. Some of this is **ultraviolet radiation**. Ultraviolet radiation can damage DNA inside living cells. If you sunbathe, your skin reacts to the ultraviolet radiation by producing extra melanin. Melanin is a dark brown pigment that absorbs the ultraviolet light before it can penetrate cells deep in your skin. The production of melanin is a defence mechanism used by your skin to stop damage to your DNA.

Recently, the number of cases of a disease called **skin cancer** have been increasing. It is likely that this is happening because more and more people can afford to go on holidays to sunny places. If a person with a naturally light-coloured skin works indoors and doesn't get much sunlight on their skin, then they have no natural protection from the ultraviolet rays when they first go into strong sunshine. The DNA in some of the cells in their skin may be damaged. Many years later, these cells may begin to divide uncontrollably, forming a lump or **tumour**. Most cases of skin cancer can be cured, but sometimes the illness is fatal. You can read more about skin cancer in Topic 70.

Ultraviolet light can also damage your eyes. It can make the lens go cloudy, so that light cannot pass through it. This is called a **cataract**.

Ultraviolet can damage plant cells, too. It can harm the pigments that are needed to absorb light for photosynthesis. Some crop plants do not grow so well in very strong ultraviolet light.

Ozone absorbs ultraviolet light

The layer of ozone in the stratosphere protects us from ultraviolet light. Much of the ultraviolet light that hits the upper layers of the atmosphere is absorbed by ozone. The ozone stops too much ultraviolet light getting down to the ground. If it wasn't for the ozone layer, there would be many more cases of skin cancer and cataracts, and many plants would not grow well.

The ozone layer has been damaged

Human activities have damaged the ozone layer. Figure 56.1 shows two satellite images, taken in 1979 and 1990. The concentration of ozone is measured in Dobson units, and if you look at the key at the side of the photographs you can see that there is much less ozone present in the second picture than in the first.

These measurements were made over the South Pole. This is where most of the damage is occurring. However, in recent years, the amount of ozone over the North Pole has been decreasing as well. Sometimes, these ozone 'holes' spread as far south as Britain. The average amount of ozone over Britain in March is about 365 Dobson units. But in March 1996 the amount was only 195 Dobson units.

Why is this happening? The culprit is a group of chemicals called **chlorofluorocarbons**, or **CFCs**. CFCs have been widely used as coolants in refrigerators, and in aerosols. When they get into the air, they remain unchanged for over 100 years. This gives them plenty of time to travel right up to the higher layers of the atmosphere containing ozone. Then they react with the ozone, and break it down. CFCs are destroying the ozone layer.

Can we protect the ozone layer?

Many countries do not use CFCs any more. Most developed countries have stopped using them completely. But some developing countries still use them, because it is expensive for them to find substitutes. And even if we stopped using any CFCs at all, it would still take at least 100 years for them to disappear from the atmosphere, because they are very stable substances.

But at least we have reduced the use of CFCs, and this will give the ozone layer a chance to recover. Ozone is constantly formed in the stratosphere, so – given time – the amount of ozone in the ozone layer should gradually increase, so long as we do not keep on releasing CFCs.

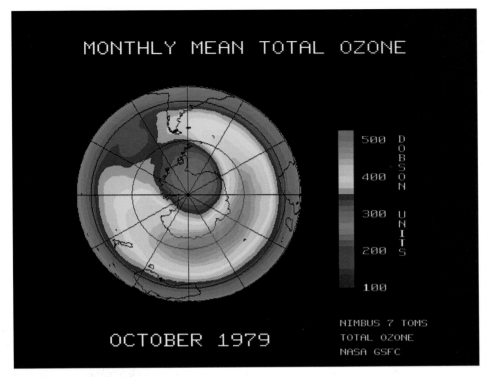

MONTHLY MEAN TOTAL OZONE

500 D
    O
    B
400 S
    O
    N
300 U
    N
    I
200 T
    S
100

OCTOBER 1979

NIMBUS 7 TOMS
TOTAL OZONE
NASA GSFC

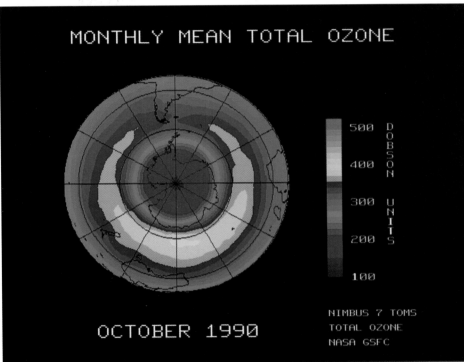

MONTHLY MEAN TOTAL OZONE

500 D
    O
    B
400 S
    O
    N
300 U
    N
    I
200 T
    S
100

OCTOBER 1990

NIMBUS 7 TOMS
TOTAL OZONE
NASA GSFC

Fig. 56.1 Maps of the ozone concentrations over Antarctica, made using data collected by the Nimbus-7 weather satellite.

Questions

1 a What is ozone?
b Describe one harmful effect of ozone near ground level.
c Explain why ozone high in the atmosphere is important to living things.

2 Suggest explanations for each of the following facts:
a Even if everyone stopped using CFCs immediately, the amount of ozone in the ozone layer would continue to decrease for many years.
b People with naturally light-coloured skin are more likely to get skin cancer than people with naturally dark-coloured skin.
c Although there has been a general increase in the incidence of skin cancer in recent years, this increase has been especially large in Australia.

3 A survey carried out in England in 1997 showed that most people believed that global warming and the hole in the ozone layer are the same thing.

Write an explanation, which could be understood by a person who has had little or no science education, to help them to understand that global warming and the hole in the ozone layer are really very different, with different causes.

You may like to use diagrams to make your explanation clearer.

4 Use Figure 56.1 to answer these questions.
a In which month were both of these images taken? Suggest why it is important to compare images taken at similar times of year, in order to determine whether the amount of ozone in the Earth's atmosphere is changing.
b Describe two differences between the two images.
c Why is the term 'hole' in the ozone layer not strictly correct?

57 THE NITROGEN CYCLE

Living things need nitrogen for making proteins. Nitrogen is cycled within an ecosystem.

Several elements are cycled around ecosystems

The molecules from which living organisms are made contain many different elements. These include hydrogen, carbon, oxygen, nitrogen and phosphorus. Molecules containing atoms of these elements are made by one organism, broken down and remade into something different, broken down again, and so on. They are passed from one organism to another. A particular atom will be used over and over again, perhaps moving between living things, the air, the soil and water. Who knows where *your* atoms have been?

Carbon is needed for almost every biological molecule. It is found in carbohydrates, proteins, fats and many other substances. The way in which carbon cycles around an ecosystem is described in Topic 53.

Phosphorus is needed to make several very important substances in all living things. One is the genetic material, DNA. Another is ATP, the energy-rich molecule made by respiration.

Nitrogen, too, is needed for making DNA. It is also a component of all proteins.

Nitrogen gas cannot be used by plants or animals

All living things need nitrogen. There is a lot of nitrogen in the air. About 79% of the air is nitrogen gas. So it looks as though there should be no problem. Living things could get nitrogen from the air.

But this is not possible. The molecules of nitrogen gas, N_2, are made up of two nitrogen atoms held together by three strong covalent bonds. These molecules are very stable. They will not easily react with other substances. When you breathe in air, the nitrogen molecules in the air go into your body, travel round in your blood, and are breathed out again. They do not react inside you. They are no use to you at all.

Before plants and animals can use nitrogen, it must be changed into a more reactive form. Plants can use nitrogen in the form of nitrates, NO_3^-, or ammonium salts, NH_4^+. Animals can only use nitrogen in the form of organic compounds, such as proteins. The changing of nitrogen gas into a more reactive form is called **nitrogen fixation**.

Fig. 57.1 The nitrogen cycle

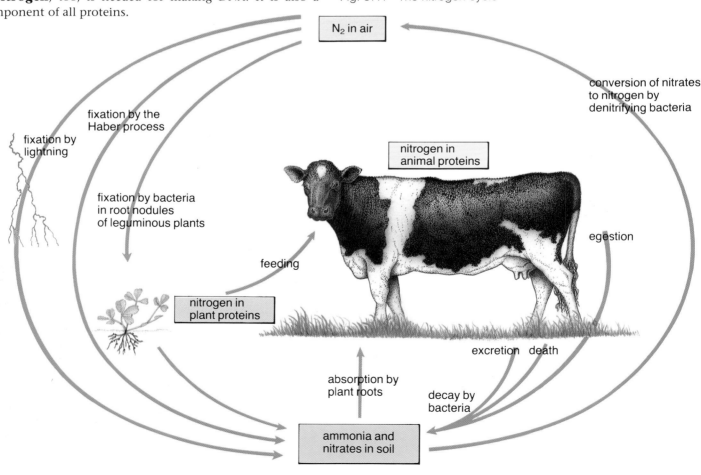

Nitrogen fixation can be carried out by some bacteria

There are several ways in which nitrogen gas from the air can be changed into nitrate or ammonium ions.

- **Lightning** provides a tremendous burst of energy as it rushes through the air. The energy can split apart the two atoms in a nitrogen molecule. Each atom can then react with oxygen in the air to form nitrogen oxides. These dissolve in rain droplets and fall to the ground. Here, they can combine with other substances to form nitrates.
- **The chemical industry** makes ammonia by combining nitrogen and hydrogen. This is called the Haber process. The ammonia is used for making fertilisers, which farmers and gardeners put on the soil.
- **Nitrogen-fixing bacteria** are able to make nitrogen gas combine with hydrogen and other elements. Some nitrogen-fixing bacteria live free in the soil. But many live in little swellings, or nodules, on the roots of some plants. Both the bacteria and the plants benefit from this arrangement. The bacteria get carbohydrates and other substances which the plant makes by photosynthesis. The plant gets nitrogen compounds which it can use for making proteins. This sort of close relationship between two different kinds of organisms, from which both of them benefit, is called **mutualism**.

Fertilisers can cause eutrophication

Farmers use fertilisers to help their crops to grow better and get higher yields. This means that they can grow more food on a smaller area of land than if they did not use fertilisers. Using fertilisers helps to keep food prices down.

Many farmers use inorganic fertilisers. These are produced by the chemical industry. They often contain three minerals that are especially important to plants – nitrogen (in the form of nitrates), phosphorus (in the form of phosphates) and potassium. So they are called NPK fertilisers (K is the symbol for potassium). Other farmers use organic fertilisers, such as waste from farm animals.

Whichever kind of fertiliser is used, it is important that the farmer makes sure that the fertiliser gets used by the crop it is intended for, and does not get wasted. If it is wasted, then not only does the farmer waste money, but the fertiliser may pollute streams, rivers and lakes. This happens because if the crop does not take up the fertiliser quite quickly, and it rains, then the rain may wash or **leach** the fertiliser from the soil and into a water course.

When nitrate and phosphate ions enter a water course, they can be used by algae and water plants. Often, the algae start to grow very fast. They may cause an **algal bloom**, where the water goes thick and green, or where its surface is covered by a thick blanket of green algae. Some of these algae produce poisons or **toxins**, which can kill animals that drink the water.

Eventually, the algae die. Their bodies provide food for bacteria. The population of bacteria increases rapidly. The bacteria respire and use up oxygen, so the amount of oxygen in the water decreases. There may not be enough oxygen for animals such as fish, so the fish either swim away to a different, unpolluted part of the water course, or they die.

This sequence of events is called **eutrophication**. Eutrophication can also be caused by other pollutants that provide food for bacteria. Untreated **sewage**, for example, might do this. Sewage does not usually contain nitrates, but it may contain phosphates, because some detergents contain phosphates, and phosphates are also used in some manufacturing industries. Untreated sewage also contains many organic molecules that provide food for bacteria.

Bacteria convert protein to ammonium or nitrate

Once nitrogen has been fixed and is in the form of ammonium salts or nitrates, plants can take it up through their roots. They combine the nitrogen compounds with molecules which have been made in photosynthesis, and make proteins. Animals get their proteins by eating plants or other animals.

The nitrogen from these proteins is eventually returned to the soil. When a plant or animal dies, decomposers, including **decay bacteria**, secrete enzymes onto their bodies. The proteins are broken down into amino acids and eventually to **ammonia**. This also happens to any waste material containing nitrogen, such as urine.

Other bacteria in the soil, called **nitrifying bacteria**, change the ammonia into nitrates. The nitrates can be taken up by plants through their roots, and used to make proteins again.

Questions

1 Explain why high levels of nitrates and phosphates in a river pose a threat to aquatic animals.
2 What are the major sources of nitrate and phosphate pollution in Britain?
3 Discuss possible ways of reducing:
  a the amount of nitrate
  b the amount of phosphate, which is discarded into rivers and the sea. (Remember that even environmentally-aware people have to make a living, and that economic incentives can have considerable effects.)

DID YOU KNOW?

Although many people think that inorganic fertilisers cause most nitrate pollution, in fact organic fertilisers are even more likely to cause this kind of pollution if they are not used carefully. And a high proportion of the nitrate leached into rivers comes from nitrates that have been naturally fixed by bacteria in the soil.

Farming provides most of our food

The first humans were hunter-gatherers. They found food wherever they could, eating naturally-occurring fruits, roots and leaves, and killing wild animals for meat and skins. Now very few people live like this. Most of us rely on farming to provide our food.

Farming means growing crops and rearing animals for food. Farming has greatly changed the environment in which we live. Natural vegetation has been cleared to make room for crop growing. Instead of many different kinds of plants and animals living in an area, we have just a few. Where there might have been woodland containing many different species of plants, there might now be a field of wheat. Where there might have been a forest containing many different species of animals, there might now be grassland

Fig. 58.1 A field of ripening wheat. A big area of just one kind of plant is sometimes called a monoculture. Monocultures provide us with plenty of food, but they greatly reduce the variety of animals and plants which live in the area. Also, the populations of pests which feed on the growing wheat can become very big, as they have so much food available.

grazed by sheep.

Left to itself, the land would go back to its wild state. If we stopped farming in Britain, much of the land would gradually become forest again. It might look wonderful, but it would not be able to provide us with much food. To support the huge numbers of people on Earth, farming is essential. Farming can support far more people on a given area of land than hunting and gathering can.

Farming changes ecosystems

Since the middle of the twentieth century, farming has become increasingly **intensive**. This means that farmers have been trying to produce more and more food from a given area of land. Governments have encouraged them to do this. Intensive farming produces a lot of food more cheaply than older methods of farming.

But intensive farming can cause problems. Many people are concerned about intensive egg production, for example, because they do not like the idea of hens being kept in small spaces with little room to move around. People are becoming more prepared to pay more for free-range eggs rather than buy cheaper intensively-produced eggs.

Intensive crop production can cause problems, too. To get the most crops from a field, a farmer must add fertilisers to the soil. These may get into streams and rivers, damaging the ecosystems there (Topic 57). The farmer must spray the crop with insecticides to kill pests which might damage the crop, probably killing other harmless animals too. The farmer must use heavy machinery to plough, plant, tend and harvest the crop. This can damage the soil by compacting it. The farmer must clear the land completely of all other plants before planting the crops. If the soil lies for a long time with no plants on it, it may erode (Topic 54).

In recent years there has been an increasing awareness of how farming may damage ecosystems. Many farmers are now taking greater care of their land. Hedges, which were torn out in the 1950s, are being replanted, providing habitats for wild plants and animals. Trees are being planted in the corners of fields. Less fertiliser is being used in many areas of the country. The use of insecticides and fungicides is being reduced. Some farms have become **organic**. This means that they do not use any artificial fertilisers or insecticides in growing crops or rearing meat. Some people like to buy food produced in this way, even though it costs much more than other food.

Questions

1 a What is meant by **intensive farming**?

b List four ways in which intensive farming may damage the environment.

c Briefly discuss ways in which this damage can be reduced, bearing in mind that we must go on producing food in Britain.

d What is meant by **organic farming**? Why do organically-produced vegetables cost more than other vegetables?

Pesticides are used to increase yields from crops

Farmers and horticulturalists have to make sure that their crops are not too badly damaged by pests. Pests such as insects or fungi may feed on a growing crop. This can reduce yields of crops such as cereals. It can spoil the appearance of plants being grown for decorative purposes, such as house plants. It can spoil the appearance and keeping qualities of fruit and vegetables.

Chemicals can be sprayed onto the crops to kill pests. These chemicals are called **pesticides**. They are expensive to make and to buy, so growers do not use them unless the increased income they will get (because of a better yield and quality of their crop) is likely to be greater than the expense of the pesticide.

Bioaccumulation

There are many different kinds of pesticides. Some pesticides are **broad-spectrum** pesticides. This means that they kill many different kinds of organisms. For example, a broad-spectrum insecticide kills not only harmful insects such as aphids, but also useful ones such as predatory beetles and hoverflies, which feed on aphids. It is better if a **specific** insecticide can be used, which is designed to kill just the pest and not other organisms. As you can imagine, it is not easy for chemists to develop and make specific insecticides, so they are not available for all pests and they are usually even more expensive than broad-spectrum ones.

Some pesticides are **biodegradable**. This means that they are broken down quite quickly, usually by bacteria and other microorganisms. But others are not broken down easily. They are said to be **persistent**.

In the 1940s to 1960s, a persistent, broad-spectrum pesticide called **DDT** was widely used to kill insect pests. At the time, people did not realise the problems it was causing. But in the 1960s some scientists began to understand that DDT was being passed along food chains and killing organisms near the end of the chain. For example, a small amount of DDT might be absorbed by an insect, which might then be eaten by a small bird. The small bird would eat many insects in its life-time, so it might eat quite large amounts of DDT. Because DDT is persistent, it did not break down, but just accumulated in the bird's body. This small bird might then be eaten by a larger bird, such as a peregrine. Once again, the peregrine would eat lots of small birds, so it could end up with very large amounts of DDT in its body. This process is called **bioaccumulation**. Between 1955 and 1960, the number of breeding pairs of peregrines in Britain fell from around 1000 to less than 500. This happened because DDT stopped the shells of their eggs from forming properly, so that fewer young birds were successfully hatched.

The use of DDT and other broad-spectrum, persistent pesticides is now banned in developed countries. But DDT is still widely used in many tropical countries, where it is the only affordable way of keeping mosquito populations under control. Mosquitoes carry the disease malaria, from which hundreds of thousands of people die every year.

Integrated pest management reduces the use of pesticides

Most farmers and horticulturalists would very much like to reduce their use of pesticides, if only they could find other ways of keeping pest numbers under control. For some crops, plans called **integrated pest management systems** have been designed. IPMs do still make use of pesticides, but they use other methods as well, so that the amount of pesticide, and the number of times it has to be applied, can be kept to a minimum.

IPMs may include a technique called **biological control**. This uses predators or parasites to keep down the numbers of pests. For example, if aphids are causing problems on some ornamental plants growing in a glasshouse, ladybirds can be introduced to feed on the aphids. Farmers can leave a strip of uncultivated ground around the edge of their fields, or even strips through the middle of a field, in which ladybirds and other useful insects can breed. These useful insects may help to keep down the numbers of pests on the crop growing in the rest of the field. Biological control does not get rid of the pests completely, but it may be able to keep their numbers quite low. Care has to be taken, however, when introducing a predator to eat the pests, that the predator itself does not become a pest!

IPM schemes may also involve **crop rotation**. Most pests are quite specific to a particular crop – if that crop is not there, then the pest disappears. So pest populations are most likely to build up to very high levels if the same crop is grown over a wide area, and if the same crop is grown year after year. Crop rotation involves growing a different crop in a particular field each year – perhaps four different crops in four years – before going back to the first crop again. So, for example, wheat might be grown in one year. The wheat crop might get infected with a fungus called rust, which spoils the grains. But the infection is not likely to be very heavy, because it will take a while for enough rust spores to spread around the crop to infect very much of it. The next year, something different is grown, such as potatoes. The rust that infects wheat cannot grow on potatoes, so its population drops back to almost nothing. By the time wheat is grown again, the rust will have to start all over again from scratch.

Crop rotation not only helps to keep pest populations low, but also means that less fertiliser can be used. Farmers often include a nitrogen-fixing crop, such as beans or clover, as part of a rotation. These crops have root nodules containing **nitrogen-fixing** bacteria (Topic 57). When the crop is harvested, the roots are left behind and ploughed into the soil. They add nitrates to the soil. So the farmer may not need to add nitrogen-containing fertiliser to the soil for the next crop.

Questions

1. Explain why persistent pesticides are more harmful to the environment than biodegradable ones.
2. How can crop rotation help to reduce the amount of pesticides that are used?

59 MANAGING ECOSYSTEMS: FISHING

We use the sea as a source of food.

The North Sea is a rich fishing area

Long before humans learned to domesticate animals and grow crops, they must have caught fish for food. When we catch fish from the sea, we are still acting as hunter-gatherers. We are predators, catching prey. Not until recently have fish been farmed in a carefully managed way. People have simply assumed that the sea was full of fish, there for the taking.

The North Sea is a particularly rich fishing area. The sea is relatively shallow and rich in nutrients. Fish caught in the North Sea include cod, haddock, herring, plaice and mackerel. All of the European countries with North Sea coastlines fish in the North Sea. They have been doing so for centuries.

Until the middle of the twentieth century, people believed that we could go on taking as many fish as we could catch from the North Sea, without doing any harm to their populations. In 1883, the well-respected scientist Thomas Huxley said, 'I believe that ... the cod fishery, the herring fishery and the mackerel fishery are inexhaustible. The multitude of these fishes is so inconceivably great that the number we catch is relatively insignificant.'

We know now that this is not true. Since the Second World War, the amount of fish caught in the North Sea has increased so much that some populations have become dangerously small. Herring stocks dropped so much that a complete ban on herring fishing had to be imposed for several years. If we wish to keep on harvesting fish from the sea, we must understand what we are doing and try to manage the ecosystem carefully.

The North Sea cod fishery

One of the most important species of fish caught in the North Sea is **cod**. Cod are found throughout the North Sea. They live in shoals and are active hunters, feeding on other fish, such as herring, and on squid. Cod spawn in early spring. The young fish grow quickly, reaching 8 cm in length when they are 6 months old. By the end of their second year, they are 25–35 cm long. Cod do not become adult and begin to breed until they are about 3 or 4 years old, by which time they are about 50 cm long.

Figure 59.3 shows the amount of cod caught in the North Sea each year from 1905 to 1985. Figure 59.4 shows the percentage of the fish population killed by fishing between 1964 and 1986. By the 1980s, it was becoming obvious that we could not go on and on increasing our catches of cod in this way. We were destroying the cod population. Something had to be done.

Fig. 59.1 A cod fish, *Gatus morhua*

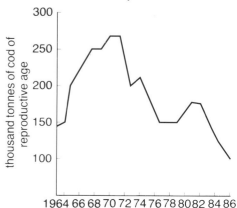

Fig. 59.2 A trawler off the west coast of Scotland

Fig. 59.3

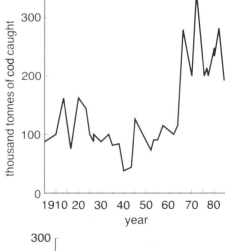

Fig. 59.4

(Source: Nature Conservancy Council)

Fig. 59.5

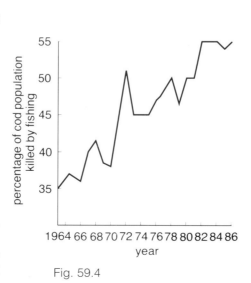

Managing the cod fishery

What can be done to limit the damage we are doing to the size of the cod population in the North Sea?

Catch fewer fish The obvious way of allowing cod populations to recover is to stop catching cod. But to put a total ban on cod fishing would be very hard on the thousands of people who make a living from catching, preparing and selling cod. Instead, a **quota** system has been introduced. All the countries involved in fishing cod in the North Sea get together to decide how much cod they can safely catch. New quotas are set each year, depending on estimates of the size of the cod population at that time.

But this is not a perfect solution. It is very difficult to make accurate estimates of the number of cod in the sea. The people who catch the fish are not happy with the quota system, especially if the amount of fish they are allowed to catch suddenly drops from one year to the next. The quota system also needs policing, to check that the amount of cod caught does not exceed the quota. This costs money.

Another problem with the quota system is that people trying to catch one kind of fish often accidentally catch large numbers of another kind. If they accidentally catch a lot of cod and go over their cod quota, they will throw the cod back into the sea. But these fish will probably still die.

Catch only bigger fish Cod do not begin to breed until they are 3 to 4 years old. If fish are caught and killed before they reach breeding age, then the reproductive rate of the population is reduced. So the size of the population falls. Catching big, fully-grown fish does not have such a big effect on the reproductive rate.

To limit the numbers of young fish being caught, a limit has been put on the size of the mesh in the nets which are used for fishing in the North Sea. At the moment, the smallest mesh size which can be used is 90 mm.

This is smaller than it ought to be for cod. Many cod caught in these nets will be below breeding age. A good mesh size for cod would be 150 mm. But we do not fish just for cod. In many areas of the North Sea, a catch will be made up of other species, such as haddock and whiting, as well as cod. A mesh size of 150 mm would be too big to allow these smaller types of fish to be caught.

Fig. 59.6   A salmon fish farm on Loch Torridon in western Scotland. The salmon are grown in cages in the clear sea water in the loch.

Fish farming allows more accurate management of fish populations

One way of making sure that we do not destroy fish populations is to **farm** fish as we farm cattle or sheep. Fish farming was a rapidly growing industry during the 1980s, especially on the west coasts of Scotland and Ireland.

Not many fish species are suitable for fish farming. Not all fish will survive and grow well in the underwater cages which are used. Farming fish is expensive, so the fish produced must be able to command a high price. For these reasons, the main fish farmed at the moment are **salmon**.

Salmon farming does help to provide plenty of fish to eat without damaging wild salmon populations. But it is causing some problems, too. The main one of these is pollution. Many salmon fish farms are in sea lochs, so any pollutants from the farms tend to get trapped in the waters of the loch.

What sort of pollutants are produced by fish farming? Faeces from the fish and any uneaten food sink to the bottom of the loch. This is rather like dumping untreated sewage in a river. Bacteria thrive on the nutrients, using up oxygen, so that animal life at the bottom of the loch cannot survive.

Another kind of pollution comes from chemicals used to kill parasites and pathogens which might damage the salmon. Salmon kept in nets are more likely to suffer from diseases and parasites than wild salmon. These chemicals spread out from the fish farm into other areas of the loch, where they may kill other species of animals.

One important parasite of farmed salmon is a **fish louse**. This lives on the outside of the fish, scraping away at its skin. The salmon are treated with a chemical called Dichlorvos to kill the lice. This chemical is poisonous to crustaceans like lobsters and to fish. It can also be dangerous to humans in large quantities. But recently it has been found that a small fish, called a goldsinny, will eat the lice on the salmon. By caging some of these fish with the caged salmon, the salmon can be kept louse-free without using harmful chemicals. This is an example of **biological control**.

Question

1   In January 1988, the cod quota allowed per fishing boat was 3 tonnes per month. In February, it was halved to 1.5 tonnes. Put yourself into the position of each of the following people, and discuss how you might feel about this.

   a a person who earns their living by cod fishing

   b a shopper wanting to buy cod

   c a fishmonger

   d a person fishing in the year 2000

60 POPULATION GROWTH

The growth of populations is limited by the availability of resources and by other factors such as disease.

The growth of a population depends on its birth and death rates

The size of a population is increased when new individuals migrate into it or when new individuals are born. In most populations, the birth of new organisms is much the most important of these two events. The rate at which new organisms are born is called the **birth rate** of the population.

The size of a population is decreased when individuals emigrate from it or when they die. The rate at which organisms die is called the **death rate**.

Common sense tells you that if the birth rate is greater than the death rate, the population will increase. If the death rate is greater than the birth rate, the population will decrease. If the birth rate and the death rate are equal, the population remains the same size.

Environmental factors limit population growth

The single-celled fungus **yeast** is often used in experiments to see how populations grow. Figure 60.1 shows what happens if a few yeast cells are put into a flask of warm, well-aerated broth. The yeast has everything it needs for survival. The cells multiply quickly and the population grows rapidly. The only thing limiting the rate of growth is the speed at which the yeast can reproduce.

But eventually the growth in the yeast population begins to slow down. There are several possible reasons for this. Food may begin to run out, or the yeast may produce so much alcohol that it poisons itself. The curve levels off.

Similar patterns can be seen in populations of other organisms. If rabbits are introduced onto an island, their population grows rapidly at first. The birth rate is much faster than the death rate. There is plenty of food and plenty of space for making burrows. But, as the population gets larger, food and living space may become scarce. The rabbits have to **compete** for these scarce resources. Not all of them will manage to get enough food, or find a place to breed. So the birth rate goes down and the death rate goes up. The population levels off.

The populations of most organisms stay roughly constant. They may go up and down a bit from year to year, but the average population size tends to stay about the same. If a population gets too large, then various factors come into play which tend to reduce its birth rate or increase its death rate.

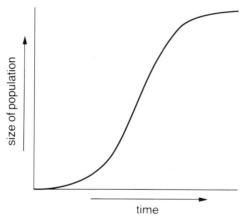

Fig. 60.1 If a few yeast cells are added to some broth, their population grows like this.

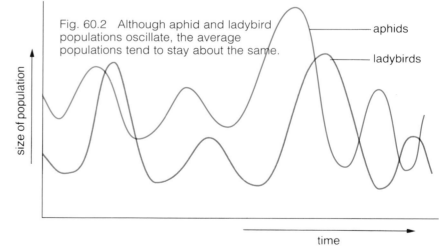

Fig. 60.2 Although aphid and ladybird populations oscillate, the average populations tend to stay about the same.

aphids

ladybirds

Predator populations are often limited by availability of prey

It is not easy to find out exactly what controls the size of a particular population, because there are usually lots of different factors involved which are difficult to sort out. But sometimes at least some of the factors seem clear. In predator populations, for example, it is often found that the size of the prey population is the main factor in deciding their size.

An example of this is the relationship between ladybird and aphid (greenfly) populations. Ladybirds are predators which feed on aphids. In a year when there are a lot of aphids, the ladybird population rises rapidly. The large numbers of ladybirds eat large numbers of aphids, increasing the aphids' death rate and reducing the aphid population. So now the ladybirds have less food. Their population will begin to decrease. This allows the aphid population to increase, which allows the ladybird population to increase, and so on. The sizes of the two populations go up and down, or **oscillate** (Figure 60.2).

The human population is rising fast

Figure 60.3 shows how the size of the human population has grown. It is estimated that 10 000 years ago, there were no more than 10 million humans on the Earth. This population remained fairly constant until quite recently. But in the last thousand years or so, the human population has been rising rapidly, and the rate of rise has been getting faster and faster. In 1950, the world population was about 2.5 thousand million people. By 1987, it was around 5 thousand million. It is predicted that by 2025 there will be 8.5 thousand million people on the Earth.

Why is this happening? Up until about 1000 years ago, death rates were so high that human populations hardly increased at all. People died from lack of food and from disease. Infant mortality rates were very high. But as agricultural methods have improved and medicine has enabled many diseases to be successfully treated, death rates are much lower. More people stay alive long enough to reproduce. Populations have risen rapidly.

Population growth cannot go on for ever

It is obvious that this growth cannot go on for ever. But what is going to halt it? Either birth rates must fall or death rates must rise. Exactly what will cause this to happen is not clear. Famine, disease or war might happen on such a huge scale that the world population will plummet. But no-one would wish for this to happen. It would be much better if birth rates were to fall.

This is already happening in some countries. It is found that, as countries become industrialised, both birth rates and death rates fall. Death rates fall first, so for a while the population increases. But then birth rates fall even more, so the population begins to decline. No-one is quite sure why birth rates fall like this, but it has happened in many countries, such as Japan, Germany and Britain.

This pattern may be repeated in other, less industrialised, countries as they become more industrialised. But it will take a long time. In many

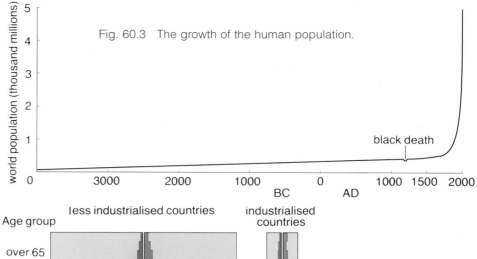

Fig. 60.3 The growth of the human population.

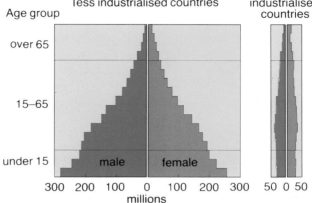

Fig. 60.4 Age distribution pyramids. The large numbers of young people in less industrialise countries show that their populations are still growing. In industrialised countries, populations are more stable.

Fig. 60.5 Birth control programmes in Bangladesh include the distribution of contraceptive pills.

countries, birth control programmes have been introduced to try to lower the birth rate. They have often been very successful. Before 1973, Mexico had a birth rate of 45 births per year for every 1000 people in the population. Then a birth control programme was introduced. Now the birth rate is 31 births per year for every 1000 people in the population. But how much of this drop is due to the programme, and how much to other, unknown, factors, will never be known.

Even with all these hopeful signs of falling birth rates, the human population will still go on growing rapidly for many decades. Our huge numbers are damaging the Earth, as we deplete its resources and pollute our environment. We must do what we can to bring population growth under control.

Questions

1 The table shows the amounts of fertiliser used in six different parts of the world for three different periods between 1964 and 1987.

Average amount of fertiliser used annually (millions of tonnes)			
	1964–67	1974–77	1984–87
South America	1.5	3.5	5.0
Africa	2.0	3.0	4.0
Asia	4.5	16.5	40.0
North and Central America	12.0	21.5	22.5
Europe	18.0	28.0	32.0

a Show this information as a graph. There are several ways in which you could do this. Choose a method which is easy for people to understand and which looks attractive.

b Which area used the most fertiliser during this period?

c Work out the percentage increase in fertiliser use by each of the five areas, between 1964–67 and 1984–87. (If you are not sure how to do this, ask for help.)

d Which area has the greatest percentage increase in fertiliser use during this period?

Two ions contained in many fertilisers are nitrate and phosphate. Both of these ions are often in short supply in the soil, and adding them to the soil can increase the growth of plants.

e Why does adding (i) nitrate and (ii) phosphate increase the growth of plants?

f Discuss how the use of nitrate and phosphate fertilisers can damage the environment.

2 Read the passage below, and then answer the questions which follow.

a Explain the meaning of the following words:
pesticide
resistant
natural predator
biological control
oscillate.

b Give four disadvantages of using chemicals to control pests.

c Name the genus of one biological control organism. Which pest does it control, and how?

d After introducing a biological control organism into a glasshouse, a grower may not have to reintroduce it for a long time. Why is this?

e At the moment, the use of biological control organisms is mostly restricted to glasshouses. They have not proved very successful against pests of crops growing outside. Discuss the possible reasons for this.

3 To answer this question, you will need to look at the graphs and other information in Topic 59.
Figure 59.3 shows the amount of cod caught each year between 1905 and 1980.

a In which year was the greatest mass of cod caught?

b Suggest an explanation for the small amount of cod caught between 1940 and 1945.
Figure 59.4 shows the **fishing mortality** between 1964 and 1986.

c Suggest what is meant by 'fishing mortality'.

d How do you think this information might have been collected and worked out?
Figure 59.5 shows the amount of **spawning stock** in the North Sea between 1964 and 1986.

e What is meant by 'spawning stock'?

f What would happen to the cod population if the spawning stock continued to follow the pattern shown by this graph?

g Discuss the possible solutions which could allow us to continue harvesting cod from the North Sea, without damaging the fish stocks.

Biological control in glasshouses

A glasshouse is a warm, sheltered environment in which plants grow well. Unfortunately, these conditions are also appreciated by many pests which live on the plants. Aphids (such as greenfly and blackfly), mealy bugs, whitefly and red spider mites, are important pests of glasshouse plants. For a grower who makes his or her living from producing crops under glass, they can pose a serious threat.

One way of destroying these pests is to spray them with pesticides. These contain chemicals which are poisonous to the pest. However, this is not a perfect solution to the problem. Some pests, such as mealy bugs are very resistant to pesticides, and so are

difficult to kill. The chemicals may also kill other harmless organisms, such as bees which pollinate the plants or ladybirds which eat greenfly. The effect of the pesticide does not last long, so they have to be reapplied many times. Many people do not like the idea of eating tomatoes or lettuces which have been sprayed with chemicals.

Another way of winning the battle against the pests is to use a natural predator. Several firms now breed and sell natural enemies for important glasshouse pests. *Aphidoletes* is a midge whose larvae are fierce predators, attacking aphids. *Cryptolaemus* is a type of ladybird which attacks mealy bugs. *Encarsia* is a tiny wasp, which lays its eggs inside

whitefly; the larvae which hatch out eat the whitefly from inside their bodies. *Phytoseiulus* is a tiny red mite which eats the eggs and adults of red spider mites.

The use of these natural predators against pests is called biological control. The predators are introduced into the infected glasshouse, where they feed on their prey and multiply. As the prey population goes down, so does the predator population. But it is unlikely that either population will be completely wiped out straight away. The predator and prey populations oscillate at a very low level.

HEALTH AND DISEASE

61 PATHOGENS

Some diseases are caused by other living organisms invading our bodies. These organisms are called pathogens.

A pathogen is an organism which causes disease

Many human diseases are caused by other living organisms. These disease-causing organisms are called **pathogens**. A few protoctista and fungi are pathogens. Several kinds of bacteria are pathogens. Viruses are also pathogens.

Pathogenic organisms live inside the human body. They may destroy cells. They may release harmful substances, called **toxins**, into your body. Both of these activities can make you ill.

protein

DNA

Fig. 61.1 A virus. Viruses are not made of cells. They are much smaller than any living cell. They are made up of a coil of DNA or RNA, surrounded by a protein coat. They are not able to reproduce unless they are inside a living cell.

Pathogens have many methods of entering your body

Before a pathogen can make you ill, it must get into your body. Different pathogens get in in different ways.

Some pathogens get in through your **skin**. The virus which causes warts can get in through undamaged skin. But most pathogens can only get through skin if it is cut. The bacterium which causes tetanus, for example, gets into your blood through cuts and grazes.

Other pathogens get in through your **digestive system**. The bacteria which cause food poisoning, such as *Salmonella*, are taken into your digestive system when you eat food in which they are growing. Cholera bacteria and poliomyelitis viruses may be swallowed if you drink contaminated water.

Pathogens can enter through your **respiratory system**. Cold and influenza viruses get into you in this way. When someone sneezes, blows their nose, or just breathes out, tiny droplets of moisture float into the air. They may contain these viruses. If you breathe these droplets in, you may get infected too.

Some pathogens enter through the **reproductive system**. The AIDS virus can be passed from one person to another during sexual intercourse. Some bacterial diseases, such as gonorrheoa, are also transmitted in this way.

Some pathogens rely on **vectors** to transfer them from one organism to another. A vector is an organism which carries a pathogen from one animal to another. For example, the protoctistan which causes malaria lives inside human red blood cells. An infected person may be bitten by a mosquito. The mosquito sucks blood and so takes the malaria

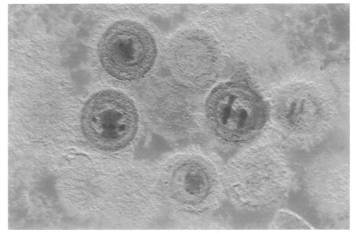

Fig. 61.2 Viruses which cause herpes (cold sores), magnified about 166 000 times.

Fig. 61.3 A male mosquito *Anopheles gambiae*. This species of mosquito carries the malarial parasite *Plasmodium* in its saliva. Only females carry the parasite, because only they feed on blood.

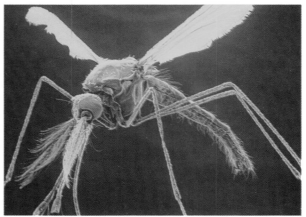

protoctistan into its body. The protoctistan lives in the mosquito's salivary glands. When the mosquito bites another person, it injects some of its saliva into the wound to make the blood flow more easily. It also injects the malarial organism, infecting the second person with malaria. The mosquito is a vector.

Pathogens reproduce inside the body

Once a pathogen has entered your body, it may begin to reproduce.

Viruses reproduce inside your cells. They take over the cell, and instruct it to make new viruses, using chemicals from your own cytoplasm and nucleus. After a while, the new viruses burst out, ready to infect other cells.

Bacteria usually reproduce outside cells, although some reproduce inside them. Pathogenic bacteria feed on organic material inside your body. They may be able to absorb some material directly from your body fluids such as blood. They may also secrete enzymes which will digest parts of your cells so that they can absorb food from them. The damage the bacteria do to your cells can make you ill. The bacteria may also release toxins into your body, which can also make you ill.

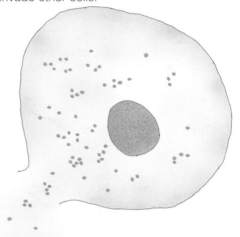

Fig. 61.5 Viruses reproduce inside living cells. They use energy and materials from the cell, and this may kill it. The new viruses burst out of the cell, and can then invade other cells.

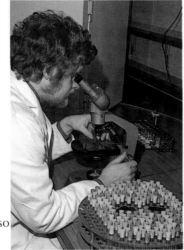

Fig. 61.4 People working in pathology labs inspect blood and other tissue samples for signs of disease. Here, blood is being investigated for any abnormalities in the red blood cells, such as the presence of the malarial parasite.

Questions

1 a Give three examples of diseases caused by viruses.

b Give three examples of diseases caused by bacteria.

2 a Name two pathogens which may enter your body through your respiratory system.

b What features of your respiratory system cut down the number of pathogens which get into your body?

c Why are smokers more likely to suffer from respiratory infections than non-smokers?

3 Read the passage on the right, and then answer the questions which follow.

a What is meant by the term 'vector'?

b Why is bubonic plague unlikely to occur in Europe now?

c Suggest measures which could be taken to control the spread of

The Black Death

In the fourteenth century, the Black Death destroyed one quarter of the human population of Europe. The Black Death was the disease bubonic plague. It is caused by a bacterium, *Yersinia pestis*. The bacterium does not normally pass directly from one human to another, but is carried by a vector. The vectors are rat fleas, especially fleas from the black rat.

When an infected rat flea bites a human, the plague bacterium travels in the blood to a lymph node. Here, it reproduces, causing the node to form a swelling or bubo. The swelling may become black, which is how the disease got its name. The infection may spread into the blood, where the bacteria reproduce rapidly, causing death.

Better living conditions and control of rats have made this disease very rare in Europe now. But bubonic plague does still occur in some parts of the world. In 1896, for example, there was an epidemic of bubonic plague in India. Over 8 million people died from the plague during the following fifteen years.

bubonic plague in other countries.

d Find out more about the Black Death in Britain. History books may help.

i How did people think the disease spread?

ii What did they do to try to prevent themselves and their families from getting the disease?

iii How did the disease affect the population of individual villages and towns?

iv Were these effects long-lasting?

Table 62.1   *How the body prevents pathogens from entering*

Method of entry	Examples	Defence mechanisms
Skin	Wart virus	Very few pathogens can get in through undamaged skin. Blood clotting prevents entry of pathogens after skin has been cut. A chemical called lysozyme is present in tears, and kills bacteria on the surface of the eye.
Digestive system	Salmonella	Food which is badly affected by bacteria may taste or smell 'off', so we find it distasteful. It may make us vomit, so any pathogens in it are removed from the body. Hydrochloric acid in the stomach kills many bacteria in food.
Respiratory system	Cold and flu viruses	Cilia and mucus in the nasal passages, trachea and bronchi help to trap dust particles and bacteria, so they do not reach the lungs. White cells patrol the surfaces of the alveoli.
Reproductive system	Gonorrhoea	We have few natural defences against this route of infection.
Vectors	Malaria	We have few natural defences against this route of infection.

White cells fight against disease

The human body is designed to prevent too many bacteria or viruses from getting in and reproducing. Table 62.1 shows some of the ways in which entry is prevented.

If pathogens do manage to get into your body, then your **immune system** goes into action. The most important cells in your immune system are the **white blood cells**. They can travel around in the blood and some can crawl around in every part of you. They are on constant patrol for invading bacteria and viruses.

The immune response kills most invaders

Despite your natural defences against the entry of pathogenic bacteria and viruses, they *do* get into you all the time. Usually, though, your immune system kills them before they have a chance to do much damage.

Some of your white cells have the job of recognising any foreign cells inside you. They do this by looking for chemicals, called **antigens**, on the surfaces of cells. Your white cells know all your own antigens. If they meet any different ones, they recognise that these are foreign, and should not be there.

If a white cell finds a foreign antigen, the white cell multiplies rapidly. The new white cells produce chemicals to kill the foreign cells. These chemicals are called **antibodies**. They can travel around in your blood and get virtually everywhere in your body. Wherever the foreign invaders are, the antibodies will reach and kill them.

Some white cells have a different way of dealing with foreign cells. They flow round them and take them into their cytoplasm. Here, they digest them. This is called **phagocytosis**. If the white cells do this to a bacterium, they may also break down the antigens on the bacterium's surface. The white cells then display these antigens on their own surface, showing them to other white cells which then learn to look out for, and deal with, these particular kinds of bacteria.

Viruses are dealt with in a similar way to bacteria. They are more of a problem because they are mostly *inside* your own cells. If they lie low, your immune system may not know that they are there. But if they start reproducing, the cell in which they are multiplying may have some of the viral antigens on its surface. Your white cells recognise these antigens as foreign, and will kill the whole cell, viruses included.

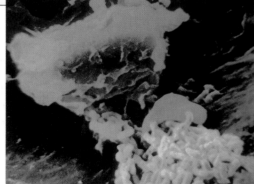

Fig. 62.1
A white cell attacking bacteria at the site of a skin infection. This picture was taken with a scanning electron microscope.

Fig. 62.2

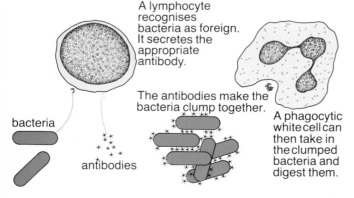

A lymphocyte recognises bacteria as foreign. It secretes the appropriate antibody.

The antibodies make the bacteria clump together.

A phagocytic white cell can then take in the clumped bacteria and digest them.

bacteria

antibodies

Producing antibodies takes time

The odd bacterium or virus getting into your body is not much of a problem. Scavenging white cells will probably get rid of it by phagocytosis before it does any damage. But imagine a whole collection of flu viruses getting into your lungs. The patrolling white cells will not be able to deal with these quickly enough to prevent them reproducing inside your body cells.

Once the viruses begin to take over large numbers of your cells, you feel ill. Your nose runs, you may have a sore throat and cough, you have a temperature and generally feel awful. For a while, the viruses win the battle.

But while you are feeling ill, your white cells are recognising the viral antigens. The ones which recognise the antigen are multiplying, producing more white cells like themselves. These white cells then manufacture and release the antibodies which will kill the viruses. This all takes time – perhaps a week before your white cells begin to get the upper hand. After this, you gradually begin to feel better as the viral infection is brought under control.

If this same kind of virus gets into you again, your white cells are able to respond more quickly. Lots of white cells already exist which can produce antibodies against the virus. The viruses will probably be destroyed before they do any damage. You are not likely to get the same sort of flu twice. You are said to be **immune** to this sort of virus.

Vaccinations give your white cells 'advance warning' about particular antigens

Having a disease is a very effective way of becoming immune to it. But it is not a very pleasant way. Some diseases, such as whooping cough, measles and poliomyelitis, are very unpleasant and can kill. To become immune to these diseases, you can be vaccinated against them.

Whooping cough is a horrible disease, in which large amounts of thick mucus make breathing difficult. About 1 in 1000 children who get whooping cough die. Whooping cough is particularly dangerous in babies.

The whooping cough vaccine contains dead whooping cough bacteria. They are injected into a child's blood. As the bacteria are dead, they cannot cause whooping cough. But they still have their antigens on them, so the child's white cells react to the bacteria as though they were alive. The white cells multiply and produce antibodies against the bacteria. If, years afterwards, the child is infected by *live* whooping cough bacteria, the white cells will be able to kill them straight away. Immunity to whooping cough lasts for many years after vaccination.

Antibiotics kill bacteria inside you

Sometimes, bacteria may get past all your defences. They may manage to reproduce so successfully inside your body that your immune system is overwhelmed. In this case, your body needs some help from outside.

Many bacterial infections can be treated with **antibiotics**. An antibiotic is a drug which kills bacteria, but does not damage your cells. Many antibiotics come from fungi. The blue mould which you sometimes see on dry bread or fruit makes one sort of antibiotic. The mould is called *Penicillium*, and the antibiotic which it produces is **penicillin**.

There are lots of different antibiotics and most bacteria can be killed by one or other of them. However, as we use more and more antibiotics, some bacteria are becoming resistant to them. So new antibiotics are constantly being sought in an effort to win the fight against bacteria.

Antibiotics are no good against viruses. At the moment, medicine can do very little about a viral infection. If you have flu, it is your own immune system which will cure you. A dose of aspirin may be able to make you *feel* a bit better, but it will not kill the viruses. Only your own cells can do that.

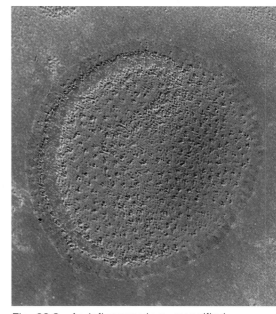

Fig. 62.3 An influenza virus, magnified about 350 000 times. The spikes sticking out from its surface help it to attach to a host cell.

Questions

1 The chart below shows the number of reported cases of diphtheria in the United Kingdom.

Year	Number of cases reported per year
pre-1940	70 000
1940	60 514
1941	61 834
1947	6672
1951	798
1967	6

a Plot these figures as a graph.
b Mass immunisation of children against diphtheria began in 1940. Describe and explain the effect that this immunisation programme has had.

Children are vaccinated against diphtheria during the first year of their life. This vaccine contains a substance produced by the diphtheria bacterium, called a toxoid. The toxoid behaves as an antigen in the child's body.
c What is meant by the word 'antigen'?
d Explain how the diphtheria toxoid makes the child immune to diphtheria.
e A booster vaccination against diphtheria is given when the child is 5 years old. Why do you think this is done at this particular age?

63 FOOD HYGIENE

Food poisoning is caused by eating food in which dangerous bacteria have been reproducing.

Several types of bacteria can cause food poisoning

Food poisoning is a very common disease. It is usually caused by bacteria.

Many bacteria live in human food. Given warm, moist conditions, they can reproduce rapidly. Some of these bacteria are harmful if you eat them in large quantities. The harmful ones include some types of *Salmonella*, *Campylobacter*, *Listeria* and *Clostridium*.

None of these bacteria are harmful to you unless you eat a lot of them. *Salmonella*, for example, is a very common bacterium, found almost everywhere. It is only when it multiplies into large populations, and you eat a sizeable dose of it, that it will make you ill. Careful treatment of food while it is being produced, processed, stored and cooked can make sure that any *Salmonella* or other bacteria do not have the chance to multiply.

Bacteria reproduce fastest at warm temperatures

Most bacteria reproduce fast at warm temperatures. If they are kept cold, they will reproduce only slowly, or not at all. If they are heated to high temperatures, many of them will be killed. The worst thing you can do with food is to keep it at warm temperatures for a long time. Any bacteria in it will have a chance to reproduce. When you eat the food, you may eat a lot of bacteria along with it.

If you keep food cold, in a refrigerator, then bacteria will only reproduce very slowly. So long as you eat the food within a few days it will be quite safe. In a freezer, where the temperature is about −10°C, bacteria don't reproduce at all. But neither a refrigerator nor a freezer kills bacteria. Once the cold food warms up, they will begin to reproduce again.

If you make food very hot, then you will kill most of the bacteria in the food. So long as you eat the food soon after it has been cooked, it will be safe. But there may still be some bacteria in the food, which have survived the cooking or have fallen into it afterwards. If you leave the food for very long, especially in a warm place, then these bacteria will reproduce.

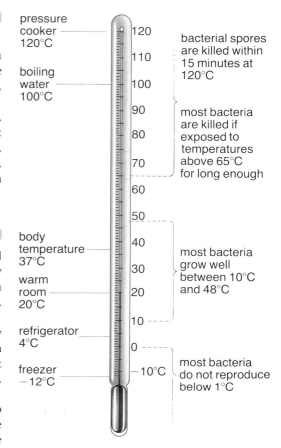

pressure cooker 120°C
boiling water 100°C
body temperature 37°C
warm room 20°C
refrigerator 4°C
freezer −12°C

bacterial spores are killed within 15 minutes at 120°C

most bacteria are killed if exposed to temperatures above 65°C for long enough

most bacteria grow well between 10°C and 48°C

most bacteria do not reproduce below 1°C

Fig. 63.1

Careful cooking and storing makes food safe to eat

Imagine you buy a frozen oven-ready chicken, which you are going to cook the next day. The chicken was in contact with *Salmonella* before it was slaughtered. Only a few *Salmonella* bacteria were in it, though – not enough to make you ill. The chicken was killed and then quickly cooled, before being packed and frozen. At these cold temperatures, the bacteria will not have reproduced at all.

The frozen chicken was transported to a supermarket in a refrigerated lorry. In the supermarket, it was quickly transferred to a freezer, which kept it at a very low temperature until you bought it.

You now put the chicken into your refrigerator to thaw out slowly. Here, at about 4°C, the bacteria may be able to reproduce very slowly. But by the next day their population is still very low. When you are ready to cook the chicken, you turn on the oven and let it heat up to 300°C. The chicken goes into the oven, and the outside of it rapidly comes up to this high temperature. The inside will take a bit longer. It will be warm for a while, and the *Salmonella* bacteria may reproduce. But even the inside of the chicken quickly gets hot. The bacteria population doesn't have time to build up much, before the bacteria are killed by the heat. The heat also inactivates any toxins produced by the bacteria. You can safely eat and enjoy your chicken with no fear of food poisoning – even though its body had *Salmonella* bacteria in its body when it was killed.

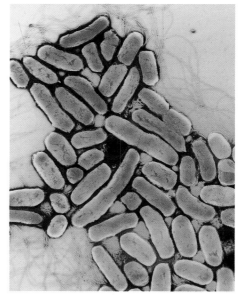

Fig. 63.2   A colony of *Salmonella enteritidis*, magnified about 4800 times.

Food hygiene can prevent food poisoning

Food producers and retailers can also do a lot to reduce the risk of infection. Food producers, for example, should try to make sure that food is produced in hygienic conditions. Chickens, for example, should be fed on *Salmonella*-free food and kept in clean surroundings, so that neither they nor their eggs are badly infected. The people who process food must provide hygienic conditions, and check their products to make sure that the levels of bacteria in them are very low. Shops must keep food cool and clean, and not keep food on the shelves for so long that large populations of bacteria have a chance to build up in it.

But we can never assume that all the food we buy is completely bacteria-free. Food must be carefully handled if we want to be sure that we are not going to get food poisoning, or poison anyone else.

Fig. 63.3 The spotlessly clean conditions in this food processing plant greatly reduce the chances of any harmful bacteria getting onto the cooked chickens. All surfaces in the room are cleaned daily. Clean clothing is worn each day, preventing bacteria, from hair, hands or clothes, from contaminating the food.

Fig. 63.4 Perishable foods such as these are stored and displayed at low temperatures before sale, to slow the growth of microorganisms. These cooled display units are expensive to run, because the cold air is constantly being replaced by warmer air which must again be cooled.

Questions

1 The following article appeared in a local newspaper in November 1989.

Hotel lamb causes outbreak of food poisoning

A chef at a local hotel has been blamed for causing stomach upsets among lunch guests. Half of a group of people attending a function at the hotel suffered diarrhoea and stomach pains, after eating rare lamb. Tests showed that they had all been infected with *Clostridium* bacteria.

The chef admitted to cooking the lamb 40 hours before it was served. A joint weighing about 5lbs was cooked for 1 hour. It was then kept in a warm kitchen for an hour, before being transferred to the refrigerator.

A written warning has been sent to the hotel, stressing the need for food hygiene education for the kitchen staff.

a Describe three things which the chef did which contributed to the infection of the hotel guests. For each of your three suggestions, explain how this allowed a large population of *Clostridium* bacteria to build up in the lamb.

b How would you explain to the kitchen staff what they *should* have done to ensure that the lamb was safe to eat?

2 How might each of the following procedures cause food poisoning?

a A frozen chicken is put into a cold oven without being properly thawed. The oven is then turned on, and the chicken cooked.

b A ready-meal of stew, designed to be reheated in a microwave, is displayed on a supermarket shelf. The thermostat controlling the temperature of the display unit is faulty, and the temperature is about 14°C. The meal is bought and eaten after being on display for three days.

c A chopping board is used for cutting up beef for a stew. The board is not properly washed. The next morning, the same board is used to slice tomatoes for a salad. The salad is left on the kitchen work surface until it is eaten for the evening meal.

3 Write a short and snappy list of dos and don'ts for people to follow in their kitchen to make sure that they do not suffer from food poisoning.

Sewage may contain harmful bacteria

Sewage is waste water from homes and industry. Your home will produce liquid waste from your washing machine, washing up water, wastes from the toilet, and dirty bath water. All of this is carried from your house into underground pipes, or sewers. Factories also produce a lot of liquid waste, which is collected in the sewers.

For a long time, sewage was just poured into rivers or the sea. In some places, this still happens. But raw, or untreated, sewage is damaging to the environment.

- It may contain harmful bacteria or viruses, which could cause disease if people swallowed them.
- It contains many substances which provide food for bacteria. If raw sewage is discharged into a river, huge populations of bacteria will develop, feeding on the sewage. They will use up so much oxygen from the river water that fish and other animals will not be able to breathe. The fish will die, or will move to other, unpolluted, areas.
- It contains chemicals which may harm living things. These include phosphates from detergents, and a wide variety of different chemicals used in industry.

So raw sewage should be treated before it is released back into the environment. Figure 64.2 shows how this may be done. Some of the most important stages in the treatment of sewage are done by bacteria! These, of course, are not the same kind as the ones which might cause disease. They help by digesting some of the harmful substances in the sewage.

Fig. 64.1 Mogden Sewage Treatment Works in London treats the sewage from 1.5 million people before releasing the effluent into the Thames. These are some of the settlement tanks.

Fig. 64.2 Sewage treatment. This is called the activated sludge method. There are several other ways of treating sewage, all of which use bacteria to break down harmful substances.

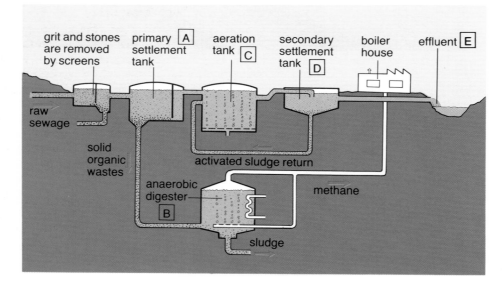

A **Primary settlement tank** Solid wastes sink to the bottom and are sent to anaerobic digester.

B **Anaerobic digester** There is no air here so all the bacteria which need oxygen are killed. Other bacteria which grow well in anaerobic conditions feed on the sludge, digesting it and producing methane gas. The methane can be used as a fuel. The digested sludge contains no harmful bacteria, and can be used as fertiliser.

C **Aeration tank** The liquid from the top of the primary settlement tank flows into here. Air is bubbled into it, so aerobic microorganisms grow, breaking down any remaining organic matter.

D **Secondary settlement tank** Here, many of the microorganisms from the aeration tank sink to the bottom. The material that sinks is called activated sludge. It is piped back to the aeration tank where the microorganisms help to digest the organic material.

E **Effluent** The liquid at the top of the secondary settlement tank is quite clear, does not smell, and has no pathogenic organisms in it. It can safely be released into rivers or the sea.

The water you drink might once have been inside someone else

The water in your tap might have been drawn from a river, or from a deep well. It depends on the area of the country in which you live. If it came from a river, then the water coming out of your tap might have been part of someone else not long ago!

In Britain, a lot of our tap water comes from rivers. This water must be treated very carefully to make it safe to drink.

River water contains bacteria, which could make you ill. In the nineteenth century, before safe drinking water was supplied to towns and cities, diseases such as cholera and typhoid were frequently caught by drinking untreated water. Now these diseases are very rare in Britain.

Figure 64.3 shows how river water is treated to make it safe to drink.

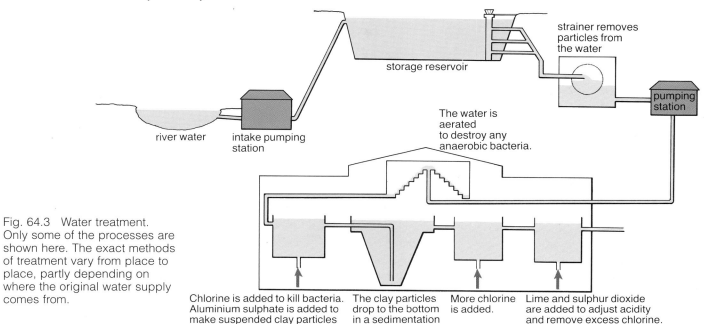

Fig. 64.3 Water treatment. Only some of the processes are shown here. The exact methods of treatment vary from place to place, partly depending on where the original water supply comes from.

storage reservoir

strainer removes particles from the water

pumping station

river water   intake pumping station

The water is aerated to destroy any anaerobic bacteria.

Chlorine is added to kill bacteria. Aluminium sulphate is added to make suspended clay particles clump together.

The clay particles drop to the bottom in a sedimentation tank.

More chlorine is added.

Lime and sulphur dioxide are added to adjust acidity and remove excess chlorine.

Questions

1 a What is meant by 'raw sewage'? Where does it come from? What does it contain?

b Why is it harmful to discharge raw sewage into rivers or the sea?

c Describe how bacteria help in the treatment of sewage.

d Name two useful substances which are produced by the treatment of sewage. What are they used for?

2 Find out where your local tap water comes from. Is it from rivers or from wells? How does your local water authority treat the water before it sends it through the pipes to your tap?

3 You drink a glass of water from your tap. Trace, in detail, the path of a molecule of this water through your body, into the sewage system, through a sewage treatment plant, into a river, through a water purification plant, and out of someone else's tap.

4 The graph on the right shows the distribution of some living things and chemicals in a river.

a Give explanations for the shapes

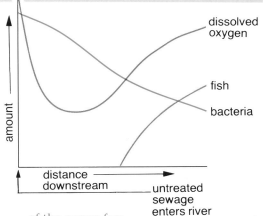

of the curves for:
  i bacteria
  ii dissolved oxygen
  iii fish.

b What shape do you think a curve showing the numbers of water plants might be? Give reasons for your answer.

c If the sewage being discharged into the river had been properly treated before being discharged, what differences would you expect to see in the shapes of each of the three curves? Explain your answers.

The Thames Water Authority is trying to improve the water quality of the river so that more living things can thrive in it. One problem is that, after a storm, a lot of sewage may be carried into the River Thames as the rain water rushes through the sewers. This can make oxygen levels plummet, especially in summer. As well as improving the efficiency of its sewage treatment plants, the water authority uses a bubbler to help to cope with this problem. The bubbler is a boat which can bubble up to 30 tonnes of oxygen a day into the river. It is used when checks show the dissolved oxygen levels in the river to be especially low.

d Why are dissolved oxygen levels more likely to become low in summer than in winter? (Think about the solubility of gases and temperature.)

e Why is it a good idea to have a *boat* which bubbles oxygen into the water, rather than a machine in a fixed position on the river?

A good lifestyle can help you to feel better, stay fitter and live longer.

Your lifestyle affects your health

Figure 65.1 shows the most important causes of death in the United Kingdom for people under 75. You can see that heart disease and cancer are by far the commonest causes of death. Infections and accidents account for only about 12% of all deaths. But, in fact, accidents are the commonest cause of death among young people.

Everyone has to die of something. But there is a lot that people can do to make sure that they die later, rather than sooner. Your lifestyle can affect not only how long you live, but also how healthy you feel now.

Cancer causes nearly one third of all deaths in Britain

At the moment, cancer is the most important cause of death in Britain. Cancer is caused when a cell begins to divide uncontrollably. The new cells also divide and divide, forming a lump or **tumour**. Many tumours are harmless. But in cancer, the cells from the tumour continue dividing and may spread around the body. Here they start other tumours, called secondary tumours. Eventually, a vital organ will be damaged, causing death.

The causes of some cancers are very well understood, and you can do a lot to reduce your risk of suffering from them. Lung cancer is caused by harmful chemicals affecting cells in your lungs. Almost everyone who suffers from lung cancer is a smoker. If you don't smoke, you stand less chance of contracting lung cancer. Smoking also increases the risk of getting other kinds of cancer.

Skin cancers are caused by contact with some dangerous chemicals, or by the effects of ultra-violet light on your skin. Taking care when sunbathing in bright sunlight can cut your risk of getting skin cancer.

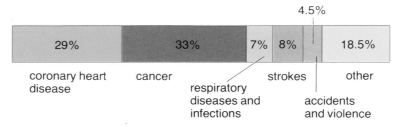

Fig. 65.1 Causes of death in the United Kingdom in people under 75.

| 29% | 33% | 7% | 8% | 4.5% | 18.5% |

coronary heart disease · cancer · respiratory diseases and infections · strokes · accidents and violence · other

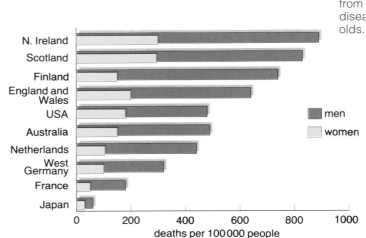

Fig. 65.2 Death rates from coronary heart disease in 55–64 year olds.

N. Ireland, Scotland, Finland, England and Wales, USA, Australia, Netherlands, West Germany, France, Japan

■ men □ women

deaths per 100 000 people

Cervical cancer is most common in women who have had a lot of sexual partners, or whose partners have had a lot of sexual partners. It seems to be associated with viruses which are transmitted during sexual intercourse. So staying faithful to one partner, who stays faithful to you, means that you are less likely to get or pass on this cancer.

Excessive consumption of alcohol also seems to increase the risk of some kinds of cancers. Keeping drinking to a sensible level can reduce this risk.

The United Kingdom is at the top of the league for heart disease

Figure 65.2 shows the death rates from coronary heart disease in several different countries. You can see where Northern Ireland, Scotland, England and Wales stand. Why do we get so much more heart disease than other countries?

There is no simple answer to this question. There seem to be several factors involved, which, acting together, can tip the balance against your heart.

Diet is important. Large amounts of fat in your diet, especially saturated (animal) fats, increase the risk of your arteries becoming 'furred up' and blocked. This can lead to a stroke or a heart attack. Overeating can cause obesity, which also increases the chance of heart disease. Cigarette smoking can double the risk of having a heart attack. In heavy smokers, the risk may be four times greater than normal. Lack of exercise is also a contributory factor. Stamina-building exercise, such as cycling or swimming, seems to be the best at reducing your risk of heart disease. Exercise can make you feel fitter, more energetic and healthier.

Drugs can be useful

A **drug** is a chemical which affects the way the body works. Drugs can be very helpful to us, especially if we are ill.

In Topic 62, you saw how **antibiotics** can help us to fight infectious diseases. Antibiotics are drugs which kill bacteria, but don't harm human cells. Until antibiotics were discovered and produced on a large scale, which happened towards the end of the Second World War, many people died of infectious diseases that don't worry us at all today. But we are constantly having to find new antibiotics, because bacteria develop resistance to them.

Analgesics also help people when they are not well. An analgesic is a pain-killer, such as aspirin, paracetamol, ibuprofen or heroin. Most people have taken an aspirin or other pain-killer at some time or another.

Many people also make use of **caffeine**, the drug in coffee, tea and cola drinks. Caffeine is a **stimulant**, which means that it stimulates the activity of the brain. It can make you feel more alert. Doctors may prescribe more powerful stimulants called **amphetamines** to patients who are ill.

Other drugs have just the opposite effect to stimulants, reducing the activity of at least some parts of the brain. They are called **depressants**. Doctors sometimes prescribe depressants called **barbiturates** to help people to calm down and sleep.

Yet another group of drugs are the **hallucinogens**. **LSD** is an example of a hallucinogenic drug. Some **solvents** are hallucinogens. These drugs are not widely used in medicine, perhaps only being of any help to people with some types of mental illness.

Drugs may be harmful

If drugs are misused, they can cause very unpleasant illnesses. Some of them can increase the risk of accidents and violence. Some of them can become addictive.

Analgesics such as aspirin and ibuprofen, for example, can damage the lining of the stomach in some people, causing ulcers and sometimes dangerous bleeding, if they are taken in large amounts over a long period of time. If a doctor thinks a person is at risk from this, but does really need pain-killers, then a different drug may be prescribed.

Stimulants, too, can cause harm if over-used. They can cause your body to overwork, using up energy supplies which cannot be replaced quickly enough. Intense activity may be followed by deep exhaustion, which can be harmful. Sometimes, the over-activity caused by stimulants may cause the body to become overheated or dehydrated, and in some cases this can be fatal.

Overuse of depressants can be fatal, too. **Alcohol** is a depressant. In large amounts, it is a dangerous poison, and a person who has drunk a lot of alcohol over a short period of time may go into a coma and even die. Taking alcohol and other drugs, such as barbiturates, at the same time is especially dangerous.

Alcohol slows down the activity of parts of the brain which normally control other areas, so you lose control over some of your activities. Some people respond to alcohol by losing all their inhibitions, and this can lead to violence. At least half of all violent crimes are committed by people who have been drinking alcohol, and a very high proportion of people in prison are there because of something they did after drinking alcohol.

Statistics also show that a very large proportion of accidents are related to drug use, especially alcohol. Alcohol lengthens reaction time and affects people's judgement. So a driver who has been drinking alcohol isn't able to size up the danger of a situation they find themselves in, and isn't able to react quickly to it. More than one thousand people die every year in Britain from alcohol-related road accidents.

Drinking large amounts of alcohol over a long period of time can cause major damage to the liver and brain. The liver is damaged because one of its roles is to break down harmful substances in the body. While the liver cells are destroying alcohol or other drugs, they may become harmed themselves.

Hallucinogenic drugs, such as solvents, can directly damage the brain. They are also responsible for many injuries and deaths caused by accidents, because people affected by them aren't fully aware of what is going on around them. Solvents can cause major damage to the lungs and liver.

People sometimes become **addicted** to drugs. This means that they cannot manage without the drug. Often, their body comes to need more and more of the drug. What began as an enjoyable activity becomes a desperate and miserable battle to obtain enough of the drug to be able to satifsy their need. People may have to steal to obtain money to buy the drug they need. Their whole life is taken over by the drug, so they have no time for any pleasures. They cannot work and earn money, so they cannot help to support a family, and may find themselves on their own with neither family nor friends to help them. Getting out of this situation is very difficult, but people can be cured of addiction if they have enough determination, and lots of help and support from others.

Many different drugs are addictive. For example, cocaine and crack are particularly likely to become addictive, and some people can become addicted to heroin. Nicotine, present in tobacco smoke, is addictive. For some people, alcohol is addictive.

Question

1   Write a short, eye-catching list of what someone can do to keep healthy. People are more likely to take note of your suggestions if they know why certain actions might help, but they won't remember it if they have to take in too much at once. So keep it brief.

Questions

1   Read the following passage, and then answer the questions which follow.

Immunity and disease

Your body is fighting a constant war against disease. Your immune system destroys invading cells by a combination of phagocytosis and the production of antibodies. It can normally do this very swiftly if you have already been exposed to a particular antigen before, either because you have had that particular disease or because you have been vaccinated against it. Either of these events provides you with **active immunity** against that disease.

There are other ways of becoming immune to particular diseases. Young babies are provided with antibodies in their mother's milk. This is important because their immune system does not become fully active until several months after birth. The mother's antibodies provide the baby with protection against diseases to which the mother is immune, until the baby's immune system can fend for itself. This type of immunity is known as **passive immunity**.

There are some diseases which affect your immune system itself. These are very difficult to treat. One such disease is AIDS. AIDS is caused by a virus, which breeds inside lymphocytes. The virus can pass from person to person during sexual intercourse, either between homosexual men or during intercourse between a woman and a man. It can also be transferred in blood, and the sharing of needles by intravenous drug users has been a major means by which AIDS has spread. The virus which causes AIDS gradually destroys the cells of the immune system so that a sufferer loses the ability to combat other diseases. A person with AIDS eventually dies from one or other of the many infections to which they are exposed.

Human lymphocytes normally recognise the antigens on your own body cells and so do not attack these cells. But sometimes this system seems to go wrong. A person's own lymphocytes may begin to attack some of their own cells. The resulting disease is called an **auto-immune disease**. In some types of diabetes, for example, the lymphocytes attack and destroy the insulin-producing cells in the pancreas. Rheumatoid arthritis is caused by the body's immune system attacking cells at the joints. Multiple sclerosis is another auto-immune disease, in which nerve cells are damaged. The progress of these diseases can be slowed by the use of drugs which stop the immune system working properly. These are called **immuno-suppressant** drugs. But their use has major drawbacks, because it exposes the patient's body to infection by any other bacterium or virus which comes along.

Immuno-suppressant drugs are also used in treating patients who have had a transplant operation. When a person is given someone else's heart or kidney, for example, their immune system recognises the new cells as foreign. The lymphocytes will kill the 'invading' cells, unless drugs are administered to stop them from doing this.

a Give brief explanations of the meanings of the following words:
  i phagocytosis   **iv** immunity
  ii antibody   **v** vaccination
  iii antigen   **vi** lymphocyte.

b i The passage suggests one reason why breast feeding young babies is better than bottle feeding. What is this reason?
  ii Suggest other reasons, not connected with immunity, why breast feeding might be better than bottle feeding.

c Intravenous drug users have an especially high risk of infection from AIDS. Suggest why this is so.

d Why are antibiotics of no use in the fight against AIDS?

e Describe what is meant by an auto-immune disease, and give two examples.

f People who have recently had transplant operations must be kept well away from any possible sources of infection. Explain why this is so.

EXTENSION

2   Antibiotics have only been known about and used since the 1930s. Find out about:
  • the way in which antibiotics were discovered.
  • the difference which the discovery of antibiotics made to the treatment of bacterial infections.
  • how antibiotics are manufactured.
  • the problems caused by the indiscriminate use of antibiotics, for example in farm animals.

3   Read the passage below, and then answer the questions which follow.
  a Explain the meaning of each of the following words or phrases:
    i vector   **iii** insecticide
    ii protoctistan   **iv** biological control.

  b Why might biological control of the number of mosquitos be preferable to the use of chemicals to kill mosquitos or their larvae?

Bacteria and biological pest control

In many parts of the world, mosquitos are vectors for malaria. They carry the protoctistan, which causes malaria, in their saliva and inject this into a person's blood stream when they bite. To control malaria, mosquito populations must be kept down.

In the past, this has been attempted with various chemicals and insecticides. In the last twenty years, however, biological control has been used. This involves attacking the mosquitos with another organism. The organism used is a bacterium, *Bacillus thuringiensis*. Several firms in different parts of the world produce large amounts of this bacterium commercially. It forms spores, which can be mixed with water, and sprayed over water where mosquitos breed. The mosquito larvae are infected and killed by the bacterium.

GENETICS AND EVOLUTION

66 GENES AND CHROMOSOMES

Chromosomes are long threads of DNA and protein, found in the nucleus of a cell.

Chromosomes contain genes

In the nucleus of every living cell are several thread-like structures called **chromosomes**. Human cells each contain 46 chromosomes.

Chromosomes are made of **DNA** and **protein**. The DNA is a set of instructions to the cell. These instructions tell the cell what proteins to make.

The DNA molecules are very long. A DNA molecule may contain instructions for many different proteins. A section of a DNA molecule which gives instructions for making any one kind of protein is called a **gene**. Each chromosome contains many genes.

By giving instructions for which kinds of proteins to make, genes determine all sorts of things about a cell, and about the organism in which the cell is found. Your genes make you a human being, rather than a cat or a tomato plant. They determine the colour of your hair and the shape of your nose. They have some effect on many of your other features, such as your height.

All the cells in your body have the same genes inside them. But not all your genes are active in every cell. The genes which give instructions for your eye colour, for example, are only active in the cells of the irises of your eyes. These same genes are in all your other cells, but they do not do anything there.

Human cells contain two of each kind of gene

The 46 chromosomes of a human cell can be sorted into pairs. There are 23 kinds of human chromosome. Almost all human cells contain two of each kind.

The two chromosomes of a 'matching pair' are called **homologous chromosomes**. They contain the same kinds of genes in the same places along their length. So you have two of each kind of gene.

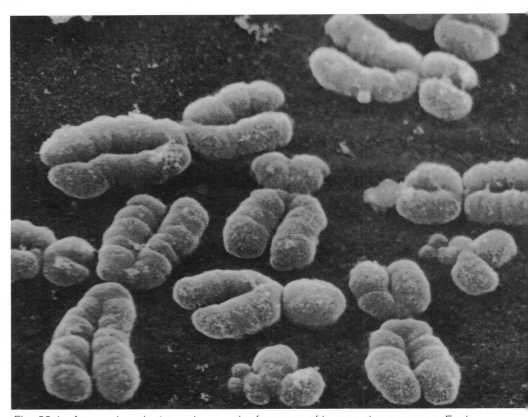

Fig. 66.1   A scanning electron micrograph of a group of human chromosomes. Each chromosome is made up of two strands called chromatids, joined together at a point called the centromere. There are 46 chromosomes in the nucleus of each of your cells.

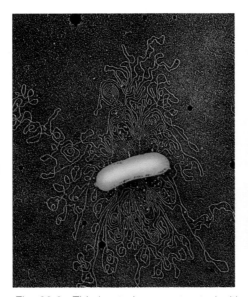

Fig. 66.2   This bacterium was treated with an enzyme which weakened its cell wall. It was then put into water, which made it burst. The long yellow thread is its DNA. The total length of the DNA is about 1.5 mm – 1000 times the length of the cell.

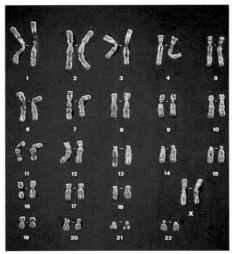

Fig. 66.3   The chromosomes of a human female, arranged in their matching pairs. Photographs were taken, using a light microscope, of the chromosomes in a dividing cell. The chromosomes were then identified and their pictures rearranged, to make this composite picture. The two chromosomes of a pair are said to be homologous chromosomes.

156

Different types of the same gene are called alleles

One kind of gene determines whether or not your skin can make the brown pigment melanin. There are two types of this gene. One type gives your skin the ability to make melanin. The other does not. The two types are called **alleles**. Alleles are the different types of the same gene. Alleles are always found in the same position on a chromosome.

Imagine that the melanin gene is found near one end of chromosome 11. You have two chromosome 11s in each cell, so you have two melanin-making genes.

Let us call the allele which allows you to make melanin **M** and the allele which does not allow you to make melanin **m**. Your two melanin-making genes could be:

MM or **mm** or **Mm.**

If your cells contain the alleles MM, then you can make melanin. If they contain the alleles mm, then you cannot. People with the genotype mm are **albino**. They have no melanin in their skin or hair. They have to be very careful in sunlight, which may hurt their eyes or damage their skin.

But what if your cells contain one of each allele, Mm? Can you make melanin in some bits of your skin? Or just make a little melanin? In fact, someone with the genes Mm can make melanin just as well as someone with the genes MM. This is because the allele M is a **dominant** allele. If this allele is present, it has its effect. The allele m is a **recessive** allele. It can only have its effect if the allele M is not present.

Your genotype affects your phenotype

The genes you have in your cells make up your **genotype**. Your genotype for the melanin genes might be MM, mm or Mm.

These genes affect your **phenotype**. Your phenotype is your observable features. The part of your phenotype which is affected by the melanin alleles is your ability make melanin. Either you can, or you can't.

If your two melanin alleles are the same, you are said to be **homozygous** for these alleles. The two genotypes MM and mm are homozygous. If the two alleles are different, then you are **heterozygous**. The genotype Mm is heterozygous.

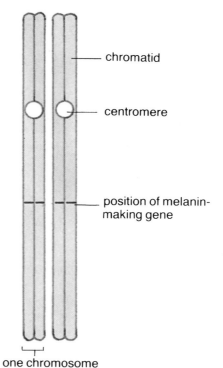

Fig. 66.4 Each one of a pair of homologous chromosomes carries the same genes at the same position. Each chromosome is made up of a pair of chromatids joined by a centromere.

Fig. 66.5 The three possible genotypes for the ability to make melanin.

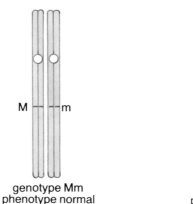

genotype MM
phenotype normal

genotype Mm
phenotype normal

genotype mm
phenotype albino

Questions

1 In gerbils, the allele for brown coat colour is dominant to the allele for black coat colour.
   a If the symbol for the allele for brown coat colour is B, and the symbol for the allele for black coat colour is b, give the possible genotypes of:
      i a brown gerbil
      ii a black gerbil.
   b What will be the phenotype of a heterozygous gerbil?

2 In peas, the allele for smooth seeds is dominant to the allele for wrinkled seeds.
   a Suggest suitable symbols for these two alleles. (Use the same letter, one capital and one small.)
   b Write down the three possible genotypes of a pea plant.
   c What will be the phenotype of a pea plant which is homozygous for the dominant allele?
   d What will be the phenotype of a heterozygous pea plant?

   e What will be the genotype of a pea plant with wrinkled seeds?
3 Dalmatian dogs have spots. The spots may be black or brown. The allele for black spots is B, and the allele for brown spots is b.
   a Heterozygous dalmatians have black spots. Which allele must be dominant?
   b What is the genotype of a brown-spotted dalmatian?

67 INHERITING GENES

Eggs and sperms carry genes from female and male parents, so a zygote gets one of each kind of gene from each of its parents.

Gametes have one of each kind of gene

You saw in Topic 36 that gametes (eggs and sperms) have only 23 chromosomes. This is so that when they join together at fertilisation, the zygote which is produced ends up with 46 chromosomes.

A human gamete contains one of each of the 23 kinds of chromosome. So gametes only have *one* of each kind of gene. They are known as **haploid** cells. Haploid cells are cells with one of each kind of chromosome. Your body cells, which have two of each kind of chromosome, are called **diploid** cells.

Think about a man who is heterozygous for the melanin making gene. His genotype is Mm. In his testes, cells divide to form sperms. When one of these sperm-producing cells divides, half of its chromosomes go into one sperm cell, and half into another. The chromosome carrying the M gene will go into one sperm cell, and the chromosome carrying the m gene into another.

There will be many sperm-producing cells dividing like this. All of them have the genotype Mm. Many sperms will be made. Half of the sperms will contain the M gene, and half the m gene. Of the hundreds of thousands of sperms made in the man's testes, half will have the genotype M and half the genotype m.

Chance decides which gametes meet each other

If this man's partner is albino, will their children be albino or not?

Her genotype must be mm. So when the cells in her ovaries divide to form eggs, all the eggs will have the same genotype. They will all get an m gene.

You can write down this information like this:

Parents' phenotypes	Normal male	Albino female
Parents' genotypes	Mm	mm
Gametes' genotypes	M or m	m

After sexual intercourse, hundreds of thousands of sperms will start to swim towards the egg in the woman's oviduct. Only chance decides which kind of sperm gets there first. It could be an M sperm, or it might equally well be an m sperm. So there are equal chances that the zygote will have the genotype Mm, or mm.

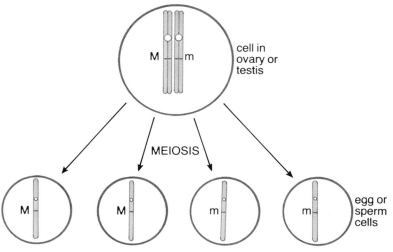

Fig. 67.1   A person with genotype Mm produces eggs or sperms, half of which have the genotype M and half the genotype m.

You can show this by continuing the chart like this:

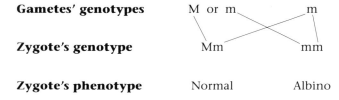

Gametes' genotypes	M or m	m
Zygote's genotype	Mm	mm
Zygote's phenotype	Normal	Albino

This means that every time the couple have a child, there is a fifty-fifty chance that it will be albino. If they have lots of children, you would expect about half of them to be albino. But don't forget that we are only dealing with *chance*. You should not be too surprised if, of eight children, two turn out to be normal and six albino!

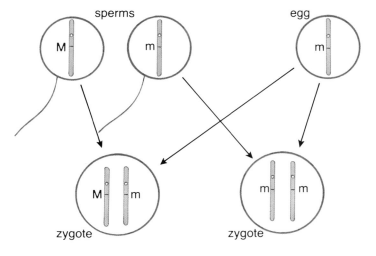

Fig. 67.2

A mating between two heterozygotes gives a 3:1 ratio

What would be the phenotypes of the children if the woman was, like her partner, heterozygous?

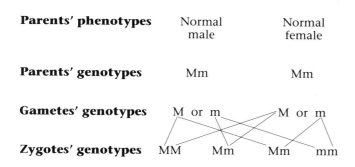

Parents' phenotypes	Normal male	Normal female
Parents' genotypes	Mm	Mm
Gametes' genotypes	M or m	M or m
Zygotes' genotypes	MM Mm	Mm mm
Zygotes' phenotypes	Normal Normal	Normal Albino

Fig. 67.3

eggs

M   m

sperms

	MM	Mm
M		
m	Mm	mm

The lines drawn to show how the gametes might join up can look confusing. But if you think about what is happening, it is very straightforward. The M sperm might join with either an M egg or an m egg. So begin by drawing lines from each of these eggs to meet lines from the M sperm. Similarly, the m sperm might join lines with either type of egg. Draw lines from the m sperm to meet lines from each type of egg.

If you find you get in a muddle when drawing these lines, Figure 67.3 shows another way of showing all the possibilities.

So what kind of children will these people have? Three of the chances produce a zygote with the genotypes MM or Mm. One chance produces a zygote with the genotype mm. So, each time they have a child, there is a one in four chance that it will have the genotype mm and be albino. There is a three in four chance that it will be normal.

On average, the couple are three times more likely to have a normal child than an albino child. If they have lots of children, we would expect the ratio of normal to albino to be about 3:1.

The sperm determines the sex of a child

As you know, human cells contain 46 chromosomes. Two of these chromosomes are called the **sex chromosomes**. They determine what sex you are.

A woman's two sex chromosomes are the same. They are X-shaped, and are known as **X chromosomes**. A woman has the genotype **XX**.

A man's two sex chromosomes are different. One is an X chromosome. But the other is an even smaller chromosome, called a **Y chromosome**. A man has the genotype **XY**.

When a woman's cells divide to make eggs, each egg gets a single X chromosome. The genotype of every egg is X. But when a man's cells divide to make sperms, half of the sperms get an X chromosome, and half a Y chromosome: 50% of sperms have the genotype X, and 50% have the genotype Y.

When a sperm fertilises an egg, there is an equal chance that the sperm will be an X sperm or a Y sperm. If it is an X sperm, the zygote's genotype will be XX. It will be a girl. If the sperm is a Y sperm, the zygote will have the genotype XY. It will be a boy.

Parents' phenotypes	Male	Female
Parents' genotypes	XY	XX
Gametes' genotypes	X or Y	X
Zygotes' genotypes	XX	XY
Zygotes' phenotypes	Female	Male

Questions

1   In rabbits, the allele for brown coat is dominant to the allele for white coat.

 a Write down suitable symbols for these two coat colour alleles.

 b What coat colours would you expect to find in the offspring of a mating between two white rabbits? Explain your answer fully, using charts such as those on this page.

 c What coat colours would you expect to find in the offspring of a mating between a brown homozygous rabbit and a white rabbit? Explain your answer fully.

 d Two brown rabbits mated. They had 12 babies, three with white coats and nine with brown coats. Explain fully how this happened.

2   In humans, the allele for brown eye colour is dominant to the allele for blue eye colour.

 a A brown-eyed man is married to a blue-eyed woman. They have three children, two with blue eyes and one with brown eyes. How might this happen?

 b The brown-eyed child eventually marries a brown-eyed woman. They have six children, all with brown eyes. What is the most likely genotype of the woman? Explain your answer.

Some diseases are caused by genes

Several different diseases are caused by faulty genes. For example, about 1 person in every 20 000 in Britain has a disease called **Huntington's chorea.** This illness is caused by a dominant allele of a gene. The disease affects the nervous system, but the person has no symptoms until they are about 40 or 50 years old. Then their muscles begin to move uncontrollably, and there is a gradual deterioration of the brain.

Because the allele responsible for Huntington's chorea is a dominant allele, every person with one copy of the allele eventually shows symptoms of the disease. So only a person who has Huntington's chorea (even if they are not yet old enough to show symptoms) can pass on the disease to their children. But some inherited diseases are caused by *recessive* genes. One such disease is **cystic fibrosis**.

Cystic fibrosis is an unpleasant disease. A person with cystic fibrosis produces large amounts of very thick mucus in their lungs. The mucus slows down the rate at which oxygen and carbon dioxide can diffuse between the air in the lungs and the blood. It also provides a breeding ground for bacteria. So, several times a day, a person with cystic fibrosis must be made to cough to move some of the mucus out of their lungs.

Cystic fibrosis is caused by a recessive allele, c. Only people who are homozygous for this allele, cc, have cystic fibrosis. Heterozygous people, with the genotype Cc, are perfectly normal. They are said to be **carriers** for the cystic fibrosis allele, because they have it in their cells but do not suffer any ill effects from it.

Fig. 68.1 Sickle-cell anaemia is a serious inherited disease, caused by a recessive allele. If both parents are carriers of this allele, there is a one in four chance that their child will have the disease. Here a genetic counsellor explains the risk to a couple with a history of sickle-cell anaemia in their family, who are thinking of having children.

Children with cystic fibrosis may be born to heterozygotes

People with the genotype CC will never have children with cystic fibrosis. The gametes of a CC person will all contain a C allele. So every one of their children will have at least one C allele. No matter what alleles the children get from their other parent, this dominant C allele will mean that they will not suffer from cystic fibrosis.

However, if two heterozygous people marry, there is a one in four chance that any child they have will have cystic fibrosis.

Until recently, there has been no way of knowing whether a person is a carrier for cystic fibrosis or not. The first indication that a couple were both carriers would come when they had a child with cystic fibrosis. But in 1989 the gene which causes cystic fibrosis was identified. This allowed a test to be developed which can tell someone whether they are a cystic fibrosis carrier, just by analysing the DNA from one of their cells.

If a couple know that they are both carriers for cystic fibrosis, they have a difficult decision to make. A **genetic counsellor** will be able to explain to them that, each time they have a child, there is a one in four chance that it will have cystic fibrosis. Should they have children? Or is the risk too great? The decision is left to individual couples. What would *you* decide?

Parents' phenotypes	Normal, but a carrier	Normal, but a carrier
Parents' genotypes	Cc	Cc
Gametes' genotypes	C or c	C or c
Zygotes' genotypes	CC Cc	Cc cc
Zygotes' phenotypes	Normal Carrier	Carrier Cystic fibrosis sufferer

Haemophilia is a sex-linked disease

Haemophilia is a disease in which blood does not clot properly. It is an inherited disease. People with haemophilia lack the allele H, which gives instructions to cells to product a chemical called Factor 8. Without Factor 8, blood will not clot. Often, blood leaks into a sufferer's joints, causing painful damage.

Only men suffer from haemophilia. Haemophilia is a **sex-linked** disease. Why is this so?

There are two alleles of the Factor 8 gene. The allele H causes normal Factor 8 to be formed. The allele h does not.

H is dominant to h, so as long as a person has at least one H allele in their cells, they will make normal Factor 8.

The Factor 8 gene is situated on the X chromosome. Figure 68.2 shows the different combinations of alleles which a man or a woman may have. A woman, because she has two X chromosomes, will always have two Factor 8 genes in her cells. But a man only has one X chromosome, so he only has one Factor 8 gene.

Let us look at what happens if a woman who is a carrier for haemophilia marries a normal man.

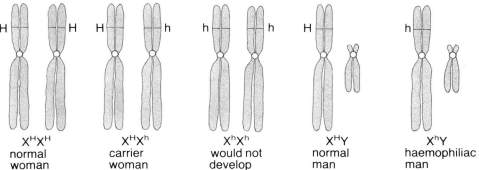

$X^H X^H$
normal
woman

$X^H X^h$
carrier
woman

$X^h X^h$
would not
develop

$X^H Y$
normal
man

$X^h Y$
haemophiliac
man

Fig. 68.2   The five possible genotypes for blood-clotting. Notice that you need to include the Xs and Ys when writing down the genotypes involving sex-linked genes.

Parents' phenotypes	Normal male	Carrier female
Parents' genotypes	$X^H Y$	$X^H X^h$
Gametes' genotypes	X^H Y	X^H X^h
Zygotes' genotypes	$X^H X^H$ $X^H X^h$	$X^H Y$ $X^h Y$
Zygotes' phenotypes	Normal female Carrier female	Normal male Haemophiliac male

So this couple has a one in four chance of having a haemophiliac son.

In theory, it is possible for a couple to have a daughter who has the genotype $X^h X^h$. (How might this happen?) But this happens only very, very rarely.

E X T E N S I O N

Questions

1 Anaemia is an illness in which not enough oxygen is carried around the body. It can be caused by a lack of red blood cells, a lack of haemoglobin, or a lack of the right sort of haemoglobin.

a What symptoms would you expect to see in someone suffering from anaemia?

b Anaemia can be caused by not having enough iron in the diet. Why might this cause anaemia?

Thalassaemia is a type of anaemia which is most common in people who originate from Mediterranean countries and some· parts of Asia. It is an inherited disease. Thalassaemia is caused by a recessive allele. This allele causes cells to make defective haemoglobin. People who are homozygous for thalassaemia suffer from severe anaemia.

c Write down suitable symbols for the thalassaemia allele and the normal allele.

d What will be the genotype of a person suffering from thalassaemia?

John has no history at all of thalassaemia in his family. Carla is a healthy person, as are her parents. But she has a sister who has thalassaemia.

e What is John's most likely genotype?

f What must be the genotypes of Carla's parents?

g What are the two possibilities for Carla's genotype?

h If Carla and John marry, might any of their children have thalassaemia? Explain your answer.

E X T E N S I O N

2 Red-green colour-blindness is a common inherited sex-linked condition. Men are far more likely to suffer from it than women. The normal allele, R, causes a protein to be produced which forms one of the pigments in the cone cells in the retina of the eye. The less common recessive allele, r, does not cause this protein to be formed. People without the allele R cannot distinguish red from green.

a On which chromosome do you think this gene is found?

b Write down the genotypes of:
   i a colour-blind man
   ii a normal woman
   iii a woman who is a carrier for colour-blindness.

c If a normal woman marries a colour-blind man, will any of their children be colour-blind? Explain your answer.

d Can a colour-blind man pass on his colour-blindness to his son? Explain your answer.

69 *DNA*

DNA is a chemical contained in chromosomes. DNA molecules contain a code that determines which proteins are made in a cell.

EXTENSION

DNA is made up of nucleotides

DNA stands for deoxyribonucleic acid. DNA is found in chromosomes. It is one of the most important kinds of molecules found in living things. DNA contains instructions which decide which proteins a cell will make. This determines the whole chemistry of the cell.

DNA molecules are made up of two long chains of smaller molecules, called **nucleotides**. So DNA is a **polynucleotide**. The two chains of nucleotides wind round one another in a helix. The shape of a DNA molecule is a double helix.

There are four different kinds of nucleotides in a DNA molecule. They are known by the letters **A, T, C** and **G**. The nucleotides can be arranged in any order along one of the DNA strands. The order of the nucleotides determines the kinds of proteins which the cell will make.

DNA carries the genetic code

Proteins are chains of **amino acids**. There are about 20 kinds of amino acid. The sequence of these different amino acids in a protein chain determines what kind of protein it is. Keratin, for example, has a completely different sequence of amino acids from haemoglobin.

Your cells make thousands of different proteins. They make them by stringing amino acids together in particular orders. The instructions for doing this come from your DNA molecules. A part of a DNA molecule which gives instructions for making one kind of protein is called a **gene**.

How does DNA do this? It carries the instructions in the form of a code, called the **genetic code**. The code is a 'three-letter' code. The letters are the nucleotides on one of the DNA strands in the double helix. A row of three nucleotides is a 'code-word', which stands for a particular amino acid.

Say, for example, that a bit of a DNA molecule has a string of nucleotides in the order CCGCAG. Reading three 'letters' at a time, CCG stands for the amino acid glycine. CAG stands for the amino acid valine. So this piece of the DNA molecule tells the cell to join a molecule of glycine to a molecule of valine when it is making a protein.

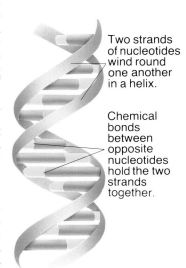

Two strands of nucleotides wind round one another in a helix.

Chemical bonds between opposite nucleotides hold the two strands together.

Fig. 69.1 Part of a DNA molecule

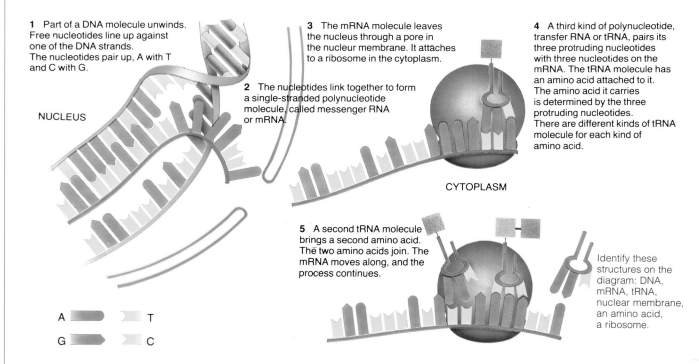

1 Part of a DNA molecule unwinds. Free nucleotides line up against one of the DNA strands. The nucleotides pair up, A with T and C with G.

NUCLEUS

2 The nucleotides link together to form a single-stranded polynucleotide molecule, called messenger RNA or mRNA.

3 The mRNA molecule leaves the nucleus through a pore in the nucleur membrane. It attaches to a ribosome in the cytoplasm.

4 A third kind of polynucleotide, transfer RNA or tRNA, pairs its three protruding nucleotides with three nucleotides on the mRNA. The tRNA molecule has an amino acid attached to it. The amino acid it carries is determined by the three protruding nucleotides. There are different kinds of tRNA molecule for each kind of amino acid.

CYTOPLASM

5 A second tRNA molecule brings a second amino acid. The two amino acids join. The mRNA moves along, and the process continues.

Identify these structures on the diagram: DNA, mRNA, tRNA, nuclear membrane, an amino acid, a ribosome.

A ▸ T
G ▸ C

Fig. 69.2 Protein molecules are made in the cytoplasm of cells, on structures called ribosomes. The protein molecules are made by stringing together amino acids in a sequence determined by the sequence of nucleotides in the DNA.

DNA makes exact copies of itself

When a cell divides by mitosis, exact copies of its DNA go into each daughter cell. The new cells contain exactly the same genes as their parent. This is possible because of the structure of DNA molecules.

The two strands of nucleotides in the DNA double helix are held together by bonds between nucleotides on opposite strands. Each nucleotide can only form bonds with one other kind. T will only form bonds with A. C will only form bonds with G. So wherever there is nucleotide A in one strand, there will be nucleotide T in the opposite strand.

When a DNA molecule makes a replica of itself, the two strands unwind and separate. This is done under the influence of enzymes.

In the nucleus, there will be many unattached nucleotides, moving around freely in solution. These free nucleotides can now bump into the exposed nucleotides on the separated strands of the DNA molecule. If an A nucleotide bumps into a T nucleotide, it will form a bond with it. C nucleotides form bonds with G nucleotides. Enzymes help with this process and link together the line of nucleotides which gradually builds up.

Figure 69.3 shows how this happens. At the end of the process, there are two DNA molecules, instead of just one. Each new molecule contains one old strand of DNA and one new one. The new molecules are both identical to the original one.

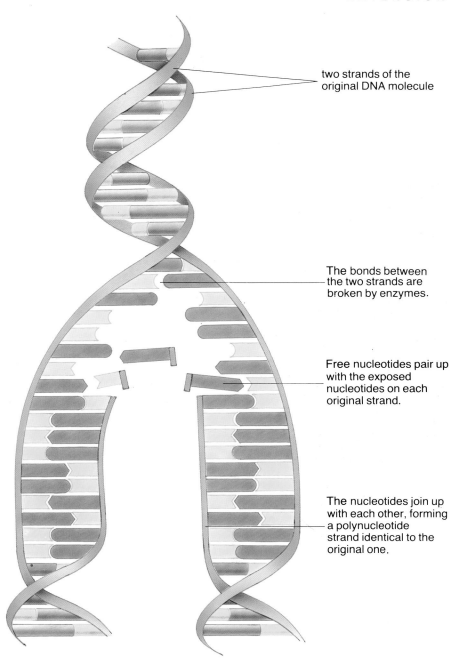

two strands of the original DNA molecule

The bonds between the two strands are broken by enzymes.

Free nucleotides pair up with the exposed nucleotides on each original strand.

The nucleotides join up with each other, forming a polynucleotide strand identical to the original one.

Fig. 69.3 DNA replication

Each person's DNA is unique

Unless you have an identical twin, the sequence of nucleotides in your DNA is different from everyone else's in the world. Although you share some parts of your DNA sequences, or genes, with other people, no-one else will have exactly the same sequences in every part of their DNA.

The uniqueness of each person's DNA can be used to identify people who have committed some types of crimes. If a person has left any of their cells – perhaps from blood, skin or semen – at the scene of a crime, the DNA from these cells can be analysed. It can then be compared with the DNA from the cells of a suspect. If the two samples match, it is almost certain that the suspect really was at the scene of the crime. This process is called **DNA fingerprinting**.

Fig. 69.4 A scientist examining DNA sequences. The bands represent the pattern of nucleotides in the DNA. If two samples of DNA show identical banding patterns, then it is virtually certain that they come from the same person.

A change in the number or kinds of genes in a cell is called mutation

Genes are lengths of DNA. DNA is a very stable molecule. It does not change easily or react with other molecules. So the genes in your cells, which are made of DNA, tend to stay the same all your life.

DNA is also able to make perfect copies of itself. So new cells contain exact copies of the genes in the cell which divided to form them. A child contains exact copies of half of the genes from their father and half of the genes from their mother. Although the *mixture* of genes is different, the genes themselves are still the same as those of the child's parents.

But things do occasionally go wrong. DNA molecules in a cell do sometimes change. This might happen for no obvious reason. Or there might be a definite cause, such as ionising radiation. This changes the genes in the cell. Or DNA might be damaged while it is making copies of itself so that the new DNA is not the same as the original. Or chromosomes might not be shared out properly when a cell divides.

All of these events are called **mutations**. A mutation is a change in the amount or type of DNA in a cell.

Down's syndrome is caused by an extra chromosome

Sometimes, when cells divide to form gametes, the chromosomes do not get shared out equally between the new cells. Occasionally both of the small chromosome 21s go into one of the new cells. One cell gets two and the other gets none.

If an egg containing two chromosome 21s is fertilised, the resulting zygote will have 47 chromosomes instead of 46. The child which

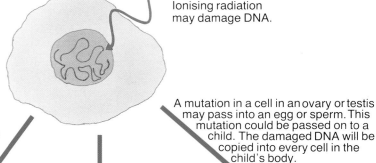

Ionising radiation may damage DNA.

The body's immune system may recognise the changed cell as being 'foreign' and destroy it.

The DNA may be changed in such a way that the cell divides uncontrollably, forming a tumour.

A mutation in a cell in an ovary or testis may pass into an egg or sperm. This mutation could be passed on to a child. The damaged DNA will be copied into every cell in the child's body.

Fig. 70.1 A mutation is a change in the DNA of a cell. Most mutations probably go unnoticed, either because the mutant cell is just one among millions of ordinary cells, or because it is destroyed by white cells. But some mutations can cause cancer. Others might happen in a cell which later divides to form gametes, and so might be passed on to children.

develops from the zygote has three chromosome 21s in their cells.

Although chromosome 21 is one of the smallest chromosomes, this extra chromosome makes a big difference to the development of the child. The child will suffer from **Down's syndrome**. Children with Down's syndrome have lower mental ability. They are more susceptible to some diseases, and commonly die as young adults.

The older a woman is, the more likely she is to produce eggs with an extra chromosome 21. So the likelihood of giving birth to a Down's syndrome

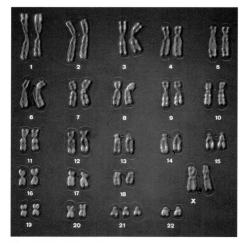

Fig. 70.2 The chromosomes of a girl with Down's syndrome. Compare this picture with Figure 66.3. What is the difference between them?

child increases with age.

Down's syndrome is an example of a mutation. It is a change in the number of chromosomes in a cell, so it is known as a **chromosome mutation**.

Ionising radiation can cause gene mutations

Ionising radiation hitting a cell can damage the DNA inside it. It can make alterations in the DNA. Often, this will not have any noticeable effects. But sometimes it will cause important changes in the genes, which in turn affect the way the cell behaves. A change in a gene is called a **gene mutation**.

An example of this is the effect that ultraviolet light can have on human skin. Ultraviolet light can damage the DNA in skin cells. It may cause alterations in the genes which control the way in which the cells divide. Normally, skin cells divide just enough to replace old cells which have worn away. But if their genes are damaged, the cells may begin to divide uncontrollably. A bundle of rapidly dividing cells, or a **tumour**, is formed. These cells with damaged genes may then spread further, causing malignant **skin cancer**.

Skin cancer is commonest in people with fair skins because their skin does not protect them against ultraviolet rays; it does not have much of the dark pigment, **melanin**. When you expose your skin to the sun, your skin cells gradually build up melanin to protect themselves. But this takes time, and in the meanwhile the cells are easily damaged. Whenever you suffer from sunburn, it is a sign that ultraviolet radiation has damaged your skin cells. You run the risk that you may have badly damaged their genes.

Most mutations cannot be inherited

A mutation like the one which causes skin cancer cannot be passed on to someone's children. The damaged genes are in the skin cells. The genes in the cells in the ovaries or testes, which will divide to make eggs or sperms, are not damaged. So any children which the person has will not inherit the damaged genes.

But a mutation in a cell in an ovary or testis *could* be passed on to a child. Great care is taken when someone is given an X ray. Large doses of X rays can damage genes. So X rays are normally kept well away from a person's ovaries or testes, unless there is a need for these areas to be X rayed. Radiographers, who work with X rays a great deal, often wear lead aprons to protect their bodies from too much radiation.

Fig. 70.4 The incidence of skin cancer has risen sharply since more people have been able to afford to go to hot, sunny places for their holidays.

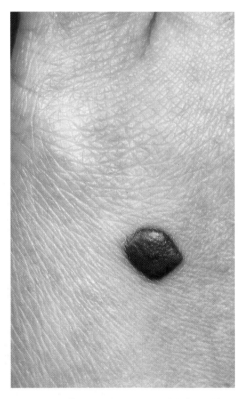

Fig. 70.3 The dark area on this hand is a malignant melanoma, a type of skin cancer. Melanoma is increasing faster than any other cancer in Britain. People who have burnt their skin in the sun, especially when young, run the greatest risk of suffering from melanoma. The cancer often does not appear until up to 30 years after the initial damage was done to the skin.

Questions

1 The table below shows the chances of having a Down's syndrome baby, for women of different ages. How does this support the theory that Down's syndrome is caused by a defect in egg formation?

Age	25	30	35	40	45
Chance	1 in 1500	1 in 800	1 in 300	1 in 100	1 in 30

2 a What is a mutation? Give two examples of ways in which mutations may be caused.

  b Why is a mutation in a cell in a person's ovary or testis more likely to have harmful effects than a mutation in one of their other cells?

  c Explain why the release of CFCs into the atmosphere may increase the frequency of skin cancer.

71

GENETIC ENGINEERING

It is now possible to take genes from one organism, and insert them into the cells of another.

Genetic engineering can be used to manufacture proteins

A gene is a piece of DNA which gives instructions for making a particular protein. The protein made depends on the sequence of nucleotides in the DNA.

It is now possible to put genes from one organism into a different organism. The cell may then follow the instructions in the DNA and make the protein for which it codes. In this way, we can persuade cells to make proteins which they would not normally make. This is called **genetic engineering**.

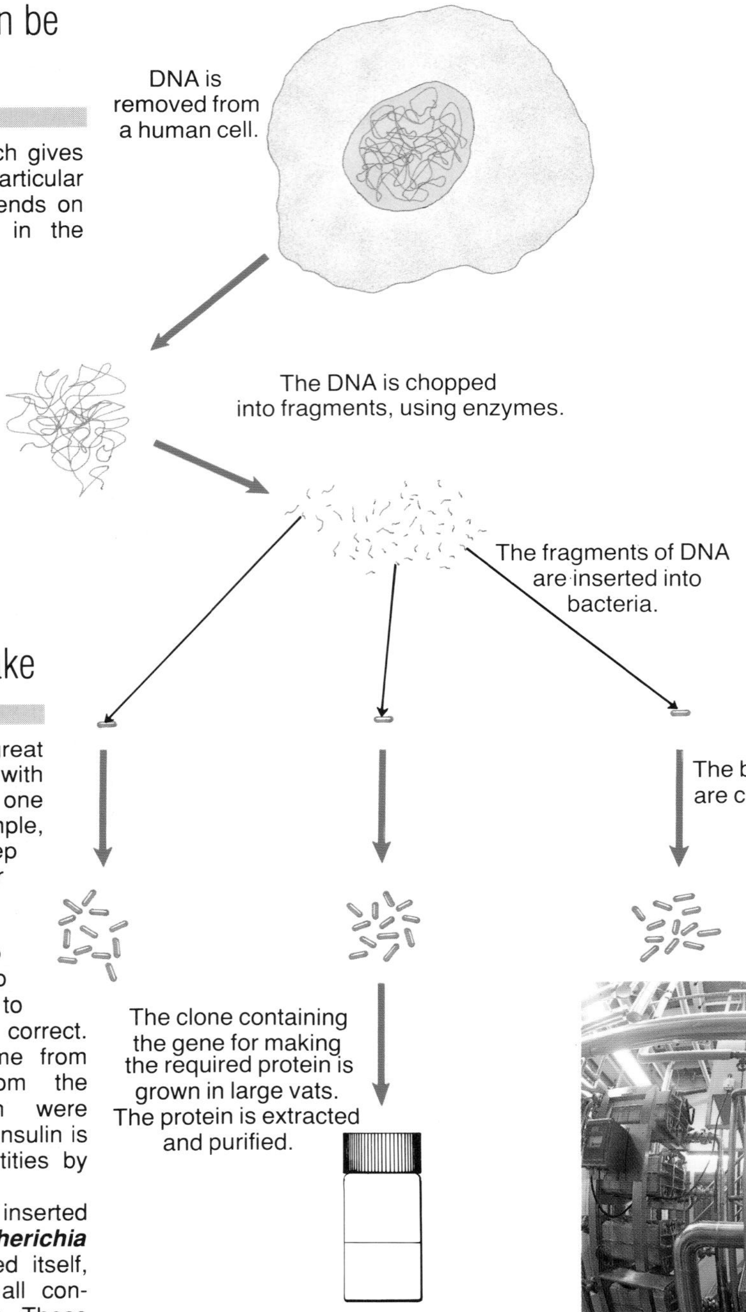

Genetically-engineered bacteria are used to make human proteins

Some human proteins are in great demand to treat people with diseases caused by a defect in one of their genes. **Insulin**, for example, is a hormone which helps to keep the amount of glucose in your blood at the right level. Insulin is made in the pancreas. But some people with **diabetes** do not make insulin. They need to be given injections of insulin to keep their blood glucose levels correct. Until recently, the insulin came from pigs. It was extracted from the pancreases of pigs which were slaughtered for meat. But now insulin is being produced in large quantities by bacteria.

The human insulin gene was inserted into a bacterium called **Escherichia coli**. The bacterium reproduced itself, forming a **clone** of bacteria all containing the human insulin gene. These genetically-engineered bacteria are grown in large vats. They follow the instructions on the human insulin gene and make insulin. The insulin is used to treat people with diabetes caused by lack of insulin.

Another human protein made by genetically engineered E. coli is **human**

DNA is removed from a human cell.

Fig. 71.1 How bacteria can be used for making human proteins.

The DNA is chopped into fragments, using enzymes.

The fragments of DNA are inserted into bacteria.

The bacteria are cloned.

The clone containing the gene for making the required protein is grown in large vats. The protein is extracted and purified.

growth hormone. A child who does not make this hormone does not grow properly. It has been possible to treat such children with injections of human growth hormone, but until recently the hormone was only available in small quantities and was very expensive. Now there is more of it, made by bacteria containing the human growth hormone gene.

Fig. 71.2 Human growth hormone is manufactured by growing genetically-engineered bacteria in large vats. Conditions such as temperature and oxygen concentration are automatically monitored and kept at the best level for maximum production of the hormone. Why do you think the biotechnologist is dressed like this?

Gene therapy could be used to treat inherited diseases

People with inherited diseases, such as cystic fibrosis, thalassaemia and haemophilia, might be cured if the correct gene could be inserted into their cells. The gene would have to be identified and then cloned, perhaps by introducing it into *E. coli*. The gene could then be put into the cells of the person with the disease. This is called **gene therapy**.

The first attempt to treat a disease in this way was made in 1990. The disease was a rare one called **ADA deficiency**. ADA is an enzyme, and people with this disease lack the gene for making this enzyme. Because of the lack of the enzyme, many of their white blood cells die and so they are unable to fight infections. At the moment, the disease can be treated by giving a bone marrow transplant. Bone marrow from a donor, containing white blood cells with the right gene, is transplanted into the sufferer. This is not pleasant for the donor or the sufferer, and doesn't always work. An alternative treatment is to give injections of the missing enzyme.

The ADA gene has now been identified. A clone of the gene has been built up. Some bone marrow cells were taken from a girl suffering from ADA deficiency. The cells were cultured in the laboratory and the ADA genes inserted into them. These cells were injected into her blood, from where they could find their way back to the bone marrow. Some bone marrow cells go on multiplying all through a person's life. So, hopefully, some of the genetically engineered cells will multiply there, making a clone of cells which will produce the ADA enzyme.

Treating cystic fibrosis, thalassaemia or haemophilia in this way would be more difficult. It is possible to identify and clone the right genes and to introduce them into human cells. But in cystic fibrosis, for example, the cells which need the gene are in several different parts of the body, including the lungs. It would not be so easy to take them out, culture them and insert the correct gene. Even if this could be done, the cells would not multiply when they were put back into the body, so most of the person's cells would still contain the faulty gene. Another problem is that, even when they contain the right gene, the cells might not use it. Cells do not use all their genes all the time. We do not yet know enough about what switches particular genes on and off in individual human cells.

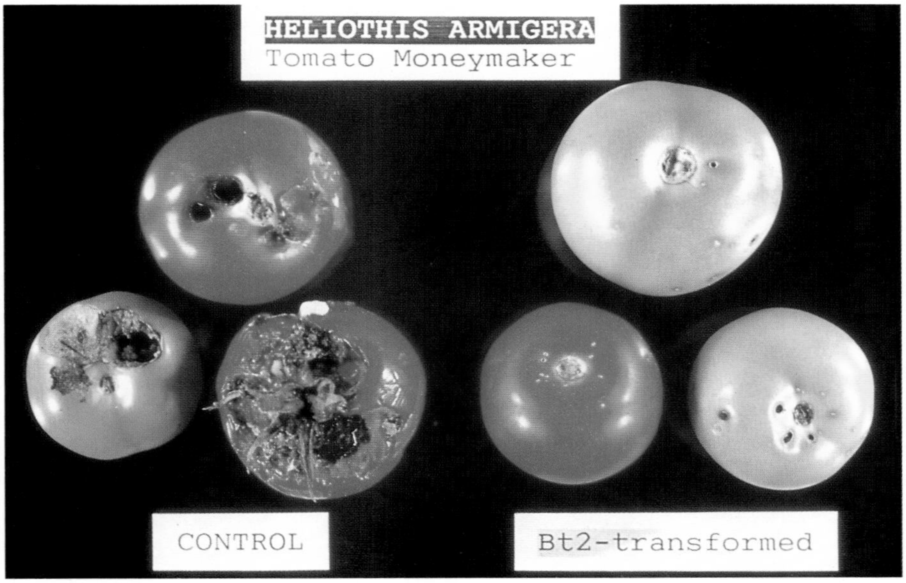

Genetic engineering carries risks

Genetic engineering is a new technology. It has been developing at a great rate since the 1970s. It could provide great benefits, but it also carries great risks. For example, genetic engineering can be used to insert new genes into bacteria. This might change a bacterium so much that a previously harmless one becomes capable of causing disease in humans. Regulations have been imposed to make sure that no genetically-engineered organisms can be released into the environment, unless it has been decided that they pose absolutely no risk to humans or other life.

Another risk might arise when new genes are inserted into human cells in the process of gene therapy. It is possible that the process of inserting the correct genes into the human cells might make them cancerous. However, if the condition which was being treated by gene therapy was going to cause the death of the person anyway, if left untreated, then this might be an acceptable risk to take.

A third possibility could raise other objections. It is possible to take eggs from a mammal, such as mouse, and to insert new genes into them. The eggs can then be fertilised and put back into the mother, where they develop into young mice. All the cells of the baby mice contain the new gene. This technique may be used to produce new strains of farm animals, such as cows which would give more milk. In theory, this could be done for humans, too. But everyone is agreed that this kind of experiment on humans would be completely wrong. No-one could be sure what the results would be.

HELIOTHIS ARMIGERA
Tomato Moneymaker

CONTROL   Bt2-transformed

Fig. 71.3 New strains of tomatoes have been developed by genetic engineering. The new varieties may be resistant to attack by a particular disease, or may last longer after picking without going squashy. These new characteristics are introduced into the tomatoes by identifying a particular length of DNA which codes for the desired feature, cloning it, and then introducing it into a few tomato cells. These cells are then grown into tomato plants, whose cells will all contain the new piece of DNA. The research involved is very expensive and companies doing this work are hoping to take out patents on the particular stretches of DNA which they have managed to identify and clone.

DID YOU KNOW?

Haemophiliacs can be given regular doses of Factor 8, which enables them to live normal lives. The Factor 8 is taken from human blood given by blood donors. Before the transmission of AIDS was understood, some haemophiliacs were infected with the AIDS virus through infected blood. Now all donated blood is carefully screened so this can no longer happen. Soon, Factor 8 may be made by genetic engineering.

72 VARIATION

Living things vary. The variation may be continuous or discontinuous. It may be caused by genes, by the environment, by a mixture of these two influences.

INVESTIGATION 72.1

Measuring human variation

You are going to measure and record an example of variation in humans. You will need a large sample to make your results valid – preferably about 30 people.

1 Choose the feature you are going to investigate. Some suggestions are: height, wrist or neck circumference, length of foot, length of index finger on left or right hand. Whichever you choose, make sure that the way in which you measure it is absolutely standard – you must do it exactly the same way each time. Write down all of your results in a clear chart.

2 Now group your measurements into categories. The sizes and range of the categories will depend on what you have measured. You should have between six and ten categories. Draw up a second results chart, recording the number of results which fit into each of your chosen categories.

3 Use this second results chart to draw a histogram. The categories go along the horizontal axis, and the number of individuals in each category on the vertical axis.

Questions

1 Describe the shape of your graph. Look at the graphs drawn by other people who have measured a different feature. Are they the same shape as yours?

2 The commonest category is called the **modal class**. What was the modal class for the feature you measured?

3 Go back to your first results chart and use it work out an average or **mean** value for the feature you measured. Does the mean value come within the modal class? Will this always be the case?

4 Think about the possible causes of the variation in the feature you have measured. Do you think it is caused by differences in people's genes? Or might it be caused by differences in their diet, or their behaviour, or anything else? Give reasons for your answer.

Variation may be caused by genes, by the environment, or by both

Humans are all different from one another. Even identical twins can be told apart by their close friends. What makes us all different?

One reason is that we have different **genes**. There are thousands of genes in every human cell. Many genes come in many different forms, or alleles. So the chances of your particular collection of genes being the same as someone else's are virtually nil – unless you have an identical twin. These genes affect many things about you and help to make you different from everyone else.

Another reason for variation between people is differences in their **environment**. Your environment is your surroundings, and all the things which affect you. Your diet is part of your environment and can affect your height, your weight, and other features.

Many of the differences between people are caused by both genes *and* environment. Your height, for example, partly depends on your genes. But it also depends on whether you have a good diet when you are growing.

Fig. 72.1   Human variation

Variation can be continuous or discontinuous

The feature you measured in Investigation 72.1 was an example of **continuous variation**. People fitted in anywhere between two extremes. There were no sharp boundaries between your measurements. You had to invent boundaries in order to put people into categories.

Some kinds of variation are not like this. People do fit neatly into definite categories. This is called **discontinuous variation**. Blood groups are a good example. Your blood group is either A, B, AB or O. Another example is sex; you are either male or female.

Fig. 72.2 What features among these dead leaves show discontinuous variation? What features show continuous variation? How many different species of leaves are there? What features would you use to decide which species a particular leaf belongs to?

Questions

1 The following are all examples of variation in humans.
    i blood groups   iv sex
    ii hair colour   v how good you are at maths
    iii eye colour   vi height
  a Decide whether each one is probably caused by genes, by the environment or by both.
  b Decide whether each one is an example of continuous variation or discontinuous variation.
  c Describe any trends or patterns you can see in your answers to parts a and b.

2 A student collected 50 fallen leaves and measured their length from base to apex. She also recorded whether the leaf margin was smooth or serrated (jagged). Her results are shown in the tables below.

a Which of the features recorded by the student shows continuous variation?
b Which shows discontinuous variation?
c Draw up a chart like the one below:

Size range (mm)	Number of leaves
35–39	
40–44	

Make a tally of the number of leaves in each category. Make your tally marks in a different colour for the serrated leaves and non-serrated leaves.

d Use your tally chart to draw a histogram of number of leaves against size range. Count all your tally marks together, ignoring their colours.

e The student decided that she must have collected leaves from two species of tree. What evidence is there that this is so?

f If you wanted to decide which of the two species a particular leaf belonged to, would you measure its length, or look at the shape of its leaf margin? Explain your answer.

g Suggest causes for the variations in:
    i leaf length and
    ii the shape of the leaf margin.

Leaf	Length (mm)	Serrated (S) or not (N)
1	75	S
2	80	S
3	40	N
4	60	N
5	42	N
6	78	S
7	50	S
8	38	N
9	74	S
10	81	S
11	45	N
12	90	S
13	46	N
14	59	N
15	98	S
16	79	S
17	76	S
18	47	N
19	71	S
20	42	N
21	39	N
22	77	S
23	40	N
24	71	S
25	68	S

Leaf	Length (mm)	Serrated (S) or not (N)
26	87	S
27	40	N
28	47	N
29	51	N
30	59	S
31	52	N
32	48	N
33	83	S
34	47	N
35	51	N
36	75	S
37	49	N
38	91	S
39	57	N
40	46	N
41	82	S
42	89	S
43	66	S
44	50	N
45	72	S
46	45	N
47	79	S
48	80	S
49	46	N
50	82	S

73 SELECTION

Within a population of organisms, many variations will exist. Some of the organisms may have variations which give them a better chance of survival.

In the wild, many organisms die before becoming adult

Wild rabbits may breed five times a year. They may have up to seven babies in each litter. So a single pair of rabbits might produce 35 young in just 12 months. If all these bred just as prolifically the next year, imagine what would happen to the rabbit population!

But the rabbit population in Britain does not increase like this. There have been sudden increases from time to time, and also sudden decreases. But, on the whole, the rabbit population remains roughly constant from year to year.

You saw in Topic 60 that the size of a population depends on the balance between its birth rate and its death rate. Rabbits have a high birth rate. But they also have a high death rate. Many baby rabbits die before they reach reprodutive age. So the rabbit population stays fairly steady.

What kills the young rabbits? There are many dangers. Predators, such as foxes, will take quite a few. Food shortages might mean that some will starve. Diseases such as myxomatosis will kill others. Only the fittest, strongest baby rabbits will live to become adults and breed.

Advantageous features may be passed on to offspring

There is quite a bit of luck involved in whether or not a baby rabbit will survive. But rabbits are not all identical. Some rabbits may have a natural advantage over others in the struggle for survival. Their chances of success may be better than others.

Imagine, for example, a litter of rabbits in which one has a white coat instead of brown. The white coat might be caused by having two recessive alleles for coat colour. This white rabbit would have less chance of survival than its brown relations. It would be more easily spotted by foxes, and so would be more likely to be killed and eaten. It is very unlikely that it would live long enough to have young of its own.

The rabbits which are more likely to survive will be brown ones. They will pass their brown coat alleles to their offspring. The white coat alleles will be lost when the white rabbit is killed and eaten. The chances of another white rabbit being born in the next generation will be quite small. It will only happen if two heterozygous brown rabbits mate.

The white rabbits, and the alleles which make them white, are at a disadvantage. They are **selected** against. The brown alleles give a rabbit an advantage in the struggle for survival.

This process is called **natural selection**. It is happening all the time. Alleles which produce advantageous variations are more likely to be passed on to the next generation than disadvantageous alleles.

Fig. 73.1 A brown rabbit is much better camouflaged than a white one, and so has a better chance of escaping the attention of predators.

Bacteria can multiply very quickly. Often, their numbers can double in 30 min. 1 cm^3 of liquid could contain 10 billion cells.

antibiotic added

Antibiotics kill bacteria without harming the person the bacteria are growing in. But one cell in millions could be genetically resistant to the antibiotic, and not be killed.

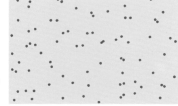

This bacterium will multiply rapidly, even though the antibiotic is present. Its descendants will inherit the resistance to the antibiotic.

Fig. 73.2 Natural selection can produce a new strain of bacteria which is resistant to an antibiotic.

Dark peppered moths survive best in polluted areas

Peppered moths are common in Britain. They spend their days on tree trunks, camouflaged against the bark. Birds prey on them, so the moths' camouflage is very important in ensuring their survival.

The colour of the moths' wings is determined by genes. There are two possible colours. One is a speckled light grey, and the other is black.

Up until the industrial revolution, in the middle of the nineteenth century, the air was unpolluted. Lichens grew on tree trunks, making them grey and speckled. Moths with speckled wings were the best camouflaged. Any moths with black wings were easily picked out by birds and eaten. So almost all the peppered moths in Britain were speckled. We know this by looking at the moths in collections made by naturalists in the nineteenth century.

But in some parts of the country, the air has become polluted. Trees no longer have lichen on them. The dark colour of the tree bark provides a better camouflage for the dark coloured moths. In these areas, it is the dark moths which are most likely to survive. So almost all the moths in these areas are dark.

This is an example of **natural selection**. In unpolluted areas, like Cornwall, natural selection acts against the dark moths. In polluted areas, like Birmingham, natural selection acts against the light moths. The proportions of the two colours of peppered moths are different in different parts of Britain.

Fig. 73.3 On lichen-covered bark, the speckled form of the peppered moth is much better camouflaged than the dark form.

Fig. 73.4a The wild boar is an ancestor of the domestic pig. In the wild, strong, fast-moving animals with a protective coat of hair for insulation are most likely to survive. The massive head and tusks of the boar help in defence if it is threatened.

Humans select animals and plants with useful variations

Humans use living organisms for many purposes. We breed crops and farm animals for food. We breed dogs for companionship, sport and appearance. We breed plants to look attractive. We breed bacteria and fungi to make foods like cheese, yoghurt and beer.

Farm animals, like wild animals, show many variations between individuals. Two cows, for example, might vary in size, colour, temperament, size of horns, ability to survive the cold, and amount of milk produced. When farmers choose which cow to breed from, they will choose the one with the most useful characteristics. They will hope that the genes for these characteristics will be passed on to the cow's calf.

This is called **artificial selection**. It has been going on ever since humans first began to domesticate animals. Over many generations, it can have big effects on the characteristics of the animals or plants being bred. You only have to look at all the different varieties of dogs to see what selective breeding and artificial selection can do!

Fig. 73.4b Artificial selection has produced modern breeds of pig, such as the Landrace, which have little hair and are much less aggressive than wild pigs. They have been bred to grow quickly, and produce large amounts of meat. This has been done by choosing to breed from pigs with these desirable characteristics.

Over long periods of time, natural selection may cause big changes in the characteristics of a species.

Natural selection may cause changes in a population

Natural selection makes sure that the best adapted organisms survive. Ones which have disadvantageous variations usually die before they can reproduce.

If the environment in which the organisms are living stays the same, then the same variations will go on being selected for. The population will tend to stay the same, generation after generation. Some kinds of organism have hardly changed at all for millions of years. The coelacanth, for example, lives in deep waters in the Indian Ocean and is the same now as it was 350 000 000 years ago.

But natural selection can also cause change. Sometimes this is because the **environment** changes. Horses were fox-sized animals, living in wet areas where they browsed on soft leaves, 54 000 000 years ago. They had spreading toes, to support them on swampy ground. But as the climate changed, becoming dryer, different characteristics were selected for. More recent fossils of horses are taller, with fewer toes. This allowed them to run faster on the firmer ground.

Natural selection can also cause change if a **new variation** turns up in a population. This could be caused by mutation. Most mutations produce disadvantageous characteristics, so that the individual possessing them dies, and the mutation is not passed on to the next generation. But a small proportion of mutations are beneficial. They give the organism an advantage in the struggle for survival. These mutations will be passed on to the next generation. Eventually, after several generations, most of the population may possess the new characteristic.

So changes in the environment or changes in the genes in a population can cause changes in the characteristics of a species of organism. Over long periods of time, a combination of these changes can produce totally different kinds of living things. This is called **evolution**.

Life first appeared on Earth about 4 000 000 000 years ago. The first living things would have been very simple, consisting of just a single cell. Biologists believe that, from these first simple organisms, natural selection has produced all the different species living on Earth. Figure 71.2 shows some of the main paths which evolution has taken.

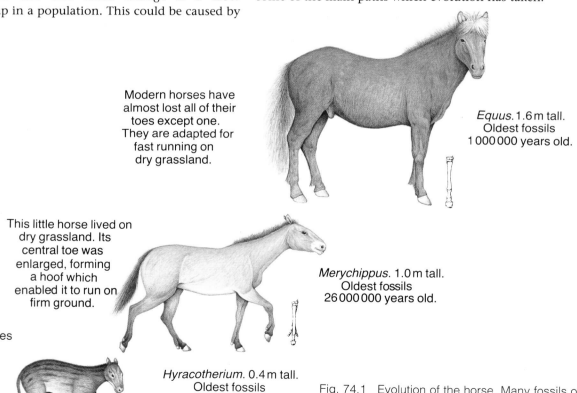

Modern horses have almost lost all of their toes except one. They are adapted for fast running on dry grassland.

Equus. 1.6 m tall. Oldest fossils 1 000 000 years old.

This little horse lived on dry grassland. Its central toe was enlarged, forming a hoof which enabled it to run on firm ground.

Merychippus. 1.0 m tall. Oldest fossils 26 000 000 years old.

The earliest horses were about the size of a fox. They lived on boggy ground, and had feet with spreading toes to give a large surface area for support.

Hyracotherium. 0.4 m tall. Oldest fossils 54 000 000 years old.

Fig. 74.1 Evolution of the horse. Many fossils of horses and their ancestors have been found in North America. The fossil sequence shows changes in the number of toes, structure of teeth, and size of these animals.

Only three examples are shown here, but there have probably been hundreds of species of horse. Each was well adapted to live in the conditions which existed at that time, in that place. As the climate changed, different features were favoured by natural selection.

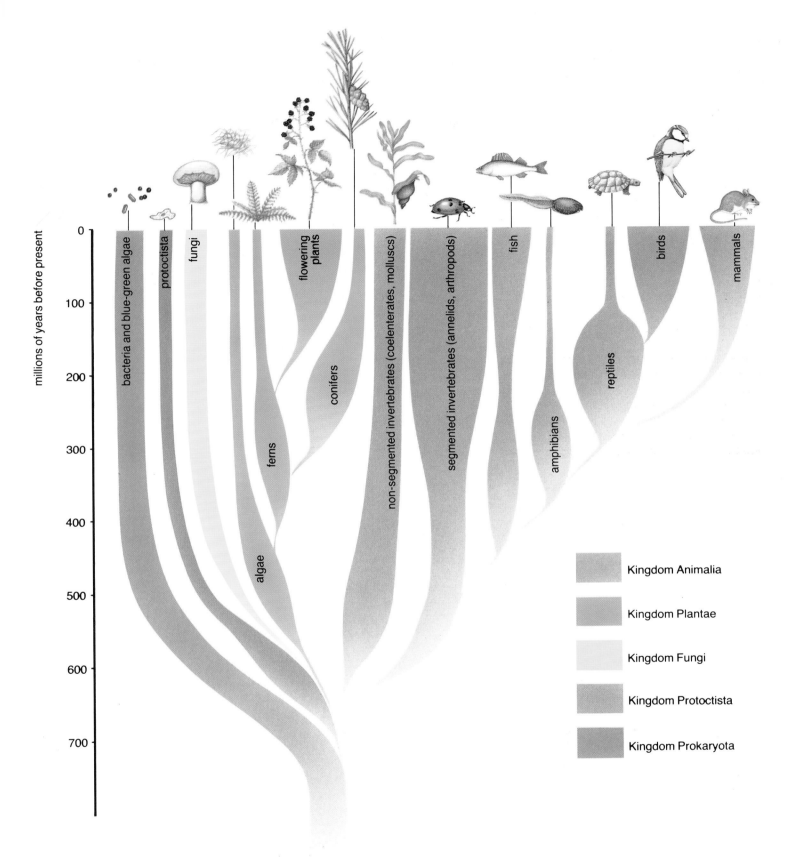

millions of years before present

bacteria and blue-green algae

protoctista

fungi

algae

ferns

conifers

flowering plants

non-segmented invertebrates (coelenterates, molluscs)

segmented invertebrates (annelids, arthropods)

fish

amphibians

reptiles

birds

mammals

Kingdom Animalia

Kingdom Plantae

Kingdom Fungi

Kingdom Protoctista

Kingdom Prokaryota

Fig. 74.2 The probable evolutionary relationships between the main groups of organisms.

Questions

1 From which group of animals did mammals evolve?
2 Which is the most recent group of animals to evolve?
3 How do you think biologists have worked out this evolutionary family tree? Why can no-one be absolutely sure that it is right?

Questions

1 In a species of flowering plant, the allele for red petal colour is dominant to the allele for white petal colour.

Pollen from a red-flowered plant is used to fertilise a white-flowered plant. Several weeks later, the seeds are collected from the white-flowered plant. They are sown, and grown into adult plants. Of the adult plants, 54 flower; 24 have white flowers, and 30 have red flowers.

a What are the genotypes of the white-flowered plants?

b What is the genotype of the original red-flowered plant? Give a reason for your answer.

c What are the genotypes of the male nuclei in the pollen grains from this red-flowered plant?

d What are the genotypes of the female nuclei in the ovules of the white-flowered plant?

e What are the genotypes of the red-flowered plants which grew from the collected seeds?

f The ratio of colours in the offspring, described above, is not exactly what would be expected. What is the expected ratio? Give a reason why this exact ratio was not obtained.

g If pollen from the original white-flowered parent had been used to fertilise the original red-flowered parent, would you expect to get similar results? Explain your answer.

h If the original red-flowered parent had successfully fertilised itself, what ratio of flower colours would you expect to get if you collected and grew the seeds produced? Explain your answer fully.

2 Phenylketonuria is a disease caused by the lack of an essential enzyme. If untreated, it causes mental retardation. Although the disease is rare, children are usually tested at birth to make sure that they have the enzyme. If they do not, treatment throughout their life can allow them to develop normally.

The chart below shows the family tree of a family with phenylketonuria.

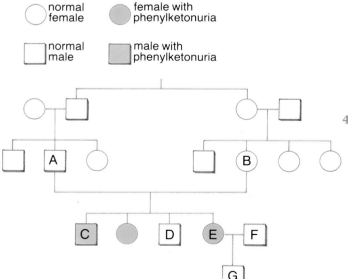

a Does this family tree suggest that the allele for phenylketonuria is a recessive allele, or is it a dominant allele? Give reasons for your answer.

b What are the genotypes of people A, B and C? Give reasons for your answer.

c What are the two possible genotypes for person D?

d Person F is from a totally unrelated family. What is his most likely genotype?

e What is the genotype of person G?

f What relationship is there between A and B?

3 Read the following passage, and then answer the questions which follow.

Sexing embryos

Farmers breeding cattle for milk production often want to produce more female calves than male ones. A portable embryo-sexing kit has now been developed, which makes it possible to choose the sex of the calves which are born to a cow.

Seven days after fertilisation, embryos are removed from a cow's uterus. A few cells are taken from each embryo. DNA is removed from these cells. The DNA is incubated with an enzyme so that it makes more and more copies of itself. The DNA copies are then tested to see if they contain a sequence which is known to be found on the Y chromosome. If they do, they are male. If they do not, they are female. This sexing procedure takes only three hours.

The embryos which are known to be female can then be split to produce two embryos. These can then be replaced in the same cow, transferred into a different cow, or frozen for future use.

The portable kit can be used on the farm, and can be used by a technician with very little training.

---

a In 1989, the cost of the embryo-sexing kit was £4800. Why might the kit be worth this much money to a cattle breeder?

b Why has the kit been developed to test for the Y chromosome, and not the X or any other chromosome?

c What is DNA?

d Suggest why the DNA is allowed to make copies of itself before it is tested.

e Would the two embryos produced by splitting a single embryo be identical twins? Explain your answer.

f What advantages might there be in transferring some of the chosen embryos into a different mother, rather than the one from which they originally came?

4 The first person to put forward the theory of natural selection to explain how evolution might have happened was Charles Darwin. Find out about:

- when and where Darwin lived, and what his profession was,
- his voyage on *The Beagle,*
- his theories about natural selection,
- how people reacted to his ideas.

CONTROL AND COORDINATION

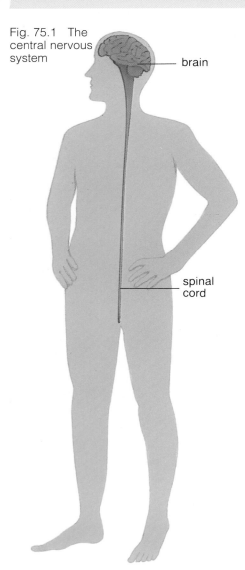

Fig. 75.1 The central nervous system

brain

spinal cord

The nervous system transfers information

Your body contains many different organs. Each organ has its own job to do. But organs must be able to communicate with each other if they are to work effectively as a team. For example, if you see a bull charging towards you, your eye must communicate with your leg muscles so that they can do the appropriate thing – make your legs run. Your eyes and muscles must also communicate with your heart and the muscles you use for breathing, so that they can work faster and provide your leg muscles with the extra oxygen they need.

You have two main ways of transferring information from one part of your body to another. One way is by sending **electrical signals** along nerves. The other is by sending **chemical signals** through the blood. This topic, and the next one, look at the first of these methods – nervous communication.

Nerve cells are adapted for quick communication

The control centres of your nervous system are your **brain** and **spinal cord**. These are known as the **central nervous system**. Their function is to receive information from all parts of your body, integrate it together, and then send messages to other parts telling them what to do.

The rest of your nervous system is made up of **nerves**. These carry messages to and from the central nervous system and all parts of the body.

The cells making up the brain, spinal cord and nerves are called **nerve cells** or **neurones**. Figure 75.2 shows one type of neurone. It has all the parts you would expect to find in any animal cell – nucleus, cell surface membrane and cytoplasm. But it also has several special features. The most obvious of these is a very long thread of cytoplasm called an **axon**. This carries electrical messages along itself. Axons can be very long indeed – possibly several metres in length! A nerve cell like this one might have its cell body in your spinal cord and its nerve endings in your big toe. The long axon can carry a message very swiftly, transferring it over this distance in a fraction of a second.

Another special feature of this nerve cell is the many small threads around the cell body. These are called **dendrites**. Their job is to make contact with other nerve cells around them, and to receive information from these cells.

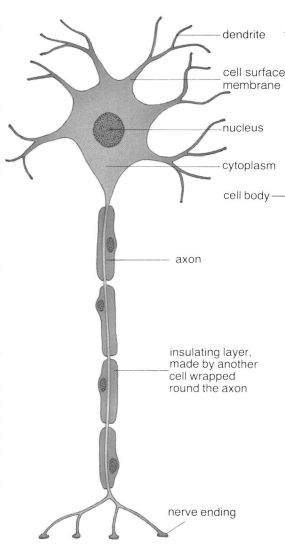

dendrite

cell surface membrane

nucleus

cytoplasm

cell body

axon

insulating layer, made by another cell wrapped round the axon

nerve ending

Fig. 75.2 A neurone. This is a motor neurone, which carries messages from the central nervous system to a muscle. Its cell body would be in the brain or spinal cord. Its axon might be up to a metre long.

Receptors collect information about your environment

Information is fed into your nervous system from **receptors** in different parts of your body. Receptors are cells which are sensitive to certain aspects of your environment. For example, rods and cones in the retina of your eye are receptors. They are sensitive to light. Table 75.1 lists the main types of receptors you have.

Receptor cells work by transferring a particular kind of energy into electrical energy. The electrical energy is then used to transmit an impulse along a nerve fibre to your brain or spinal cord. Rods and cones, for example, transfer light energy into electrical energy. Receptor cells in your ear transfer sound energy into electrical energy.

Receptor cells are often part of a **sense organ**. Rods and cones, for example, are part of the eye. The sense organ contains many other cells besides the receptor cells. These other cells may help the receptor cells to collect and transfer the type of energy to which they are sensitive. In the eye, the cornea and lens help to focus light onto the rods and cones.

Receptor	Type of energy receptor is sensitive to
rods and cones	light
cells in cochlea	sound
taste buds	chemical
smell receptors	chemical
temperature receptors	heat
touch receptors	movement

Table 75.1
Receptors

INVESTIGATION 75.1

Taste and smell

You have probably noticed that, when you have a cold, you cannot taste food as well as you normally can. This is because you use receptors in your nose, as well as in your tongue, to taste food. If your nose is blocked, then these receptors get no information from the food you are eating.

Design and carry out an experiment to test the hypothesis that **the ability to tell the differ- ence between foods is reduced if the nose is blocked.**

A good way to block your nose is to pinch it hard together between a finger and thumb.

Don't forget that the appearance and the texture of different foods also help you to tell the difference between them – you will have to design your experiment to take this into account.

Questions

1 a What is a receptor?
In which sense organ are each of the receptors listed in Table 75.1 found?
b Which types of receptor would send electrical signals to your brain:
  i to tell it that you were about to eat a hamburger?
  ii to tell it that you were eating a hamburger?
  iii to tell it that your friend was eating a hamburger?
c To which type of energy is each of

these receptors sensitive?
2 Figure 75.2 shows a motor neurone.
  a What features of this cell tell you that it is an animal cell and not a plant cell?
  b What special features of this cell tell you that it is a motor neurone and not any other type of animal cell?
  c How do these special features enable it to perform its function efficiently?

INVESTIGATION 75.2

The distribution of touch receptors

1 Choose two different parts of your skin which you can easily test for sensitivity – for example, the back and palm of your hand, your elbow, or your ear lobe.
2 Read through the experiment and draw up a results chart.
3 Take a paper clip, and pull it out so that the two ends are exactly 0.5 cm apart. Get your partner to turn away, or close their eyes. Touch them gently on the first area, either with one end or both ends of the paper clip. When they tell you how many ends they can feel, record in your chart whether they are right or wrong.
Do this 20 times on the same area. Sometimes use one end, and sometimes two. To make it as fair a test as possible:
- use one or two ends in a random order
- touch very gently, so that only the touch receptors, not the pain receptors, are stimulated
- hold the paper clip very still – if it wobbles, it is easier to feel
- don't tell your partner if they are right or wrong.

4 Now repeat step 3 on the other area you have chosen. Keep the paper clip ends 0.5 cm apart.
5 Repeat steps 3 and 4 with the paper clip ends 2 cm apart.
6 Summarise your results so that it is easy to see any differences which you found.

Questions

1 Which of the two areas you tested was the most sensitive? What evidence do you have for this? Can you suggest any reasons why it is useful for some areas to be more sensitive to touch than others?
2 Was there any difference in your results for the paper clip ends at 2 cm apart, and at 0.5 cm apart? If so, suggest why this might be. (Think about the number of touch receptors in a certain area of different parts of your skin.)
3 Are you happy with the accuracy of your experiment? Can you suggest any ways of making it even more accurate?

76 RESPONDING TO STIMULI

A stimulus is picked up by a receptor, and passed to an effector which responds to it.

Receptors pick up stimuli; effectors react to them

A **receptor** is a cell or group of cells which is sensitive to a particular type of change in the environment. Your receptors collect information about what is happening around you.

Receptors transfer the energy of the stimulus into electrical energy. This sets up an electrical impulse in a nerve fibre, which carries a signal to the brain or spinal cord. The signal is then sent on to a part of the body to tell it to respond to the stimulus. This might be a muscle or a gland. The part of the body which responds is called an **effector**.

A reflex action is an automatic response to a stimulus

An example of the way in which you respond to a stimulus is your reaction to touching a very hot object. Very quickly, and without thinking about it, you pull your hand away. This sort of very fast, automatic response is called a **reflex action**.

Figure 76.1 shows the pathway taken by the impulse in this reflex action. The **stimulus** is the pain you feel when you touch the hot plate. It is sensed by a **pain receptor** in your hand. The receptor triggers an impulse in a **sensory neurone**, which transmits the message to the spinal cord. Here, the impulse is passed on to a **relay neurone**, which in turn passes it to a **motor neurone**. The motor neurone passes the impulse to a muscle in your arm, which contracts and pulls your arm away. The muscle is an **effector** – it responds to the stimulus.

This pathway along which the impulse travels is called a **reflex arc**. This one has three neurones. Some reflex arcs have only two – there is no relay neurone involved. Some reflex arcs have more than one relay neurone. Some reflex arcs involve the brain, rather than the spinal cord. They are called **cerebral reflexes**. Reflexes like the one shown in Figure 76.1 are **spinal reflexes**.

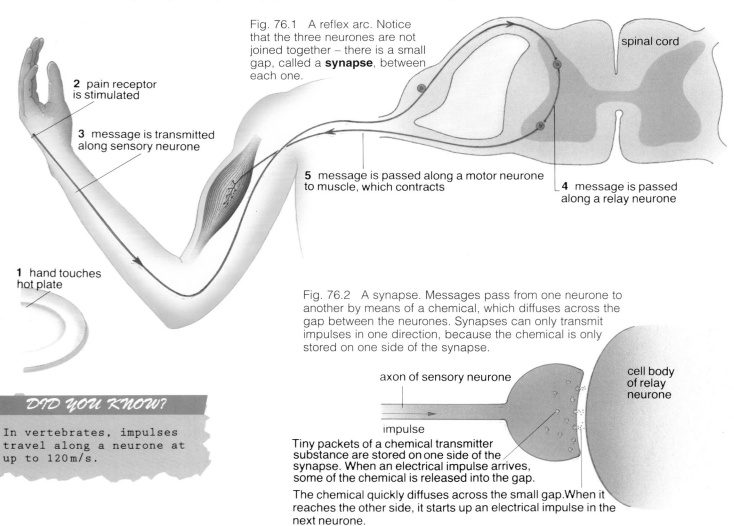

Fig. 76.1 A reflex arc. Notice that the three neurones are not joined together – there is a small gap, called a **synapse**, between each one.

spinal cord

2 pain receptor is stimulated

3 message is transmitted along sensory neurone

5 message is passed along a motor neurone to muscle, which contracts

4 message is passed along a relay neurone

1 hand touches hot plate

Fig. 76.2 A synapse. Messages pass from one neurone to another by means of a chemical, which diffuses across the gap between the neurones. Synapses can only transmit impulses in one direction, because the chemical is only stored on one side of the synapse.

axon of sensory neurone

cell body of relay neurone

impulse

Tiny packets of a chemical transmitter substance are stored on one side of the synapse. When an electrical impulse arrives, some of the chemical is released into the gap.

The chemical quickly diffuses across the small gap. When it reaches the other side, it starts up an electrical impulse in the next neurone.

DID YOU KNOW?

In vertebrates, impulses travel along a neurone at up to 120 m/s.

The brain and spinal cord coordinate your actions

The reflex action shown in Figure 76.1 is a very simple one. One receptor is receiving one stimulus, and only one impulse is being sent to the spinal cord. In reality, though, many receptors are constantly sending many impulses to your brain and spinal cord. Your brain and spinal cord have the job of putting together all the information coming in from all the different parts of your body, and then sending impulses to appropriate effectors. They **coordinate** the information coming in to them.

For example, imagine you had picked up the hot plate, rather than just touching it. Before you picked it up, your eyes had sent impulses to your brain telling it that your favourite meal was on the plate. Other impulses told your brain that you were hungry. So, when the impulse from your pain receptors arrived in your central nervous system, there were already other messages there saying 'food' and 'hungry'. The central nervous system weighs up all this information. Instead of sending impulses to your muscles telling them to contract quickly, it might tell different muscles to contract carefully, putting the plate down gently – even if you do burn your fingers!

Fig. 76.3 As Nelli Kim balances on the beam, her central nervous system receives information from all her muscles, as well as her eyes and ears. Her brain then sends out messages along her nerves to the appropriate muscles, correcting any slight imbalance. Years of patient training are needed to achieve this type of perfect coordination.

Questions

1 Read the passage below, and then answer the questions. (You will find a diagram on page 182.)
  a Which part of the eye contains the receptors which sense the brightness of the light?
  b Put the following statements in order, to describe the sequence of events in this reflex action:
  • impulse sent along motor neuron to iris muscles
  • impulse sent along sensory neu-
rone to brain
  • pupil gets narrower
  • impulse sent along relay neurone
  • bright light enters the eye
  • circular muscles in iris contract
  • receptors detect bright light
  c In this reflex action what is:
  i the stimulus,
  ii the effector?
  d What is meant by:
  i a reflex action,
  ii a cerebral reflex?
  e Summarise the sequence of events which you would expect to happen if your eyes were suddenly subjected to very dim light, after being in bright light.

2 Below is a list of stimuli. For each one, say:
  i which receptor will detect it
  ii which effectors will react to it and how.
  In each case, consider only your immediate reflex actions – not actions that you might take after having time to think.
  a a fast-moving object travelling towards your eye
  b a sharp tap on your knee, as you sit with one leg crossed over the other
  c a very loud, sudden noise just behind you
  d the smell of food when you are very hungry

The pupil reflex

The iris is the coloured part of your eye. In the centre of it is a hole, called the pupil. The iris contains two sets of muscles – radial and circular. When the radial muscles contract, they pull the iris into a thin shape. This makes the pupil wider. When the circular muscles contract, they squeeze the iris into a wider shape, making the pupil narrower.

The muscles of the iris react to light. A bright light shining into your eye might damage the cells in the retina. So the iris responds by contracting its circular muscles, making the pupil smaller and cutting down the amount of light which enters the eye.

This reaction is a reflex action. It happens very fast, and without you thinking about it. It is a cerebral reflex action, because the messages are sent through the brain, not the spinal cord.

Ears convert sound energy into electrical energy in nerves

A human ear has an **eardrum**, which behaves like the diaphragm on a microphone. Sound waves make the eardrum vibrate.

The vibrations of the eardrum set up vibrations in a chain of three small bones. The bones are arranged in a lever-like manner, so that the vibrations in the third bone, the stirrup, are greater than the vibrations set up in the eardrum. The bones **amplify** the vibrations.

The stirrup vibrates against a membrane on the outside of the **cochlea**. This is a coiled tube filled with fluid. The membrane makes the fluid vibrate. Inside it are cells which are sensitive to vibrations. They respond to the vibrations by setting up tiny electrical signals, which travel along the auditory nerve to the brain. The brain interprets these signals as sound.

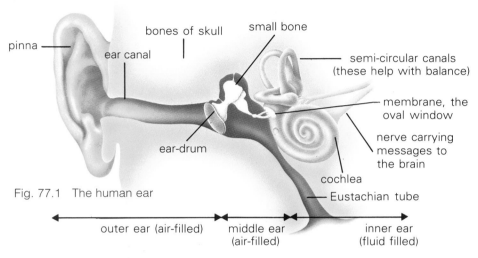

pinna
bones of skull
small bone
ear canal
semi-circular canals (these help with balance)
membrane, the oval window
nerve carrying messages to the brain
ear-drum
cochlea
Eustachian tube

Fig. 77.1   The human ear

outer ear (air-filled)   middle ear (air-filled)   inner ear (fluid filled)

Deafness has many causes

Anything which stops the passage of vibrations through the eardrum into the cochlea, or which stops the sensitive cells from sending messages to the brain, will make you deaf.

A common cause of deafness is a build-up of **wax** in the outer ear. Wax is made by the ear to stop dust and bacteria entering it. But sometimes such a thick layer builds up that the eardrum cannot vibrate. This sort of deafness is easily cured by dissolving the wax. Because the deafness does not last long, it is called temporary deafness.

The **eardrum** itself can be damaged by a blow to the head, by very loud sounds or by sudden pressure changes. Any of these can make a hole in the drum. Small tears in an eardrum can often heal themselves, but sometimes the damage is permanent.

Infections in the ear may cause damage in the three small bones. If these get jammed firmly together, vibrations cannot pass into the cochlea. Infections may also damage the cochlea or the auditory nerve. Long exposure to very loud sound can also cause this type of damage. People working in noisy environments should always wear ear protectors, or they may find that they become deaf as they get older.

Hearing aids amplify sound

A hearing aid is an electronic amplifier. It has a microphone which collects sound. The sound is amplified, and delivered to the ear by a small receiver, often worn inside the ear canal.

In deafness caused by damage to the eardrum or the small bones, hearing aids often produce very good hearing. But if the deafness is caused by damage to the cochlea, hearing aids may not be as successful. This is because the message sent to the brain by the cochlea is still not clear, even if the sound is loud. Sound may seem distorted, so that it is difficult to pick out important sounds like speech. Background noise is amplified as well, so the person may have problems in sorting out 'useful' noises from unwanted ones.

Questions

1 Match each of these functions with a structure labelled on the diagram of the human ear in Figure 77.1.

   a contains cells which convert vibrations in fluid into tiny electrical signals

   b vibrates when sound waves reach the ear

   c amplify the vibrations as they cross the middle ear

   d transmit the vibrations from the air in the middle ear to the liquid in the cochlea

Two ears help you to judge where a sound comes from

When you hear a sound you usually have a good idea of the direction it is coming from. You can do this because you have an ear on each side of your head. If a sound is coming from immediately in front of you, or immediately behind you, the sound arrives at each ear at the same time. Your brain gets identical messages from both ears at the same moment.

If a sound comes from your left-hand side, your left ear receives the sound before your right ear. The brain gets the message from the left ear first, shortly followed by the message from the right ear.

The human eye

A human eye is a bit like a pinhole camera with two lenses. The 'pinhole' is the pupil. There are two converging lenses. One, the cornea, is at the front of the eye. The other, the lens, is in the middle of the eye. The 'screen' in the eye is the retina.

Figure 77.2 shows a vertical section through a human eye. As light hits the cornea, the light is bent inwards. The cornea is a converging lens. The light rays continue through the pupil, and are bent inwards again by the lens. The rays are brought to a focus on the retina.

The retina contains light-sensitive cells, rods and cones. These send messages along the optic nerve to the brain. The brain sorts out the messages, so that you see a picture of the image formed on your retina.

Like the image on the screen of the pinhole camera, the image on the retina is upside-down. The brain automatically interprets the image the other way up.

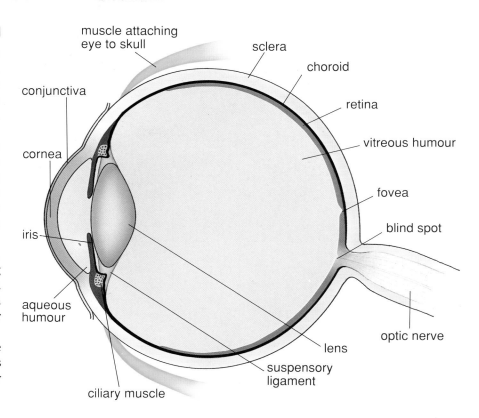

Fig. 77.2 Section through a human eye

The lens adjusts the focusing in the eye

If you have done experiments with pinhole cameras, you will have found that you could adjust the focus of the image on the screen in the pinhole camera by moving the lens backwards and forwards. Some animals use this system. Fish, for example, focus images onto the retina of their eye by moving their lens backwards and forwards.

But mammals, such as humans, adjust the focus by changing the shape of their lens.
The lens can be made thinner, which increases its focal length and makes it bend the light rays less. This enables you to focus on objects at a distance. Or it can be made fatter, which decreases its focal length. This makes it bend light rays more, and enables you to focus on nearby objects.

The lens shape is changed by a ring of muscles around it. The muscles contract to make the lens fatter, and relax to make it thinner. So when you are looking at close objects, such as writing on a page, these muscles in your eye are contracted. Some people find this makes their eyes tired, especially if they are working in dim light.

To focus on a distant object, the lens is pulled thinner, so that it bends the rays only slightly.

To focus on a nearby object, tension on the lens is slackened. This makes it fatter, so that it bends the rays more.

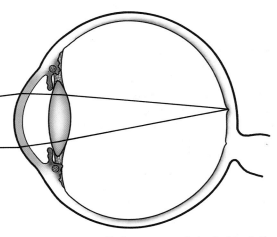

Fig. 77.3 In the human eye, the cornea, humours and lens all act as converging lenses, bringing the light to a· focus on the retina. Fine adjustments are made by changing the shape of the lens, which alters its focal length.

The amount of light falling onto the light-sensitive layer must be adjusted

The retina at the back of your eye is very sensitive to light. If too much light falls onto it, particularly over a long period of time, it may be permanently damaged. The very bright light reflected from snow can cause snow blindness.

The film in a camera is also very sensitive to light. If too much light falls onto it, then the picture you get is too 'white', instead of having a good contrast between the different colours and different light and dark shades. Your picture is over-exposed.

So both cameras and

eyes have systems for regulating the amount of light allowed to enter them. In dull conditions, a lot of light is let in. In bright conditions, less light is let in.

In the eye, this is done by the **iris.**

The iris is the coloured part of your eye. The colour in it absorbs light, and stops it passing through. Light can only pass through the circular hole in the middle of the iris, the **pupil.** Muscles in the iris can contract and relax to make the iris wider or narrower. The wider the iris, the smaller the pupil, and vice versa.

In a camera, the amount of light falling on the film is controlled by the width of the **aperture,** and by the time for which the shutter is open – the **shutter speed.** In very bright light conditions, you should use a small aperture and fast shutter speed. Successful photography partly depends on getting the balance between aperture size and shutter speed just right. Many cameras will do this automatically, but some professional photographers prefer to do it themselves, as it gives them the opportunity to achieve many different effects.

In dim light, the circular muscles relax while the radial muscles contract. This makes the iris narrower.

radial muscles

circular muscles

iris

pupil

Fig. 78.1 The iris can change the size of the pupil, by contracting or relaxing its muscles. There are many muscle fibres in the iris, but only two of each kind are shown in the diagrams.

In bright light, the circular muscles contract while the radial muscles relax. This makes the iris wider.

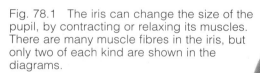

Fig. 78.2 Several adjustments can be made to the lens of a single-lens reflex (SLR) camera. The numbers from 22 (in red) to 1.8 (in white) are f-numbers. Turning the ring with these numbers on it alters the **aperture** of the lens. The larger the number, the smaller the aperture. The yellow and white numbers on the rings nearer the front of the lens represent the **focusing distance**; this lens is focused at about 0.9m. **Shutter speed** is usually adjusted on the body of the camera.

Looking at a human eye

You can either look at your own eyes, using a mirror, or work with a partner. Step 3 can really only be done successfully with a partner.

1 Make a large diagram of the front view of a human eye. Using your own knowledge, and Figure 77.2, label the following: eyebrow, eyelashes, eyelid, entrance to tear duct, conjunctiva covering cornea, sclera, blood vessels, iris, pupil.

2 Briefly suggest functions for each of these structures.

3 Get a friend to shut their eyes. Make the conditions around them as dark as possible, perhaps by putting a jumper over their head. After a few minutes, remove the jumper, and ask them to open their eyes and look at a bright light.

What did their pupils look like when they opened their eyes? What happened when they looked at the light? Explain what happened to cause this change, and why.

Fig. 78.3

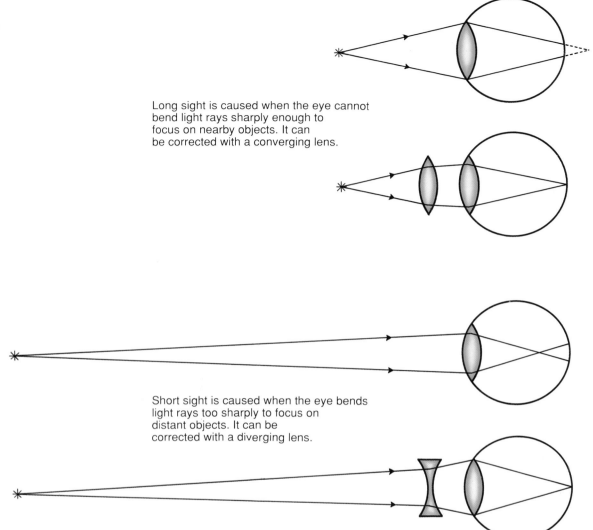

Long sight is caused when the eye cannot bend light rays sharply enough to focus on nearby objects. It can be corrected with a converging lens.

Short sight is caused when the eye bends light rays too sharply to focus on distant objects. It can be corrected with a diverging lens.

Lenses can help faulty eyes to focus

Many people have problems with focusing. The commonest problem in young people is **short sight.** You can see well close up, but cannot focus on distant objects. This is caused by having a lens which cannot be made thin enough, or an eyeball which is too long. The lens bends the rays too sharply, bringing them to a focus in front of the retina. Short sight is corrected with **diverging lenses.**

Long sight is the opposite problem. You can see well at a distance, but can't focus close up. The lens cannot be made fat enough to bring light from nearby objects to a focus on the retina. Long sight is corrected with **converging lenses.**

As people get older, their lenses become stiffer, and cannot change shape much. They may have problems with both close and distant vision.

They may need two pairs of glasses – one for distant vision and one for reading. Or they may have glasses with lenses in two parts. The top part is used for distant vision, and the bottom part for reading. These are called **bifocal lenses.**

Contact lenses lie on the surface of the eye

Contact lenses are preferred to glasses by many people. They give excellent all round vision, and are not obvious to other people.

There are several different types of contact lenses. Hard lenses are made of glass or plastic. They are usually small, less than 1 cm in diameter. They are curved to fit the surface of the conjunctiva and cornea, and sit on the front of the eye over the pupil. The space between the lens and the conjunctiva fills with fluid from the tear ducts. The lens is held in position by surface tension.

Soft lenses are usually larger, and made of a softer, absorbent plastic. Some people find them more comfortable to wear than hard lenses. They are also less likely to fall out! But their absorbency may cause problems if they are not properly cleaned, as bacteria can grow on them, causing eye infections. Modern contact lenses are permeable to gases. Oxygen must be able to get through the lens to reach the cornea, which has no blood supply.

Questions

1 Your friend can read perfectly well, but cannot see the board unless she sits on the front row in class.
a Is she short sighted or long sighted?
b What type of lenses – converging or diverging – would an optician prescribe for her?

183

79 COLOUR

Light is electromagnetic radiation with wavelengths of between 0.0004 mm and 0.0007 mm. We see light of different wavelengths as different colours.

The shape of a glass block affects the way in which a ray passes through it

When a light ray passes through a Perspex block, the ray is refracted as it enters and leaves the block. If the two sides of the block are parallel, the ray emerges parallel to the direction in which it entered. But if the two sides through which the ray enters are not parallel, then the direction of the ray is changed.

Fig. 79.1

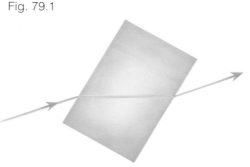

The two opposite sides of a rectangular block are parallel. A light ray passing through them is **displaced**, but its direction is not changed.

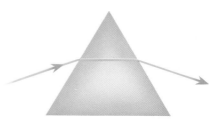

There are no parallel sides on a triangular prism. A light ray passing through it is not returned to its original direction. The ray is **deviated**.

Fig. 79.2 A rainbow is produced when sunlight is refracted by water droplets in the air.

A prism splits light into different colours

When a beam of light hits the surface of a triangular prism, it slows down. Its wavelength changes. If the light is made up of a number of different wavelengths, each wavelength is altered by a different amount, so each wavelength is bent by a different amount. The shorter the wavelength, the more it is bent as it enters the prism.

As the light leaves the prism, it is bent again, back towards its original path. But, because this face of the prism is not parallel with the first face, the light is not bent back onto its original path.

White light contains light of many different wavelengths. A prism splits up the light into all these different wavelengths. We see the different wavelengths as different colours. Each colour leaves the prism at a slightly different angle. The pattern of colours is called a **spectrum.**

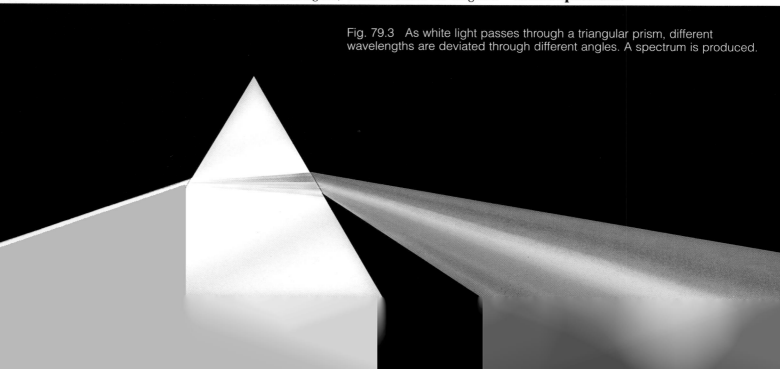

Fig. 79.3 As white light passes through a triangular prism, different wavelengths are deviated through different angles. A spectrum is produced.

Objects absorb and reflect the light which falls onto them

Sunlight, and the light from electric lighting, is white light. White light contains most of the different wavelengths from 0.0004 mm (violet) to 0.0007 mm (red). But some of the objects around you look coloured. Why is this?

Look at something red – a book perhaps. You can see the book because light from it is going into your eyes. The light from the book is reflected light. The light has come from the Sun, or from the electric lights in the room.

It is white light. When the white light hits the book, some wavelengths are absorbed by the book. The green, blue, yellow and violet wavelengths are absorbed. But the red wavelengths are reflected. This is why the book looks red. It reflects only red light into your eyes.

Objects which look white to us reflect light of all wavelengths. Objects which look black absorb light of all wavelengths.

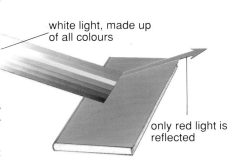

Fig. 79.4 A red book reflects red light, and absorbs all other colours.

Fig. 79.5

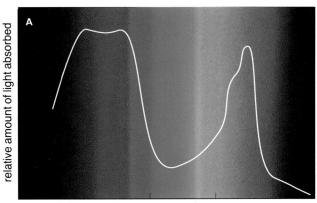

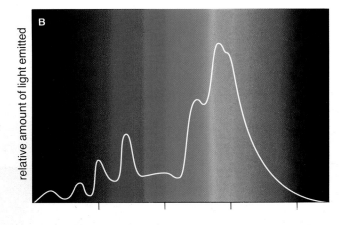

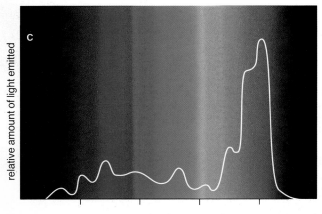

Chlorophyll does not absorb green light

Plants are green because they contain a pigment called **chlorophyll**. Chlorophyll is used in photosynthesis. Chlorophyll absorbs light, and transfers the light energy into organic molecules such as glucose.

However, chlorophyll cannot absorb all the different wavelengths in the sunlight which hits it. It can absorb red and blue light, but it cannot absorb green light. This is why chlorophyll is green. All the green light which hits it is reflected from it, or passes through it.

Some plants, such as copper beech trees, or red seaweeds, do not look green. They do have chlorophyll, and the chlorophyll reflects green light, just as in other plants. But copper beech trees and red seaweeds also contain other pigments which absorb green light and reflect red light. The mixture of green light from the chlorophyll, and red light from these other pigments, looks to us like a reddish-brown colour.

Questions

1 Look at Figure 79.5. Graph A shows the wavelengths of light which are absorbed by chlorophyll. Graph B shows the wavelengths of light which are emitted by an ordinary tungsten filament light bulb. Graph C shows the wavelengths of light which are emitted by a special type of fluorescent light.
   a What colours of light are absorbed by chlorophyll?
   b Why does chlorophyll look green?
   c Why do plants need chlorophyll?
   d Plants growing in a room lit only by tungsten filament lights will normally only survive for a few weeks. Plants growing under the special type of fluorescent light used in graph C thrive. Explain why you think this might be.

2 Investigation 19.1, on page 48, is an experiment to find out how light intensity affects the rate of photosynthesis of a water plant.
   Using this investigation as a guide, design an experiment to investigate how the **wavelength** of light affects the rate of photosynthesis.
   Using the information from graph A in Figure 79.5, predict the results you would expect to obtain.

80 SEEING COLOURS

We see colour because we have cells in our eyes sensitive to different wavelengths of light. The colour we see depends on what combination of these cells is stimulated.

The human retina contains cells sensitive to different colours of light

At the back of each of your eyes is a layer of cells called the **retina.** The cells in the retina are sensitive to light. When light hits one of these cells, it sets up a tiny electrical impulse which travels along the **optic nerve** to the brain. The brain sorts out the pattern of impulses coming from all the hundreds of thousands of different cells in your retinas, and makes them into an image.

There are two types of sensitive cells in the retina. One type are called **rods.** Rods respond in the same way to all wavelengths of light. No matter what colour light falls onto them, all the rods in your eyes send the same message to the brain. So rods cannot help you to tell what colour anything is. If only your rods are working, you just see in black, white and shades of grey.

The other type of sensitive cells in the retina are called **cones**. Most people have three types of cones. One type is sensitive to red light, one type to blue light, and one type to green light. If red light falls onto a 'red-sensitive' cone, it will send an impulse to the brain. But if green light falls onto this cone, it will not send an impulse. By analysing the messages from all the cones in your retinas, your brain can work out exactly what colour light is falling on which part of the retina. It can build up a colour image of whatever you are looking at.

Cones do, however, have one big disadvantage over rods. Cones will only respond to bright light. Rods will respond to quite dim light. So cones are useless in the dark, or even at dusk. Many night-active, or **nocturnal,** animals do not have any cones at all. They just have rods. They do not have colour vision.

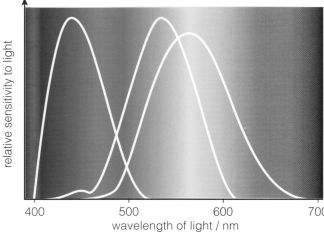

Fig. 80.1   There are three types of cone cell in the retina of the eye, each sensitive to different wavelengths (colours) of light. The three lines on the graph show the colours absorbed by the three types of cone.

Fig. 80.2   The huge eyes of a bush baby collect as much light as possible, because it hunts at night. Like many nocturnal mammals, it has few cones; the retina contains a high density of rod cells, which are sensitive even at low light intensities.

186

Any colour can be made from red, green and blue light

Any colour may be made by adding together red, green and blue light in the correct amounts. If a mixture of red and green light hits your eye, your red-sensitive and green-sensitive cones send impulses to your brain. Your brain interprets this as yellow light.

A colour television works in this way. The picture on the screen is made up of dots of light. The colours are made up of red, green and blue dots, in different combinations and of different intensities. If you look closely at a television screen, you can see these dots.

Red, green and blue are called the **primary colours of light.** You can make any colour from red, green and blue light. But you cannot make red, green or blue light from any other coloured light.

Colours which can be made by adding any two of the primary colours of light are called **secondary colours of light**. Figure 80.3 shows how the three secondary colours – yellow, magenta and cyan – are made.

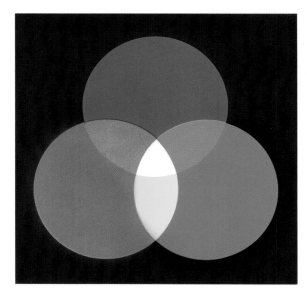

Fig. 80.3   Mixing red, green and blue light produces white light. Which coloured lights produce cyan (turquoise), magenta and yellow?

Objects look different in different colours of light

If you shine white light onto a red book, the book looks red because it reflects only the red light into your eyes. If you look at the book in red light, it still looks red, because it reflects the red light. But if you look at the book in green light it looks black. There is no red light for it to reflect, so it does not reflect any light at all, and it looks black.

What happens if you shine yellow light onto the red book? Yellow light is a mixture of red and green light. The book will absorb the green part of the yellow light, and reflect the red part. So it still reflects red light into your eye, and still looks red.

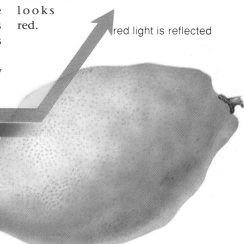

red light is reflected

white light

magenta filter allows red and blue light through

blue light is absorbed by the yellow pigment in the lemon

Fig. 80.4   A lemon appears red under magenta light. What colour would it appear if you used a cyan filter?

Questions

1   Pigeons can be trained to peck at a panel to make it open and allow them to reach food inside. If different patterns – for example, a circle or a square – are drawn on the panels, the pigeons can learn which pattern to peck in order to find food.

Design an experiment, using a similar method to that described above, to find out if pigeons have colour vision.

2   A car accident happened in a street lit by sodium lamps. A witness reported that a green car pulled out of a side road. It caused a red car to swerve into the path of a black car.

The following day, the three drivers were interviewed. Driver A has a blue-green car. Driver B has a blue car, and driver C has a magenta car. Could the witness' report have been accurate? Explain your answer.

3 a   What colours does a magenta filter allow through?

 b   What colours would a cyan filter allow through?

 c   What colour would be produced if a floodlight producing white light had cyan and magenta filters placed together in front of it?

The skeleton is a complex structure, built to withstand high compressive and tensile forces, and yet allow free movement.

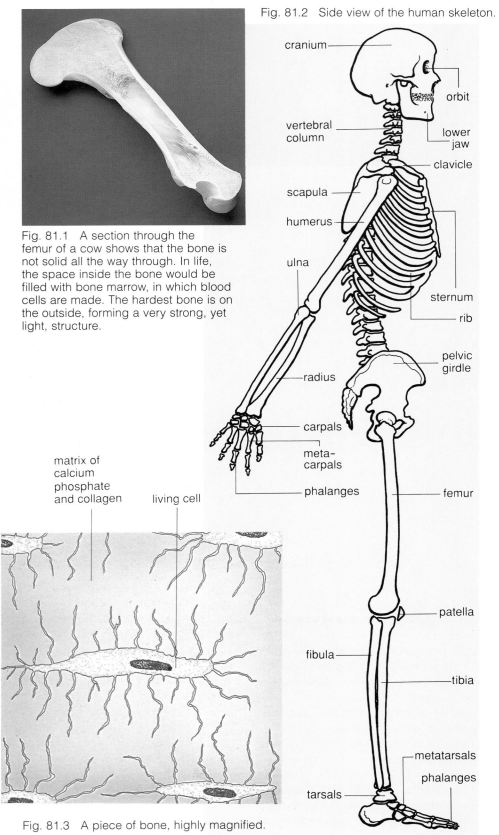

Fig. 81.2 Side view of the human skeleton.

cranium
orbit
vertebral column
lower jaw
clavicle
scapula
humerus
ulna
sternum
rib
radius
pelvic girdle
carpals
meta-carpals
phalanges
femur
patella
fibula
tibia
metatarsals
phalanges
tarsals

Fig. 81.1 A section through the femur of a cow shows that the bone is not solid all the way through. In life, the space inside the bone would be filled with bone marrow, in which blood cells are made. The hardest bone is on the outside, forming a very strong, yet light, structure.

matrix of calcium phosphate and collagen

living cell

Fig. 81.3 A piece of bone, highly magnified.

The human skeleton has many functions

Imagine yourself without any bones. You would be a heap of jelly on the ground. This immediately tells you one function of your skeleton. It *supports* your body. The vertebral column (backbone) and the leg bones are especially important for support.

The skeleton has several other functions. The bones in the arms and legs are designed to allow free *movement*. The bones of the skull, the vertebral column, and the rib cage all *protect* soft tissues inside them. Several bones, especially the ribs, skull, sternum and pelvis, contain bone marrow in which *red blood cells are made*.

The skeleton is made of bone and cartilage

The human skeleton is made mostly of **bone**. Bone is a living material, containing living cells. It contains blood vessels, which bring food and oxygen to the cells. If you cut a living bone, it will bleed.

But living cells only make up a very small part of bone. These cells are surrounded by a **matrix**. (A matrix is a kind of background material, like the cake around the cherries in a cherry cake.) The matrix is made of **calcium phosphate** and **collagen**. Calcium phosphate makes bone hard, and collagen gives it elasticity. As people get older, they may lose some of the elasticity in their collagen, so their bones break more easily.

Another important material in the human skeleton is **cartilage**. Cartilage is sometimes called gristle. It is much softer and more elastic than bone. You have cartilage at the end of your nose, and in the pinna of your ear. You also have cartilage covering the ends of moveable bones. The surface of the cartilage is slippery, so it reduces friction as the bones move past each other.

The vertebral column

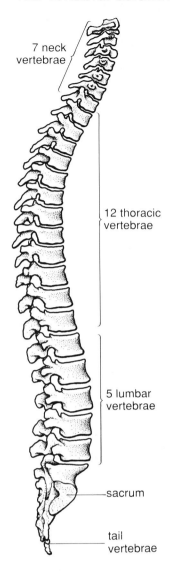

7 neck vertebrae

12 thoracic vertebrae

5 lumbar vertebrae

sacrum

tail vertebrae

Fig. 81.4 The vertebral column is made up of a stack of vertebrae, separated by discs of cartilage. As well as providing support and flexibility, the vertebral column protects the spinal cord, which runs through holes in each vertebra.

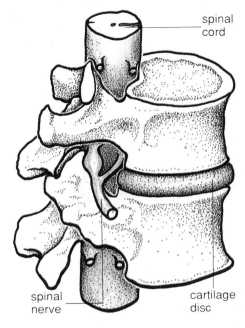

spinal cord

spinal nerve

cartilage disc

Fig. 81.6 Spinal nerves branch out from the spinal cord, between the vertebrae.

Fig. 81.5 A single vertebra

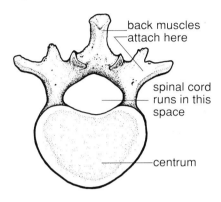

back muscles attach here

spinal cord runs in this space

centrum

Fig. 81.7 Lifting a heavy weight puts large forces on your vertebral column. If you lift with a straight back, as in diagram a, the forces are relatively small. But if you lift with a bent back, as in diagram b, the forces on your back can be enormous. Lifting a 90 kg weight can put a force of around 6000 N on the lower back muscles. These forces can damage the cartilage discs between the vertebrae, or even the vertebrae themselves.

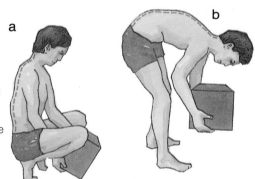

a

b

All organisms have skeletons

All organisms must be supported somehow. A skeleton is a structure which provides support, so all organisms have some kind of skeleton.

You are a **vertebrate**, and your skeleton is a vertebrate skeleton. Vertebrates have skeletons inside their bodies, called **endoskeletons**. All vertebrates have a **backbone** or **vertebral column**. Most vertebrates have skeletons made of bone, but sharks have only cartilage in their skeletons.

Invertebrates are animals which do not have a backbone. But they do have skeletons. There are many different kinds of invertebrates, with many different kinds of skeletons. Perhaps the most familiar are the **arthropods**. These are invertebrates with jointed legs. They include insects, crustaceans, centipedes and spiders. They all have a skeleton on the outside of their bodies, called an **exoskeleton**. These exoskeletons are made of a material called **chitin** (pronounced ky-tin), sometimes hardened with calcium carbonate.

Plants have skeletons too. The xylem vessels which carry water up through the roots and stems to the leaves of a plant make a strong skeleton. These xylem vessels have walls made of **lignin**. Tree trunks are made of lignin. The veins in leaves contain xylem vessels, and help to hold the leaf's shape.

DID YOU KNOW?

The upper end of your femur can withstand a compressive force of nearly 10000N. This is more than twice the load you normally put onto it, even when performing vigorous sports.

Muscles transfer chemical energy to movement energy ■

Almost all the movement of your body is produced by **muscles**. Just under half of your body weight is muscle. If you eat meat, almost all of the lean meat is muscle.

Muscles are made up of lots of fibres running side by side. These fibres are themselves made up of even smaller fibres, too small to see without a microscope. Each of these small fibres is a cylindrical cell with many nuclei. The cells may be several centimetres long.

Muscle cells are very special. They are able to transfer the chemical energy in glucose into movement energy. They break down the glucose in the reactions of respiration, releasing energy from it. They then use this energy to **contract**, or get shorter. If most of the muscle cells in a muscle contract together, then the whole muscle contracts.

Muscles are attached to bones by tendons ▭▭▭▭

Figure 82.1 shows two of the muscles in your arm. They are attached to the bones by tough cords called **tendons**. When the muscles contract, they pull on these tendons and make the bones move.

Tendons are made of a protein called **collagen**. Collagen is a fibrous material. The fibres run lengthways along the tendon, in bundles. Each bundle is slightly wavy, so when a muscle pulls on.the tendon it can give a little as it is straightened out. This helps the tendon not to snap if the muscle contracts very suddenly and unexpectedly.

But tendons must not be too stretchy. When a muscle contracts, you want the bone to which it is attached to move. Imagine what would happen if the tendon was made of elastic.

Fig. 82.1a Bending the arm

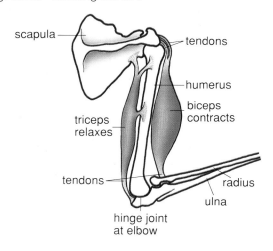

- scapula
- tendons
- humerus
- biceps contracts
- triceps relaxes
- tendons
- radius
- ulna
- hinge joint at elbow

Fig. 82.1b Straightening the arm

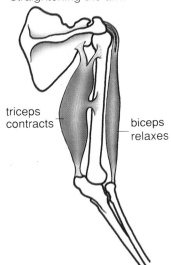

- triceps contracts
- biceps relaxes

Muscles often work in pairs ▬▬▬▬▬▬▬

Figure 82.1 shows how two muscles work together to bend and straighten your arm.

To bend your arm, the **biceps muscle** contracts. It is attached to your scapula at one end, and your radius at the other. So when it contracts, it pulls on both of these bones, bringing them closer together. This makes your arm bend at the elbow. This is called **flexing** your arm, so the biceps is a **flexor muscle**.

When you want to straighten your arm, you relax your biceps muscle. But this is not enough to make your arm go straight. The biceps muscle cannot push your arm back again, because muscles cannot push. Muscles can only pull. To straighten your arm, the **triceps muscle** contracts. This movement is called **extending** your arm, so the triceps is an **extensor muscle**.

These two muscles are **antagonistic muscles**. By working together, they can make the bones move in both directions. When one of the muscles is contracted, the other one automatically relaxes. You have many other pairs of antagonistic muscles in your body.

Joints are formed where two bones meet

The place where two bones meet is called a **joint**.

Sometimes, the two bones are joined tightly together by fibres, producing an immoveable **fibrous joint**. You have fibrous joints between the bones which make up your cranium.

The bones of the vertebral column are joined together by cartilage. These joints are called **cartilaginous joints**. The cartilage holds the bones firmly together, but allows some movement between them.

But the joints of which you are probably the most aware are **synovial joints.** These are joints like your shoulder, elbow and knee joints, where the bones can move a lot.

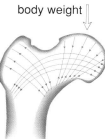

Fig. 82.2 The heads of your two thigh bones (**femora**) carry the weight of your body. This produces compressive (red) and tensile (blue) forces in the bone.

body weight

Synovial joints are designed to cut down friction

Bone is a very hard material. Bone moving against bone generates a lot of friction. So synovial joints are designed to reduce friction.

Figure 82.3 shows the structure of a human elbow joint. The ends of the two bones are covered with a smooth layer of **cartilage**. Cartilage is much smoother than bone. It is almost three times as slippery as ice.

This super-smooth surface is made even smoother by a thin layer of lubricant, called **synovial fluid**. This fluid is made by a membrane which surrounds the joint, the **synovial membrane**.

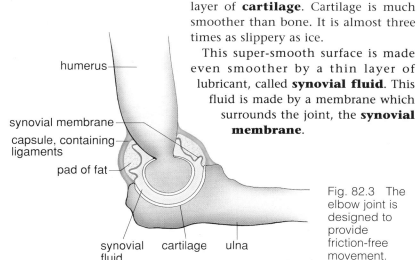

humerus

synovial membrane

capsule, containing ligaments

pad of fat

synovial fluid

cartilage

ulna

Fig. 82.3 The elbow joint is designed to provide friction-free movement.

Fig. 82.4 This photograph of a section through the head of the thigh bone shows the lines along which the hard, calcified matrix is laid down. The lines match, almost perfectly, the lines along which the forces act on the bone.

Questions

1 Read the passage on the left, and then answer the questions below.

	strength in tension kg/mm²	strength in compression kg/mm²
human bone	7–10	14–21
cast iron	7–21	42–100
mild steel	42–63	45
mahogany	8	4

Look back at Figure 82.2.

a Name one or more bones which are being subjected to tensile forces.

b Name one or more bones which are being subjected to compressive forces.

c Is bone stronger under compression, or under tension?

d Which components of bone provide:

  i its strength in tension?

  ii its strength in compression?

e Briefly describe three ways in which the structure of a bone such as the femur provides for both strength and lightness.

The Strength of Bones

The human skeleton is subjected to a variety of compressive, tensile and twisting forces. It is designed to be able to withstand these forces, yet to be light, and to allow movement.

The table on the right shows the strength of bone in comparison with three other materials renowned for their strength. Although the strength of bone in tension may not appear very high in comparison with steel, it compares very well with the other materials. This strength is provided by the protein, collagen, which is found everywhere in the body where tensile strength is required. The compressive strength and rigidity of bone is provided by calcium phosphate.

The strength of a bone is due not only to the materials from which it is made, but also to the way in which the whole bone is constructed. For example, the collagen fibres are often arranged in different directions in different layers, rather like plywood. And in order to combine strength with lightness, bones are built like tubes, with hard bone on the outside and soft marrow in the centre. At the ends of the bones, for example at the head of the femur, the bone is quite spongy in texture, with interconnecting strips of hard bone separated by spaces. These strips grow according to the stresses put on the bone, and can change if the bone is subjected to different stresses.

83 THE ENDOCRINE SYSTEM

The endocrine system is made up of glands, which secrete chemicals known as hormones.

Hormones are secreted by endocrine glands

Electrical impulses travelling along neurones are not the only way in which information is transferred from one part of your body to another. Information can also be transferred by means of chemicals, carried in your blood. These chemicals are called **hormones**. They are made by glands known as **endocrine glands**.

Adrenalin prepares your body for action

When you are nervous or in a frightening situation, your **adrenal glands** secrete a hormone called **adrenalin**. You have two adrenal glands, one just above each kidney. They each contain many blood capillaries, and pour the adrenalin directly into the blood.

The adrenalin dissolves in the blood plasma, and is carried to all parts of the body. The parts of the body which react to it are called its **target organs**. Adrenalin has many target organs.

- The **heart** reacts by beating faster. This pumps the blood around your body faster, delivering more oxygen to your muscles, to help you to run from or face up to the danger.
- The **intercostal muscles** and **diaphragm muscles** also respond by contracting and relaxing faster, so that you breathe faster.
- The **muscles around arterioles** carrying blood to your digestive system and skin contract, closing off the arterioles and diverting blood to your muscles.
- The **liver** is stimulated to break down its glycogen stores, releasing extra glucose into the blood.
- Your **brain** becomes more alert.
- The **muscles attached to hairs** in your skin may contract, making the hairs stand on end. (This is not much use to you, but in an animal like a cat it makes it look bigger, and more frightening to an attacker.)

Fig. 83.1 In this sort of situation, adrenalin is useful. It helps to provide a faster supply of oxygen to the muscles, and can speed up reactions.

Fig. 83.2 For many people, the secretion of adrenalin before and during examinations is a nuisance. It can spoil your concentration, and make you forget things you would normally remember. Steady, non-panicky preparation for exams can help to keep you calm.

Hormones stay in the blood for some time

Why does your body have *two* ways of transferring information from one part to another? The answer is that both ways have their advantages. The two systems enable different kinds of responses to be made in different situations.

In the reflex action described in Topic 76, the message is transferred very swiftly along neurones. It reaches the effector, causing an almost immediate reaction. Then it stops. The whole thing is over very quickly.

In the reaction to fear described above, the message is transferred rather more slowly, in your blood. It reaches a whole range of effectors all over your body, causing a fairly quick reaction. But, unlike the reflex action, this reaction goes on for a little while. This is because the adrenalin does not disappear immediately. It stays in the blood for a while, so its effects last longer than the effects of a nervous impulse.

But you do not want to go on feeling frightened for ever. So adrenalin is broken down within a short time of being released. If the frightening situation continues, so that you do need to keep on reacting to it, then your adrenal glands will release more adrenalin.

Hormones and the menstrual cycle

Both men and women secrete **sex hormones**. In men, the main sex hormone is **testosterone**, which is secreted by the testes. In women, the two sex hormones **progesterone** and **oestrogen** are secreted by the ovaries. These hormones are responsible for the changes that take place at adolescence, which are described in Topic 40.

The female sex hormones are also responsible for the regulation of the **menstrual cycle**. Both oestrogen and progesterone help to build up the lining of the uterus, ready to receive an egg if it is fertilised. When a lot of oestrogen or progesterone is secreted, the uterus lining gets thicker or stays thick. When little or no oestrogen or progesterone is secreted, the lining breaks down.

The events that occur during a menstrual cycle are described in Topic 37. Figure 83.4 shows how the secretion of oestrogen and progesterone varies during the menstrual cycle. The cycle shown is 28 days long. But it is common for women to have cycles which are several days shorter or longer than this. Day 1 of the cycle is the first day of menstruation.

At the beginning of the cycle, both oestrogen and progesterone are at very low levels, so the lining of the uterus breaks down and menstruation takes place. Over the next few days, cells in the ovary secrete oestrogen, and you can see that the oestrogen curve rises during this time. The oestrogen is secreted by cells surrounding a developing egg, which is inside a **follicle** in the ovary. The oestrogen stimulates the lining of the uterus to begin to get thicker.

At about day 14 of a 28-day cycle, oestrogen secretion suddenly drops. At this time, **ovulation** (the release of an egg from the ovary) takes place. The follicle, which no longer contains an egg, fills up with yellow cells that begin to secrete progesterone. The progesterone keeps the lining of the uterus thick, in case the egg is fertilised.

If the egg is *not* fertilised, then these yellow cells begin to disintegrate, and they stop secreting progesterone. As the level of progesterone falls, there is no longer any stimulus for the uterus lining to stay thick. So the lining begins to break down, and menstruation begins.

If the egg *is* fertilised, then the yellow cells carry on secreting progesterone. They keep on doing this until the embryo has implanted in the uterus and a placenta has developed. Then the placenta starts to secrete progesterone, and carries on doing this all through pregnancy. The progesterone ensures that the uterus lining stays in the correct condition until the baby is born.

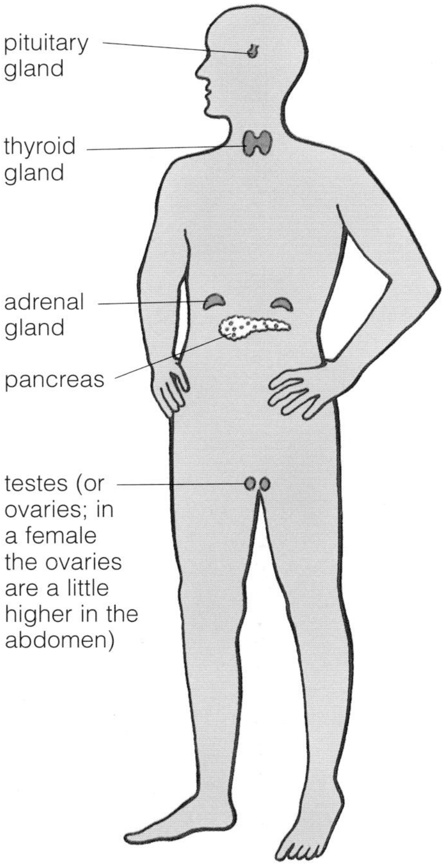

pituitary gland

thyroid gland

adrenal gland

pancreas

testes (or ovaries; in a female the ovaries are a little higher in the abdomen)

Fig. 83.3   The main endocrine glands

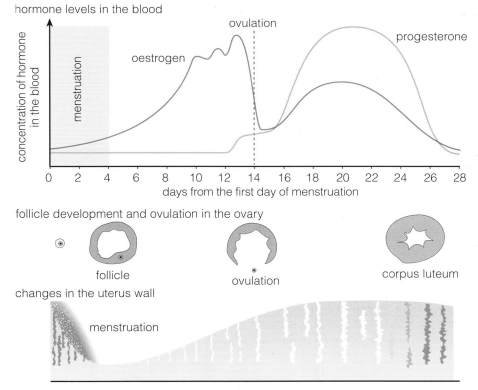

hormone levels in the blood

Fig. 83.4   Hormones and the menstrual cycle

Questions

1   You are walking across a large open field, when you suddenly see a furious bull charging towards you. Adrenalin surges through your blood, as you race to reach the fence before the bull does.

   a What are **i** the receptors, **ii** the effectors involved in your reactions to the bull?

   b On the previous page is a list of some of the effects of adrenalin on your body. Explain exactly how each of these effects might help you to be more successful in your flight from the bull.

   c This reaction involves your endocrine system. Does it also involve your nervous system? Explain your answer.

84 HOMEOSTASIS

Homeostasis means maintaining a constant internal environment. This allows cells to work efficiently.

Homeostasis is the maintenance of a constant internal environment

Cells in your body are bathed in tissue fluid. This is their environment. To allow the cells to work efficiently, this environment must be kept constant. Glucose levels, temperature and water levels in the tissue fluid are all carefully controlled. This is called **homeostasis**.

Tissue fluid is liquid which has leaked out of blood capillaries. So if the composition of the blood is correct, the composition of the tissue fluid will also be correct. Receptors monitor the glucose levels, temperature and water levels of the blood. They then transfer information about this to effectors, which do something about it if necessary.

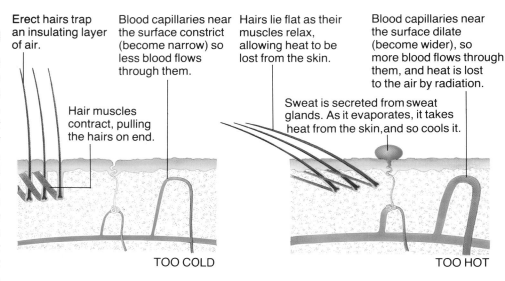

Erect hairs trap an insulating layer of air.

Blood capillaries near the surface constrict (become narrow) so less blood flows through them.

Hair muscles contract, pulling the hairs on end.

TOO COLD

Hairs lie flat as their muscles relax, allowing heat to be lost from the skin.

Blood capillaries near the surface dilate (become wider), so more blood flows through them, and heat is lost to the air by radiation.

Sweat is secreted from sweat glands. As it evaporates, it takes heat from the skin, and so cools it.

TOO HOT

Fig. 84.1 Sections through the skin, showing how it responds if your body temperature becomes too high or too low.

The hypothalamus monitors blood temperature

Enzymes work best at around 37 °C. If your body temperature is kept close to this level, the enzymes in your cells can work efficiently.

A part of the brain, called the **hypothalamus**, constantly monitors the temperature of the blood which flows through it. If you have been doing a lot of exercise, the heat released by your muscles will raise the temperature of your blood. If it is a very cold day, loss of heat by radiation from your skin will lower the temperature of your blood. If the hypothalamus detects an increase or decrease in blood temperature, it sends impulses along nerves to various parts of your body.

One of these parts is your **skin**. Figure 84.1 shows how the skin responds to these impulses. **Muscles** will also receive impulses. If you are too cold, they will contract and relax very quickly – you will shiver. This generates heat.

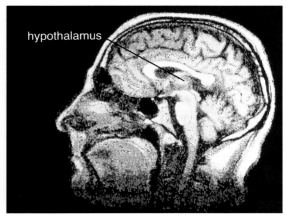

Fig. 84.2 A magnetic resonance image of a section through a human head

Water content is also monitored by the hypothalamus

The water content of the fluids surrounding your cells is very important. If there is not enough water, your cells will lose water by osmosis. Important reactions inside the cells may slow down or stop. If there is too much water, the cells may take in water and swell. Very large intakes of water may even make them burst.

The water content of the blood is monitored by the hypothalamus. If there is not enough water in your blood, then the hypothalamus sends messages to the **pituitary gland**. The pituitary gland releases a hormone, called **ADH (anti-diuretic hormone)**, into the blood.

The target organ for ADH is the **kidneys**. The kidneys make urine by filtering out water and waste substances from the blood. (This is described in Topic 85.) ADH makes the kidneys keep back most of the water. So they do not make as much urine as usual. The water will stay in the blood, instead of being lost in urine.

If there is too much water, the hypothalamus detects this and stops signalling the pituitary gland to secrete ADH. No ADH arrives at the kidneys, so they do not keep back the water. The water is allowed to flow out of the kidneys, into the bladder. So a lot of urine is produced.

Insulin reduces the amount of glucose in your blood

Insulin is a hormone secreted by the **pancreas**. The pancreas is a soft, creamy-coloured organ just below your stomach. Besides secreting insulin, the pancreas has another, completely different function – it secretes pancreatic juice into the duodenum, helping with digestion.

In the pancreas are receptor cells which detect the level of glucose in the blood. If this level rises too high, these cells respond by switching on the secretion of insulin into the blood. The insulin, dissolved in the blood plasma, is carried all over the body. Its main target organs are the **liver** and **muscles**. It causes these to take up extra glucose from the blood, which lowers the blood glucose level. The liver will change some of this glucose into the polysaccharide **glycogen**. Some of the glucose will be used up in respiration.

As the blood glucose level drops, the pancreas detects this. Insulin secretion is switched off. The liver responds to the absence of insulin in the blood by reducing the amount of glucose it takes up and uses. It may also break down some of its glycogen stores, releasing extra glucose back into the blood.

Negative feedback helps to keep blood sugar levels constant

The switching on and off of the secretion of insulin is an example of **negative feedback**. Figure 84.3 shows how this system works. The pancreas receives information about the blood glucose levels, and responds by either secreting or stopping the secretion of insulin. The effect of this action alters the blood glucose levels, and information about this **feeds back** to the pancreas. This information causes the pancreas to stop doing what it was doing before, and to switch to doing the opposite. So it has a *negative* effect on the activity of the pancreas.

Negative feedback is an important part of many control systems, including many in the human body. Blood sugar levels, body temperature, and water content are all controlled by negative feedback.

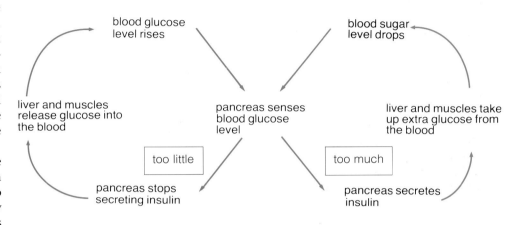

Fig. 84.3   The control of blood glucose levels by insulin

Questions

1 a Explain what is meant by **homeostasis**.
  b Name three properties of the blood which are kept constant.
  c For each of these properties, explain why it is important for it to be kept constant.
2 Explain why:
  a sweating helps to cool you down.
  b a person who has been exercising hard, on a hot day, is likely to excrete less urine than a person who has been less active.
3 Both temperature and water content are controlled by negative feedback. Using Figure 84.3 as a model, draw diagrams to show how each of these control processes works. In both cases, the central box will begin 'Hypothalamus senses ...'
4 a A normal person eats a meal containing a lot of carbohydrate. The carbohydrate is digested, and absorbed into the blood in the form of glucose. This raises the level of the blood glucose to a much higher level than normal. Briefly describe what happens to restore the level to normal again.
  b Diabetes mellitus is a disease in which a person's blood glucose levels are not kept constant. This could be because their pancreas does not secrete insulin, or it could be because their cells do not respond to insulin. If a person with diabetes eats a meal containing a lot of carbohydrate, what will happen to their blood sugar level?
  c How might high blood sugar levels damage cells in the body? (Think about osmosis.)
  d Insulin stimulates the conversion of glucose to glycogen in the liver. How would you expect the levels of glycogen of a person with diabetes to compare with those of a normal person?
  e If a normal person goes without food for a time, their liver will break down glycogen stores, changing them into glucose which goes into the blood. What would you expect to happen to the blood sugar levels of a person suffering from diabetes, if they go without food for a long time?
  f Why might very low blood sugar levels be dangerous? (Think about respiration.)
  g Most diabetics are able to keep healthy by carefully controlling their diet. What sort of precautions do you think they need to take?

195

85 THE KIDNEYS

The kidneys help to excrete waste products of metabolism from the body.

The urinary system

The kidneys are part of the human urinary system. Figure 85.1 shows the position of the kidneys, and the rest of the urinary system, in the body. Your kidneys are near the back of your body, just above your waist.

Figure 85.2 shows a section through one kidney. You can see that it is made up of three main areas – the **cortex**, **medulla** and **pelvis**. Urine is made in the cortex and medulla, inside thousands of tiny tubes called **nephrons**. The nephrons empty the urine they have made into the pelvis of the kidney, from where it flows along the **ureter** to the **bladder**. Urine can be stored in the bladder for a while, before it is released to flow out of the body through the **urethra**.

The kidneys make urine out of waste products in the blood. Figure 85.3 shows how this is done. Blood is brought to the kidneys in a branch of the **artery**. As the blood passes the **renal capsule** (or Bowman's capsule) at the end of a nephron, it is **filtered**. The cells in the blood, and big molecules such as proteins, stay in the blood, but small molecules are squeezed through the filter and into the nephron.

Although many of these small molecules are waste substances (such as urea and excess water), many of them (such as glucose) are not. So that these substances are not lost, the blood capillaries run alongside the nephron, and **reabsorb** any of the filtered substances that are needed by the body. All of the glucose is reabsorbed, and also most of the water.

Urea and carbon dioxide are excreted

The urea which is excreted by the kidneys has been made in the liver. It is made from excess amino acids. If you eat more protein than you need, your body is unable to store it. So it changes the amino acids into something else, such as fats or carbohydrates. To do this, it has to remove nitrogen from them. The nitrogen is made into urea. As urea is poisonous, it is removed from the body by the kidneys.

Urea is an **excretory product**. An excretory product is a waste product made by reactions in your body. Another important excretory product is **carbon dioxide**. It is made by all your cells, in the reactions of respiration.

The removal of excretory products from your body is an important part of keeping the environment of your cells constant. If levels of urea or carbon dioxide build up too much, they could damage or even kill body cells.

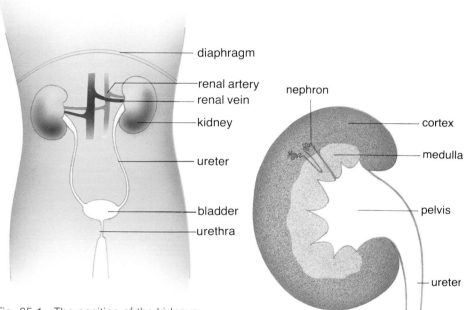

Fig. 85.1 The position of the kidneys

- diaphragm
- renal artery
- renal vein
- kidney
- ureter
- bladder
- urethra

nephron
- cortex
- medulla
- pelvis
- ureter

Fig. 85.2 A longitudinal section through a kidney

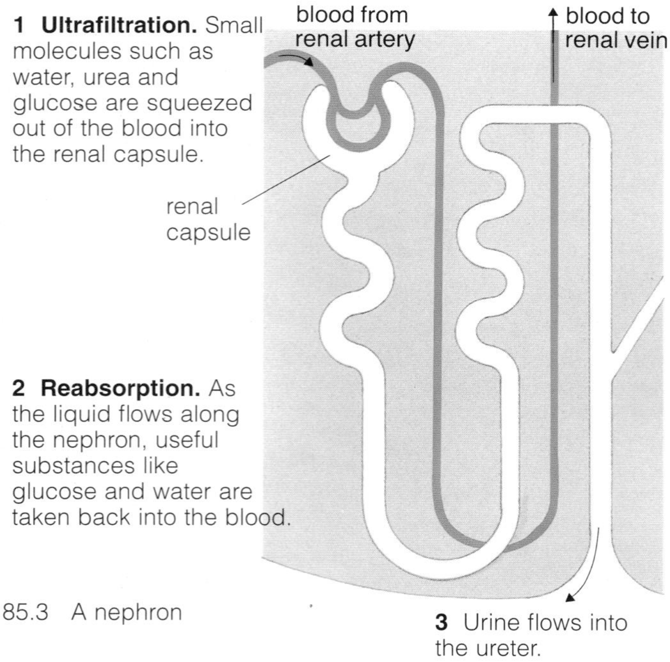

1 Ultrafiltration. Small molecules such as water, urea and glucose are squeezed out of the blood into the renal capsule.

blood from renal artery

blood to renal vein

renal capsule

2 Reabsorption. As the liquid flows along the nephron, useful substances like glucose and water are taken back into the blood.

3 Urine flows into the ureter.

Fig. 85.3 A nephron

Nephrons make urine by ultrafiltration and reabsorption

Figure 85.4 is a more detailed diagram of one nephron and its associated blood capillaries. The renal capsules of all the nephrons are in the cortex of the kidney. The tube then leads down into the medulla of the kidney, before looping back up again into the cortex, and then once more turning down into the medulla.

Inside the cup of the renal capsule, there is a knot of blood capillaries, called a **glomerulus**. The contents of the blood inside the glomerulus are squeezed against the walls of the capillaries, because the blood is at a fairly high pressure. The capillary walls have gaps in them, so the blood plasma (but not the cells) are squeezed out. The capillary walls are right up against the walls of the renal capsule, and these walls also have holes in them. However, these holes are very small, and they only allow relatively small molecules to get through and into the space inside the renal capsule. This process is called **ultrafiltration**.

The substances which *do* get through, and into the beginning of the nephron, form a liquid called the **glomerular filtrate**. This is mostly **water**, and also contains any other small molecules or ions which are present in the blood. These will include **glucose**, the waste product **urea**, and inorganic ions such as **sodium** and **chloride**. It does not contain any blood cells, nor large molecules such as proteins, because these cannot get through the 'filter' between the blood and the nephron.

This liquid now flows along the nephron. As it does so, some of the substances in it are taken back into the blood, which is being carried alongside it in capillaries which wind around the nephron. Because only some substances are taken back in this way, the process is called **selective reabsorption**. All of the glucose is reabsorbed, most of the water, and as much of the sodium and chloride ions as is needed.

By the time the liquid reaches the end of the nephron, it is made up of water in which urea and various inorganic ions are dissolved. The liquid is called **urine**. The amount of water

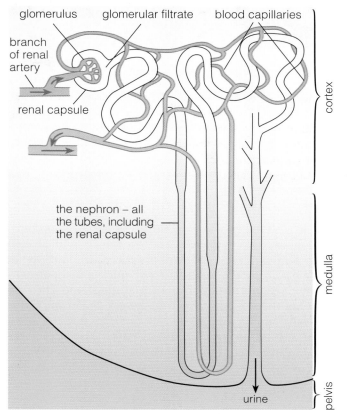

Fig. 85.4   One nephron and its associated blood capillaries

in the urine is very variable, depending on whether the body needs to lose water, or to conserve it. This is controlled by the hormone **ADH**, and is described in Topic 84.

Kidney failure can be treated by dialysis or transplants

A person's kidneys sometimes stop working, perhaps because of an infection or other disease. If only one kidney is affected, then the person can manage very well with just one. But if both kidneys fail, then urgent treatment is needed.

The best long-term solution to kidney failure is a **transplant**. The useless kidney is removed, and replaced by a healthy one from another person. The operation to insert the new kidney, although not easy, does not usually cause any problems. The problems come afterwards, when the recipient's white cells may attack and destroy the 'foreign' cells on the transplanted kidney. This is called **rejection**. The chance of rejection can be reduced if the transplanted kidney is taken from a close relative of the recipient. Another way to help the body to accept the new kidney is to give the recipient drugs called **immunosuppressants**, which stop the white cells from reacting strongly to it.

Another difficulty with transplants is that there are not enough kidneys available. While someone with kidney failure is waiting for a kidney to become available for them, they will need regular treatment called **dialysis**.

A dialysis machine, or kidney machine, filters a person's blood in a similar way to a real kidney. The blood flows through the machine in tubes, rather like the visking tubing you have may have used in osmosis experiments. On the other side of the tubes, there is a liquid called dialysis fluid. The dialysis fluid contains water, glucose and salts, in similar concentrations to those in normal blood.

As the blood flows along the tubes, small molecules and ions such as glucose, urea, water, sodium and chloride are able to pass through. Because there is no urea in the dialysis fluid, virtually all of the urea moves out of the blood and into the fluid, down its concentration gradient. But because the dialysis fluid contains glucose, there is no concentration gradient for glucose. So the blood does not lose its glucose as it passes through the machine.

Dialysis needs to be carried out regularly, and most kidney patients do not find it very pleasant. Because it takes several hours, and has to be done several times a week, it restricts what they can do – it is difficult for them to go on holiday, for example. They also have to be very careful what they eat, so that the amounts of unwanted substances such as urea or too many sodium ions do not build up too much between dialysis sessions. But at least dialysis can keep a person with kidney failure alive until a transplant becomes available.

86 PLANT HORMONES

Hormones in plants help to control growth and development.

Plant hormones regulate growth

Plants, like animals, produce chemicals called hormones, which are involved in the control of many different activities and processes. Plant hormones help to control growth, flowering, fruit production, fruit ripening and seed germination.

Unlike animals, plants do not have special glands that produce the hormones. And, as plants do not have a blood system, the hormones clearly cannot be transported in the same way as in animals. Plant hormones are produced in particular regions of the plant, and then move to other parts by diffusion or active transport, or in the xylem vessels.

Auxins stimulate growth in shoots

Plants, like all many-celled organisms, grow by a combination of producing new cells, and by the individual cells getting larger. New cells are produced by mitosis in particular parts of the plant. For example, in a shoot, new cells are made in a region at the tip of the shoot. The cells just behind the tip grow by getting longer (Figure 86.1).

The cells in the region of cell division make a plant hormone called **auxin**. The auxin passes back down the shoot, and stimulates the cells behind the tip to get longer. If you cut the tip off a shoot, so that the part which makes auxin has been removed, then the rate of elongation of these cells slows down and may stop completely.

The auxin has another function. So long as one main shoot has a tip which is producing auxin, buds further down the shoot will not grow. The presence of the auxin stops them. However, if the main shoot is cut back, then the side buds are not inhibited by auxin any more. They begin to grow, so the shoot grows side branches. Gardeners use this fact when they want plants to grow in a bushy shape, rather than tall and thin. If you prune the tips off the shoots, then several buds that previously were being prevented from growing will begin to produce side branches.

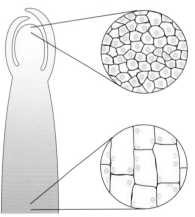

Cells divide rapidly at the tip of a stem. The new cells are small.

As the cells get older they grow larger. The increase in stem length is mainly due to the elongation of cells.

Fig. 86.1   How a shoot grows

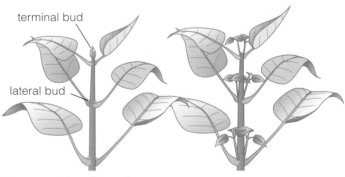

In many plants only the terminal bud grows a new stem. Lateral buds may lie dormant for a year.

If the terminal bud is removed, the lateral buds start growing new stems.

terminal bud

lateral bud

Fig. 86.2   The effect of pruning on a shoot

Fig. 86.3   By pruning the top branches from the laurel bush, the gardener encourages the bush to produce many side branches. The laurel bush will become thicker and less straggly.

Tropisms

Plants have no nervous system or muscles, yet they can respond to stimuli. Often, they respond by the way they grow.

For example, shoots usually grow towards the light. This helps the plant because it provides more light for the leaves to use in photosynthesis. Roots usually grow in the direction from which gravity is acting. This is useful because roots hold the plant in the soil, and also absorb water and mineral salts from the soil.

These growth responses are called **tropisms**. A tropism is a response where a plant grows towards or away from a stimulus. The growth response of a shoot towards the light is a **positive phototropism**. It is positive because the shoot is growing *towards* the light, and a phototropism because 'photo' means 'light'.

Auxin is involved in phototropism. If light is shone onto a shoot from one side, then more auxin builds up on the shady side of the shoot than on the well-lit side. As you have seen, auxin stimulates cells to get longer. So the cells on the shady side lengthen more than the ones on the bright side. This makes the shoot bend towards the light as it grows.

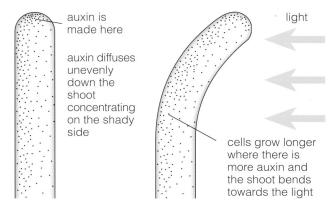

Fig. 86.4   How auxin is involved in phototropism

Using plant hormones

Many plant hormones are used commercially, or by people who garden for pleasure. Perhaps one of the commonest uses is as **selective weedkillers**. Plant hormones can be sprayed onto a lawn or a field of growing wheat, to kill the weeds, but not the grass or wheat. The hormones are carefully selected so that they affect the weeds, which are broad-leaved (dicotyledonous) plants, but they do not harm the grass or wheat, which are narrow-leaved (monocotyledonous) plants. They disrupt the normal growth patterns of the weeds, making them grow very fast for a while and then die.

A different type of plant hormone is used to help cuttings to root. These hormones are sold as **rooting powder**. When a cutting has been taken, as shown in Figure 35.2, the end is dipped into rooting powder, which stimulates roots to grow from the stem.

Plant hormones are also used by growers of some types of fruit. They can be sprayed onto a fruit tree when the flowers are out, to stimulate the ovaries of the flowers to develop into fruits even if the flowers are not fertilised. This means that the fruits develop without any seeds inside them. Not only does this mean that more fruits develop on the tree, but it also increases their commercial value, because many people prefer to eat fruits that do not contain seeds. Some varieties of grapes and citrus fruits, for example, are treated in this way.

Fig. 86.5   Auxin has been used to make this grapefruit develop without seeds.

Fig. 86.6   These two cuttings were taken at the same time, and treated in identical ways, except that the one on the right was dipped into rooting powder containing auxin and other plant hormones.

APPARATUS LISTS

3.1 Using a microscope
any student microscope (with lamp if needed)
a prepared slide

3.2 Making a microscope slide
clean microscope slide and cover slip
microscope
object to mount on slide, e.g. filamentous alga
dropper pipette
access to water
mounted needle or similar for lowering cover slip
filter paper

3.3 Looking at plant cells
clean microscope slide and cover slip
microscope
scalpel, fine forceps and mounted needle
dropper pipette
access to water
filter paper
small piece of onion bulb
small piece of pond weed
Iodine solution can be used instead of water for mounting the plant tissues.

4.1 The effect of heat on plant cell membranes
fresh raw beetroot
Bunsen burner, mat, tripod and gauze
sand tray with sand
access to water
cork borer
Pyrex beaker
thermometer
The sand tray is not essential, but does make sure that the water heats gently. This makes it easier for students to catch the exact temperature at which colour begins to leak out of the beetroot.

6.1 How quickly do scent particles move?
Students will ask for their own apparatus, but are likely to need:
a small container of a strongly-scented substance
stopwatch or clock
metre ruler or tape

6.2 Diffusion of two gases
The apparatus is shown in the diagram on page 19. Concentrated hydrochloric acid and ammonia solution give the best results, but care must be taken not to expose students to fumes at close quarters, or for very long. A small amount of each liquid can be poured into a watch glass in a fume cupboard, and a piece of cotton wool (held with forceps) dipped into each. If the soaked cotton wool is quickly pushed into the tube ends, and

then immediately held in position with a bung, only a relatively mild smell will be noticed by students.

7.1 Osmosis and visking tubing
a piece of visking tubing, roughly 15 cm long
cotton
dropper pipette
a fairly strong sucrose solution
capillary tubing – fairly long if possible
retort stand, clamp and boss
beaker
access to water
stopclock, or the sight of a clock with a second hand

8.1 Osmosis and raisins
a few raisins
Petri dish
access to water
This experiment can be made quantitative. Each student should be given ten raisins, and asked to measure them. An average length is then calculated. The raisins are then soaked for a set length of time, and remeasured. Different methods of measuring could be tried – e.g. measuring the lengths of each individual raisin, measuring the length of a line of raisins, or massing the raisins.

10.1 Looking at a mammal's heart
Any mammal's heart. Sheep, pig and cattle hearts are readily available from most butchers. If asked for in advance, you may be able to obtain one with all attached vessels intact.
dissecting board
instruments

11.1 How does exercise affect the rate at which your heart beats?
stopwatch

15.1 Using a potometer to compare rates of water uptake
Any style of potometer will do – the simplest version is a capillary tube to which wide plastic tubing is attached in an air tight manner. The tube is filled with water and the plant stem inserted in the plastic tubing. More complex versions may have graduated capillary tubing and a reservoir.
secateurs for cutting plant stems
leafy plant; young, strong shoots from shrubs or trees often work well
stopclock
vaseline

18.1 Is light needed for photosynthesis?
a healthy potted plant; pelargoniums are ideal
glass beaker
Bunsen burner, mat, tripod and gauze
boiling tube
forceps
glass rod
white tile
ethanol
iodine in potassium iodide solution with dropper
black paper
scissors
paper-clips
access to a dark cupboard and a sunny window sill

18.2 Is carbon dioxide needed for photosynthesis?
two healthy pot plants, e.g. pelargoniums
starch testing apparatus as for 18.1
two conical flasks fitted with split bungs
two retort stands, clamps and bosses
two small containers to fit inside flasks
sodium hydroxide solution
access to a dark cupboard and a sunny window sill

19.1 Does light intensity affect the rate of photosynthesis?
apparatus as in diagram
sharp scalpel
stopclock
lamp, preferably with 100 W bulb
material for shading the lamp if necessary

20.1 Getting energy out of a peanut
raw or dry-roasted peanut
mounted needle
Bunsen burner and mat
retort stand, clamp and boss
boiling tube
thermometer
access to water

21.1 The structure of sheep lungs
A set of lungs – these are obtainable from most butchers, especially if you give them a few days' notice.
dissecting board and instruments
length of Bunsen burner tubing

22.1 Pressure and volume changes in a model thorax
See diagram for apparatus.

22.2 Does breathing rate increase with exercise?

Students will ask for the apparatus they require. They should need little more than a stopclock.

Check that no-one risks illness if they exercise strenuously. Asthmatics will probably be able to do this experiment but with care.

23.1 Comparing the carbon dioxide content of inspired and expired air

See diagram for apparatus.
limewater
hydrogen carbonate indicator solution
Make sure that the breathing tube is thoroughly disinfected after use.

23.2 Comparing the temperature and moisture content of inspired and expired air

thermometer
blue cobalt chloride paper
forceps
Warn students not to put the thermometer into their mouth. Homemade cobalt chloride paper often gives a much more convincing colour change than commercially prepared paper.

25.1 Anaerobic respiration in yeast

See diagram
boiled, cooled water
dried or fresh yeast
glucose or sucrose
limewater
paraffin oil
If the yeast is not very active, the experiment may need to be left for more than 30 min. It can be speeded up by using a water bath at around 38 °C.

27.1 Testing foods for carbohydrates

small samples of foods, some which do and some which do not contain carbohydrates
knife or scalpel
tile
Petri dish to hold food samples
several boiling tubes and rack
Bunsen burner and mat
Benedict's solution
iodine in potassium iodide solution, plus dropper
Heating is safer if a water bath is used (a beaker of boiling water on a tripod and gauze). However, the ability to boil a tube of liquid safely in a Bunsen burner flame is useful, and this gives a good opportunity to learn or assess this skill.

27.2 Testing foods for fats

clean, dry filter paper
a range of foods, some which do and some which do not contain fat
Different syllabuses may specify different fat tests. The other one commonly used at this level is the emulsion test. The food is 'dissolved' in absolute ethanol, and the ethanol then poured into distilled water. A milky emulsion indicates the presence of fat.

28.1 Testing foods for proteins

a range of foods, some which do and some which do not contain protein
knife or scalpel
tile
Petri dish for holding food samples
several test tubes with corks or bungs to fit
20 % potassium hydroxide solution
1 % copper sulphate solution
The difference between the purple 'positive' colour and the blue 'negative' one is not always easy to see. Students could begin by testing water to give the blue colour, and cheese to give the purple one. These two tubes can be left in a rack for comparison against other results.

28.2 Testing fruit juices for vitamin C

Students will ask for the apparatus they require. It is likely to include:
test tubes or beakers
syringe or measuring cylinder
dropper pipette
They will also need:
a standard ascorbic acid (vitamin C) solution – this can be made up using vitamin C tablets, obtainable from chemists, and normally stating the amount of vitamin C in each tablet
1 % DCPIP solution, freshly made up, and covered to prevent excess contact with air
a range of fruit juices, e.g. different types of lemon squash, lemon juice, freshly squeezed fruit juices etc.
Different types of juice produce different colours with DCPIP; some of them produce a completely clear solution while others cause a pink colour. The disappearance of the blue colour should be considered to be the end point.

31.1 Catalysing the decomposition of hydrogen peroxide with an enzyme

20 volume hydrogen peroxide solution
syringe, measuring cylinder or pipette and filler to measure 20 cm³
4 boiling tubes
glass marking pen
fresh liver
kitchen knife
tile
pestle and mortar
Bunsen burner, mat, tripod and gauze
glass beaker
stopclock
forceps
stirring rod
splint
Fresh liver reacts very fast, and it may be found that the froth rises too quickly to be measured. Most living tissues contain enough catalase to make this experiment work successfully, so pieces of apple or potato, or a yeast suspension, could be used as an alternative.

32.1 The absorption of carbohydrates from a model gut

two lengths of visking tubing, each about 15 cm long
starch solution
glucose solution
cotton
access to warm water
dropper pipette
beakers
iodine in potassium iodide solution
Benedict's solution
Bunsen burner and mat
boiling tube

33.1 Human teeth

mirror

43.1 Investigating the structure of a flower

an insect pollinated flower preferably with a simple structure, e.g. wallflower, geranium, buttercup
white tile
scalpel, forceps, mounted needle
hand or bench lens
adhesive tape and paper or card (if parts are to be mounted)

43.2 Comparing an insect pollinated and a wind pollinated flower

Two flowers, one insect pollinated and one wind pollinated. Grass flowers are probably the best to use for wind pollinated flowers, but these vary greatly from genus to genus. The grass *Stipa gigantea*, grown in some gardens, is ideal. Oat flowers are also very good. Examples of insect pollinated flowers are given for investigation 43.1.
white tile
scalpel, forceps, mounted needle
hand or bench lens

44.1 Investigating the structure of a seed

a large, soaked seed – beans are readily available, and the parts are easy to see
tile, mounted needle, hand lens

44.2 What conditions do mustard seeds need for germination?

Students will ask for their own apparatus, but are likely to need some or all of the following:
about 50 mustard seeds each
test tubes or Petri dishes
bungs for test tubes, or lids for Petri dishes
cotton wool, filter paper or soil
black paper or plastic
boiled, cooled water, oil, or alkaline pyrogallol to absorb oxygen
access to incubators at different temperatures, or areas at different temperatures within the laboratory – for example a refrigerator, the top of a radiator, a draughty window ledge
means of marking test tubes or Petri dishes

45.1 Adaptations to the environment
tape measures
light meter if available

46.1 Identifying and counting organisms in a habitat
keys and identification books
a variety of collecting and sampling equipment appropriate to the habitat, e.g. quadrats, sweep nets, waterproof paint and brushes for mark-release-recapture, pooters, Longworth traps and bedding, pitfall traps
Tullgren funnel if soil invertebrates are to be sampled
This is a very wide-ranging investigation and, unless a lot of time is available, it will be best to limit the 'how many' part to just a few organisms in the habitat. However, as many organisms as possible should be identified. All but the most observant students fail to find many of the less obvious organisms, and their discovery and identification using keys is a very useful exercise.

48.1 Growing bacteria
sterile Petri dishes, containing sterile nutrient agar jelly
a sample of material from which bacteria are to be grown – e.g. soil, pond water
sterile pipette or inoculating loop
sticky tape
marker pen or labels for dishes
Care must be taken with this experiment, to ensure that the chances of growing harmful bacteria are kept as low as possible. A source such as soil or pond water is fairly safe, but do not attempt to grow bacteria from anywhere on the students themselves, or from environments such as toilets. Keep the plates at room temperature, not in an incubator, as warm temperatures encourage the growth of the types of bacteria which thrive in the human body. Once the lids have been fastened on the plates, they should not be removed at all; examination of colonies must take place through the lid.

52.1 Working out food chains
list of organisms in the habitat being studied
reference books giving information about feeding habits
This is not an easy investigation. It can take a long time for students to find out about what different organisms feed on, and you may like to shorten this time by providing them with a certain amount of information. The extension part of the investigation is very difficult to do satisfactorily, but students who are particularly interested in this topic will enjoy the challenge.

55.1 The effect of sulphur dioxide on plants
4 margarine tubs or other containers, with drainage holes
general purpose compost, e.g. John Innes Number 2
viable barley and maize seeds
means of labelling containers
4 watch glasses
cotton wool
sodium metabisulphite solution
access to water
4 large, transparent polythene bags
ties or rubber bands for bags

72.1 Measuring human variation
rulers, including metre rulers
string, or tape measures, for measuring circumference

75.1 Taste and smell
Students will ask for their own apparatus. They are likely to need:
blindfolds
noseclips (or they can just hold their nose with their fingers)
a range of foods of similar texture, but different flavours – e.g. potato crisps, mashed potato flavoured with different food flavourings, pieces of fruit cut into cubes

75.2 The distribution of touch receptors
paper clips
ruler

78.1 Looking at the human eye
mirror
something with which to cover eyes
bright light

ANSWERS TO QUESTIONS

Topic	Question			Topic	Question		
14	**a**	1s		46	**1a**	20 m²	
	b	60			**1b**	20 m³	
	c	3/10			**1c**	0.20 m³	
	d	136 mm mercury			**1d**	10	
	e	14.5 mm mercury			**1e**	1000	

muscles, intercostal, 56–57
mushrooms, 67
mussels, 119
mutation, 164–165
mutualism, 135
mycelium, 115
Myriapoda, 120

N
Natural selection, 170–172
nectar, 103
nectaries, 102
negative feedback, 195
nephrons, 196–197
nerve endings, 176
nerves, 176
nervous system, human, 176–177
neurones, 176
niches, 108
night blindness, 71
nitrates, 49, 134–135
nitrifying bacteria, 135
nitrogen cycle, 134–135
nitrogen fixation, 134, 137
nitrogen oxides, 130–131, 135
nodules, root, 134
nuclear membrane, 10
nucleotides, 162–163
nucleus, 10, 14
nutrition, 8
nutrition, autotrophic, 67

O
Obesity, 73
oedema, 37
oesophagus, 74
oestrogen, 97, 99–100, 193
oils, 49, 69
omnivores, 124
optic nerve, 181
organ system, 16
organs, 16
organelles, 16
organic substances, 43, 66
osmosis, 20–23
osmosis, water uptake by roots, 39
ovaries, 89–90, 92, 193
ovaries, in flowers, 102, 104
overgrazing, 129
oviduct, 90
ovulation, 90, 193
ovule, 102, 104
oxidation, 53
oxygen debt, 63
oxygen, as a product of photosynthesis, 42–50
oxygen, as a raw material of respiration, 53–54
oxygen transport, 34, 94
oxyhaemoglobin, 34, 55
ozone, 132–133

P
Pacemakers, 28
pain receptors, 178
palate, 74
palisade cells, 11, 15
palisade layer, 44–45
pancreas, 74–75, 193, 195
pancreatic duct, 74–75
pancreatic juice, 75
partial permeability, 14, 20, 22
passive immunity, 154

patella, 188
pathogens, 114, 144–145
pelvic girdle, 188
pelvis, of kidney, 196–197
penicillin, 147
Penicillium, 115, 147
penis, 91
pentadactyl limb, 112
peppered moth, 171
pepsin, 78
peptidase, 79
peristalsis, 74
permeability, partial, 14, 20, 22
pest management, 137, 139
pesticides, 137
petals, 102
pH, in digestion, 78
phagocytes, 35, 60, 146–147
phalanges, 188
phenotype, 157
phenylketonuria, 174
phloem, 38, 45
phosphate, calcium, 188
phosphates, 49
phosphorus, 134
photosynthesis, 8, 14, 41–50, 66, 114, 124, 126–127
phototropism, 199
physical factors affecting organisms, 109
Pisces (fish), 122
pituitary gland, 193
placenta, 93, 95
plant cells, 22, 23, 39
plant growth, 198
plants, classification of, 116–117
plants, desert, 39
plants, flowering, 117
plants, leguminous, 134
plaque, 81
plasma, 33
Plasmodium, 144
plasmolysis, 23
platelets, 35
pleural membranes and fluid, 54
plumule, 104
poisoning, food, 148–149
pollen grains, 102–104
pollination, 102–103
polynucleotides, 162–163
polypeptides, 70, 79
ponds, as a habitat, 108
population, 98, 108, 138, 140–141, 172
potassium, 49
potato cells, 15
potometers, 39
precipitation, 128
predators, 140, 142
pregnancy and birth, 94–95, 106
premature babies, 95
premolar teeth, 81
pressure and volume changes in thorax, 56–57
prey, 140, 142
primary consumers, 124
primates, 113
producers, 116, 124–125
production of food, 136–139
progesterone, 99, 193
Prokaryota, 114–115
prokaryotic cells, 114
prostate gland, 91
proteases, 78–79
proteins, as products of photosynthesis, 49

proteins, blood, 33
proteins
   in chromosomes, 156
   in human diet, 68, 70, 196
proteins, structure of, 70
proteins, synthesis of, 162
proteins, transporter, 19
Protoctista, 114–115
protozoa, 114
pruning, 198
pulmonary arteries and veins, 24–26, 30–32
pulp cavity, 80–81
pulse, 28
pupil reflex, 179
pus, 81
pyramids of numbers and biomass, 125

Q
Quadrats, 110
quotas, fish, 139

R
Radiation, ionising, 164–165
radiation, sunlight, 42–44, 47–48, 124, 127–128
radicle, 104
radius, 188
ragworms, 119
rain forest, 109
reabsorption, selective, 197
reactions, metabolic, 9, 14
receptors, 177–178
recessive alleles, 157
rectum, 74
red blood cells, 33–36
   and osmosis, 22–23
   and oxygen transport, 34, 55
red-green colour blindness, 161
reflex arc, 178–179
reflexes, cerebral, 178
rejection of transplants, 197
relay neurones, 178
renal artery and vein, 31–32, 196
renal capsule, 196–197
reproduction, 9, 85–106
reproductive system, human, 90–91
Reptilia (reptiles), 122
resistance to antibiotics, 170
respiration, 9, 52–64, 126–127
retina, 181, 186
rhizoids, 116
rhizomes, 116
rhythm method of birth control, 98
ribs, 54, 56, 188
ribosomes, 162
rickets, 71
rod cells, 186
root hairs, 19
root nodules, 134
roots, 80
rooting powder, 199
roughage, 72, 74

S
Sacrum, 189
salivary glands, 74
salmon farming, 139
salts, bile, 79
Salmonella, 148
sampling techniques, 110–111
sap, cell, 10–11
saprotrophic nutrition, 67, 114

ACKNOWLEDGEMENTS

The authors and publishers would like to thank the following for permission to reproduce their photographs:

Part-title photograph for 'Cells and Transport' Chuck Brown/Science Photo Library; 1.1 Oli Tennent/Allsport; 2.4b, c & e John Adds; 2.4d Gene Cox; 3.3 Sinclair Stammers/Science Photo Library; 4.1 and page 15 John Adds; page 17 Q4 Mark Colyer; page 17 Q6 Biophoto Associates; 6.2 Andrew McClenaghan/Science Photo Library; 8.4 and 8.7 M.R. Crow; 11.3 Leicestershire Health Authority, Health Education Video Unit; 12.6 Biophoto Associates; 13.1 Dr Tony Brain/Science Photo Library; 13.3 John Adds; 13.5 Biophoto Associates; 13.6 and 14.3 St Bartholomew's and The Royal London School of Medicine and Dentistry; page 40 Q1 Gene Cox; page 40 Q5 Biophoto Associates; part-title photograph for 'Photosynthesis' G.I. Bernard/Oxford Scientific Films; 16.1 Planet Earth Pictures/Andrew Westcott; 16.2 Australian Tourist Commission; 17.1 Planet Earth Pictures/Mark Mattock; 18.2 and page 50 Q4 Dr Jeremy Burgess/Science Photo Library; part-title photograph for 'Respiration' Stephen Dallon/NHPA; 20.1 Bob Thomas Sports Photography; 24.2 CNRI/Science Photo Library; 24.3 Dr Arnold Brody/Science Photo Library; 24.4 James Stevenson/Science Photo Library; 24.5 BOC Gases; 24.6 St Bartholomew's and The Royal London School of Medicine and Dentistry/Science Photo Library; 25.1 Dr Jeremy Burgess/Science Photo Library; 25.3 Brewers and Licensed Retailers Association; 25.4 R.Bond/Zefa; 25.5 Bob Thomas Sports Photography; 26.1 Mushroom Growers' Association; 26.2 Vaughan Fleming/Science Photo Library; 26.3 Biophoto Associates/Science Photo Library; 27.1 Leicestershire Health Authority, Health Education Video Unit; 28.3 St Mary's Hospital Medical School/Science Photo Library; 28.4 Biophoto Associates/Science Photo Library; 29.1 Martin Dohrn/Science Photo Library; 29.2 Zefa; 29.3 J. Hartley/Panos Pictures; 30.3 St Bartholomew's and The Royal London School of Medicine and Dentistry; 33.3 Science Photo Library; 34.2 CAFOD/Liba Taylor; part-title for 'Reproduction' Ben Osborne/Oxford Scientific Films; 35.3 Nigel Cattlin/Holt Studios; 35.5 Sinclair Stammers/Science Photo Library; 35.6 CNRI/Science Photo Library; 37.4 Gene Cox/Science Photo Library; 38.5 James Stevenson/Science Photo Library; 39.1 Sally and Richard Greenhill; 39.3 SIU School of Medicine/Science Photo Library; 39.4 Neil Bromhall/Science Photo Library; 39.5 Simon Fraser/Princess Mary Hospital Newcastle/Science Photo Library; 40.1 The Hutchison Library; 40.2 Colin Milkins/Oxford Scientific Films; 40.3 Stadler/Frank Lane Picture Agency; 41.2 LRC Products; 42.1 Zefa/Schaefer; 42.2 Hawk Morgan/Science Photo Library; 42.3 Martin Dohrn/IVF Unit, Cromwell Hospital/Science Photo Library; 42.4 and 42.5 Animal Biotechnology Cambridge Ltd; 43.3 Phil Jude/Science Photo Library; 43.4 Heather Angel; part-title photograph for 'Organisms in their Environment' Laurence Gould/Oxford Scientific Films; 45.1 and 45.3 Heather Angel; 47.1 Royal College Physicians of London; 47.2a Biophoto Associates; 47.2c David Fox/Oxford Scientific Films; 47.3a Michael Leach/Oxford Scientific Films; 47.3b Mark Pidgeon/Oxford Scientific Films; 47.3c Stan Osolinski/Oxford Scientific Films; 47.3d Mike Birkhead/Oxford Scientific Films; 47.3e Photo Library International; 48.2 Ron Boardman/Life Science Images; 49.3 J. Hutchings/Frank Lane Picture Agency; 49.6 Heather Angel; 50.2 G.I. Bernard/Oxford Scientific Films; 50.3 Laurence Gould/Oxford Scientific Films; 50.5 Heather Angel; 50.7 G.I. Bernard/Oxford Scientific Films; 50.8 Rudie H. Kuiter/Oxford Scientific Films; 50.10 Mike Birkhead/Oxford Scientific Films; 50.12 Vaughan Fleming/Science Photo Library; 50.14 Dick Jones/Frank Lane Picture Agency; 50.16 Dr Jeremy Burgess/Science Photo Library; Dr Tony Brain & David Parker/Science Photo Library; 51.1 Kathy Tyrrell/Oxford Scientific Films; 51.4 Werner Layer/Silvestris/Frank Lane Picture Agency; 51.5 E. Robinson/Oxford Scientific Films; 51.6 Ian Tait/Biofotos; 51.7 Stephen Dalton/Oxford Scientific Films; 51.8 R. & G. Wustig/Okapia/Oxford Scientific Films; 54.2 M. Wendler/Okapia/Oxford Scientific Films; 54.3 Colorific!/Penny Tweedie; 54.4 Landform Slides; 55.1 Frank Lane Picture Agency; 55.2 reproduced by kind permission of the Dean and Chapter of Lincoln; 56.1 NASA GSFC/Science Photo Library; 58.1 David M. Campione/Science Photo Library; 59.1 Roy Waller/NHPA; 59.2 Holt Studios/Michael Mayer; 59.6 Michael Marten/Science Photo Library; 60.5 Paul Harrison/Panos Pictures; part-title photograph for 'Health and Disease' Sean Sprague/Panos Pictures; 61.2 CNRI/Science Photo Library; 61.3 Dr Tony Brain/Science Photo Library; 61.4 Biophoto Associates; 62.1 Ron Boardman/Life Science Images; 62.3 CNRI/Science Photo Library; 63.2 A.B. Dowsett/Science Photo Library; 63.4 J. Sainsbury plc; 64.1 Thames Water; part-title photograph for 'Genetics and Evolution' Phillipe Plailly/Science Photo Library; 66.1 Biophoto Associates/Science Photo Library; 66.2 Dr Gopal Morti/Science Photo Library; 66.3 CNRI/Science Photo Library; 68.1 Sally and Richard Greenhill; 69.4 Sinclair Stammers/Science Photo Library; 70.2 CNRI/Science Photo Library; 70.3 James Stevenson/Science Photo Library; 70.4 J. G. Fuller/The Hutchison Library; 71.2 Pharmacia & Upjohn; 71.3 Plant Genetic Systems N.V.; 72.1 Sally and Richard Greenhill; 73.1 (top) G.I. Bernard/Oxford Scientific Films; 73.1 (bottom) Avril Ramage/Oxford Scientific Films; 73.3 David Fox/Oxford Scientific Films; 73.4a Frank Lane Picture Agency; 73.4b Holt Studios/Gordon Roberts; part-title photograph for 'Control and Coordination' G.I. Bernard/Oxford Scientific Films; 76.3 Allsport/Steve Powell; 79.2 Phil Jude/Science Photo Library; 80.2 Carol Farneti/Partridge Films Ltd/Oxford Scientific Films; 82.4 John Watney Photo Library; 83.1 Allsport/Dan Smith; 83.2 The Hutchison Library/David Hodge; 84.2 CNRI/Science Photo Library; 86.3 MJK/Photos Horticultural; 86.5 Harold Taylor/Oxford Scientific Films; 86.6 Holt Studios/Nigel Cattlin.

Figures 49.1 and 72.2 are © Geoff Jones. All other photographs were taken and supplied by Graham Portlock, Pentaprism. All artwork is by Geoff Jones with the exception of Figure 81.7.

The authors and publishers would also like to thank the following: The Nature Conservancy Council for supplying the data on fishing used in Topic 59 and in Q3 at the end of the section on 'Organisms in their Environment'; Thames Water for supplying information used in Q4 of Topic 64; and the Health Education Council for supplying the data on heart disease shown in Topic 65.

Every effort has been made to reach copyright holders; the publishers would be very pleased to hear from anyone whose rights have been unwittingly infringed.